THE WATCH
THAT
ENDS
THE
NIGHT

The Watch That Ends the Night

a novel by Hugh MacLennan

Macmillan of Canada
Toronto

ISBN 0-7705-1050-7
Printed in Canada for
The Macmillan Company of Canada Limited
70 Bond Street, Toronto, Ontario   M5B 1X3

Tibi, ubicumque sis aut qualiscumque,
gratiae et hic liber

PART ONE

Chapter I

THERE are some stories into which the reader should be led gently, and I think this may be one of them.

One evening at the beginning of a cold February, the first winter of the Korean War, I left my classroom in the university and made my way along the corridor to the stair. It was five o'clock and the best time of my days that winter was about to begin. I love Montreal on a fine winter night and I was looking forward to the walk home along Sherbrooke Street with the evening star in the gap at the corner of Guy, then to a drink before my fire, to dinner and after dinner to a quiet evening with my wife, a little more work and a good night's sleep. That evening I was happy.

Now I suppose I should introduce myself. My name is George Stewart and I come from what might be called an old Montreal family. But I also come from an impoverished family and even now I think of myself as a product not only of Montreal but also of the depression, scarred by it like so many of my friends. For this intricate, fostering city was a bad place in the depression.

I have done various things for a living, but radio has been the only thing in which I have gained any reputation. For years before the Korean War I had been a political commentator over the radio and a writer of free lance articles on political topics for our magazines. In a huge country like the United States a man with a reputation such as I had here would have been prosperous. But Canada is a country with a small population, and the pay for my kind of work is proportionate. Hundreds of thousands of Canadians knew my name from coast to coast, but most of them were better off than I was. I had never known financial security. But at least I managed to get by and was not in debt.

I have never felt safe. Who of my age could, unless he was stupid? Quite a few people thought me successful, but in my own eyes I was no more successful than the old Greek who pushed boulders up the hill knowing they would tumble down the moment they reached the top. Some people thought me calm, but inside I knew I was not. I have often heard myself described as a "mature" commentator, but I have never seemed mature to myself. The young seem more so because they know nothing of the 1930s. The young have the necessary self-confidence and ignorance to feel mature, and that is why I like them so much better than I like my own generation. Was there ever a crowd like ours? Was there ever a time when so many people tried, so pathetically, to feel responsible for all mankind? Was there ever a generation which yearned to belong, so unsuccessfully, to something larger than themselves?

That winter I truly thought I had begun to relax for the first time since I was a boy. I thought I had come to terms with myself and with the peculiar fate which controlled me owing to my wife. I even thought I might have become self-confident. And I had loved this part-time job in the university, because it had brought me into touch with the young.

These post-war students seemed to me a new breed on earth. They were so much freer in their souls than we had ever been, and so much easier in their emotions. Also, unless the world goes crazy again, they were luckier. For not one of them could remember the depression or what it had been like when Hitler was the most powerful man in the world. Not one of them was corroded by the knowledge that nobody wanted them. They all expected to get jobs and marry young and to raise families young, and now as I walked down the corridor I felt joy flood me as I heard the happy noise they made at the end of their day. A student asked me a question about my lecture; I gave him an answer and stopped at a window and looked out.

Powder snow lay deep and white on the slope of Mount Royal and was flecked with the foot and tail marks of the squirrels who lived on the mountain. On this clear winter evening after sunset there was a green blink in the sky, and as I looked up through the boles of the bare trees I saw a flash of bright color and recognized a pheasant which also lived on the mountain and survived the winters on scraps thrown to him out of apartment windows by old ladies who loved him. This pale twilight bathing the city erased time: it called me back to the Montreal which once had been one of the true winter cities of the world, with iced toboggan slides on the mountain and snow-shoers in scarlet sashes and tuques and gray homespuns bright against the snow and shacks with rank coffee and acrid air where you warmed your half-frozen feet in front of Quebec heaters and felt young and clean and untroubled. It was gone now that we were learning to live like New Yorkers.

The porter was at the foot of the stair and I saw from his expression that he wanted to speak to me. He was an Englishman, a former Grenadier, and he had a ramrod back, waxed gray moustaches and a voice husky and formidable.

"A gentleman 'as been calling you, sir," he said in that voice of his. "Most important 'e said it was, sir, so I left you 'is number in your box."

I went into the staff room, took the number out of my box and waited for an elderly professor to finish using the phone. The number was unfamiliar, but from its exchange I knew it was located downtown and this suggested that it might be more important than an unknown lady who wanted me to give a political talk at a suburban women's club. So I sat and waited, looking out the window at the clean northern twilight feeling easy and relaxed.

Must one remember or is it better to forget? Certainly that winter it had seemed easier to forget than ever before. Sleep had come easily, and sometimes the nights were like quiet oceans where I woke after five hours of profound sleep and lay happy in the dawn. We lived in the heart of Montreal but inside our apartment home it was always quiet and we never seemed conscious of the city. Nor is anything quite like the silence of a northern city at dawn on a winter morning. Occasionally there was a hiss or whisper and a brushing against the windows and I knew it was snow, but generally there was nothing but a throbbing stillness until the street cars began running up Côte des Neiges and I heard them as though they were winds blowing through old drains.

Must one remember or can one forget? Those trams of Montreal were history to me, and when the day came when they would be replaced by buses I had the feeling that history itself would disappear with them. Whenever I sat on one of their straw-yellow seats, hearing the bilingual conductor chant "Mountain Street—de la Montagne," I was apt to have a total recall and remember exactly how I had felt in those same cars when I sat reading the news from Mukden, Chapei, Addis Ababa, Guernica, Sudetenland, Eben Emael and Forges-les- Eaux. What a terrible lesson in geography my generation had learned! Those place-names of our lost passions and fears! No wonder there were moments when I felt like a survivor, for those names which could still send a shiver through me meant nothing to these students I taught three hours a week. Most of them had never heard of them.

Can one forget through another human being? That winter I loved so many things, and one of them was the thought of Catherine in the dawn. She was always asleep then in her separate room, but I would lie and be conscious of her presence. I would watch one of her paintings grow visible on the wall and some of the joy she had when she painted it became mine and I was so happy because she had discovered this wonderful thing before it was too late, and I was proud, too.

I had made Catherine the rock of my life. As a boy, at least for a time, I had been religious and believed that God cared for me personally. In the Thirties I had said to myself: There is no God. Now I had Catherine and Catherine's fate and that winter, feeling confident of being equal to it, I said to myself: "What difference does it make if there is no God? Or, if God exists, why worry if He is indifferent to justice?"

For on account of Catherine I could not believe that if there is a God He is just. Catherine had a rheumatic heart which had handicapped her from childhood and it was not on account of her sins, or of her parents' sins, that the seeds of this obscure disease had singled her out among hundreds of thousands of others who went free. A rheumatic heart is fate palpable and unavoidable. It cannot be contended against, it cannot be sidestepped and until very recently it could not be cured. Twice within the last few years Catherine had nearly been killed by it, and for such time as remained to her she must live with the sword dangling over her head every minute of every day. So had she to live and so had I. And I was proud that winter because—so I believed—I could do so without begging for help from a Power which, if It existed, I could not respect because It had allowed this to happen to the woman I loved.

Now as I sat looking out the window at the twilight darkling on the snow, thinking idly as I have described—how many thoughts you can have while waiting to get to a telephone!—inevitably I remembered the man I always remember when I think about the 1930s, the man who would always epitomize that time to me. He at least I had all but forgotten. He had been dead for a decade now and I had put him behind me, I thought, forever. I had put him behind me as a grown man puts behind him his predecessor, his father. He had <u>not</u> been my <u>actual father but</u> for a time in the Thirties, when I was <u>spiritually and emotionally</u> fatherless, I had virtually allowed him to become so.

The professor rose from the phone, smiled and apologized for delaying me, and left the room with his head on one side. I took his place and dialed, and immediately a harsh voice spoke to me in French: "L'hôtel Eduard Sept."

"What?" I said, and was sure the porter had copied the number wrong. I continued in French: "My name is George Stewart. Is there anyone there who wants to speak to me?"

"Moment, s'vous plaît," and I was left with an idle line.

So I waited and wondered if I wasted my time in doing so, for it seemed inconceivable that anyone I knew would be staying at a place like that. Before the war I had known several who had frequented the Edward VII, for it had been a famous institution where respectable men had gone to sleep off a bender; it had been disreputable, but to its disreputableness there had been a certain *cachet* in pre-war Montreal. It had no *cachet* now, for the war had ruined it. During the war years it had rented its rooms to soldiers and their girls by the hour, and so many soldiers requiring penicillin had mentioned its name to battalion medical officers that the army had put it out of bounds for troops. Now it was a place you never heard mentioned unless somebody died or was arrested in it.

I heard a noise at the end of the line, heavy breathing and then a voice spoke which made my hair prickle.

"Is that George Stewart?"

No! the thought crashed through my stunned mind. No, this is impossible. Things never happen like this.

"Yes," I heard my own voice say, "this is George."

"Really you? Really old George?"

"Really me."

"This is Jerome. Jerome Martell."

"I know," I said. "I recognized your voice right away."

Then I began to shake and felt myself turning pale. Telepathy is more common than we care to believe. Jerome Martell was the man I just mentioned, the one I had thought dead for a decade.

Chapter II

I WAS shocked and startled into utter banality. "When did you get back?" I asked him.

"If you mean Montreal, I got back this morning. I've just been talking to Harry Blackwell."

Another name from the past and I said: "Good God!"

"He told me about you and Kate and I phoned your apartment."

"You mean, you've talked to Catherine?"

"No, there were so many George Stewarts and G. Stewarts I gave up after the fourth try and called Blackwell instead. He told me you had this university job. Look George—he told me you've all thought I was dead."

"That's right. We did."

"Kate, too?"

"What else could she think?"

A pause and then he said in the voice of a man who can be surprised by nothing.

"Truly, I thought I'd got word out."

"Word out of where?"

"I've been—" another pause, I heard his heavy breathing, and he went on. "I've been in Russia and I've been in China. I got out of China into Hong Kong and I spent a year there getting my health back. I wrote several letters from Hong Kong, but they were all returned. On the odds it would be surprising if Kate were still alive, but inside me I was sure she was. I had this inside feeling all the time about her. How long have you been married?"

I took out a packet of cigarettes, spilled one onto the table beside the phone, put it between my lips and lit it. My right hand shook when it snapped the lighter.

"I suppose this must be a shock," he said.

"That's one way of understating it."

"Harry Blackwell kept repeating, 'But it was in the papers you were dead!' That poor sorry little man, he always believed the papers."

For a moment the wire sang between us and then I said: "Harry has done pretty well lately. We all under-rated him. We under-rated so many people who have done well since the war."

Jerome did not seem to hear me. "Didn't even one of my letters get back?" he said.

"Nobody has had a single word from you since 1939."

Again the wire sang between us.

"Did Blackwell tell you *how* we thought you had died?" I asked.

"He just said it was in the papers I was dead."

"Does the name Lajoie mean a thing to you? A French aviator? Captain Lajoie?"

He waited a moment and said no.

"Well," I said, "this Captain Lajoie was over here for a time in the war and he said he knew you in the French underground. What he told us wasn't pretty."

"He might have known me under another name," Jerome said. "What did he say?"

"He said the Nazis spent two days torturing you and afterwards they hung up your body on a meat hook in the square of a French market town."

"Was all that in the papers?"

"No, just that you'd been killed in the French underground. The *Gazette* wrote you a very nice obituary, considering what they thought of your politics."

There was another silence.

Then Jerome said: "Did everyone believe this story of the torture and the meat hook?"

"Yes."

"Did Kate believe it?"

"Yes."

"Well," he said, "it came pretty close to being true. Did Kate believe it?"

"I said so, Jerome."

Looking out the window I saw the darkness visibly flooding down over the snow with its squirrel tracks, and now a light was on and there was a yellow track from it across one part of the snow. I felt numb, unreal, and heard myself say, "Where have you been? What have you been doing?"

"George, I can't tell you all that now. Russia—China—the war—everything. You see I was caught with the Spanish in France in 1939 when we came over the Pyrenees and my passport was stolen. When I was in Hong Kong I read a book about one of those French concentration camps written by a man called Arthur Koestler. Did you ever read that book?"

"Yes."

"Then you know what it was like." I heard him breathing so heavily that I wondered if he was sick. "When the Nazis came in, the French let me out and I had to go underground. I lasted till 1943 before they caught me. They didn't kill me because I was a doctor. They shipped me around for a while, but I ended in Poland after I was caught escaping."

"Auschwitz?"

"Yes," he said simply.

There was another silence and I felt even more unreal as I tried to imagine what he looked like.

"When the Russians came in they shipped me east. The Russians wanted doctors too, and after a stretch in one of their arctic camps I was a surgeon in a Siberian town. They promised to let me go home but they never did. But they did let me go to China. It's too long a story and it's too commonplace. What happened to me has happened to millions of others. The Chinese let me out after I got sick. They let me out to Hong Kong." He paused, and then he said with an intense calm more powerful than any note of passion could possibly be, "All I ever wanted was to come home. All I lived for was to come home to Kate and Sally."

I felt as tired as a man after a fainting spell.

"How long did you say you and Kate have been married?"

"I didn't say, but we've been married nine years."

Another pause before he said: "How is she?"

At last I recovered something of myself, for this question was the one I was most frequently asked. Whenever I met a friend on the street his first question was apt to be, 'How is Catherine?' I began to talk about her and with dramatic suddenness his tone changed to that of a doctor.

"What, precisely, are the symptoms now?"

For the next five minutes I recounted them, and from time to time he interrupted me with questions.

When I was done he asked: "Did I understand you to say *two* embolisms?"

"That's right." And noting the doubt in his voice I added: "She's had the best opinions, Jerome. Jack Christopher is her physician now."

"I guessed he would be. I'm glad he is."

But he was, at least partially, still the same Jerome, for he cross-questioned me further about her symptoms. I assured him that to look at her casually you would never guess she had even been sick, and I asked him if he was out of touch with recent medical developments. He said he supposed he was out of touch to an extent, but that he had worked for a year in a hospital in Hong Kong, having obtained the post through a chest surgeon he met there whom he had known years ago in Edinburgh. I explained to him about a new drug which had helped her, one which had been used for the first time in such cases here in Montreal, and he admitted that he had never heard of it. A professor entered the room to hunt for mail, inhibiting me by his presence, and looking out the window I saw that it had become totally dark.

"How's Sally?" I heard Jerome say.

"She's in her last year in the university."

"Tell me more about her, George."

It was then that I became haunted by the thought that I must know what he looked like if I was to continue talking to him. His age I knew—he was fifty-two. But what a fifty-two years of life he had spent! Was he white? Was he scarred? Did his eyes have that look of the men who had been in the camps? Did his face have that holy expression that sometimes comes from just the right amount of starvation?

I tried to describe Sally to him.

"Little Sal a biologist!" He gave a soft, wondering laugh. "Remember how I used to set up the microscope for her when she was a kid? The things she used to say when she looked through it!"

When he said this my eyes burned and I nearly wept. Those last words of his had jumped the years, had picked him up and brought him back alive as I had known him in those depression evenings in Montreal when he was the center of rabid discussions in apartments when we sat on the floor and drank beer and talked politics and economics and dreaded the coming war and reviled Baldwin, Chamberlain and the capitalists. He was right in front of me now, Jerome Martell in the mid-Thirties, ugly-handsome with muscular cheeks, a nose flattened by an old break, hair cropped short because it defied a brush, a bulldog jaw, nostrils ardent like those of a horse, mouth strongly wide and sensual, but the eyes young, hungry and vulnerable, quick to shame as a boy's, charming with children and the weak, quarrelsome with the strong. There he was, that oddly pure sensualist so many experimenting women had desired, the man so many of us had thought was wonderful in those depression years when we were all outcasts.

"George," I heard him say, "you're probably thinking a lot you're not saying."

"I suppose you're doing the same."

"Does she hate me?"

"She never did."

"Then she hasn't changed! Then she's just the same! Then what I saw in my sleep was true! Does she still talk about me?"

"Not any more."

There was a long silence after I said this. Then I heard him whisper, "Kate! Kate!" And I heard him sob, and the pity of the moment was almost too much for me. I had never doubted that he loved her.

"I've got to see her, George. I've got to see her and Sally."

I'm not a man with much self-confidence and when I was young I took it for granted that nobody respected me or paid me any attention. When I was young I was just another of those people who are around, for I had, and still have, a clumsy body of which

I was never proud and when I was young I was timid. But living with Catherine had matured me a little and my work on the radio had taught me how to control my voice. I realized now—for I have learned to listen to my own voice as though it came from somebody else, I have learned what it sounds like from listening to play-backs in the studio—I realized now that it was resonant and steady.

"Are you in a fit condition to see her, Jerome?"

"What do you mean, a fit condition?"

"Mentally and physically is what I mean."

He seemed surprised by the question. "I've got a constitution like an ox," he said.

"But Catherine hasn't."

He did not seem to have heard me. "I know this must seem strange and sudden to you, but listen, George—I've gone over most of the frontiers and I tell you, I'm still a doctor and a reasonably good one. It will be all right. I must see her, George. I think it would be quite wrong if I didn't. I'm not in trouble with the police or anything like that. I spoke with the police in Vancouver. It was Kate who kept me alive and I tell you, George, I believe she will know it. Once in a dream she said, 'I've never left you.'"

"When did she say that to you in a dream?"

"Does it matter?"

"I think it may."

"Well"—he seemed to be making an effort to calm himself—"well, it was quite a while ago. But it was real. Those things—if you've had them yourself you'll know they can be real sometimes." Another pause. "Of course the Nazis had me in their power, and of course they did torture me, but it could have been much worse even though my hands have been damaged so there are a few operations I can't do any more. Except for my hands the other scars are all covered by my clothes. I don't think I'm shocking to look at. Children don't stop and stare."

"I see."

But I didn't; not really. How could I even pretend to understand a man who had lived as he had lived these dozen years?

After a while I said: "Jerome, you must understand this. Catherine has no reserves at all. There's been a certain amount of neurological destruction, if I'm using the right words. Besides, she's assumed these last nine years that you were dead."

Then I felt a wave of feeling that astounded me. I realized that I was glad, that I was thankful and very glad that he was back and not dead.

"She may refuse to see you," I said.

"Forgive me for saying this, but I don't think she will."

"I'll try to talk to her tonight. I'll call you tomorrow around noon."

"Can't I see her tonight?"

"No, you can't." Then another idea struck me. "What about money? Do you need any?"

"Oh, money! No, I still have some I earned in Hong Kong and the ship passage cost me nothing because I signed on as a surgeon. The rail fare from Vancouver ran into a lot, but I have a little left and I'll soon be on my feet again."

"You intend to live in Montreal?"

"I don't know where I intend to live. I haven't even thought about it. I suppose things have changed. The whole country seems to have changed."

"Jerome, please don't call the apartment. I'll be in my office tomorrow at ten in the CBC building and you can call me there. Otherwise I'll call you in that ghastly hotel you're staying at. But I will have to talk to Catherine first. I can't have her hearing your voice over the phone without any preparation for it." I gave a laugh out of sheer tension. "Do you by any chance remember that it was you who got me into radio work?"

"Did I? Oh yes, so I did. I remember all sorts of things, George."

"Well, I'll call you tomorrow."

Chapter III

THERE it is just as it happened, my conversation with Jerome Martell after twelve years in which a war had been fought and the British Empire had crumbled and Europe had become like the succession states of ancient Greece and America had turned into a new Rome. I looked at my watch and it was hard to believe that only twenty-five minutes had passed since I had given my students a pleasant and at times witty lecture on the witty and at times pleasant eighteenth century.

The staff room was still empty and I went into a small lavatory adjoining it and bathed my face and eyes, and after drying my hands I surveyed myself in the mirror.

I suppose I am a presentable enough person, but my Aunt Agnes, the dominant female in our family when I was young, had long ago made me self-conscious about my face and general appearance. I was not fat, but I was not thin, either. Aunt Agnes had believed I would run to flesh and had told me I must think of myself always as a thin man, and so I tried to do. I was too clumsy ever to be an athlete but I had always enjoyed walking and physical exercise like digging in gardens and chopping wood and paddling canoes. But I was certainly not a man people notice in a crowd. I was no Jerome Martell, whom everyone had noticed wherever he was.

Going to the phone I dialed my own number and after three rings Catherine's voice came to me warmly. I had always loved that contralto voice of hers with its cello note and hint of gaiety.

"I've felt so well today, George, I've felt so well it's been glorious."

"That's grand."

"And the light this afternoon—were you too busy to see it? It was delicious. That's the only word for it—delicious. In spite of the cold and everything, I walked down to the gallery and I crossed the street afterwards and bought a new record you'll hear after supper and it was so lovely there should have been birds singing in the snow. Now—how was *your* day?"

"Not bad." Then I remembered a call that had come in the Radio Building early that afternoon. "External called me from Ottawa and it seems that the Minister wants to talk to me the day after tomorrow. I suppose that means I'll have to leave on tomorrow afternoon's train, for the appointment's for ten in the morning."

Her voice rose to the news: "But that's simply marvellous. George—I'm so proud of you!"

"I don't think it's all that important, but this is the first time the Minister has ever wanted to see me for a private interview. I wonder what he wants?"

"You'll find out and then you'll tell me. I'm getting excited already."

But the truth was that this invitation meant only one thing to me: it was one more small reassurance that I had recovered from the depression. It was a tiny indication that in my work I had done well enough to know that I would always be able to earn a living.

"Did you paint after you got home?" I asked her.

"Well, first I lay down and tried to sleep, but after a few minutes I felt so well I got up and got busy. I liked what I did, too."

"I can't wait to see it. Were there any phone calls?"

"All day long the phone has been beautifully behaved. It didn't let out a single peep."

I was going to hang up when she suddenly called: "Oh yes, one thing more—Sally just telephoned to say she's changed her mind about staying out for supper, so if you look around the hall you'll probably find her there and you can walk home together."

Outside in the hall students were coming and going, standing in small clusters in front of the notice boards or sitting on benches talking together. It was perfectly normal and I had become such a creature of habit that I had to prod myself and repeat that Jerome was alive and back. I wanted to walk home in that quiet winter evening looking at the evening star at the end of Sherbrooke Street, I wanted my quiet drink and supper with Catherine and to see her new picture and to listen to her new record, and then to do a little home work and sleep in the silent city as I had done all winter long. I wanted no crisis. For years now Catherine and Sally and I had lived knowing that at any instant Catherine might collapse with her face twisting up and her insides writhing and that I would have to rush to the phone for the doctor, then the ambulance would come and there would be the pain, misery and shame of a fearful illness, and possibly even death. I wanted no external crisis to disturb the calm spells.

Sally was sitting on a deal table in the hall with a huge youth beside her and the pair of them were swinging their legs. The boy, as was obvious from their mutual expressions, was teasing her about something and she was liking it and pretending not to. I recognized him, for several times she had brought him around to the apartment. His name was Alan Royce and I knew he was popular on the campus, if not a big wheel at least a sizable one. When they saw me they both got off the table and I noticed that Sally's neat little head did not even reach the shoulder of this huge bear of a boy. He brushed a loose lock off his forehead, gave a hitch to a shapeless garment he had probably bought in some place which sold surplus navy stores, and grinned.

"Hi, sir," he said.

"Hi."

"You've arrived at precisely the right moment," Sally informed me. "Alan and I were about to quarrel."

"What about? The usual thing?"

"I told her about the bees and the birds long ago, sir."

"You told *me!*" she said. "And since when have you known the elements of biology?"

He gave her an amiable slap on the backside and we stepped outside and there from the front of the Arts Building was downtown Montreal like a fleet at anchor in an arctic port with all its lights on and the smoke going straight up. The campus was dark with its elm fountains lean and bare, but long rhomboids of light from the library windows fell across the snow and I saw students passing through them with their breath puffing out and heard their heels creaking on the packed snow. This campus was an island of quiet in the city's roar, and at night it was an island of dark in the city's blaze, and on this particular night it felt very cold. I buttoned up the collar of my station wagon coat and pulled my fur cap down over my ears and forehead, and Alan Royce, who was bareheaded and rosy-cheeked, gave me another of his grins.

"Sir, you look like a pall bearer at a Soviet funeral."

"I feel like one."

A heavy step crunched behind me and I turned and saw Roberts, the former Grenadier who had become the college porter.

"Did you get my message, sir?"

"Thanks, I got it."

He sniffed noisily and contemplated the scene. "Ten below it is at present and twenty below before dawn. 'ard to believe the glaciers are melting on a night like this, isn't it, sir?"

"Are they melting?"

"Oh yes, sir, indeed they are. The other day I 'eard Professor Chown explaining to a foreign gentleman that the glaciers are on the melt. Professor Chown is a world-renowned authority on glaciers."

"Well, well."

We said good-night all around, and while Sally and I went down the campus avenue, Alan Royce turned off toward his fraternity house on University Street to the left of the campus. The porter stayed where he was, hands locked behind his back, waxed moustaches bristling, shoulders on parade with his breath puffing out. It was exciting on the campus with the sound of creaking feet as the students hurried past clamping their ears; there was the recurrent excitement an extremely cold night gives you even in Canada. The evening star was yellow in a tiny green corona caught in a net of bare branches over the little observatory and behind us, high over the university and the hospitals that hug the city's crest, the hospitals I had come to know so well, Mount Royal slumped like a stationary whale in an arctic sea, the huge lighted cross in its brow blazing eastward toward the Catholic end of the city.

"You're exceptionally taciturn tonight," Sally told me.

"Considering what you think about my talking too much, nothing could please me more than to hear you say that."

"All I meant was that when you talk too much it's because you do it compulsively."

"Sally darling, I love you."

"Now you're teasing me."

Sherbrooke Street throbbed with its usual traffic jam and the cars and buses were stalled solid all the way from University Street to Côte des Neiges with a fume of exhaust hanging over them in the still air and their windows so frosted it was impossible to see through them. Horns were snarling impotently.

"I wish you liked Alan Royce," Sally said, and from her guarded tone I knew it mattered to her that I should.

"What gives you the idea that I don't?"

"You think he's dumb."

"I hardly know the lad."

"I know he's indecently gigantic and wears his hair like an oaf, but he happens to be one of the most intelligent people I've ever met. He's another product of divorced parents, but the marvelous thing about him is that he's *not* one of the sad young men. I suppose you know his awful family?"

"I've a vague idea who they are. What's his father do?"

"Investments, I suppose. Alan and I met him once in the Ritz and he took us to lunch. He reminded me of one of those leathery officer types you see in the British liquor ads—you know, very distinguished and all that, but distinctly B-minus. During lunch he told us how good his squash game was and how soft our generation is and he asked me to feel his abdominal muscles. 'They're as hard now as they were when I was twenty-one,' he said, as if I cared how hard his stomach was. Alan calls him the sexual career man."

"You're giving this boy a terrific build-up."

"I am, as a matter of fact. In spite of that awful family, I've been trying to tell you that Alan is not one of the sad young men. And he's got this terrific intelligence if only he'd use it. His mother is pleasant enough, but she's absolutely helpless and clinging, and now she's living in Ottawa married to a civil servant who's a Jew. His name is Lubliner and I suppose you know him, for you know everybody in Ottawa."

"If he's Jack Lubliner, I do know him and he *is* nice."

"Alan's got everything under control now, but in the crucial years that turn people into neurotics he had a pretty bad time. He's come right out of it. Perhaps I shouldn't mention this, but he told his father once he didn't think he was his real father."

I trudged along with my face feeling as though a thousand needles of ice were massaging it.

"You know, Sally, Alan was by no means the first youth to make that suggestion to a perfectly legitimate parent."

"Please don't depreciate him and tear him down, George."

"Darling, I can't afford to tear anybody down."

There was another burst of horn blowing from the packed automobiles and Sherbrooke Street looked like an army in retirement. I lost interest in Alan Royce and barely listened while Sally explained his latest theory about the effect of the somatotype on the human character. I was thinking of Jerome and Catherine and what I would say to Catherine after dinner, and I was wishing I could afford to say nothing.

"Alan thinks I'm somewhat mixed up," Sally was saying, "and he insists I ought to talk my background out of my system. He says that's the only thing to do if you're the product of a broken family. What we were really talking about when you came along, in case you're interested, was Dad."

I started. "I thought you said you were getting into a fight?"

"That was just covering up in front of you. I was shy."

"I see."

We stopped at an intersection and waited while a few cars nudged their way into the traffic jam, the light changed and we crossed.

"Alan thinks each period of history favors the emergence of a special human type," Sally told me. "And that made me think of something I'd never thought of before. The depression was Dad's real time, wasn't it? I mean, he was a real depression type—wasn't he?"

"What about me? I'm a depression type and I was never like him."

"Oh, you're just old George. What I meant about Dad was that he really fitted in and symbolised that whole awful period. Those appalling adolescent he-men like Hemingway and all those naive idealists thinking they were so terrific because they went to bed with each other to prove the capitalist system stank. That's what I meant."

"Is this Alan's diagnosis, or yours?"

"His, mainly. But I think he's right. Don't you?"

We were passing under a light and I saw her face like a cameo under the scarf she wore over her hair. She walked and stood as straight as a rush, and when she was on her feet you never thought of her as short. Sally resembled neither of her parents, though she had Catherine's fair skin and a good deal of Jerome's vitality and impatience. I knew she was sensitive about the shape of her jaw, which was rather long, for a week ago she had asked me if she would look like a horse when she was my age. But she was not alarmed about the prospect, for this winter she had been having too wonderful a time. To her surprise she had become one of the most popular girls on the campus, and our apartment would have pullulated with youths if Catherine had been well enough to receive them.

"Just how well do you remember your father, Sally?"

"Too well."

"He was very fond of you, you know."

"Is that why he walked out and left us?"

Suddenly I found myself on Jerome's side against this girl I loved, this member of the generation I liked so much better than my own.

"Your father didn't just walk out," I said. "He went to the war."

"Before it began?"

"That particular war began long before Mr. Chamberlain got around to declaring it."

"I wonder if it did? Alan says it was the death-wish that produced men like my father. The war too for that matter."

We trudged on, slipping on icy patches, passing clusters of office girls shivering at the bus stops, passing an art gallery with a minor Dutch master ruby-red in its window.

"Among other things, Sally, your father was a great doctor."

"Come, George! 'Great' is a big, big word."

"I admit he wasn't a Penfield, but he was a very good doctor and he was a very brave man."

"Couldn't a man be brave in your day without making a career out of it?"

The traffic crawled twenty yards closer to Côte des Neiges, the horns wailed when it stopped again, and through a momentary gap I saw, a jet of pure excitement in the night, a slim woman dart out of the Ritz with her mink a-flutter and one hand trailing a graceful adieu to an iron-gray, European-looking man bareheaded in front of the revolving door.

"When your father went away you were only eight," I said, "but you can't possibly remember what things were like then. None of you kids can. Hitler was around then. Call people like your father anything you like, but if there had been no people to walk out to the horns, Hitler would be around still."

We passed the Museum, a church, and then in front of another church we found ourselves on the corner of Simpson Street with the light against us and a snarl of traffic blocking our way.

"What I remember about Dad," she said, "isn't what he felt about Hitler, but how he made Mummy cry. I remember it so well sometimes I can't sleep. And I was talking to Alan about it and he said, 'What do you expect? All our parents were balled up about themselves.' But Mummy wasn't, and you know she wasn't. He *made* her that way that time."

A taxi trying to muscle its way into the mainstream had hooked its bumper onto a Cadillac, and now the taxi driver and the chauffeur of the Cadillac were out in the cold arguing, and a cop was looking at them unable to get through to put in his two cents' worth. The jam at this corner would be solid for another ten minutes.

"Let's climb through," I said.

We did so, and just as we were about to turn up Côte des Neiges hill, Sally stopped and faced me.

"Why do you stand up for him?" she said. "Once before I talked about him and you did the same thing."

"Because I admired him. Because he did a great deal for me once. Because he was brave and I wasn't."

It was strange having such a conversation on the corner of Côte des Neiges and Sherbrooke in the cold with the traffic snarling beside us. Strangest of all was the fact that Sally, just after I had been talking with Jerome, should have begun to speak of her father. Or was it really as strange as I fancied? Underneath her banter she had been disturbed lately and in one way or another she had been asking me questions about the 1930s. I had not realized that her motive had been to lead me on to talk of Jerome. "Who am I? Whence come I?" Of course, I thought, the child has fallen in love, but she is not a romantic, she has a scientific mind and she wants to know the answers. And possibly something else: possibly she is frightened of herself, of feelings in herself she cannot control, and so she wants to talk about her father.

"George," she said, "please don't laugh. If you do I'll never speak to you again. But there's something I want to say. I've wanted to say it for years but it seemed—I don't know, but I just couldn't. George?"

"Yes, Sally?"

"I wish you were my real father and not him. I think of you as my real father."

Coming on top of everything else that day, this was too much. It was the nicest thing anyone had ever said to me and tears scalded my eyes before they turned to icy liquid. I put out my gloved hand and brushed her cheek.

"Thank you, child," I said, and we began walking up the hill.

The headlights cascading down Côte des Neiges were like two rivers of light and it was so cold the whole north seemed to be breathing quietly into my face. This air had come down from the empty far north of spruce and frozen lakes where there were no people, it had come down from the germless, sinless land. Winter days like this were hard on Catherine, each year they were harder, but I could not help enjoying them, for they reminded me of my youth and of the time before the glaciers began to melt.

"Sally—" I began, and stopped.

For suddenly I was frightened by an entirely new element in this bizarre situation in which I found myself: I was frightened by what Sally might do to her father when she met him. She would be polite and competent in the situation, for she was a polite, competent girl except on certain occasions with me and her boy friends. But when she met her father I was afraid she might wither him with hostility or even with something worse, which I imagined might be the terrible indifference the young can show to their elders. What had happened to Jerome I could not even guess. What he was like now was probably something I could not even imagine. But he had always been a man who lived passionately because that was the only way he had been able to function. He had not been raised in a city apartment like this girl, and if he had survived the camps of the Nazis and Russians it could only have been because of that passionate, rash and irrefragable strength I recalled in him. He was not wise; he was not shrewd; he was not even clever; he had never learned or been taught how to adjust.

"Transferences aren't really so difficult," I heard Sally say.

"Freud and you little girls."

"Oh, we take him in our stride."

"You take so much in your stride."

Chapter IV

I DON'T know how a man can describe his wife to somebody else unless he dislikes her—there is nothing like dislike to make a character appear vivid—but the very things in a woman that makes a man love her escape language. Women seem able to recognize with perfect candor the flaws in the men they love. Men lack this ability. And besides I had known Catherine so long and in so many circumstances that I could describe half a dozen entirely different women and they would all be her to me.

Now in the living room with a glass of whisky in my hand, feeling the coldness of the glass and the warmth of whisky along my veins, I watched Catherine and Sally preparing the table for supper. How lucky I had been, I thought, to have lived with two women like these. They were quiet with each other as they always were when doing something together about the house. They were unusually close for mother and daughter. Yet they were so different it was hard to believe they were even related.

Sally was rush-straight, quick and impetuous, with crisp, blonde curled hair and she looked at ease in her undergraduate's sweater and tweed skirt. Catherine had never looked well in tweeds or woolens. Now in a limegreen housecoat she appeared slow and deliberate, her movements adagio. Her hair had once been sable with a suggestion of lightness of weight, of airiness, and it was still mostly sable despite the suggestion of silver-steel which now was beginning to show. She was shorter than her daughter. She had a small waist and a classically formed figure almost but not quite plump, and the sweep of her shoulders was so bold it made me think of the clarity of a Picasso-line. Her face was heart-shaped, large gray eyes and sensitive mouth. If you could think of a queen as small you could think of Catherine as queen-like.

During her life she had seemed many things to many people. As a girl lonely, shy, and reserved, but this had been because she had suffered so much sickness as a girl. In her early twenties gay, reckless, and to some almost desperate in her eagerness to live and enjoy. Then as a young wife fulfilled and quiet, with a sparkling sense of humor and a wonderful capacity for making friends. But now when people thought of Catherine—this I knew—they thought of her as tragic because of the condition of her heart. Though she looked no older than her age, they thought of her as old because they knew—at least her friends did—that her time was limited.

She was also an artist, and had become so first out of loneliness and now because art was her chief hold on a world she loved and saw slipping away. She had come late to painting and had much to learn. She believed—I knew this—that if she could live long enough she would leave behind her some pictures the world would value. This Catherine was ambitious. This Catherine was also strangely solitary in her core and—I dare say this now—there were days when she seemed totally to exclude me because of this communion she had established with color and form. Yes, she was also ruthless. All artists are.

And finally there was the Catherine which had never died, the little girl who came out in her wistful smile, the little girl who had been alone and longed to be appreciated. Alone, and as a little girl knowing it, with her fate.

Her fate was that rheumatic heart of hers. Her strength, her essence, her mystery in which occasionally I had almost drowned— this I can only call her spirit, and I don't use the word in a sentimental sense. Far from it. For to me this has become the ultimate reality, so much so that I think of this story not as one conditioned by character as the dramatists understand it, but by the spirit. A conflict, if you like, between the spirit and the human condition.

Some people have within themselves a room so small that only a minuscule amount of the mysterious thing we call the spirit can find a home in them. Others have so much that what the world calls their characters explodes from the pressure. I think of it as a force. I have recognized—and I am no mystic—an immense amount of this spiritual force in people whose characters, judged by the things they do, are bad. In others who are blameless I have found hardly any. Probably I will never be able to know what its real nature is; all I do know is that I know it is there. Call it the Life-Force if you prefer the modern term; call it anything you like. But whatever it is, this thing refuses to be bounded, circumscribed or even judged. It creates, it destroys, it re-creates. Without it there can be no life; with much of it no easy life. It seems to me the sole force which equals the merciless fate which binds a human being to his mortality.

Catherine had more of this mysterious thing than anyone I ever knew with one exception, and the exception was Jerome Martell. Is this another way of saying that she was not easy to live with? Or is it another way of saying that it was so impossible for me to imagine myself living without her that—without realizing I did so—I sometimes dreaded her because of my dependence on her?

Yet I loved her. She was my rock, she was my salvation, but I also loved her for herself. When she moved like a queen I was proud. When she smiled like a little girl I melted.

Have I described Catherine? I don't think so. Probably I have only described myself.

They called me to supper and I was so preoccupied and silent that Sally said, "What is this, a funeral?" and took over the conversation, talking about a debate she planned to attend at the Union that night when all along she knew that I knew she intended spending the evening with Alan Royce if he called her up and asked her. I saw Catherine's eyes twinkling, then contemplating me without twinkling, and I knew she had sensed I was disturbed. That was another reason why she was at times difficult to live with: she was so empathetic she could almost read my mind, and Sally's mind, just as years ago she had been able to read Jerome's.

Supper ended, and while Sally stacked the dishes to be cleaned in the morning by the woman who came in, Catherine and I took our coffee to chairs on either side of the hearth. I looked into the flames and was aware of her probing silence.

Then I heard her say: "Something is worrying you, George."

"Is my face so obvious?"

She smiled again: "When you want to talk about it, I'll listen."

"My face is a Rorschach test. It says more about whoever looks at it than it says about me. And speaking of my face, it's beginning to worry me. Inside the year they'll be starting television in this country and my face on television—my voice may sound like Roosevelt's, but my face!"

Again that smile of hers: "All right, dear."

"All right what?"

"What do you think the Minister will want to talk to you about when you go to see him?"

"I haven't the slightest clue, and I don't think it means a damned thing. All they're doing is going through the motions, even the Minister, and he's the best of the lot."

I looked across at her small, beautifully formed figure, at her heart-shaped face under that dark hair, at the strange serenity that came to her so often these days and had—I refused to admit it but I can admit it now—the odd effect of excluding me, as though she had gone to some place to which I would eventually arrive and knew all about it, while I did not. And yet she was happy tonight. She was at ease. Her health had been good all that winter, and winter had become her difficult time. She began talking about the spring and the garden in our country place, and mentioned that the seed catalogues should have arrived long ago. She planned and re-planned the gardens with an efficiency which would have exasperated me if I had not enjoyed gardening. Everything she did she tried to do perfectly, and if there were some things she wanted to do and lacked the strength to do herself, she still planned that they be done perfectly and I carried out her orders.

Sally returned dressed to go out with a different scarf over her yellow hair, and with an expression unwontedly shy she glanced at her mother.

"Is it all right if I use your phone?"

When she left, Catherine twinkled: "I wonder why she bothered asking? She never does."

A few minutes later Sally reappeared looking like a secretive but very pleased kitten.

"I trust everyone here will be sleeping peacefully when I come home?" she said.

"Will you be late?" Catherine said, her head lifting over her shoulder.

"I hope so," Sally said, and bolted.

Now Catherine and I were alone at last and how good it might have been. But I knew from her manner, if not from her expression, that she was aware that I had not told her the truth when I said I was not worried. She got up and put a piano concert on the phonograph and we listened without speaking. When it ended I took the record off the machine and sat down again.

"I suppose Sally has gone out with Alan Royce again?" Catherine said.

"I suppose so. Do you like him?"

"I think they may be good for one another."

"Can you get used to it?"

Again she twinkled: "The hardest thing to get used to is Sally's idea that I'm so old I've forgotten how she feels. I used to think the same of my own mother, remember."

She got up and searched the record shelves and I felt desire as I watched the curve of her back, the lovely line of her shoulders, the full swell of her hips as she bent. Always, when I saw Catherine like this these days, these sensual images were touched with poignancy and I remembered and loved even better the image of her in a hospital bed five days after her second embolism when she had suddenly recovered from the paralysis.

"Look!" she had cried. "*Both* hands work today. Watch me tie this ribbon in my hair."

Like a proud little girl she had tied the ribbon while I watched.

And then she had said: "It's nice to know I'm not going to be a cripple. Don't I keep on fooling them?"

And this expression had reminded me of still another I had seen in her childhood after her first attack of rheumatic fever when I had come to visit her.

"Here I am again!" her little girl's face had seemed to say. "Here I am again in spite of everything, and please nobody mind for I hated being sick."

She came back to her chair and the music began playing and it was Louis Armstrong. This quiet, stately woman, this mysterious combination of so many characteristics, also loved New Orleans jazz, and as Louis' bell-like trumpet rang into the room I thought that if her heart had been normal this would have been the music she would have preferred above all others, the kind which best expressed her.

I got up and held out my hands to her and she rose as I tugged and melted against me, and then I asked to see her new picture. I followed her into the bedroom where she painted and there it was on her easel, another of her joyous outbursts of color and form.

She had said to me once: "People with nothing to worry about can afford to paint the tragic pictures. I'm like the colored people. I'd rather be gay."

And still I thought: How can I bring up the subject of Jerome? She thinks he's dead. She has grown accustomed to that fact. She has even stopped dreaming about him. He will drain her vitality. He will bring up all that ocean out of the past and what will it do to us? I had no ordinary vulgar fears of Jerome taking her away from me. The truth was I did not know exactly what I feared. Perhaps myself? Perhaps her? Perhaps the knowledge of what life had done to us all? Perhaps having to face that knowledge again when all I wanted was peace and quiet?

"Catherine—" I began, and would have forced myself to tell her. And she, sensing that this was important, turned to me calmly. But at that instant the phone rang stabbing into the room, and as she was nearest she picked it up, spoke and then handed it over to me.

"Yes?" I said into the instrument.

Then I heard a voice I had not heard in years, a colorless voice deceptively humble.

"This is Harry Blackwell, George."

I cursed myself for not having called Harry from the university, for I should have realized, after Jerome had told me he had been speaking to him, that the chances were good that he would want to get in touch with me.

"He's back!" Harry cried in the voice of a man with an obsession.

"I know. He's talked to me, too."

Harry must be bald now, I thought. I had seen him only once in the last dozen years, and then only in passing, and the years had not been kind to him. Nothing had ever been kind to Harry. And yet I knew that since the war this nonentity had become a prosperous business man, and was probably worth several hundred thousand dollars.

"I've got ulcers," Harry said, "and when he called me we were in the middle of inventories and they were bad. I mean the ulcers, not the inventories. And the gas pains got so bad I couldn't think, and anyhow I thought he was dead. So I just answered a lot of questions he asked and let him go and then I took a pill and I still feel pretty bad. I never got to ask him where he's staying and that's why I'm calling you, George, for I guess you know. He asked about you and I told him about this college job you have. I've followed your career with genuine interest, George. Can I see you tonight?"

"I'm sorry. Tonight is impossible."

"When can I?"

"Is it really necessary?"

After a short silence Harry said: "I always liked you, George."

"I always liked you, Harry."

"I'm going to do something this time. I know I'm not important like you, but I'm not a push-over any more, not like I used to be. Now it's going to be different."

The undertones in his voice made me frightened. Frightened of the unknown, for clearly I knew nothing important about this little man I remembered as an unemployed radio mechanic who now owned a thriving business just off St. Catherine Street.

I glanced sideways at Catherine but from her face I could tell nothing. Presumably she knew this was not a usual call, but in my work I met a lot of men she never saw, and it was reasonable to suppose that some of them were called Harry. All the same I wished she were not in the room.

"There's the police," Harry said, as though that settled everything.

"They know about him anyway. He saw them in Vancouver."

"Where is he staying?"

"Look Harry—all that business went over the dam years ago. Don't you think it would be better to leave it that way?"

"No, I don't. And I'm not going to. Where is he, George?"

"I don't know."

"I think you're lying."

"Okay," I said.

Catherine rose and went out of the room, and as soon as she had gone I went over to the door, the telephone in my hand on the end of its long extension wire, and closed it.

"There's Joan," Harry said in that obsessed voice.

My memory for names was never good and it let me down.

"Joan," he repeated. "*My* daughter, George, no matter what you may think."

"I never thought otherwise."

I had though.

"She's Norah's image, and it's just like having Norah in the house having her here. She's in the best girls' school in the country, George, and soon she'll be going to college, and she's going to have a good and decent life."

"That's fine, Harry."

"She's going to have a good and decent life, and nobody's going to bring up all that—that dirt."

I breathed heavily. Was I getting old, or was I simply exhausted by crises and emotions?

"Harry, listen to me just for a minute, will you? What good will it do going to the police or starting anything? I suppose you can guess that his return has churned me up too. But there's nothing I can do or want to do. He's been in the camps, Harry. He's been worse than dead for years. Whatever he did in the past, my God, he's paid for it."

There was a short silence.

Then Harry said: "He's alive, and Norah's dead."

The implacable hatred in Harry Blackwell's voice frightened me all the more because Harry, as I remembered him, had been such a gentle, mild and ineffectual little man. I looked at Catherine's painting and what it represented was the exact opposite of this thing I heard in Harry Blackwell's voice.

"Whatever else he may have come home for," I said, "I'm sure it was not to make trouble for anyone. He's a tired, beaten man. Probably he's come home like a lost dog to his basket. You can be sure he's bitterly sorry for any harm he may have done."

Harry Blackwell answered as a Jew might answer a man who informed him that Hitler was sorry.

"Do you think a man like him can come back and say he's sorry and that makes it all right? Do you think it's going to be that easy?"

I shrugged and waited. He went on slowly and very deliberately.

"Joan doesn't even know he exists. His name has never been mentioned in her presence. What she knows about her mother is just what I've told her. I've told her that her mother was a lovely little lady who died when she was very young. I've told her Norah was wonderful." His flat voice went hard. "And so she was before he came along and corrupted her, and made a whore out of her, and took her away, and left her like she was a whore."

"He didn't, Harry. He didn't do it like that!"

"Don't talk to me about what he did or didn't do. Joan is her image. Joan is a pure and innocent little girl and she doesn't know about that dirt."

I thought this remark gave me an opportunity. "Why should she know now? If you ignore him, she will never know him."

"His name is going to be in the papers."

"What if it is?"

"She'll hear about it."

"I doubt it. She's a schoolgirl, and I doubt if she will."

"You don't know how bad and cruel some people are, George. When the talk starts, she'll hear. She'll be asked questions about this man they'll all be talking about. Some kind friend will give her the idea."

I had nothing to say to this, for I realized that he was quite possibly right.

"All I want is for you to tell me where he's staying," Harry said.

"I've told you already I don't know that." God, but I was tired of talking to Harry Blackwell. "But I'll tell you the best I can do. He's going to ring me in the morning and quite possibly he's going to tell me he's leaving town for the States. I'll let—"

"Don't give me that, George. Him go to the States! The Americans are smart. Do you think they'd let a man with his record into their country?"

"Anyway, I'll call you tomorrow."

"Just so long as you do," he said, and the tone and words were a threat.

I hung up wondering what kind of image this deprived mollusc in the Great Barrier Reef of Montreal had formed of himself in the years when he had surprised himself by becoming a success-ful business man. But this was no question I could answer. I had little difficulty understanding the mentalities of famous

politicians, but the minds of the individual common men they
served and pretended to worship I understood no better than they
did themselves.

Chapter V

COMING back from the kitchen with a drink in my hand—and this
was tell-tale because I almost never drank after dinner—I sat
opposite Catherine and saw the flutter in her carotid artery and
marvelled how any human being could endure living with such
extra-sensory perceptions as she had always had. No wonder
Jerome had exploded against her. No wonder he had dreaded
this capacity of hers virtually to read his mind. Had I possessed
his violent vitality I would have dreaded it myself.

"That was Harry Blackwell," I said. And I added grimly: "You
will recall the name."

The heart-shaped face turned to mine, gray eyes wide, and I
swallowed half the whisky at a gulp.

"I was going to tell you this anyway," I said. "It isn't easy."
Still her lips and eyes were open. "Catherine dear"—I forced out
the words—"there's no easy way to say it. Jerome's alive. He's
just come back to Montreal."

Her face went the color of chalk and she trembled.

"I haven't seen him," I hurried on, and wondered why I felt so
guilty. "He phoned me at the university and I talked to him
there."

She neither spoke nor moved, but her face stayed the color
of chalk.

"I haven't seen him," I hurried on. "He phoned me at the
university and I talked to him over the phone. That's why I was
late for dinner."

Out of a huge silence came her voice in a whisper: "How is
he?"

"He tells me he's all right."

But a door had swung open in her mind and the expression on
her face said: "This is too much. I'm not equal to this. Please,
God, why don't You leave me alone?"

Yet her expression softened and her eyes blurred with tears and she looked younger. She had loved Jerome with all her heart and with all her soul and with all her mind, had relied on his enormous vitality, had been the mother of his daughter and the center of his home. He had loved her, too; I believe he had loved her equally. And then something had happened to this marriage so many of their friends had thought perfect. Of course they all had blamed Jerome and called Catherine a saint, but she was not a saint nor . . . it is so easy for an unimaginative man to say that all Jerome need have done was his duty. "What is my duty?" I had remembered him crying out. So he had gone to Spain and become involved, and for years Catherine had lived with the recurrent vision of his splendid male body being lashed, twisted, torn and broken. In the silence of her mind she had heard his screams. In the secret places of herself she had wondered if she had failed him, and by failing him had driven him abroad to this end.

"Is he alone?" she asked me.

I knew it was another way of asking if there was a woman with him, and I told her yes, so far as I knew he was alone.

"Has he any money?"

"I think so, but he's staying at the King Edward Hotel."

She gave a little laugh of anguish: "Let me have some of your whisky, George."

"Do you think whisky's a good idea?"

"No. Get me some of that red liquid, though."

It was a sedative and I brought it to her from her bedroom and she made a little girl's face as she swallowed it. Tears came after that and relieved her and she whispered through them.

"I can't talk now. I can't think now. I'd better go to bed."

I saw that small, graceful figure in the housecoat rise, sway slightly as it moved down the hall and a few minutes later I knew from the sounds that she was in bed. I sat down in my long chair and tried to read a political magazine but could not even see the print. Then like a dentist's drill the telephone snarled at me and I rose and answered it.

"André? André?" called an angry female voice.

"*Vous avez le mauvais numero, Madame,*" I said.

I flopped back in the chair and looked around and saw Jerome's face staring at me from a photograph on top of the corner bookshelf. We always kept it there for the sake of greater naturalness, but I seldom looked at it, or really saw it if I did. I looked at it now and it conveyed little of my sense of its original: it was simply a correct photograph of a surgeon in a white jacket. I got up and joined Catherine in the bedroom, where I found her propped against a pile of pillows with a book on her lap.

"Thank you, George," she said.

"What for?"

"Just for being yourself."

I shook my head, sat on the edge of the bed, stared at the floor and felt her fingers in my hair.

I heard her say very quietly: "It's all come back to me."

I looked at her enquiringly and she looked away.

"Not the things that happened," she said, "but how I felt at the time they happened."

"I understand that."

"Bless you for understanding that."

Meanwhile my fingers, lightly holding her wrist, had found the pulse and I did not like the feel of it at all.

"Don't you think I'd better call Jack Christopher?"

She shook her head: "What can he do but tell me to do what I've done already—take a sedative and rest? But I wish so much he hadn't come back."

I sat helplessly holding her hand in mine.

"I used to see him sometimes in the cellars with those Nazis."

"I did, too."

"But you thought he was stronger than he really was. He was so frightened inside. Just like me."

"Just like everyone."

"I love you," she said simply. "Most of all I've loved you because you never tried to take those old days away from me. And at the same time because you gave me so many new, good days."

"I didn't give them to you. They just came."

"Time heals everything, doesn't it? So long as you don't have to go back and discover it's healed nothing."

"You may go back and discover it's healed more than you think."

"Yes, perhaps I will."

I saw a wry smile cross her face masking the strength I also saw there. I felt her pitying: pitying Jerome, me, herself, pitying all of us whom life presses in middle age. Personal she was as only a woman can be, yet at the same time she had acquired in recent years a capacity to feel with almost everyone she met, a capacity so catholic it was almost impersonal. Jerome would find her different from the eager woman he remembered. Sometimes this impersonality of her feeling for others, for life itself, made me resentful because I felt myself excluded. She understood what it is like to die and I didn't, and that made the difference.

I looked at her and said: "Dear, I must tell you this. I'm glad he's back. I'm glad he's alive."

She gave me a strange glance in reply: "I'm not sure that I am."

What did that mean? Certainly not something obvious. Silence came over us as we companioned one another, two people still wanting to feel young at heart but unable to.

"You see," she said, "I'm still responsible for him. And he feels he's still responsible for me. We're both right. I don't want to feel responsible, but I do and I must. I wonder if he looks old? I almost hope he does. I could never think of him as growing old."

Then, so amazingly fast were the changes in her, she gave a sudden smile that was entirely personal and as female as it could be.

"Tell me something—did he ask if he could see me tonight?"

"He did."

"Oh Jerome!"

Crossing to the window I peered through the slats of the Venetian blind and saw moonlight on the glass roof of a conservatory whose owner was an old lady wintering in the Bahamas. I saw squirrel tracks and the humped shapes of dormant rose bushes wrapped in sacking and drifted over with snow. The snow shrouded everything from here to the pole and the moon shone on it. All the way down the frozen St. Lawrence the moon gleamed on the steeples of the parishes, it threw the shadows of horses pulling farmers' sleighs home from bingo parties in church basements, it brought down into the valleys the huge shadows of hills.

"Dear," she said, "do you know what I'm going to do now? I'm going to try to go to sleep."

"Bless you."

I kissed her forehead, tucked her in and turned out her light.

Chapter VI

LIKE most people who have lived through the last twenty years, I had become a reasonably successful schizophrene so far as my work was concerned. I had acquired the ability to concentrate on a job no matter where my thoughts were. On half a dozen occasions when the world seemed to be falling apart, I had managed to summon up enough concentration to do a job. But tonight it was hard.

For the truth was that I was sick of politics, that I had come to the conclusion that however important politics might have been a decade ago, they had ceased to be fundamental now. In the Thirties I had thought most politicians were scoundrels and in the Forties I had taken a few of them at their own face value as genuine makers of history, but now I believed that nearly all the real history was being made by the scientists and that the politicians merely held posts and inherited situations. So far from being scoundrels or geniuses, most of the ones I knew were depressingly normal: indeed they seemed the best adjusted men I had ever met, for they were at ease in situations which any clear-eyed neurotic would instantly recognize as insane. They must have realized that the control was out of their hands, yet somehow they contrived to give the necessary illusion that it was not. They had a marvellous capacity, at least so I thought, for recognizing the importance of whatever seems obvious to the voters, and for neglecting the importance of almost everything else. If it was obvious to the voters that they were in control, it was equally obvious to them.

But I knew that few of them were. The capital cities where they worked had become colossal Univac machines grinding out more statistically-based information in a month than any trained mind could comprehend in a lifetime. The statesmen went to their desk in the morning and the papers were there. They cleared their desks for more. The harder they worked the less time they had to think, and now that they travelled to see each other in aircraft their lives had turned into a rat race. Every election since 1945 had convinced me that it made little difference who was prime minister or president so long as he was sane and could make the public believe he was leading instead of following. Elections would be held and new faces would appear, but they would soon look just like the old ones and their owners would soon be doing precisely what their predecessors had done. They would over-work and under-think, they would travel too much by air, they would see the importance of the immediately obvious and after a while they would disappear.

But it was no part of my job to philosophize about the effect of modern communications on politics. I was fairly good at my work and had a sixth sense I trusted, and this sixth sense had told me all along that this Korean War would not blow up into the big one everyone feared. My problem was purely technical: how could I reinforce this hunch with evidence? But a trained journalist can reinforce any idea with evidence, so I set to work and around midnight I had finished a job I knew would be adequate in terms of the assignment.

I went to the kitchen, poured myself a glass of milk and tried to relax and think. But instead of thinking I felt, and felt scared and unnatural and became very lonely. I was still feeling lonely when a key scratched and Sally came in on tip-toe.

"What are you doing awake? Is Mummy all right?"

"She's asleep."

While I blew up the fire, Sally went out to the kitchen for milk for herself, and when she came back and sat down she said: "If I don't talk, I'll burst."

Chapter VII

NEVER had I seen Sally look as she did then. Her whole presence shone and she was encased in such a brightness that neither Jerome's return nor my own present mood could dim it. Her cheeks were pink from the cold, her curls were glossy and tight and all about her was this radiance. She set down the milk and came over and kissed my forehead and rubbed her smooth cheek against the back of my hand.

"George!" she whispered. "Comfortable old George!" And then she said: "It's happened at last and if you laugh I'll throw this milk into your face, for it's just as wonderful as all the bad novels say it is."

She dropped onto the sofa so hard she bounced, and she sat there with her legs curled up, shining and glowing at me.

"You're sure about this?" I said.

"But absolutely and positively and completely."

"You've compared your somatotypes? You've gone through the checklist on your neuroses? You've discovered that they fit each other!"

She picked up her milk and held it threateningly, then she gave a gurgle of joy and swigged down half the glass. Even her jaw, which was going to be formidable when she was my age, was soft and gentle tonight.

"In case you'd like to know," she said, "it happened on the top of Mount Royal."

"At eighteen below? Yours is a hardier generation than Alan's father thinks."

"It's only sixteen below as a matter of fact. But to fall in love at sixteen below ought to prove pretty clearly to certain oafs in the Engineering Faculty that I'm not a frigid woman. It was so lovely." A luxurious sigh. "We walked up the mountain through the trees above Pine Avenue and when we got to the top—have you ever been on the top of Mount Royal on a winter night?"

"When I was your age the top of Mount Royal had genuine prestige. Once I was there with a girl and she asked if this meant we ought to get married."

"Don't boast, George. Let me do the boasting tonight." She leaned back and clasped her hands behind her head. "It really was unbelievable, if you'd like to know."

"It always is."

"I'm sure it always isn't. But it was so lovely just the same."

"Have a cigarette?" I suggested.

She shook her head so strongly that her curls trembled.

"It was just as if the whole sky had turned upside down and fallen flat all around the mountain without putting the stars out. Millions and millions of kilowatts lying there all quivering like an electric jelly. At the very moment when it got so beautiful I couldn't stand it, do you know what the idiot boy said? He said I was beautiful, too."

"You told me he's the most intelligent man of his time."

"He's an oaf, of course, but such a sweet one!" She gave me a quick frown. "*I* happen to know it's nonsense, him thinking me beautiful, and it worries me because pretty soon he's sure to take another look. I think it's much safter to have a marriage rest on a solid basis of sex-attraction and compatibility than on some youth's idea that a girl is beautiful, don't you?" Then the raptured smile came back. "But it was lovely just for once. All my life I've wanted to be beautiful, or at least to believe that some man thought I was, and all my life I've known I wasn't, and I've taken it for granted that no man would ever think I was. If any man mentioned I was even pretty, I just took it for granted he had designs for a lost weekend. Men are such awful crystallizers. The nicest of them are the worst of the lot. Look at those sweet neurotics who go up to the Arctic every summer and grow beards and dream about women until they crystallize some little mouse they met at a dance the winter before into a goddess." A sigh. "Well, at least Alan's not one of them. It's not as if he's without experience."

There was a crack from the fire and another ember shot out. I rose and extinguished it, then drew the wire guard in front of the flames.

"One thing puzzles me, Sally. Just what gave you the idea you aren't a pretty girl?"

"Oh, Mummy, of course."

"Now don't be silly."

"I don't mean anything she said. I mean just her. What man could possibly waste a look on me with her in the room?"

I was amazed and said: "I think you really mean that."

"Mummy's passionate and I don't think I am."

"Give yourself time, darling."

"You don't know this but quite a few youths of my acquaintance have informed me pretty bluntly that I'm cold. Did you have affairs when you were Alan's age?"

"When I was his age there was a depression and I was broke and anyway my appearance was against me."

"But you must have had *some*. How many would you call a lot?"

"There's probably an American sociologist with statistics on that. Why don't you look him up the next time you're in the library?"

"I'm being serious, George. You see—" The frown-line struck between her eyes and I hoped that somebody, maybe Alan Royce, would cure her of this habit. Inside another ten years the line would be permanent and it would not help her at all. "You see," she went on, "Alan has built up quite a reputation for himself around the campus and around the town. He started cavorting at a pretty tender age, in my opinion. Now don't misunderstand me, George—I'm not judging him. Growing up in that family what else could have been expected? But I've made a few enquiries about Alan, and I'm not exactly enchanted to learn that for his age he's supposed to be one of our most accomplished swordsmen."

"You persist in giving this lad a terrific build-up."

Then she smiled softly. "But isn't it a fact that a swordsman like Allan is the safest type for a little bunny like me to marry?"

She was so serious, she was so much in love, and underneath her facade she was so moral.

"You mean you got engaged tonight?"

"Well no, and anyway 'engaged' isn't a word we use much any more, and I rather think Alan intends to scout around a little bit, but maybe inside another week or two things will settle themselves, if you know what I mean. But I *am* a bunny, George. In case you're interested, I'm still a virgin."

"That really shocks me, Sally."

"I wish you'd stop laughing at me when I'm being serious for a change. But isn't it true? I mean, isn't it better for somebody like me to marry a man who knows his way around instead of some pure boy who'll want to look around later on? Aren't the pure ones the worst later?"

"I was a pure boy. *Faute de mieux,* but on the whole a pure boy."

"But you wouldn't have had Alan's temptations."

"Why Sally, you insult me."

"I'm not insulting you. I'm just stating a fact. Some men look permanently available and some don't, and you don't, and besides you've been in love with Mummy from the Year One."

Part of the log had collapsed and the fire had ceased flaming. Its glow was sleepy and the apartment so still I could hear her breathing.

"Yes," she said dreamily, "I think we ought to get married as soon as we graduate. We'll both be getting jobs, and the sooner Alan settles down the better. I wouldn't change him for worlds, but I do think he ought to settle down." A look of exquisite, tender pleasure suffused her determined little face. "Who was it wrote, 'Come live with me and be my love and we will all the pleasures prove'? It must be wonderful to be able to *prove* pleasures."

The fire glowed, Catherine's pictures loomed on the walls, in a dismal room downtown where hundreds of whores had labored and hundreds of alcoholics had seen snakes, Jerome Martell was either asleep or staring into the darkness. And outside, according to Sally, the temperature was sixteen below zero.

"But of course," she said slowly, "there's always some gimmick."

"And what may be this particular one?"

"Children," she said. "We don't intend to make the mistake your generation did and put off children till we get neurotic or it's too late."

"Is this your idea or Alan's?"

"He didn't mention it yet, at least about us personally, but it's his idea I'm sure, for he thinks the biological aspect of marriage should be settled as quickly as possible. With life-expectancy rising constantly, we should live till we're well over eighty. There's so much to learn these days we should get the biological side of marriage out of the way when we're too young to be any good at anything else. But the trouble is money. I absolutely refuse to consider Alan turning himself into a corporation slave at the very moment in his life when he ought to be as mobile as possible. I want him to sit the exams for External

Affairs. With his understanding of human nature, he'd be wonderful in External."

I gave my jaw a rueful rub.

"Well," she said, "wouldn't he?"

"He'll have to wait awhile before he reports direct to Mike Pearson."

"Well, what *will* he have to do if he gets into External?"

"My dear girl, tell him to ask his step-father. Jack Lubliner's been in External for twenty years."

"Does Mr. Lubliner report to Mr. Pearson?"

"I suppose he does sometimes. But the pay isn't going to be astronomic in External. What about Alan's father? Is there any money there?"

Sally shook her head. "His father has to pay alimony to his second wife, and there are his mistresses and cars and clubs and trips to Florida and his golf and his liquor and his clothes and the general corruption of his entire personality. Alan doesn't hope for a dime from his father, and that's all right with me."

Silence fell again and we both stared into the fire. I felt young with the sweet, lovely, sad joy of youth, the soft creative sadness of youth I thought had left me forever and I remembered Catherine coming out of the lake when she was eighteen with the summer water streaming off her shoulders and thighs, and myself, later that day when the sun had set, watching a grain boat silhouetted against the western sky and feeling the sweet pain all through me, too innocent even to guess that what I craved was physical love with Catherine.

"George," she murmured, "you're so nice and easy to talk to."

"Come over and kiss a used-up man on the brow."

"But you haven't answered a single one of my questions."

"That's why I'm so nice and easy to talk to."

We were silent again and I stole a glance at her rapt profile and felt a flash of resentment because she was well and Catherine was not.

"George," she said, "I wish I wasn't so shy. There's something pretty personal I want to ask and I'm shy." She flushed slightly and did not look at me. "Do you think I ought to spend a weekend up north with Alan? You know what I'm talking about, I suppose."

"What do you think yourself?"

"How is he going to know if he really wants to marry me unless he's found out first if I'm any good? It was your generation that first had that idea, wasn't it?"

"My generation was wonderful, but it's my impression that the first people who had that particular idea were Adam and Eve."

"It's the accepted thing in Sweden, you know."

"I know. And the Swedes are such a joyous people."

"What are you making fun of now?"

"Only the plans of mice and men."

"Have you gone old-fashioned now you're middle-aged?"

"Probably."

"The trouble would be Mummy, of course. I hate lying, George, I hate lying, and if I went up north with Alan I'd have to lie to Mummy and it wouldn't do any good if I did, for she'd know anyway. She knows everything, doesn't she?"

"Not quite, but you're right that she'd know that."

"If she wasn't Mummy I wouldn't care. Lots of people I know go north and it's kind of a conspiracy between them and their parents. They tell their parents it's just for the skiing, and their parents pretend to believe it because they did the same themselves once. Children hate embarrassing their parents these days."

"They always did, Sally."

"But I couldn't do that to Mummy. Somehow I think it would make her miserable. It would bring all sorts of things up. Dad, and stuff like that."

"I see," I said, and looked away and found myself staring at Jerome's picture.

"I've never understood why she was in love with a stinker like him," Sally said. "But she was—wasn't she?"

"Of course."

"Was he in love with her, too?"

"Of course."

"Then why did he behave like that?"

"I suppose because he was a man."

"That's no answer."

"No, it's not much of an answer."

My expression must have betrayed me, for it was two in the

morning and we were both tired from excitement and from being so close and perceptive.

She said sharply: "George, why is this the second time tonight that you and I have talked about Dad? It's more than a year since we've even mentioned him."

I shrugged.

"You're hiding something," she said. "I can always tell when you are."

"So can your mother," I said. "And she was able to tell the same thing about me tonight." Our eyes met and I took the plunge. "Sally, you're right. It's not been entirely an accident that we've both talked of your father tonight. People are more mediums than they guess, at least some are. Since I've got to tell you in a day or two I'd better tell you now."

She sat upright and looked about five years older, for she knew this was important.

"It's going to startle you and shock you and I wish I didn't have to say it, but you'll have to know sooner or later and I'd better be the one who tells."

Her level glance met mine.

"It's certainly been no accident that I've been talking about your father tonight, for I've been thinking of nothing else. Sally—" I paused and then I jumped in. "Sally," I said quietly, "your father isn't dead after all. I just discovered that today."

Her expression did not alter.

"He's back in Montreal. He telephoned me at the university and just before I met you and Alan, I talked to him over the phone."

She turned slightly pale and became a little more tense but she said nothing.

"I gather his story is not as unusual as you might think. Or at least as I might think. You knew he was in the French underground and you were told—we all were told—he'd been killed there. Well it seems he was captured instead and his life was spared because he was a doctor."

Quickly I went through the same story I had told Catherine. While I talked, her pallor changed to a bright flush and I saw her little fingers clenched hard. Still she did not speak.

"There's only one more thing I want to say," I said. "I'm glad he's back and so is your mother. I liked him and I respected him."

"Then you've told Mummy?"

I nodded.

"George," she flared at me, "why didn't you tell him to go to hell? To go to the States. To go anywhere. Why did you tell Mummy?"

Our eyes locked and after a time she looked away. "Okay, I guess you win. Now I'll take one of your cigarettes, if you don't mind."

I gave her one, lit it for her, and lit another for myself. I had smoked far too many that day and my mouth tasted like the rim of a porthole.

Suddenly Sally broke down and cried. Not in years had I seen her cry, but now she sobbed like a child and I sat beside her with my arm about her slim shoulders trying to comfort her and doing no good whatever.

After a while she looked up, wiped her eyes and blew her nose and turned away.

I heard her say as though she were ashamed: "Did he happen to ask about me?"

"He asked about you almost at once. And very, very fondly."

She began to cry again. "He was such a damned fool!"

"Yes, dear, he was all of that."

"Didn't he ever guess how much we all loved him?"

"He didn't guess. He knew."

"And still he went away and left us?"

"He was a strange man and that was a strange time."

She turned and stared into the fire, her two little fists hard under her chin, her neat little legs pressed together.

"I wish he *was* dead. I never want to see him again."

Then she rose and went to the window and pulled the cord on the draperies, parted them, and stared out at the moonlit snow. The moon had gone far around and there were only a few patches of light where it struck the snow. But it still glimmered from the glass roof of the conservatory.

"Please be nice to him when you meet him," I said.

Still staring out into the night, she answered: "How do I know how I'll be to him?"

"Just don't shut the door in his face, that's all."

"I may even slam it in his face. He slammed it in ours." She turned and her face had the fighting look I had seen so often on her father's. "How do I know anything? All I know is tonight I came home happier than I ever was in my life and walked into this and now I feel horrible. How do I know how I'll behave if I meet him? I may break down and weep like a baby or perhaps I'll simply not care. He's old and I'm young. Why should I feel responsible for him?"

We looked at each other and felt sad.

"Why does everybody stand up for him?" she said.

"Everybody doesn't."

"But you do. I think there's something neurotic in your whole attitude. It's all mixed up with how you feel about Mummy. She loved him and you want to kid yourself you love him, too. You want to share him with her the same way you shared me."

I shook my head.

"I know I'm sounding awful and I hate to sound awful, but why don't you admit that Mummy's human and isn't perfect? Why don't you admit that she made a mistake?"

"Because she didn't. Not in marrying your father."

She stamped her foot. "You're hopeless."

I became angry not because she had called me hopeless but because suddenly her whole attitude angered me.

"You're talking like a child," I said. "Do you think my generation invented neuroses? Do you think things in the Thirties were the same as now? Mistakes? For God sake, of course we made them! But let me tell you something, Sally. You haven't earned the right to despise your father. You may *have* that right, but by God, you've not earned it."

Our eyes met and she looked away, still headstrong, considerably upset, resentful and guilty because she was. Truly I thought this girl felt guilty whenever she detected a trace of neurosis in herself and this made me smile grimly. Was neurosis the new word for sin?

"I'm sorry, George."

"That's all right."

"What are those pills you take to make you sleep?"

"Seconal. Why don't you take a couple?"

"One will be quite enough. I hate dope."

I got up and went down the hall to the bathroom found the seconal and came back with two little capsules in my hand. I got a glass of water in the kitchen and came back to the living room with it and handed Sally the tablets and the glass. She was kneeling on the sofa as stiff as though she were out cold, as silent as though she were in a trance. Automatically she took one tablet and the glass and swallowed the tablet and took a sip of water and handed the glass back. I returned it to the kitchen and came back to the living room and saw it was a quarter past two.

"I'm going to bed," I said. "I'm tired out and I've got work to do in the morning and tomorrow afternoon I have to go to Ottawa."

God knows I was tired. Right down into the bones, as I often told myself I was during the worst of Catherine's crises, and as sad as a folk-song. But when I had undressed and washed and gone to bed and turned out the light I was still wide awake and unable to sleep.

After a while—it may have been half an hour—lying with my eyes closed I became aware of somebody in the room.

"It's only me," Sally's voice whispered. "I'm sorry, George, for some of the things I said to you."

I felt the edge of the mattress go down as it took her weight and a moment later I felt her hand on my forehead. It was gentle and healing and I had never felt it there before. So this girl was motherly after all. I had always suspected she was. This girl was motherly, and how lucky a boy Alan Royce might be.

"You said I hadn't earned the right," she whispered, "and that really reached me. It must be awful to be middle-aged and remember so much and know that everybody thinks it's natural for middle-aged people to be dull and put up with everything."

"Some of us get used to it before we die. At least that's what I'm told."

Out of a sea-deep silence I heard her say: "Why did Mummy marry Dad?"

"Why do you want to marry Alan?"

"I want to marry Alan because I think I love him. And I want to marry him because I want children and a home of my own."

"That's why your mother and father wanted to marry each other."

"Him too?"

"Of course him too. He wanted a home and children as much as any man I ever met."

"You mean he wanted *me?* You mean I wasn't born just because he came home drunk and took a chance?"

"My God, girl, where is your backside? I want to slap it."

"But I thought none of you people wanted children."

"Oh brave new world!" I said.

From Sally there came a sigh, a rending noise of a sigh, and it was followed by a sob.

"You mean he really wanted me? He really did? Oh George, thank you for telling me that! Thank you, thank you, thank you!"

I felt her going away from me, and me going away from her, and I went all the way out to the Rocky Mountains where I saw foothills shaped like the bodies of brown females and a snow-covered mountain spire rose-hued in the distance and heard a waterfall and felt the coolness in the air about a waterfall in the high mountains. Then darkness flooded over the scene with a roll and a fox walked out of the lodgepole pines and watched me.

I heard Sally: "But long before Dad appeared, you and Mummy were in love, weren't you?"

"Yes."

"Why didn't you marry her then? Why didn't you?"

"That would be a long story for three o'clock in the morning."

"But why?"

"No money. No job. No prospects. Too much pride. The depression. But mostly not enough courage."

Again her hand came over my forehead, rested there, and I wondered which was the child, she or myself.

"What was Mummy like when she was my age?"

"How do I know? I was too much in love to know."

"It must have been nice on the Lakeshore when you and Mummy were kids."

"Very nice. No airport. A minor journey into Montreal. French Canadian farms with stone houses and old barns."

"The first time you saw her, what did she look like?"

"The first time I saw her—really saw her—she was all dressed in green."

"Aren't those the words of a song?"

But after Sally left me and all was quiet I was still unable to sleep. Lying in bed with my eyes open, the snow outside a *tabula rasa* now that the moon no longer made shadows in the squirrel tracks, the city silent, lying there in the extreme precariousness of three o'clock in the morning I remembered the first time I had really seen Catherine. It was true what I had told Sally, the first time I saw her she was all dressed in green.

PART TWO

Chapter I

I WAS a seventeen year old boy standing just inside the screen door at the back of our house in Dorval on the shore of Lake St. Louis west of Montreal. An August morning was rising in full tide with cicadas shrilling and a heat haze was building over the lake and I was feeling the heat, especially the humidity of it, for only the night before I had returned from a canoe trip through a region where the days were astringent and the nights were cold. I had been one of eighteen boys led by a schoolmaster from Frobisher and we had paddled from Port Arthur along the north shore of Lake Superior into Huron to Georgian Bay, whence we had gone our several ways home by bus and train. We had looked at those stone islands since made famous by the painters of the Group of Seven, we had paddled into lonely little villages called Jackfish and Marathon, we had broiled fresh trout and whitefish over camp fires, had got up with the sun and fallen asleep when the western sky was the color of a burnt orange.

Now I was in the best condition of my life and was home smelling the flat fresh water and sedge of Lake St. Louis and feeling the heat and recognizing for the first time how lush was this country around Montreal. I was home and was proud and grateful. I was a religious boy, and being acutely conscious that I was clumsy in athletics, and that other boys did not take me seriously, I had prayed to God that I might be strong and popular like the rest. On that trip I had discovered that though I was clumsy I was at least strong, and the other boys had liked me. I had found myself able to carry heavier weights than most and to paddle for hours without a rest. Now, home from the adventure on the water and in the bush, having seen wild bears and heard timber wolves bark, home on the flat shoreline in the familiar heat of a Montreal August, I had found my mother more charmingly feckless than ever and my father more of a boy.

Father was back at his old games. An archery butt with circles of red, white and blue rose over our peony bed and twenty-five yards in front of it was Father surrounded by a bevy of children. Under our lone apple tree Catherine Carey stood with a basket of phlox, roses and late delphinium on her arm, she was laughing infectiously as she told my mother not to concern herself, that nothing had happened to her and that it would have been her own fault if something had. My mother was chattering in her usual way without listening to a word anyone said and my father—whom I had never been able to take seriously as a father—had a sheepish expression on his sheep dog's face and was leaning on a cross bow of his own manufacture which was certainly as lethal as any used at Agincourt. The actual color of Catherine's dress that morning I do not know—it might have been white or red or blue—but with the sunlit green of the garden around her, with the dappled green of the shadowed grass under her feet, green was her color at that supreme moment of my youth.

The cause of the commotion was not unusual in the Stewart household. Once again Father had nearly hit somebody with one of his arrows, and this time the somebody had been Catherine. He had his archery range directly across the lawn beside the house, and anyone entering by the back gate walked right into it. It had been my mother's frightened cry that had brought me to the back door, and now both my parents were talking in the way they had, not angrily (they never got angry) but without listening to a word the other said.

"Hastings, what if you'd killed poor Catherine!"

"But Carrie, we weren't using the Parthian arrows, we were using the English ones."

"You don't get gangrene from English arrows," one of the children said.

"But Mrs. Stewart—" this from Catherine—"don't you see it's perfectly all right. Nothing hit me."

"But something very nearly did. And Hastings, if you'd killed poor Catherine, what would you have said?" Without waiting for an answer she turned to Catherine and bubbled, "It was so darling of your mother to send me delphiniums because they're my favorite flowers. They always remind me of naval officers. Look out, Hastings, here come the dogs!"

Our four dogs, all named after British admirals and generals, all dangerous to strangers, all large, had come charging out and now they surrounded Catherine barking and leaping and barking again, and she tried to fend them off because they were violent, and Beatty and Haig, bull terriers trained by Father to go straight for a marauder's throat, caught hold of her flower basket with their teeth and tried to tear it away from her.

"Down!" shouted Father. "Down and to heel."

Those dogs sitting down around Catherine, their tongues hanging out and their flanks throbbing like bellows, looked slightly more alarming than they had looked before.

"There was no danger to Catherine," Father explained. "She knew all about the archery range. Don't you remember the time we played William Tell? It was Catherine who shot the apple off Billy Aird's head."

"I wish it had been Catherine who shot the apple," said Catherine. "But the year you played William Tell, Catherine was such a sick little girl she couldn't even eat an apple."

"Catherine dear," said my mother with that exaggerated anxiety which always made me nervous, "how is your poor little heart today?"

"It's so much better I don't even know it's there."

"It's so horrid to know it's there, isn't it, that ugly little thing bumping up and down inside of us. Hastings, make the dogs go away. They make me nervous."

Father commanded the dogs to depart and they went. Animals and children always liked to please him. Then, while Catherine and my mother tried to talk to each other, Father turned to the children and resumed a monologue I had heard many times before.

"The reason for the shape of this English arrowhead," he explained, "is very simple. The Parthians made their arrowheads with barbs so you had to tear the flesh to get them out and a man got gangrene every time. But the English liked to kill clean." Father's loving finger stroked the hard smooth blade he had made in his workshop in the barn. "When this kind of an arrow hit a French knight, it shot right through the eyeball into the brain. That's the English way every time. When they kill, they kill clean."

"What's the difference between killing clean and killing dirty?" one of the children said.

"Killing without gangrene."

"Tell us more about gangrene."

Father did so, with detail, accuracy and gruesomeness. I did not listen because I had heard it before, along with the difference between getting bitten by a rattlesnake and a cobra, and between fighting Wellington and Napoleon, and between the size of the bites made by lions and grizzly bears. My world turned upside down as I looked at Catherine enveloped in the sunshine pouring down through the branches of the apple tree. The air began to sing and I felt faint from beauty and from something new I could not understand.

She left before I revealed myself and I saw her back pass through the gate to the road, but I was shy and did not want the others to see me follow her. So I went back into the house and out by another door and through a neighbor's property and came by a roundabout route to the highway where a farmer's cart creaked past me loaded with fresh vegetables, the farmer nodding in the heat. Catherine was twenty yards ahead walking slowly and now she was no longer dressed in green but in light itself, and I tell you I saw a nimbus around her.

She turned as she heard my steps and cried out: "George! I didn't know you were home!"

I came up to her and looked at her face and then at the ground. "Oh, I got home last night."

"Was it wonderful?"

"I guess so."

"Of course it was wonderful! And so were you to make a trip like that. I wish I could, but of course I can't. But I've got something new to show you just the same. Father bought me a sailboat and I've learned how to sail. That's not bad for Catherine. I'm really improving at last."

I blurted out: "Improving? You're perfect!"

We looked at each other and Catherine stepped quietly forward and placed her hands on my shoulders and looked up. Her eyes grew soft and large and her voice sounded like a cello.

"What a silly thing to say! But what a lovely thing to say!"

Then she rose on tip-toe and I felt her full arms go about my neck and her full lips warm and soft on mine, and in a flood of shyness we were looking at each other and it was my first experience of a miracle. I saw her hand pass over her sable hair, that sable hair that seemed so light and alive, and the queen-like serenity return to her heart-shaped face, and I knew, though I had never seen a woman, how the white fullness of her breasts would contrast with the tan fullness of her upper arms, and all these sensual images were so sacred that I blushed lest my knowledge of them would seem a profanity, and I looked at the ground and saw her sandaled feet, very small feet, and how her toes were a little too big because the joints had been swollen and gnarled by rheumatism.

"If there's a breeze this afternoon, would you come out sailing and try my new boat?"

"You mean you really want me?"

"George," she said gently, "why do you talk about yourself that way?"

"Well—"

"I won't let you do it again. You see, compared to me you're —well, apart from being pretty small to handle a boat, I'm not allowed out alone in case a squall comes up and the sails have to be taken in in a hurry. Besides, I want to hear about your trip."

"But all sorts of people will want to go out with you."

Her hand rested on my arm and her eyes on mine. "Do you really think so?"

"Why sure."

"George, you're so sweet." She turned away. "Haven't you ever noticed that the boys are afraid of me. And why not? They've been taught by their mothers to think of me as 'poor Catherine.' They've been told to be nice to me, but at the same time they've been warned not to become fond of me for fear that one of these days they'll find themselves engaged to an invalid."

"Oh no! That's not true."

"If I was a mother and saw my son falling in love with a girl like me, I'd do the same." She took her hand away and gave me a teasing smile. "So now! I've warned you myself. So let's not argue any more. I've always loved your parents because they never warned you against me. Remember the time when

I was a little girl and had the rheumatic fever the first time? All that winter, you were the only boy who ever came to see me. Do you remember?"

I did remember: that January morning when my mother had virtually ordered me to go down the road to see poor little Catherine Carey who was sick and had such a hard time. It was a day of white and green frost with the whole of Lake St. Louis like a Saskatchewan prairie when the arctic wind sweeps it under the sun. The wind swept up whorls of shining snow crystals and the sun flashed through them and the dry snow blew into my eyes as I walked the lakeshore road to the Carey house. After I was let in by the maid, I saw Mrs. Carey coming down the stairs in an apron and from the tone in her voice I knew she was glad I was there.

I had never liked Catherine's mother; in the way children have of knowing such things, I had sensed that she was a resentful woman. She was also much younger than her husband, whom everyone liked.

"Isn't it nice," she said to Catherine, and at that moment there was no love in her voice, "for George to come to see you on a day like this? Not every little boy would do that."

Catherine was sitting up in bed with a ribbon in her hair and a shawl about her shoulders and her face white and thin with enormous eyes. Is there any human expression as wise, as utterly knowledgeable, as poignantly aware as that of a child who longs to live but knows it is crippled? Who longs to please but knows that its body—its very self—makes it impossible to please? It was there on her face, that expression I was later to see so often, and it said as clearly as words: "Please don't anybody mind. Please don't. I don't want to be sick. I want to be like everyone else."

Mrs. Carey left us and Catherine said: "The doctor told me I had the biggest temperature he ever saw."

"That must be pretty big."

"I had one of the biggest pains he ever saw, too." Then she gave me the odd smile with the tiny droop of the left lid and her face said: "I'm *glad* to be here. Please nobody mind because I want to live so much."

"I guess you'll soon be getting out," I said.

"Oh yes."

"We were going to play hockey this afternoon, but the snow drifted all over the rink so I guess we don't."

"But can't you shovel the snow off? It must be such fun, playing hockey. Are you good at it?"

"Oh, I'm no good at stuff like that. They always pick me last on the teams, and sometimes they don't even give me a game in."

"They're mean."

"No, I guess it's just because I'm clumsy, like my Aunt Agnes said. She says I'll always be clumsy."

Our conversation went on like this and then she gave a little wiggle of joy in the sheets.

"No-pain is the loveliest feeling in the world," she said. "And there's one thing you'll never know that I know—what it feels like to see the squirrels come back."

"The squirrels?"

"Of course. I thought I'd never see them again, but this morning my old gray squirrel came to the window to see me and Mummy gave him nuts. Mummy does everything for me. She's wonderful."

Since that January the years had passed and Catherine had become a woman. And now it was as a woman that she smiled at me.

"I'm going to be well from now on, George. I promise."

"To look at you, nobody'd ever think you'd ever been sick."

"Of course I can't take long walks or go swimming, so all I can do is float in the water and get cool. But I can sail. I feel perfectly wonderful, as a matter of fact."

She was so small and yet in a way so stately; so dignified and yet in a way so sensuous. That year I had been reading a book about Mary Queen of Scots and though I hadn't the slightest idea how Mary had actually looked—indeed I believe she was tall—the idea of her was the idea I now had of Catherine: dark hair and high color, a certain gallant despair, a flame in the dark.

But she was also practical and matter of fact; she could be naturally gay as I never could, and she wanted to be gay. She felt my muscle and made a face pretending to be terrified of how strong I had become from my summer's paddling.

"Well, I guess I can hang onto a jib-sheet in a blow. Do you really want me to crew for you?"

"I'm a selfish, hard-headed little woman, George. Yes, I want you."

"What time?"

"As soon as possible after lunch. Whistle for a wind, will you George? You ought to know how to whistle for a wind. Your father's the best wind-whistler on the lake."

"He can always do damned fool things like that better than anyone else."

"But whistling for a wind isn't a damned fool thing. All the best sailors do it." Her face broke open with happiness. "I can't tell you how wonderful it is to have a boat of my own when I never dreamed I could ever have anything like that. It's like being"—suddenly her gray eyes filled—"George, it's almost like being normal."

Chapter II

So THAT summer I entered Arcadia and the pipes played and the glory of the Lord shone round about. The colors of that summer's end are with me yet: the heavy greens of the land and the lighter greens of the gardens, the pinks of the phlox and the ripening apples, the scarlets and tulip-yellows of tremendous sunsets when the clouds stood high as the Himalayas over the pastel-colored lake where yachts lay becalmed. Even the nights were visible. They were dark velvet before the moon rose and later, when the moon was up, Catherine and I along the shore smelled the sedge and the plants, the summer smells of growth and decay, and I thought of her as a whiteness in the dusk.

But that summer more happened to us than falling in love. If childhood is a garden, the gates closed on us then and ever afterwards we were on the outside, on the outside even of the community in which we were born.

Montreal is a world-city now with most of the symptoms of one, but in those days it was as a visiting Frenchman described it, an English garrison encysted in an overgrown French village.

We belonged to the outer fringes of this garrison where the soldiering was done in the banks and trust houses and national insurance companies, the generals being the board chairmen, while the lower officers were the executives who kept things running. The English-speaking garrison of Montreal, absolutely sure of itself in the heart of the French island in North America, was a place where people knew most of the things they needed to know without having to think at all. If you were born in it, and your nature fitted it, your path was clear from childhood. Catherine and I were born in it, but neither of us fitted, and neither did our families.

Mr. Carey would have been happier as a college professor than as an officer in the trust house to which a domineering parent had consigned him. If ever a man lived a life of quiet desperation, it was he. He was quiet, small and dignified, he never raised his voice, he loved growing roses and reading books, and he quietly loathed the work he did for a living. Also he had married in early middle-age, and was unequal to his wife, who had been only twenty years old when she became his bride. Catherine was their only child.

Though I never liked Mrs. Carey, I know now that she was worthy of respect or at least of sympathy. Handsome in the Edwardian style, she was a woman who would have thrived on a busy social life and was permanently frustrated by her husband's bookish habits. She was tactless, passionate and impatient; she was devoted to Catherine even while she resented her for the demands the child's illnesses had made upon her.

That summer, with Catherine grown into a young woman, Mrs. Carey went into the change of life and saw herself with despair as a person who had thrown her youth away. She became snappish and impatient with Catherine, who reacted against her with the sudden ruthlessness of youth.

"I'm going to McGill this fall," Catherine told me. "Mummy says no, but I say yes. I'm going to Europe and I'm going to work and I'm going to do everything Mummy should have done herself when she was young. Mummy says I'm not strong enough, but I won't be an invalid, I won't! Even if I live only ten years, I mean to *live* those ten years." And she talked about the candle that burned at both ends and gave out the lovely light.

Toward the end of August she said to me: "George, you must go to McGill with me this fall."

I protested that I had to go back to Frobisher.

"You made your junior matric last spring. You can go to McGill. Go to McGill, George. Grow up and go."

"But if I go back to Frobisher I'll be a prefect."

"And what difference will that make?"

At the time it seemed to me to make a lot of difference. My Aunt Agnes, who was married to a cadaverous canon with hair growing out of his ears, (he was one of the spiritual guides of the upper echelons of the garrison), had always insisted that I become a prefect at Frobisher. So far as McGill was concerned, she considered it an admirable university because she knew everyone on the Board, but it was also a place which received among its students what she called the ragtag and bobtail of the city. In other words McGill had no social status. But Frobisher had it, and my aunt was determined that I become a prefect at Frobisher.

Catherine laughed at all this.

"But it's so frightfully old-hat, as though Montreal were the the center of the world. And it's so ghastly dull. Look at your friend Jack Buchanan. Whenever I think of Frobisher I think of him. I could write a biography of Jack right now. He'll go to R.M.C. and be a senior cadet. Then he'll go into some St. James Street office and join the mess of a regiment. Then he'll marry exactly the kind of girl that kind of boy always marries, and by the time he's twenty-eight he'll have three children. Inside ten years he'll be having one mistress after the other and getting heavy around the waist. By the time he's fifty he'll look just like his father looks now, and by the time he's seventy he'll be on all sorts of boards, and his grandson will be exactly as he is today. I can't stand a life like that, George, and I'm not going to let you think you can stand it, either."

Catherine was imperious that summer; inside she always was, yet with this wayward little girl's feeling that if she ever wanted anything badly it was going to be taken away from her. In her desire to spread her wings and fly, she was in revolt against her whole background, and even then I knew she was unfair to Montreal. For this old city of French, Scotch and English is wiser than she seems. Ruthless on the exterior, she is inwardly kind; love her, and she will give you her heart, though not her purse. A wise woman said to me not long ago that Montreal's real character is reflected in the faces of the women of its older families, so many of whom, even if not beautiful, contrive to give that illusion of beauty which comes to a woman who knows she has been admired, perhaps even loved, by more than one man, yet is discreet, guarding her own enrichment. The silence of Montreal people about the things that matter most to them is not really hypocritical; it is a protection of the quiet and deliberately chosen intricacy of their lives. But Catherine was in revolt that summer and so was I. I allowed her to become my judge, and I decided to go to McGill in spite of my Aunt Agnes, who seemed less terrifying because I was in love and because she herself was in Europe that summer.

It is time to speak of my family. I have already said enough to suggest they were preposterous, but not enough to explain how a pair like my father and mother were able to survive in a world where people must live in houses and pay their bills. I had one sister six years older than myself, Edith, who had left home two years previously and now is married to an engineer living in San Francisco. It is fifteen years since I have seen her, and I mention her merely to indicate that I was not an only child. Edith has no part in this story. According to my Aunt Agnes she resembled my grandfather on my mother's side, but as I never saw this grandfather, I must take my aunt's word for that.

My grandfather on my father's side is more vivid, and there are still a few people in Montreal who recall him. He was a ruthless business man, but eccentric, a great reader of eighteenth century literature, and after making a sizable fortune he ruined himself by trying to build a railway in South America. In his will he left his house and its furnishings to Aunt Agnes, and the remnants of his financial assets to Father. My two uncles he cut out entirely, and comforted them by the following cryptic sentence: "I know that you, Arthur and James, will wonder why you have been left nothing. The fact is that you are the only ones who have been left anything that counts. I have bequeathed you two priceless assets: my own acquisitive instinct and a grudge against your father which I have no doubt will spur you both toward success."

If my uncles had played on Father's good nature they might have got the estate away from him, but they had always despised him and made the mistake of bullying him. Also, my Aunt Agnes stood up for Father and forbade him to give his brothers anything. The family was permanently split, and though I have two rich uncles still alive in Montreal, all I know about them is that they both suffer from arthritis.

With a modest competence behind him, Father established himself on the Lakeshore and began inventing things. He filed nineteen patents, all of them military and a few rather ingenious, but there was some flaw in all of them but one. The magnetic mine he invented twenty-five years before the Germans invented a workable one was detonated by a barn rat and nearly killed us all. Father's machine gun fired so fast it melted. His one practical invention was a huge steel claw which could be fixed to the back of a locomotive and lowered in such a way that it ripped up the sleepers as the engine advanced. Its purpose was to wreck railways behind retreating armies, and in the British War Office people were so interested they might possibly have bought it had not Father gone to London to discuss it with them.

After this disappointment, Father relapsed into the life that was natural to him. From time to time he filed a new patent, but his real occupation was playing with children, reading boys' books and battle stories and anything he could find dealing with the habits of snakes, soldiers, sailors and savage beasts. His favorite killer among humans was Genghis Khan, among reptiles the African black mamba, and among animals the Canadian grizzly bear, which he insisted could break the back of a lion if it got in the first blow. He was also the gentlest man I ever knew. He never saw a man die a violent death, he never struck a person in his life and the only animal he ever killed was a groundhog that ate Mother's asparagus. The look of reproach in the eyes of the dying animal haunted him for years, and though rifles and muskets were suspended all over our house, he never bought much ammunition for them and when he did so his targets were bottles and tin cans which he pretended were enemy battleships. He infested our property with traps for skunks, muskrats, otters, squirrels and ground hogs, but when he caught them he always released them. Indeed, so many skunks sprayed father when he performed acts of mercy on them that during one summer he smelled like a dead skunk whenever he got wet. Mercy was the cause of the one invention he patented which might have been useful had it not been too expensive. This was an animal trap equipped with a hypo- dermic needle which automatically injected its victim with morphine.

Such was my family. I don't expect you to believe them, but this happens to be what they were like. One more fact completes the picture: Father and Mother loved each other from the day they met.

August passed into September and it was still warm. The moon left us for its fortnight on the other side of the world and the moonless nights were as soft as warm milk. Then after Labor Day, suddenly as happens so often in Quebec, there came a storm followed by a rush of cold air from the arctic and one morning we woke to see the ground white with a flash frost, the lake steaming with fog and the sun shining through it like a copper disk. For two days the shore was bare of children and everyone huddled around wood fires in the houses. Then with equal abruptness the cold front retired before a flood of warm air from the United States and it was Indian summer. Wind- lasses creaked as yachts were hauled out of the lake, boys put their tennis rackets away and went back to school, the oaks and the maples turned copper and gold. The moon was crescent again and one morning I went to town over a plain hazy with the smoke of burning leaves and registered in five courses at McGill, bought my text books and returned for the last days of holiday.

A kind of inner trembling had come simultaneously to Cath- erine and to myself and we found it hard to speak to one another. We became shy now that the moment of truth was near. It came on the night of the hunter's moon.

The moon rose imperiously out of the haze to the northeast

where the city lay, it rode clear of the wrack into an enormous sky emptied of stars by its own might and it moved southward until it stood over the lake. There it hung with a ring glittering about it and dominated the world. Catherine and I met and touched hands and went down through the dewy grass to the sailing dock, knowing that nobody would be there, now that the season was over and the yachts were high and dry. The benches where the people watched the finish of the sailing races gleamed as though quicksilver had been spilled, and I found an old sack and wiped one of them dry. We sat down together, our hands in one another's, and the glory of the world entered us. Catherine's hand trembled in mine and mine in hers, and I could not believe it was myself beside her, myself feeling this mysterious power and beauty, for myself was as I had thought, a more or less fat boy at school with the face described by my Aunt Agnes as a cross between a muffin and a goblin, with a kindly idiot for a father and no confidence. Myself was the person who wished he was a hero, and had been born clumsy and had grown up without much courage. But Catherine's hand was in mine and I saw her profile against the moon with the strong bones under the petal-skin, and I saw her wide, calm eyes and the delicate upward sweep of her brows, and something broke inside me and I was a boy no longer.

Catherine's head turned, it turned as though at that instant she had heard my boyhood break, and the next moment I was kissing her. I thought of an orchard with dew on it, but her lips were soft, giving and receiving, and she took my head in her hands and bent it downward until my ear was against her, and I felt her breasts lifting and falling and lifting as she breathed, and this was the first time I had ever touched a woman so. She took my hands and drew them to where my head had been and I held her as though my hands were receiving two holy cups. "George!" she whispered, and I whispered "Catherine!"

She said: "Last night I couldn't sleep for telling myself we're too young to be in love. But we are."

"Yes."

"I suppose this means we've grown up?"

"Yes."

The hunter's moon stared down, the St. Lawrence lapped so gently at the reeds that its sound was barely audible, and far out in the channel were the riding lights of a moving ship.

"George?"

"Yes."

"Unless I can tell the truth I can't live. I love you, and that's the truth."

"Yes."

"And you love me, and that's the truth, too."

"Yes."

"George, I've been so unfair!"

She turned away, her hand clasping mine convulsively, and I felt the emotion strike out of her like a physical power. I tell you, I felt her soul. My body longed for hers, but my soul thirsted for her essence. Fearfully, wonderingly, pretending it was a caress, I lifted my hand to her cheek and found it wet. She surged against me with a kiss and I felt her tears warm and salt, and I knew she was not crying as a girl but as a mature woman, and I did not know why.

"I've wanted to live so much," she whispered. "I've wanted to live so much I've been unfair for I've made you fall in love with me. I wanted you to love me so much. And I've been so unfair."

"Why?" I whispered. "Why?"

"Because I can never get married, Never, never, never."

"Why?" I repeatedly blindly.

"Because I can never have children."

Again I asked her why and she said: "Please don't pretend. Pretend with anyone else you like, but never with me."

"But isn't your heart better now?"

There was a silence and then she said with her odd factuality: "Dear, put you head here and listen to it."

Again I bent my head and felt the warm, sacred, living fullness of her breasts receiving its weight, and all I could think of at the instant was how beautiful she felt, and all I could feel was this wonder inside of myself that it was I who was holding her.

"Listen, dear," she said.

Then for the first time I heard the stroke of that hidden,

treacherous organ, Catherine's heart. Chunka-ha, chunk-ha, chunk-ha, and then a pause with no sound at all, and then a little stutter, and then the heart took up its litany again—chunk-ha, chunk-ha, chunk-ha.

"It's enlarged," she said simply, "and both its valves have been damaged. With that kind of a heart I can never have children, so I can never get married."

"But why?"

"Because I would die even before they were born."

"How do you know that?"

"Last year the doctor came and I heard him talking to my father when they didn't know I was in the house. 'I suppose Catherine could marry,' the doctor said to Father, 'but only if it's clearly understood that she never attempts to have a child. The labor of carrying a child, much less giving it birth, would finish her with a heart like hers.' Afterwards when he went away I saw Father sitting in the garden and I saw from his face he had been crying. He hasn't had much happiness in his own marriage, but he knows what happiness can be, and he wants it for me and that's why he was sad. Someone like me, George, can bring nothing but sadness to anyone who loves her. Father knows that, and so he cried."

I stared out at the lake and smelled the reeds and followed the lights of the ship ploughing up the channel toward the Soulanges Canal.

"Catherine?" I whispered.

"Say anything you feel like saying. Say it. That's all I beg. Just that you tell me the truth always."

"It's not as if I was any first prize," I said.

She surged against me. "Never, never let me hear you say a thing like that again about yourself. You're lovable."

"I'll never be able to believe that about myself, Catherine."

"Then believe it because you've heard me say it. Listen to me, George. I'm not like these other girls you know. I'm far older than any of them, really. If I had health I sometimes think there's nothing I couldn't do. I don't care whether I live a year or thirty years—oh yes I do, though. But I know that what counts is what you do with your life and not how long you live. I want to live, but I don't want to hurt anyone just because I want to live. Not you, not you least of all the people in the world. But you're lovable and I know it, and if I say so, then you must believe that you are, for I want you to love me, and nobody can ever love another person if he despises himself. There's only one person I hate, and that's your Aunt Agnes. And I hate her because of what she's done to you."

Then she held her face away from mine and looked at me in the bright moonlight.

"Don't be frightened, George. Take what I can offer you. Take me and use me, please. Let me help you stop being a frightened little boy, and then you can grow older and marry somebody who is strong and healthy."

She kissed me with a maturity of passion equal to any I ever found in her afterwards. The moon continued to stare down on us and we sat on the cold damp bench in one another's arms until at last a wandering cloud covered the moon and the lake gave a shiver and went dark.

She said: "You're the only person who ever made me feel I was a woman and not a sick little girl."

And I said: "You're the only person who ever made me feel I was anything."

People talk of calf-love with wistful disdain, but mine was as intense as any emotion I knew until I crossed the frontier, years later, when I discovered that all loving is a loving of life in the midst of death.

We rose and went home with our hands entwined.

The next day I woke with the feeling that I was in a different world and so, outwardly, I was. The house trembled and shook, and I looked out the window and saw waves on the lake four feet high. They smashed against the shore in short, sharp volleys, the wind whipped off their tops and blew water like hail against the front of the house, the trees screamed and groaned in the wind and rain, their trunks turned black and sleek, their dying leaves stained the air scarlet and bronze as they streamed through it and the light was weird on account of the carpet of wet leaves on the ground. Indian summer was over, and with it my time in Arcadia. Another set of gates swung to and locked, and when I came down to breakfast I found my parents looking at one another, and then at me, like a pair of guilty children.

"Your Aunt Agnes has just telephoned from the city," my mother said, "and I'm afraid she's coming out to spend tomorrow with us."

"Oh?" I said, and sat down at the table.

"She's heard about you and Catherine. I thought I'd better warn you. She's heard about McGill, too."

That was quite a house to grow up in, one where my parents turned into a pair of frightened children at the arrival of an aunt.

Chapter III

THE next morning was clear and cold and Aunt Agnes came at noon. The moment she entered the house she behaved as though she owned it, and because I was accustomed to this, I did not think it exceptional that she should say to Father, "I'll speak to you alone," and that he should follow her into his own library and come out of it ten minutes later looking sheepish and shifting from one foot to another while he stood and told us that lunch was ready, though it wasn't.

While lunch was being served Aunt Agnes was dramatically silent. When lunch was over she turned to me:

"I've come out to talk to *you*, George," she said, and added to my parents: "I don't wish to be disturbed when I talk to George."

Then it was my turn for the library, an absurd room filled with boys' books and military histories and a stuffed python.

"Sit down, George," said Aunt Agnes, and she herself sat down on a horsehair chair with her back straight.

The four uncles I never knew loathed Aunt Agnes, and the most ribald of them is supposed to have said that she would have made an excellent madam of a bawdy house. As a masterful character is traditionally associated with that position in life, it is possible that my Uncle Leslie was right. Aunt Agnes wore her hair in bangs like Queen Alexandra and she dyed it. She wore small, black-buttoned shoes and dresses that rustled. I believe she also wore whalebone stays, because without them her body could hardly be as stiff as it looked. As I see her in retrospect it occurs to me that had she been another kind of woman she might have been attractive to men, as some *belles laides* are, for she had a well-turned bosom, a wasp waist, a melodious voice and her height was five feet and one half inch; even the tiny mole on her chin might have been an asset if she had wished to attract. But she didn't.

"George," she said, in her melodious and oh so reasonable voice, "I understand that you've made a double fool of yourself this summer."

I mumbled something negative.

"First it was this Carey girl and then it was McGill."

"What's the matter with Catherine?" I said defiantly.

Aunt Agnes looked at me as my Grandfather had looked at me and created a moment of dramatic silence.

"You mean to say you don't *know* what's the matter with her?"

"Catherine's not sick any more," I said.

Aunt Agnes looked out the window and my eyes, following her glance, saw Father scuttling past the house holding something bulky under each arm.

"In normal circumstances," said Aunt Agnes calmly, "a childhood infatuation is no more serious than the measles. But the situation between you and this Carey girl is quite dangerous enough to be nipped in the bud."

"What do you mean, Aunt Agnes?"

"It might easily grow into something very serious indeed."

"It's serious right now. I love Catherine."

She gave me a pitying smile. "At seventeen?" And then she surprised me. "That's why I'm here. I believe you really do love this little invalid. And I should not be surprised if she returns your infatuation. The both of you are lame ducks. Yes." Her beady eyes fixed themselves on mine. "I expect she's the first girl who ever liked you?"

I nodded.

"She's similar to a cripple, of course, with that heart of hers. I'm told she's quite good-looking, though I can't see it myself. It would be much better, actually, if she had a wooden leg than a heart like that. Naturally the child is grateful to you for even noticing her. Cripples are always grateful for affection, especially if they're female. Yes. I can see how she might be grateful for the attentions even of someone like you."

I felt myself flushing with rage and hatred, but could think of nothing to say.

"I have made enquiries," Aunt Agnes continued serenely, "of a doctor who understands about cases like hers. They're quite incurable. She will be a burden on others as long as she lives. Of course at the moment she *appears* quite all right. But she knows she is not all right. Did this Carey girl," asked Aunt Agnes in the same serene tones, "mention any of this to you, by any chance?"

"Of course she did."

"What a fool you are! You're not an idiot like your father, but you're a fool."

I looked at her sullenly.

"I believe I've under-rated Catherine. She's shrewder than I thought. She's played on your chivalry. Women are apt to do that, and men are always fools about it. I suppose it was she who suggested that you go to McGill in spite of my plans?"

I did not answer.

"So it was! I knew it. Yes."

A long silence during which I felt my ears on fire.

"George," said Aunt Agnes after a time, "I suppose you are aware that the time has come for you to think seriously about your future?"

"I have been thinking about it."

"Indeed? What do you intend to be?"

"I don't know yet, Aunt Agnes."

"What do you think you could be successful at?"

"Well, I guess there'll be quite a few things."

"There will *not* be quite a few things, George. You would be useless in business. Business does not attract you, does it?"

"No."

"Well? I can't see you as a lawyer. You lack the kind of intelligence and drive for the law, and you would quickly be bored by it. There is only one profession where I can imagine you even earning a living, and that's schoolmastering. In the *right* kind of school, of course."

There was a ragged volley of shots outside and Aunt Agnes lifted her chin.

"What's that?" she said.

"It's only Father."

She raised her eyebrows for more specific information. And feeling ashamed and resentful because Father let this woman come into his house and bully us, I spoke spitefully.

"He's firing off brass cannons with the kids. He made them himself. He's made models of German battleships and he and the kids are shooting at them. They're playing the battle of Jutland."

Aunt Agnes surveyed me. "George," she asked sweetly, "have you any idea what kind of man your father seems to adults?"

I let the question go and she did not press it.

"George," she said next, "before I sailed to Europe last June I thought you and I had come to a clear understanding. You were to return to Frobisher and become a prefect. Montreal is a man's city and being a prefect will be like joining a good club. But as a freshman at McGill you'd be just one little boy in a herd of Jews.

"I have spoken with your headmaster and he believes that with diligence you will be able to get a second-class degree at the university later on. That will be adequate for you to obtain a position in a good private school."

Another pause.

"As a schoolmaster, what will you earn?" She continued. "Do you know the answer to that question?"

I, who had no wish to become a schoolmaster, mumbled that I did not expect it would be very much.

"You will start at about a thousand a year with keep," said Aunt Agnes. "In time you will work up. In schoolmastering, the clergy and ships the pay is never large, but there are other compensations. A clergyman, a ship's captain and a headmaster has a position. At forty-five, if your cards are played right, you might become a headmaster.

"For a career like that—and it's the only possible career for someone with your disadvantages—you must be scrupulously careful in your choice of a wife. Obviously it is absurd for you even to consider marriage for at least ten or a dozen more years. But when the time comes, you must marry the right kind of girl.

"For you, the right kind of a girl is a wealthy young woman who has always considered herself plain. Your appearance will improve in the twenties, and after you are thirty it will deteriorate until you are fifty, when it will no longer matter what you look like.

"You must plan to marry a plain girl with money. You must be realistic and disciplined. There are many such girls and I have my eye on several who may turn out to be suitable. They make the best wives because they are grateful to be married at all. With a plain girl of good family and a private income, you could make a tolerable success out of life in a modest way, our family would not die out and perhaps you would have children who would amount to something.

"There is no other alternative that I can see. I have talked things over with your Uncle Harry and he agrees with me.

"So you must return to Frobisher this fall. Yesterday I visited the Registrar at McGill and cancelled your enrollment there. So everything is decided."

I lost my temper and flushed and got to my feet.

"I won't!" I said. "I'm going to McGill. I'm going to do as I please."

"Sit down, George, and stop being silly."

"I won't sit down."

"You will please stop behaving like a child."

"Then stop treating me like one."

She eyed me and I felt the steel of her will. Since I had been a baby I had felt it, and it paralyzed me. I sat down and looked sullenly at the floor.

"Actually, George, you have no choice in this matter. Your Father will advance the money for Frobisher. He will not advance it for McGill. I have already spoken to him and the thing is settled."

Then she rose and with a perfectly-timed exit she left the room.

A few minutes later I followed her. The banging of cannons continued on the shore and I saw Father's little boats sailing in line ahead and the shot splashing around them. None of the boats seemed to be in any danger. Mother fluttered downstairs and began talking to Aunt Agnes. I passed them, red-faced and sullen, and walked out of the house and down the road to the Careys. I knocked on the door and nobody answered and then I remembered Catherine saying that she and her Mother were gong into town that day. Wretched and despising myself, I killed the rest of the afternoon alone.

At tea time I returned and found that Aunt Agnes had left and that my mother and father were eating buns in the living room. Father gave me an evasive look and then became boyish and hearty.

"George, you should have been with us this afternoon. We sank four German ships, the boys and I. The cannon worked perfectly. We sank the *König*, the *Kaiser*, the *Prinz Regent Luitpold* and a cruiser. That's more big ships than Beatty and Jellicoe sank at Jutland."

I sat down and said nothing.

"George dear," said my mother, "have some tea and a bun?"

I shook my head and my parents looked as uncomfortable as a pair of schoolchildren caught by the teacher in the wrong place.

Finally I said: "Why does Aunt Agnes have to come out here and treat us like that?"

"Well," said Father, "well, you know her bark's worse than her bite. Old Aggie," he went on to Mother, "you know what she's like. But I'm afraid she knows best. She's a clever woman, you know, a very clever woman. Always was."

"She's a horrible woman," I said.

"George," said my mother, "that's no way to talk about your aunt."

"She told me you won't let me go to McGill," I said to Father.

"Well now, I wouldn't put it quite that way, old man. Your Aunt Agnes has your interests very close to her heart and in spite of her bite—I mean her bark—she knows best, old man."

"So she's bullied you, too?"

"Now then, old man, that's putting it pretty rough."

"Can I go, Father? That's all I ask. Can I go to McGill?"

He swallowed nervously and tried to look wise.

"George old man, when your Aunt Agnes explained things to me, I realized I'd not given the matter sufficient thought."

I looked at him the way a boy looks at his father when he knows his father is afraid of doing what he wants.

"After all," Father went on, "she's a very clever woman, your aunt. I don't know where we'd be without her. When your grandfather died she said to me I must always take her advice about important things and it's a lucky thing I did or long ago we'd have been without a roof."

I stared sullenly at my plate.

"After all, old man," said Father with forced cheeriness, "what's a year in a boy's life? You go back to Frobisher like a good boy, now. You'll be a prefect and that's more than I ever was. Next year you'll go to McGill and that's a promise."

"If I don't go now," I said, rising to my feet, "I'll never break loose."

"Break loose from what, dear?" My mother asked.

"Oh my God!" I said and headed for the door.

Behind me I heard my mother's plaintive voice: "I do hope you won't swear like that in front of Catherine, she's so delicate."

"Oh my God!" I repeated, outside in the hall I hit the newel post so hard with my fist that I broke the skin over my knuckles.

Chapter IV

MY AUNT AGNES was a thorough woman; years later I met an elderly lady who told me, in speaking of her, that she was a political hostess *manquée*. She was married to this cadaverous canon with the hair growing out of his ears, who was partially deaf, and was lazy and insensitive as well, and she had no children of her own and hardly any outlets for her energy. She was too snobbish to have anything to do with women's clubs—she regarded them as middle-class and American—and she probably felt herself snubbed by people with more money than herself. She had met Catherine's parents and despised them, and had met Catherine herself and disliked her. Whether or not she liked me I never knew, but she certainly resented the fact that I disliked her.

No sooner was Aunt Agnes back in Montreal than she wrote Catherine the kind of letter an experienced woman can write to a young girl. She was courteously cruel, and she struck Catherine exactly where she knew she would hurt her the most. She expressed sympathy with her heart-condition and admiration for her courage in living with it. But she made it very clear to Catherine that she and everyone else assumed that Catherine would accept realities and understand that it would be sinful and destructive for her to try to live as other women did. She told her that I was weak and she spoke very frankly about the kind of people my parents were. She did not blame Catherine for influencing me, but pointed out that she had.

Catherine showed me this letter and watched my face while I read it, and I felt unequal and alone. I was only seventeen and I had never had any confidence in myself. My expression betrayed me, and for the first time Catherine became formal with me.

"I never intended to intrude into your life, George."

Strange, elderly words from a girl of eighteen, and I was too weak to face their implication. I became tongue-tied, and when I left her that day her face was frozen.

Two days passed and we did not see each other. Then word came from Aunt Agnes that all had been arranged for my return to Frobisher even though the autumn term had already begun. Feeling like lead I packed my bags and walked out alone along the lakeshore in an autumn wind, and all the intimate places where I had known life and joy were dead and sad. Night fell and I ate a silent, sullen meal with my parents.

"Cheer up, old man," said Father, "It'll only be one more year."

"Why don't you go out and say good-bye to Catherine tonight?" Mother suggested brightly.

"No," I said.

But an hour later I was walking along the road in the dark to the Carey house in a wind that whipped my hair and blew moisture from the lake through half-bare trees. The leaves had begun to fall early that year and only the oaks were fully clad and now, hearing that wind screaming through the ragged birches and maples, I could almost hear the voice of the winter.

When I reached the Carey house there were only two lights burning and I rang the bell and waited. Several minutes passed and I was about to go away, when suddenly the door opened and there was Catherine in a silk dressing gown looking tiny and dark against the dim light behind her.

"George!" And in her voice was that note of fatality which some women have when, after a long inner struggle, they have made up their minds to surrender to some decisive force. "Come in, dear."

I followed her in and this new Catherine made me afraid. The door closed behind me and I went into the living room ahead of her, smelled the pleasant aroma of Mr. Carey's tobacco, looked out the window at the end of the room and saw nothing but darkness. One of the lights went off behind me and I turned around.

"I'd gone to bed," Catherine said. "Mummy and Dad are in town at some reception and Yvonne won't be back for a couple of hours. When I heard the bell I hoped it was you."

I sat down and she was little more than a presence in the dim light. She sat beside me, her head turned away, relaxed and tense all at once. I was aware that her hand lay beside me and I took it and felt its pressure.

"George!" she whispered, and I felt her will, her woman's will, taking possession of my weaker male one.

Then we were in one another's arms on the sofa and she had nothing on but her dressing grown and the nightdress underneath it. I held her and felt the house quiver and saw strange images and she was alive and stirring against me, alive and embracing me with an instinctual female knowledge wonderful and frightening.

"George!" she murmured. "Dear George! Dear George!"

Then she sat up and looked at me and I saw her eyes grave in the dim light. She slipped out of her clothes and I saw her naked and strange with the white and immense wonder of a woman's beauty the first time a man or a boy sees it. Then again she was in my arms and I held her blindly.

"Yes," she whispered, "yes, yes. We must, we must."

But I trembled and was afraid not merely as a boy is who

fears to make a girl pregnant, but because I was not yet a man.

She waited for me, she held me, she was as quietly restless as a quiet sea.

Finally I sat up and heard myself say: "No, I can't."

And when I said this I felt a kind of virtue go out of me, and became an utterly defeated boy and less of a man than I had been for months.

Silence for at least five minutes while the house quivered in the storm and then, suddenly, I was aware that the room was bright. Catherine, looking calm and now dressed again, her face appearing as though nothing unusual had happened, sat down on the chesterfield and said nothing. Neither did I.

"George," she said finally, "I wanted it to be you. *You* George."

I could say nothing, could think of nothing to say.

"I've got to live, George. When I go to McGill I'm not coming back here. Mummy resents me. She always has. I've held her down and spoiled her life. At least, that's what she thinks. Actually she's spoiled it herself because she's selfish and at the same time she's afraid not to do what everyone thinks is her duty."

Catherine could talk like this even then, possibly because she had been alone so much that she had read far more than most of us and had not picked up the loose and easy speech rhythms the rest of us used.

She smiled at me with a gentleness for which I was grateful: "George, who ever told you that women are delicate and gentle? I'd have been good for you, dear. I'd have protected you. Don't let some other woman spoil . . ." And then with a little shrug and another smile she said: "Have you got a cigarette?"

I didn't, and she knew I didn't because I had not yet begun to smoke.

"Daddy usually smokes pipes, but he has some stale old Three Castles around somewhere. Let's smoke a cigarette and then I'll send you home."

She found a tin of her father's cigarettes and they were stale and dry and we smoked one apiece and coughed and then, with a new formality, she extended her hand and I took it.

"Good-night, dear. A year from now I'll see you at McGill."

I left the house like somebody escaping from he knew not

what, and the wind tearing at my hair and the rain lashing my face were grateful as I walked home.

The next morning I returned to Frobisher after failing in my first effort to be a man. A fortnight later the headmaster announced to the assembled school that I had been made a prefect, and a week later I received a letter from my Aunt Agnes congratulating me and reminding me how wise her decision had been. My last year at Frobisher was not a happy one and that is all I can remember about it. It was almost a blank in my life because of what I had lost, and I lived through it in the hope of seeing Catherine again the following summer.

But I did not see her the following summer because she had gone to Europe. We had exchanged a few letters in the interval, but hers had been correct, the kind of letters a woman writes to a man when she has closed the book on a might-have-been. It was mid-summer before I learned anything about her first year at McGill, and I learned it from Jack Buchanan, the boy Catherine had taken as an example of all that was stuffy in the life of the Montreal garrison.

"She went wild last year," Jack told me with a knowing smile.

"What do you mean by that?"

He gave me another knowing smile: "She certainly surprised a lot of people. Nobody ever noticed her out here. Out here she was my idea of a mouse, but at McGill she certainly got herself talked about."

"What for?"

"Late parties. She was in with quite a crowd. I heard she was on the carpet before the Dean of Women."

But this rumor of Jack's was untrue. Certainly she had burned her candle at both ends and had lived with a kind of desperation, but she had also worked hard and done well in her exams. From other students I learned that she had become a considerable figure on the campus for a first year girl. Boys who had never seen her before had thought her attractive and she had been given quite a rush. And one of the girls I knew, who was wiser than Jack Buchanan or any of the boys, told me with perfect candor that she envied her.

"I know a lot of people criticized her, but that's only because she doesn't care. She doesn't expect to live more than ten years, but she intends to *live* those ten years. I think she's wonderful, even though she can't see me across the street."

I knew then that I had lost her and with her the best of myself, and I was afraid of going to McGill as a freshman because of the pain I would feel when we met and she was somebody and I was nothing. But this was one humiliation which turned out to be baseless, because I did not go to McGill that fall.

During the past twelve months my father had at last contrived to do what my Aunt Agnes had always predicted he was bound to do—he had lost his money. This was one more evil for which my own failure had been responsible, for after I returned to Frobisher, Father was ashamed of his weakness before his sister. He had always consulted Aunt Agnes before making an investment, and she in turn had always consulted the best investment broker in the city. Now Father decided to be his own boss and get rich quickly.

It was an ore development which sunk him, and like most of Father's projects the idea behind it was eminently practical. The ore was located in the Ungava Peninsula, there was a large steel plant in Sydney hungry for it and the ore could be brought to Sydney by sea more cheaply than the ore of the Mesabi could be brought to Pittsburgh. But as in all Father's ideas there was one fatal defect, and the defect here was that he was exactly one generation ahead of the times. Without bulldozers and aircraft it was impossible to exploit the Ungava ore, because the region was not opened up. Father sank his money and lost it.

It was not from him, but from my Aunt Agnes, that I learned what this meant to our future. It meant the sale of the old graystone house that had been our home. It meant that Father would have to become a clerk in a commission office in the city, and that he and Mother would have to live in a small flat in Nôtre Dame de Grace. And it meant that I, instead of going to McGill, would have to go to work to earn a living.

In mid-September Catherine returned from Europe and discovered that our house had been sold and that we had been ruined. She wrote me a letter I still have. She wanted to see me. She begged me to borrow money—she promised that her Father would arrange it—and go to McGill anyway. But my pride had already driven me out of Montreal to Toronto, for I did not want to live where I had been happy for a time and where all my old friends were rich and I was as poor as a grocery clerk. I did not answer Catherine's letter, or the one she sent after that, or the card she sent to me at Christmas. I did not see her again until years later.

PART THREE

Chapter I

FIVE hours after my late night talking with Sally I was up and
bathed, making my breakfast and trying to think about the day
ahead of me. I left the apartment before either Catherine or Sally
were awake and went down in the elevator and out into the
street. My eyes were stiff from lack of sleep and felt too large
for my face and when I stepped outside the air was so cold I
gasped. It was a cruel day, twenty below zero with a high wind
blowing bright from the north under an electric blue sky. No
taxis were in sight and I kept walking down Côte des Neiges
turning my head to watch for cabs coming down the hill but
seeing nothing but private cars slithering on the hard ice with
little rabbit tails of smoke blowing back from their exhaust
pipes. Montreal in this north wind looked harsh and angular
and the edges of the roofs smoked with snow that made rainbows
as the sun struck through them. The light hurt my eyes and
I wished I had remembered to wear my colored glasses. By the
time I reached the radio building my nose was running and my
briefcase seemed frozen to my hand.

Ten minutes later my skin was on fire in the dry heat of the
office, and when I unlocked my filing cabinet the key made
a spash of light from the static charge and the papers I took
out crinkled in my hands. While waiting for Connolly, the man
who produced my broadcasts, I tried to work on an article I
had agreed to write for a national magazine. But I needed more
sleep for a job like that, and it was a relief to drop it when the
mail was delivered. I began reading the papers, worked through
one French and one English paper from Montreal, then the edi-
torial pages of *The Ottawa Citizen,* the Toronto *Globe and Mail,*
the India paper edition of the *Times* (London), *The New York
Times* and I was about to pick up *The Chicago Tribune* when
the door opened and Connolly came in.

"I feel like hell," he said.

"Fine. So do I."

"Yeah," he said, "I certainly do feel like the bottom of a bird
cage on this lovely winter morning."

Connolly slumped into a chair and scowled at me. He was a

big man thick through the shoulders and hips bulging in an unpressed tweed suit. He was a salaried servant of the CBC who hated his work but did it because he had a family and believed he was buying time for his great novel about the war in which he himself had been a genuine hero and casualty, for he had flown forty-seven missions with Bomber Command and won a bar to his D.F.C. for staying at the controls of a flaming Lancaster long enough for the rest of the crew to escape. He limped from a shattered leg and one side of his face was shiny from a skin graft and unnaturally pink and white under his shock of black hair. But the post-war Connolly was more seriously a casualty of Ernest Hemingway. He had entered Hitler's war so steeped in *A Farewell to Arms* that the Australians, Englishmen and Canadians he wrote about all talked like Italians trying to think in English, just as he in his ordinary life tried to talk like a character out of a Hemingway short story. He had showed me his script and I had not known what to say about it, for I liked and respected the man. You couldn't call his novel a plagiarism; he was such a prisoner of the master that his script read like a parody of the later Hemingway parodying the Hemingway of the Twenties.

"I certainly do feel like hell," he repeated. "Do you feel like hell?"

I shrugged.

"What's new?" he said. "You finished that script? I better read it if you finished that script."

I pushed the papers over the desk and while I read the *Chicago Tribune* I heard him grunting angrily and after a while he pushed the script back at me and asked if I believed all that crap.

"The Americans are carrying the ball," he shouted at me, "and this country that used to be a real country what's it turned into but a hog with its snout in the trough? What the hell are we doing out in Korea to make you talk so smug? Time was this country did the fighting and the Americans did the talking, but times sure have changed. No wonder this sweet little show of ours gets a higher rating every week with you talking about patience and time. I read my Tolstoy too."

"Well, what's your policy?"

"Go in with all we've got. Go in for Christ's sake and kick those goddam Chinks in the teeth."

I looked at him and felt irked. He knew nothing whatever about international affairs and he thought himself a realist. In a way I suppose he was.

"This crap about the importance of Indian opinion," he went on. "The Americans could give those Indian bastards the whole goddam U.S. Treasury and that Nehru would make a speech about American imperialism. For Christ's sake, the Indians! Why can't you ever tell the truth for a change? I bet in the 1930's you were all for Chamberlain and appeasement. I bet the night of Munich you said it was peace in our time."

I raised the *Tribune* between him and me. "Bill," I said, "I'm tired of you."

"You're tired of *me*? What the hell do you think I am of you?"

He went out slamming the door behind him and I looked at the ashtray beside me and saw it was piled with butts. I reached into a drawer for a stick of gum, a sure sign my nerves were bad, for I only chew gum when I smoke too much and I usually don't smoke too much unless I am over-tense. Now I chewed and smoked at the same time and felt the bile rise as I thought about Connolly, and went on reading an editorial in the *Chicago Tribune* that made Connolly sound mild in comparison. It was developing into a thoroughly bad morning.

Then the phone began ringing. The convener of a woman's club wanted me to address the ladies about Korea and I gave her my regrets. A sub-editor of a national magazine wanted to buy me a lunch and talk over a few ideas and I told him I was sorry. There were some more calls, all more important to the caller than to me, but not important enough for a sensible man to have wasted his time on them, before the switchboard notified me that Ottawa was on the line and that Mr. Arthur Lazenby wanted to speak to me if I was able to speak to him.

"Put Mr. Lazenby on," I said, and waited for half a minute before his voice reached me.

"Hullo, George. Do you remember me?"

"Of course, Arthur."

"It's been a long time."

"It certainly has."

"I hear you're coming up to Ottawa tomorrow," he went on, "and after you've seen the Minister I was wondering if you could have lunch with me?"

"That would be fine, Arthur. Anything special?"

"Nothing you could call special in the official sense. But I think we ought to have a talk."

"That would be very nice."

"How are things with you? I've been so out of touch with Montreal I hardly know my way around there any more."

"Things with me are about the same."

"But a little different from the old days?"

"Not as different as with you."

"Well, I'll meet you outside the Minister's office tomorrow morning. Your appointment is for ten—you should be through around eleven."

"Is he going to give me all that time?"

"You never can tell. But I don't think I'm being indiscreet if I mention that your attitude in this Korean affair has been much appreciated by our department. And all the more so because everyone knows you're independent."

"Why thank you, Arthur."

"I'll meet you outside the Minister's office then, in the East Block?"

"Let's make it later if you don't mind. I've promised to look in on an old friend in the Press Gallery."

"Then we'll meet in the lobby of the Chateau at noon? Right?"

As I put up the phone my feeling of unreality deepened. It was months since I had thought of Arthur Lazenby and years since I had seen him, but he was another of those figures who would always be associated in my mind with the depression. In the old days he had been silent, less obviously insecure than the rest of us, an adherent to the group around Jerome Martell, and on the last occasion when we had met he had made me realize how much one can see of a man without knowing the first thing about him. His career since then had been spectacular. No sooner had he joined External than he rose like a rocket. In the war he had been stationed in London, and using London as his sally-port he had completed some confidential and even dangerous missions with great distinction. The talk in Ottawa was that he could have a top ambassadorial post for the asking, but that he probably would not ask for one yet because he was so important where he was. Remembering what he once had been like, I found it hard to believe that this was his career, but it was.

I went back to my papers and read a few more before the door opened and Connolly came back, this time looking sheepish and apologetic.

"I'm sorry about sounding off, George. Forget the crap, eh?"

"That's all right."

"It's not all right at all. Why do I have to shoot off my mouth at a nice guy? Why not at a bastard?"

"I'm not so sure I'm a nice guy, Bill."

Connolly went on to explain that his novel had been rejected by another publisher, that he'd had a fight with his wife and got drunk afterwards and was badly hung over.

"So I see a calm guy like you and I feel inferior and that's why I get sore. I feel like a coated tongue."

"I thought you felt like the bottom of a bird cage."

"I feel like that, too."

"You were right about my script," I said. "It's crap all right. But it's not crap for the reason you said. It's crap for a different reason."

Then I told him about my trip to Ottawa and asked if he could put my broadcast onto tape that afternoon. Connolly was as helpful as possible: he said it would be easy to tape it and run it at the usual hour as though it were live. This was not often done without the public being told it was a recorded broadcast, and my stuff was always supposed to be live, but Connolly said there would be no need to make any mention of the technical difference this time.

"Jacques will be free at three o'clock," he said, "and we'll shoot it through in time for your train. Say, that's swell about the Minister wanting to see you. That's real recognition."

"I'd hardly call it that. But I don't mind admitting I'm pleased."

Connolly went out and I remembered some calls I had to make. I phoned the university and told the porter to put up a notice saying I would be unable to meet my students at the usual hour next day. Then I called the King Edward Hotel and was temporarily alarmed when the clerk told me there was no Dr. Martell registered there. But I guessed at the explanation and asked if anyone had left a message for George Stewart.

"*Moment, s'vous plaît,*" said the clerk and went into his routine of the night before.

After a minute he came back on the line and asked if I was George Stewart personally—those were his words—and when I said I was, he told me there was a Dr. Armstrong who had left a message an hour ago saying I could meet him in the lobby of the King Edward at 12:30.

"Tell the Doctor I'll be there at 12:45," I said, and hung up.

I sat before the phone with my elbows on the desk and thought about Catherine and felt guilty because I had left the house without seeing her that morning. It was absurd to feel guilty because of this, for I had not opened her door lest she awake, and with her heart she needed more sleep than most people. And what did I know about the possible hours in the night when she had lain awake in the dark?

I thought about Jerome and wondered what he had done the night before, and I thought of him as I remembered him in the past. What is time anyway? The past seemed part of the present today. Time had lost its shape. Time is a cloud in which we live while the breath is in us. When was I living, now or twenty-five years ago, or in all those periods of my life simultaneously?

The electric clock showed 12:25 and I picked up the phone, dialed my own apartment, the phone rang four times and I heard Catherine's voice, but there was nothing vibrant in her voice today as there had been the night before. It sounded tired and half alive.

"How are you?" I said. "How was your night?"

"Not very good. How was yours?"

"Not very good. I stayed up till all hours talking to Sally."

"So she told me."

The wire sang between us.

"Look dear," I said, "I can call this Ottawa thing off. I don't have to go if you want me here."

Again the wire sang between us.

Then she said: "Jerome telephoned this morning."

I waited.

"What do you want me to do, George?"

"Whatever you want to do yourself."

Again there was silence.

"Are you all right, Catherine?" I said.

"I don't know."

"Listen, dear," I said, "anything you do is perfectly all right with me."

"I'm not sure that anything I do will be perfectly all right with me, though."

"Catherine!"

There I was, a husband pleading for comfort, but none came.

"When will you be going to Ottawa?" she asked me.

"I'd thought of taking the train after dinner, but—no, if it's all right with you, I'll take the one this afternoon. I'll be home after lunch and pick up my bag."

"I'll have it packed for you."

"Please don't waste any energy doing that. Rest. You sound tired."

"Please don't insist that I'm tired when I'm perfectly all right."

When our conversation was over I put on my fur cap and coat and went out into the hall toward the elevator. There was a mixed chatter in French and English among the usual cluster of engineers, stenographers, actors, singers, producers and executives who were waiting for the elevator to take them down to their lunch. They all seemed younger than me and when one of them addressed me I answered in the discouraged monotone of a veteran in a trade where the accent has always been on youth and novelty. The future was theirs and they knew it with the ruthlessness of the young. In the elevator I listened to a television engineer telling a girl that any time now the first TV studio would be ready for experimental shows and I wondered if this would mean the end of my work and if I would even be able to earn a living three years hence. I was an incurable product of the depression. In my heart I never believed that a job would last.

Outside in the streets it was just as cold as it had been earlier and the noonday sun was so bright it blinded me. The roofs still smoked with snow and people on Dorchester Street kept turning their backs against the wind. I walked to the King Edward Hotel with my gloved hands deep in my pockets and my fur cap well down against the iron-cold hand of that wind. Montreal on a day like this was unfit for human beings.

When I reached the hotel it looked worse even than I remembered it, for it had been given a false front popular in cheap establishments in French-Canada with a lot of opaque glass bricks and shining chromium and harsh angles without any obvious purpose. But inside was the same old lobby.

Blind from the sun I found my way through the lobby by my nose. It smelled like a used ash tray and it was so dark it took nearly half a minute before my pupils adjusted and I saw the shiny, black-leather chairs, the stained carpet, the small desk, a gray clerk with a pencil clamped-between his ear and his temple, a gold ring on one of his fingers and an expression that looked as though he had seen nothing sweet, pleasant or happy in the last fifty years.

"Moment s'vous plaît," he said when I asked for Dr. Armstrong.

What a place for Jerome to have returned to, I thought as I dropped into one of the chairs and felt a stickiness on the leather and heard squeaking sounds overhead and continued to smell the used ash trays. This hotel haunted by the nightmares of alcoholics and stale with the sweat of a thousand whores, what a place for a man to reach when he came home!

"Monsieur?"

It was the gray clerk and I turned my head.

"Dr. Armstrong has checked out," he said.

"Did he leave any message for me?"

"Non, Monsieur."

"Thank you."

I left the hotel and walked two blocks to a restaurant where I ate a fillet of flounder (called sole on the menu) and watched a young French-Canadian with a face like a hawk dining with his fiancée, who was fragile, lovely, convent-bred and clearly unequal to a life with a man like him. I knew they were engaged because I had seen their pictures while leafing through the pages of *La Presse.* I have that useless kind of memory which stores up such images and never loses them.

After lunch I walked back to the studio wishing I had taken two drinks before lunch instead of one. I met Connolly, and Jacques the engineer who put me onto tape, and when I listened to the play-back my Rooseveltian voice seemed to have no connection with me. But Connolly said it was a good broadcast, a dandy, and I thanked him for putting it onto tape, went out, found a taxi and drove home.

Catherine was lying down and we had little to say beyond repeating, both of us troubled, that we loved one another.

"I was supposed to have lunch with him," I said, "but he'd checked out of the hotel. I don't know where he is. Do you?"

She shook her head. "He'll come to see me. Perhaps this afternoon. Perhaps tomorrow. He called to ask if he could come."

"How did he sound to you over the phone?"

"Familiar."

"No more than that?"

"Oh, it was such a long time ago, George."

Going up to Ottawa that evening in the train, lying back in the chair car with the blind up, seeing the lights coming on in the barns where farmers were milking their cows, the snowy plain merging gray with the twilight and occasionally a stand of trees visible against the sky in the west, I wondered vaguely about Catherine and Jerome and myself and all the years. I knew that Catherine loved me and that I loved her. I had no vulgar anxieties about this situation. She and I had protected and touched and greeted each other reasonably well in the past nine years, but Jerome was a part of her core, the great part of her life as a woman, and now he was alive and life is dangerous. No wonder people commit suicide, I thought, for death is so safe. Catherine would never kill herself, that I knew. She had fought so hard for life she would fight to the end. She had done infinitely better than my Aunt Agnes had predicted, better far than even she herself had dreamed. She had defied all the medical prognoses and she was still here. Yet I knew that Jerome's return would bring close to her consciousness the knowledge that the time left her was short.

And I still felt young. Young and old. Old and young together.

"Are you only forty-four?" I asked my reflection in the glass. "Are you actually forty-four?"

The train drummed toward Ottawa and I closed my eyes. O Lord, give us some peace. Give us rest from ourselves, O God.

Chapter II

THE next day in Ottawa I was a fair facsimile of the professional character I had pasted together out of various bits and pieces during the past dozen years. My interview with the Minister went pleasantly, and I had never seen him more friendly and charming. He amazed me, this man. There can't be any department in a modern government where a minister must deal every day with more aspects of sheer villainy and horror than in the department of foreign affairs, yet this minister, deeply serious inside and absolutely honorable, was outwardly gay. He was an excellent politician and yet I could never think of him as a politician at all. He told me little new, but I left him with a feeling that I knew much more than when I entered his office.

An hour later my temporary euphoria was dampened when I shook hands with Arthur Lazenby in front of the main desk of the Chateau Laurier. At first I did not recognize Arthur, but he recognized me and came over to shake hands with a diplomatic smile on his diplomatic face. His shake had once been hard and aggressive, but now it was so limp that I wondered if the limpness was calculated. Many people when offered a limp hand feel themselves rejected, and this leads some of them to offer more of themselves than they normally would. The new Arthur Lazenby looked like a man who might think of such things, but he may merely have been tired.

"If you don't mind," he said, "we shan't lunch at the Rideau Club. I was thinking of the cafeteria."

"That's where I'd have eaten if I'd been alone."

We went downstairs and after we had piled our trays, he led the way to a corner table where he sat with his back to a pillar.

"I don't want us to be disturbed. I'd like to be invisible."

It occurred to me that in this city of civil servants he was almost invisible anyway. He looked like the public idea of a modern Ottawa hand: dark pinstriped suit, dark horn rimmed glasses, just the right amount of flesh on his cheeks and just the right amount of gray on his temples. A big change from the lean, hungry and generally silent young man I had known during the depression. Even more changed was his manner. In the old days

Lazenby had been so unobstrusive that you hardly noticed him. Now, once you had noticed him, once you found yourself engaged with him, he was dominant. He talked suavely of politics for fifteen minutes, dropping just the right number of names in just the right way, and if there was any civil service cliché I had ever heard, he did not miss it. Yet his performance was a competent one, for he was almost entertaining, though both he and I knew that he had said nothing that could be quoted against him and nothing I did not know anyway.

"You've changed, Arthur."

"So have you, George," and his ever-so-slightly-conspiratorial smile left me wondering why he had asked me to lunch.

We were on our dessert before I found out.

"Do you ever find yourself thinking about Jerome Martell these days?"

"Yes, I think about him occasionally."

"When was it he went away?" asked Lazenby smoothly. "Was it twelve years ago, or thirteen?"

I permitted my eyebrows a slight lift, for Lazenby knew as well as I did when Jerome had gone away.

"You heard he was killed in France, I suppose?" was his next question.

"Tortured as well, was the story I got."

"I was in England when that story got out. We tended to disregard some of the more grisly details, but there's no doubt he was presumed dead officially."

"That ought to make him pretty dead."

This time it was Lazenby's eyebrows that lifted, but his voice continued smooth.

"I'm in a position to tell you that the official report of Martell's death was inaccurate. He's turned up. He's here in Canada at this very moment."

His eyes met mine and I knew that he knew that I knew this. "Yes," I said, "I've talked to him."

"I rather thought you might have."

"How did you find out he was back, Arthur?"

"From the R.C.M.P. One of their security men called around a few days ago to ask what I remembered of Martell before the war."

"How do they know you knew him then?"

"The same way they know you knew him."

"I've often wondered if they had a dossier on me."

"They've got one, all right." He smiled. "However, there's no cause for concern here. The R.C.M.P. are quite happy about Martell, actually. They wanted to check a few facts with me, but chiefly they wanted to know if he'd be of interest to us in External."

"Is he?"

Lazenby took a cigar case from his inside pocket, offered it to me and when I refused he took a cigar himself, cut off the end and inserted it into his white face.

"Intelligence-wise, and therefore possibly External-wise, he may be of *some* use. One checks such cases as a matter of routine. But it's surprising—or is it, really?—how little there is to be learned from people with his kind of experience. They've come out of hell. They've seen little that isn't common knowledge. Their minds are apt to be distorted and they tend to confuse fiction with fact. They're in a state of shock and so forth. During the war I interviewed several dozen escapees from Nazi camps and I never learned anything that mattered." He paused and asked casually: "How did Martell seem to you—bitter?"

"He sounded sad but he didn't sound bitter."

"Did he ask about any of his old friends?"

I shook my head. "It was a personal call, Arthur. You probably know why it was."

Lazenby nodded, puffed on his cigar and laid it down. Still using his professional voice, he recounted some of the facts Jerome had already told me and added a new one. According to him, Jerome had been married to, or living with, a young Russian woman who later got into trouble with the Soviet authorities on account of her connection with him.

"So apparently his life-style hasn't altered radically," he said. "He always attracted women and he never seemed able to protect himself against them."

I let this go and we were silent for nearly half a minute while we both remembered things. I was waiting for Lazenby to take off the mask and be natural, and I was beginning to wonder if there was anything natural left in him. He knew that I knew a lot of things about Arthur Lazenby in the old days, but he was still holding me off.

"Doctors are an odd lot," he said reflectively. "With a lawyer or an engineer you know what you're dealing with, but you can never be sure of a doctor outside of his work. They're rather like soldiers in that way. I suppose it's the life-and-death aspect of their professions." A gentle shrug of the padded shoulders. "Whatever it is, it makes most doctors and soldiers impossibly inept in politics."

"MacArthur, for instance?"

"I was talking to MacArthur's chief of staff only three weeks ago, actually." Another smooth shrug. "Yes, he'll do as a case in point. Politically, Truman's paying him out enough rope for him to hang himself." He paused and smiled. "Which doesn't alter the fact that he's one hundred percent in his assessment of the Far Eastern situation."

"That doesn't sound like the thinking in your department."

"I don't know about the *thinking* in my department." Another suave smile. "I merely said he's one hundred percent right in his assessment of the situation at the moment. That's the trouble. In democratic politics it's absolutely fatal to be one hundred percent right about anything. I'm not being cynical, I'm merely stating a fact. Think it over."

I thought it over, looked across the table at Lazenby, and waited.

"Of course MacArthur wasn't on my mind when I made that remark about doctors and soldiers in politics. I was thinking about Jerome Martell in the Thirties. Judged by the standards we use here—and I think you'll agree they're pretty basic—Martell in the Thirties was a fanatic. Not a crackpot exactly, but absolutely a lone wolf out of line with everyone. He wasn't in with the intellectuals, though they hung around him. He wasn't a political show-off like Laski. You found him in all those places where we used to go and talk, and you often found him doing a lot of talking himself."

"Yes," I said, interrupting him, "you don't have to remind me what he was like in those days. I also remember what you and I talked about the last time we met, Arthur. To be precise, it was the night of May 27, 1939."

The mask came off at last and he flushed slightly and looked down at his plate.

"He got you your job in radio and he got me mine in External," he said.

"Not quite yours in External."

"But without him I'd have gone to Spain. Without what he told me about Spain, I mean. God, I was young then. He was absolutely right in what he told me. He was absolutely right about everything then. But because he was so absolutely right, he was absolutely wrong so far as the politics of the time were concerned. If he'd only been patient and waited. But of course he wasn't patient."

"No," I said.

"Look at you." Suddenly the emotion was naked in Lazenby. "You're a success. Look at me—I'm a success. And look at him— years of misery, concentration camps, exile, sickness and hopelessness."

"Yes," I said.

"He was born ahead of his time. Or perhaps behind it. He didn't fit. Types like you and I, we fitted."

The sudden change in Lazenby's manner was understandable to someone who knew as much about him as I did, but as I saw a civil servant from another department pass us, I thought how astonished he would be if he knew that Lazenby's mask could crack like this. For Arthur Lazenby was a new man in a new Canada; he was a type we had never produced until the war. He was as polished, as hard and as expert as any of his opposite numbers in the British Foreign Office, he was at home in any capital in the world. He was competent, he had turned in a remarkable record during the war in our London office, he had come a long way from the place where we first had met and had turned himself into a being different in kind from the self-effacing young man I had first seen filling glasses with beer in the apartment of one of Jerome's friends.

"It's a miracle he's alive, of course," Lazenby went on. "The torture story was at least three-quarters true. The Gestapo gave him a pretty bad working over. The R.C.M.P. man told me his back's a mass of weals from their steel whips. It's quite useless even to try to guess what kind of a life he's led since. He used to have a home. He used to have a wife and child and a first-class medical reputation and he threw it all away. Why? Those God damned commies, I hate them so much I almost distrust my judgment when I deal with them. I'd like so much to see them wiped off the face of the earth I'm afraid I'm going to make a mistake one of these days."

He picked up his cigar, puffed rapidly and looked around.

"You see—I was a card-holder myself once."

"I know. You told me."

"Did I? When?"

"That night in 1939 when you talked to me about Jerome."

"I was off my head that night. I can't remember much of what I said. I didn't think I told you that."

Now I knew why he had invited me to lunch, and also why I disliked him. By showing such an interest in me, he had made it clear that my meeting with the Minister, which had flattered me, had been arranged by himself. But I disliked him because he could not think of Jerome, or of anything, except in terms of his own political interests.

"It would be inconvenient if my name came up before one of those American congressional committees," he said as casually as he could.

"I suppose your department knows you held a card?"

"Naturally. I told them before I entered. It was a big chance, but it would have been fatal if I hadn't, for they'd have found out. I argued that I'd be useful for that very reason. I argued that I could read the commie mind, and so I could. Old Dr. Scrimgeour bought it. He was a shrewd old man. Did you know him?"

Ignoring his last question, I said: "I suppose you're worrying that Jerome may spill the beans in the States?"

He nodded.

"Do you think he's that kind of man?"

Lazenby gave me a hard, shrewd look. "How do I know what kind of a man he is now? He's been through the camps. The quickest way for him to win sympathy and rehabilitate himself would be to go to one of those damned American committees and give them some names."

The unpleasant thought came to me that if Lazenby were in a similar spot he would do that himself. There was a mess of dirty dishes on our table and they bothered me, so I picked them up and laid them on the empty table beside our own.

"For what my judgment is worth," I said slowly, "I think Jerome is lonely, and I don't think he wants to talk to anyone even about Russia, much less about that old pre-war stuff."

Lazenby appraised me, shrugged and sighed.

"You're probably right," he said. "Yes, you're probably right." And then: "Do you ever have the feeling that time stopped in 1939?"

"Often."

"We were alive before then, weren't we?" And his voice was wistful.

"I suppose we were."

"And since then we've had our careers. Successful careers!" He gave a contemptuous laugh. "One of these days I'd like to meet an intelligent man who really believes that it matters what any of us does any more. But the odd thing is, I'm good at my job. It doesn't say much for the worth of the job, does it?"

Out of the corner of my eye I saw Jack Lubliner, the step-father of Sally's boyfriend Alan Royce, emerge from the counter with a tray in his hand and seat himself at an empty table in the center of the room with his back toward me.

"Well," Lazenby said, "I'd like to see Martell again. I owe him more than even you can guess. If I'd gone to Spain I'd have been ruined forever. It's an odd thing—that was the one move a man could make in those days that was never forgiven afterwards. I'd like to repay some of my debt to Jerome."

"How do you propose doing that, Arthur?"

He shrugged. "I'm not exactly without influence, and he's not exactly in the position of not needing any. If you see him in town, would you tell him I'd be glad to help in any way I can?"

"As you like."

"I mean it, George."

"I'll tell him that if I see him."

We finished our coffee and the professional mask slid back over Lazenby's face. He changed the subject, gossiped a little more about politics, and precisely at one-twenty-five he looked at his watch and said he had an appointment at two and would have to con some papers in preparation for it. We both rose and made for the door, and by the time we reached the lobby Arthur was as suave as when I had met him.

"It's been good seeing you, George. And let me repeat this—the Minister was really gratified by your talk this morning. As you know as well as I, External has to tread a delicate line at the moment with the Americans and . . ."

He went on with compliments which meant nothing to me because they meant nothing to him, and then we shook hands and he went out the revolving door into the arctic wind blowing across Confederation Square, leaving me feeling stale, flat and unprofitable. There but for the grace of God, I thought, went something. And what a generation I belonged to, where so many of the successful ones, after trying desperately to hitch their wagons to some great belief, ended up believing in nothing but their own cleverness.

If it had not been so cold I would have gone to the National Gallery and spent the remainder of the afternoon with the pictures, but it was twenty-three below. I bought a magazine and sat in a corner to pass the time before my train left. I wished I were home. I wished I were home with Catherine, my rock and reason for being. I wanted the good feeling to return.

"Well," I said to myself, "perhaps it will."

But that evening on the train returning to Montreal, looking out at the lights coming on in the barns, at trees stark against the orange afterglow of a winter sunset, at snowfields dead-white and lustreless, looking out, depressed by Lazenby, I had the feeling that after all my work and minor success I had come full circle and was back where I had started with the unemployed trudging the sidewalks and the professors talking and Hitler screaming. Canada was rich now; she also was feeling the oats of success, but when I thought of Arthur Lazenby I wondered whether she was finding herself or losing herself.

I closed my eyes and hoped for sleep and I may have dozed a while for I became aware of a numbness in my legs and of a train whistle miles away. I was tired right down into the tissues of my brain and my soul felt exhausted. I was tired of the responsibility for Sally's education, of having to write stuff which would earn us a living when I knew it did not really matter whether it was written or not. Oh my God, I was tired of Catherine's illness and of myself for being tired of it.

The trained stopped after a while and I looked out at a small station platform where three men in mackinaw caps stood beside a pile of farmers' milk pails under the naked overhead lights, their faces red with cold and their breath in clouds around their heads. Suddenly I sat up straight, realizing that I knew one of these men. He was Ti-Jean Laframboise and this was the station which served Waterloo School where I had taught for five years during the depression. This was Lachance, and Ti-Jean Laframboise was probably still the porter at Waterloo. How many times had he driven me over the dirt road to this station to catch this same train coming down from Ottawa to Montreal? Sometimes the landscape was gorgeous with autumn and sometimes it was brown and sodden in the spring break-up, but I remembered it best as it was now—clean, white and cold with the smoke of farm chimneys going straight up.

The train creaked and crept forward, its interior hot but its window panes like ice, and Ti-Jean's face, older now and wizened like a monkey's, slid backward out of view. It was uncanny. Nothing in this world is so permanent as a school; nothing is like a school to bring you back full circle. Forty years on is today when you return to the school where you sung it.

I stared out the window at the shroud of the snow and remembered how I used to sit in this train, not in the parlor car where I was now but in the day coach with the gritty green plush and the hard seats, sometimes with Shatwell when we escaped from Waterloo for our weekends in Montreal, sometimes alone. Shatwell——my God, he must be seventy now!

The train rolled down the valley and soon it was so dark I could see nothing but the reflections of other passengers in the window panes. On this line running down from Lachance I was familiar with every curve and the rumble of every culvert we crossed. I thought of Waterloo in the snow and its lights sending the shadows of bare elms over the snow-covered playing field, of the boys coming up from their supper in the long dining hall paneled by Dr. Bigbee and I thought that there but for the grace of God might I be still. Waterloo had changed hands and become an entirely different school from the one I knew; it had a fine reputation now. But a school is always a school, good or bad, and time stands still in it. It might have stood still for me. There is no man I respect more than the schoolmaster born to the job, but none I pity more than the man not born to it who falls into its trap and stays till the chalk dust passes through his pores into his bloodstream and soul. Such a man I might have been myself had I not escaped on those weekends to Montreal, and during one of them met Jerome Martell.

PART FOUR

Chapter I

THE road which brought me to Waterloo was too drab and long to waste time talking about. For ten years after my father lost his money I lived in Ontario, mostly in Toronto. My first job was in a bank and I stayed with it for five years during which, out of a small salary, I saved enough money for two years in the university. I left the university in order to work again, and the year I returned the depression settled in. When I obtained a degree I was twenty-seven years old.

During this long, drab hiatus three things happened to me, as they happened to millions of other young men at that time. I lost my faith in religion; I lost my faith in myself; I lost my faith in the integrity of human society.

My last year in the university ended and there was no job in Toronto. My degree was worthless and there was no job anywhere. So in late June I returned to Montreal, and lived with my parents because there was no other place to go.

Somehow Father had survived. People had always liked him, some of his old friends had rallied around and all through those years he had held a petty job in a commission office, his innocence preventing him from knowing that the job was pure charity. He had never abandoned hope in himself. He and Mother lived in a three-room apartment in Nôtre Dame de Grace and he used one room for a workshop and still believed he would invent something that would make him rich and famous.

No sooner had I come home than he put on his little boy's expression and led me into the bedroom—I was to sleep on the living room couch—and showed me his latest invention.

"Feel her," he said. "Handle her. Isn't she a beauty?"

I felt her and handled her and asked him what she was.

"You mean you don't know? This can hit harder than a Mannlicher. After supper we'll go out into the park and test her. You wait—it can hit harder than an elephant rifle."

Father took the contraption from me, settled it against his shoulder and at last I realized what it was. It was a crossbow made of light alloys with a shoulder fitting butt.

"This will stop the charge of an elephant," said Father. "It will knock a rhino backwards. It will split a lion's skull in two. If this weapon had been invented two thousand years ago, it would have changed the history of the world."

I took the invention from him and laid it on the bed.

"Father," I said, "this is 1933 and what the hell is the use of a crossbow in 1933?"

"Hunting, of course. What's the use of a rifle if you're a serious hunter? It scares the game for miles around. But this"—he patted the bow affectionately—"is as silent as a baby's breath. A hunter with a rifle meets up with a pair of rhinos and he wants 'em both, and he's lucky if he bags even one. The second one bolts at the shot. But with this crossbow, the first goes down and the second just stops and stares. It's a repeater, too. Have you ever heard of a repeater crossbow? You haven't, for this is the first in history."

"Oh my God!" I said, and turned away.

A little later Father came back into the living room and sat down silently in a corner and I realized how much I had hurt him. I realized also how much older he looked, and how much older my mother looked, and I was sad and ashamed. But I was bitter, too, and unforgiving, and began to fill the silence with the kind of talk young men used in the depression.

"There'll never be the slightest hope of anything improving until the whole system is changed. Here we are—for the first moment in history we are really able to abolish poverty. But there's never been so much poverty as now. Have you seen it? Have you seen the men riding the rods? Have you seen the flat cars crossing the prairies loaded with unemployed? Meanwhile"— I was working myself up the way we used to do—"look at this city with the same people sitting on top of the nation's wealth like incubating hens. I saw in the paper this morning that Huntley McQueen's worked another merger. Yesterday there was a housing riot in St. Henri and when the police arrested the poor devils the jail was the first roof they'd had over their heads in weeks. Nobody does a thing. No, that's not quite fair, Father. You've invented a crossbow that would have changed the history of the world if it had been invented two thousand years ago."

Father looked away and then back again and I saw tears in his eyes.

"It's just a little thing," he mumbled. "I don't suppose anything will come of it. Nothing ever does seem to come of my ideas. But I thought it might help your mother and you if it came off. It really does work, you know."

I left the apartment and walked the streets until seven o'clock, when I returned hungry and ashamed and ate some of the sausages and mash my mother had prepared for me.

That summer I walked the sidewalks day after day, I searched the want-ads and soon gave up because no employer even bothered to advertize for help. I found nothing to do, absolutely nothing. I applied to every teachers' agency in Canada and to half a dozen in the United States. I made a few semi-friends about the town, but most of the time I was alone. And the sexual loneliness which had been growing in me became as sour as the Dead Sea.

Summer passed into autumn and the leaves began to fall. And then one evening in mid-October I came home and found a telegram. It was from a teachers' agency and informed me that a job was waiting for me at Waterloo School, the salary ninety dollars a month, room and board included, and that I was to report for duty immediately.

This was the middle of October and even the private schools had been in session for a month, so I was sure there must be a mistake. I wondered what to do and asked Father about it.

"Why, call them up long distance, of course, and find out."

"Long distance calls cost money."

"But this is a job, George. You have to spend money before you can make it. I discovered that years ago."

I telephoned to Waterloo and after a wait of seven minutes an English voice, speaking as though all telephones were its personal enemies, boomed into my ear.

"Stewart, did you say? Of course you're wanted here. What's been keeping you, I'd like to know? Be here tomorrow morning."

Without giving me a chance to ask another question, the speaker hung up. I presumed that he was the headmaster of Waterloo, but as he had not introduced himself I did not know that his name was Dr. Lionel Bigbee, much less that his doctorate was purely imaginary, and that he called himself Doctor because he believed that all headmasters should be called Doctor for the sake of morale. I tried to recall what little I had heard of Waterloo, and the little I was able to remember did not sound so good.

The only person I knew who had gone there was an eccentric who had been at Frobisher when I was in the middle school, and he had only gone to Waterloo because Frobisher had expelled him. His name was Adam Blore and he claimed to be a sculptor; for a living he sold carpets in Eaton's.

"My God," Adam whispered, when I called him up. "Have you been reduced to *that?*"

I mentioned the pay, the room and the food.

"You'll get berri-berri from the food. Those Englishmen out there eat like convicts. They don't know any better. Those Englishmen out there never ate a decent meal in their lives. If old Bigbee hadn't expelled me, I'd have died of malnutrition."

The next day I got off the train at Lachance and was met by a gnome-like creature in a flat cap driving an Model-A Ford he called the Waterloo bus. He was Ti-Jean Laframboise and he drove me over three miles of bumpy dirt road and then up a weedy driveway to a building the like of which I never saw before or since.

Originally, I suppose, Waterloo School had been the house of a prosperous French-Canadian landowner. Now a cascade of marble steps poured down in front of it surmounted by a portico which in turn was decorated by four angels who gesticulated at one another and looked as though they had been stolen from a Catho-lic cemetery. Over the door was a shield with a coat of arms and the strange motto, *Caveat Gallus.*

"Where did the steps come from?" I asked Laframboise.

"The Doctor put them in seven years ago. Him and me. They're beautiful."

After my luggage was inside, Laframboise led me upstairs and along a corridor that boomed like a sounding board to a cell-like, rugless room where the pipes were exposed, the plaster flaking and the smell ratty.

"I guess this is your room," he said. "Now I guess you better see the Doctor."

I followed downstairs once more, then along another corridor where the stuffed heads of lions, tigers, impallas, rhinos and African buffalo stared at each other like family portraits in an English country house.

"Did the Doctor shoot these?" I asked Laframboise.

"He bought them at an auction. But you wait till you see his birds. They're beautiful."

He knocked on a door, a loud voice boomed, "Come in!" and I entered to make the acquaintance of the man described by hundreds of old boys of Waterloo as the greatest personality they had ever known in their lives.

Dr. Lionel Bigbee was as thin as a stork's neck and stood five feet five in his socks. But at that moment he was not standing; he was leaning back in a wooden chair with his feet on his desk, his left hand stroking a pink, bald, shining skull, a pair of watery blue eyes peering out from under tufted white brows, his right hand flapping as though I were a taxi and he were hailing it. He was entirely surrounded by stuffed birds. Quails and geese perched on the floor, on the window sill were an eagle and an owl, an albatross spread wings in one corner and a swarm of lesser fowl clustered on tables and shelves.

"Well Stewart," said Dr. Bigbee in a male alto boom, "you've taken your own good time getting here, I'm bound to say. You should have been here five weeks ago. What have you been up to? Missed your sailing?"

"I beg your pardon, sir?"

"I'm not seasick or any other kind of sick myself, but I notice a lot of men are. Were you?"

"I beg your pardon, sir."

"There's no chair for you, so don't look for one. The other chair's fractured and Laframboise is mending it. But standing never hurt a man. Speak up, Stewart. What have you got to say for yourself?"

I muttered that I was sorry, but that I had only heard from him the day before and did not understand what he meant by ships and seasickness. The Doctor listened, rubbed his skull and stared out the window.

"You aren't from home, not with that accent, Stewart."

"I beg your pardon, sir."

There was a knock and Laframboise entered with another wooden chair, which I sat on. I looked past the Doctor's head to bookshelves containing some battered school texts, the complete Oxford Dictionary from A to E, and five bound volumes of Punch, 1888 to 1892 inclusive. Behind the doctor was the room's sole decoration apart from the birds; it was an engraving of a seventeenth century battleship firing a broadside.

The Doctor spoke: "These agencies aren't worth the price of a stamp. I know picking a new master's pretty much a matter of putting one's hand into the poke and coming out with what it grabs, but at least the agencies understand that I take my men from home." His blue eyes appraised me. "Where did you say you were from, Stewart?"

"Montreal."

"Mmmm," said the Doctor. His eyebrows jumped quickly up and down and settled themselves. "Well, I must have a master and you're here. I suppose you have some kind of a degree?"

I told him I had an honors degree in history from Toronto University.

"Mmmm," said the Doctor. "Well, you can't teach history here. Ponson does it in the uppers, McNish in the lowers. Ponson's old Boer War and McNish is Royal Navy. The socialists axed him and the poor chap had to come out here. What else can you teach?"

I told him my French was pretty fair and that I could probably teach English as well, but the Doctor did not seem to listen.

"We'll find plenty for you to teach," he said as he stared sideways out the window. "Don't you worry on *that* score. Do you know any French?"

"Yes, sir," I repeated.

"Then I fancy you'll teach some French in the middle school where there are always gaps that need stopping. Far better not having a Frenchman for French, the boys can never understand a word he says. I expect you'll stop that particular gap very nicely." The Doctor swung around and his voice became confidential. "Let me tell you something, Stewart. When you've been in this profession as long as I have, you'll understand that the least important part of schoolmastering is teaching. Show the flag, set an example, give a tone. Can *you* remember anything you were taught in school? *I* can't. But I jolly well remember my school, and a jolly good school it was, too."

The Doctor took a silk handkerchief out of his sleeve and blew his nose with such violence that dust spurted from the head of the nearest owl. Then he recrossed his legs on the desk, and with both hands clasped behind his head and his body tilted so far back he was almost prone, he rattled off the schedule, which he described as "Ponson's timetable," adding as he did so that Ponson was the kind of chap who understands timetables.

Rising bell was at 6:45, breakfast at 7:15, prayers at 7:45, and then there was a half-hour break.

"Bowels," said the Doctor. "Give 'em plenty of time to move 'em. The secret of a good school's a happy boy, and the secret of a happy boy's a comfortable intestine."

From 8:30 to 12:30, with a fifteen minutes' break in the middle, were classes. Then came lunch, followed by a half hour break and then more classes till 3:30. These were followed by detention and/or games. If the master was on duty he took detention and if he was not he supervised games. If he was on duty he also patrolled corridors, attended the prefects' court where junior offenders were caned by senior boys, took the two-hour evening prep and when that was over he put the junior and middle schools to bed.

"Keep 'em on the hop and you have no moral problem," explained the Doctor. "But give a boy time to think and you know as well as the next man what he'll think about. Have you ever used a cane?"

"No, sir."

"Then go to Cutler—he's our sergeant-at-arms and an old Green Jacket—and ask him for one. Preaching at a boy, chivvying him, making him ashamed of himself, there's nothing worse for the character. But give him six of the best if he deserves it and you've made a friend for life."

The Doctor contemplated the eagle which stood on his window ledge and rubbed his head some more.

"Well, Stewart?" he said after a while, genially.

"Yes, sir?"

"I've noticed you've been admiring my ship-of-the-line." He jerked a lean thumb over his shoulder at the engraving of the seventeenth century battleship and his voice became excessively cordial. "She's *H.M.S. Terrible,* first of the name in the Navy List if I'm not mistaken. An ancestor of mine had her once, an ancestor on the maternal wing, Prisser, Admiral of the Blue. I don't expect you've ever heard of him. My full name actually is

Prisser-hyphen-Bigbee, but Prisser won't do in a school for obvious reasons, so I drop both the Prisser *and* the hyphen out here. Did you ever notice the motto over the school door?"

"Yes, sir."

"It was Prisser's. *Caveat Gallus*—'Let the French Beware!' I rather fancy with good reason, for they never came out to fight him. He watched 'em for years and they never came. I'd wanted a naval name for the school, but it wasn't as simple as it looked. Nobody out here's ever heard of Camperdown. If we called us The Saints in this province they'd think we were Roman Catholics. The Nile? Copenhagen? Obviously wouldn't do. Trafalgar naturally—but do you know, Stewart? In Montreal there's a *girls'* school called Trafalgar. So I settled on Waterloo willy-nilly, though it wasn't the Duke's best battle. Salamanca was that, but out here who's heard of Salamanca?"

With a crash the Doctor dropped both feet to the ground and rose towering among his birds, and with an expression disconcertingly roguish he pointed his finger at me and wagged it.

"Stewart, you're the first native, I mean the first man not from home we've ever had here. So go in and win."

"I'll do my best, sir."

"Of course you will. And by Easter, instead of being the wrong Stewart, you may have proved you're the *right* Stewart."

Chapter II

So BEGAN five years of servitude. I liked the boys and got on with them and I was thankful to have a job of any kind, but I was nervously exhausted most of the time, for Waterloo was as wild a jumble of improvisations as a British army in the first year of a war, with life a constant emergency.

"The Duke," Dr. Bigbee said, "preferred to do the business himself."

So did Dr. Bigbee: I truly believe that if it had been possible he would have run the school with no masters at all. He taught a full schedule, and did so with such enthusiasm that the masters in the rooms next to his were unable to teach because his voice boomed through the paper-thin partitions and drowned them out. He liked boys and had an uncanny understanding of them, and at least three-quarters of the boys worshipped him. He played cricket, rolled the pitch himself, watered the rinks and was busy every instant of the day. For recreation he cycled, and I can still see him peddling on his English cycle, which he rode very tall in the saddle, singing sea chanteys out of tune. He would have been a great schoolmaster if he had possessed an education, or even if he had enjoyed reading. But he was too busy, so he said, even to read the newspapers.

That may have been why the staff was what it was. The contrast between Dr. Bigbee and the rest of us, I thought in my bleaker moments, was the contrast between the Duke and the troops he once described in a famous phrase. Only one of us had ever wanted to be a schoolmaster; the rest of us were like me. We had *ended* at Waterloo.

There was Ponson, who was old Boer War and composed the timetable: he had come to Canada after a commercial misfortune in Portugal. There was Callendar, who taught Latin, had been trained as a church organist, and whose hobby was brass rubbing; Callendar was bitter because in Canada there were no brasses to rub. The science master had once been purser of a P. and O. Liner. The mathematician was a militant pacifist who infuriated Ponson by his nasal reiterations that England was dying and that he intended to dance at her funeral. There was a shaggy youth—the only one who had wanted to be a schoolmaster—who believed in the Montessori System. There was a trio of vague young men who had obtained degrees from British provincial universities and, in the words of one of them, "taught odds and ends to the odds and sods in the middle school." There was a former clergyman who looked like the archbishop of Canterbury and insisted that Webster's Dictionary was no authority for the English language. There was McNish. And finally there was Shatwell.

Jocelyn McNish, the axed naval officer, was forty-two years old, lean and tall. He had black hair surrounding a twitching scalp rendered horseshoe bald from years of wearing a naval cap, and his black brows were as straight as a gridiron's bars. McNish lived for the outbreak of war—any war—which would restore him to active rank as a lieutenant-commander with full pay, and the only times I saw him cheerful were the days when the headlines were terrifying. He was not a bad schoolmaster when he was sober, but he hated weekends and duty days and drank on them, and liquor made him surly and savage. He used to prowl the corridors on duty days with a waxed rope's end he called a starter, and the boys when he was on duty padded the seats of their pants with towels. He never got wise to this shop-worn trick and their fortitude under his starter had given him an admiration for my countrymen unshared by any of my other colleagues.

"Say what you like," McNish used to announce with a twitch of his scalp, "say what you like, but these local yokels take a flogging Dartmouth-fashion. That's more than you can say for the little buggers at Eton."

McNish's combination of names seemed so bizarre to me that I once asked him how a man with such a surname had come by the Christian name of Jocelyn.

"Nothing to that," said McNish with a twitch of his scalp. "Jocelyn was the Pater's name, and the Pater was no bloody Scotchman."

He then informed me that the Pater was a Somerset viscount who had begotten him during a grouse season in Kintail.

"Naturally the old boy couldn't acknowledge me publicly," McNish explained, "but he always showed an interest. He put up the necessary to send me through Dartmouth, and the day I was commissioned he sent me his check for fifty guineas. I've never heard from him since, but I've always thought that was jolly decent. Not many chaps'd've been so handsome if they'd knocked up the chambermaid on a weekend."

And there was Randolph Shatwell.

When I first saw Shatwell's ramrod back, bullet head, clipped moustache and walnut countenance, I thought he must surely have been cashiered from the Bengal Lancers. But Shatwell had never got as far as that. His soft mouth and calf's eyes, his raffish smile and his languid voice, together with his air of cheerful and perennial defeat gave him a kind of saving grace wherever he went, and (he said it himself) women had always been kind to him.

"A chap with the name of Shatwell," he explained, "learns

rather early on that things are likely to go against him, you understand. I thought of changing the old name once, but I'd become rather attached to it, you understand, so I decided to make do."

Shatwell had emerged from an English public school (I think it was called Lancing) into Sandhurst, where he had gone because his father had gone there before him, but all he learned at Sandhurst was how to keep a straight back. Leaving Sandhurst without a commission, he had spent several agreeable years in Smyrna in raisins and dates, but something had gone wrong in Smyrna so down he went through Suez to Kipling country, where over a period of twenty years, broken by a stretch in the Army Service Corps during the war, he had failed in teak in Calcutta, in jute in Madras and in rubber in Kuala Lumpur. He had spent a year in Java in an enterprise he described as ephemeral, and six months in Bali ("Absolutely the best time of my life, old boy.") doing nothing at all. For a year after that he had been a shipping agent in Brisbane, but something had gone wrong in Brisbane and he had been toying with the idea of South America ("Just turning the Argentine over in my mind, you understand.") when the long fingers of Dr. Bigbee, scraping the bottom of some teachers' agency barrel, closed on Shatwell and dragged him without protest halfway round the world to Waterloo, where his natural inertia had held him ever since. It was his dream to return to Cheshire where he had been born ("I know of a rather charming cottage near Knutsford."), but he never expected to bring it off.

"A chap has to be rather a brain-wave to get along in England, you understand. It's not at all as it is out here, where anyone can get along."

Shatwell differed from my other colleagues in one respect; he was the only one of them who had seen anything of Canada beyond what was visible around the school and from the windows of the trains that conveyed them to and fro between Lachance and Montreal, their sally port and escape hatch. The moment the summer term ended, all of them except Shatwell made a concerted rush for the first steamer home, and when they reached England I suspect that most of them eked out their funds by tutoring backward boys in coastal resorts. But in June Shatwell could never afford the passage money and had to get through his summers as best he could. Once he lived with a woman he did not particularly like, but who liked him; another year he went as far west as Winnipeg, from which he returned with the comment that there didn't seem to be much out there; generally he got through his long vacation in a shack beside a Laurentian lake, eating out of tins. When I knew him he lived for his weekends in town, where he was acquainted with a widow he liked so well that once or twice he toyed with the idea of marrying her. But always, after weighing the pros and cons, Shatwell decided against this.

"If I had her out here all the time there'd be nothing to look forward to, you understand. But as things are, I can always look forward to the weekends."

As I said elsewhere, the character of Waterloo has changed out of recognition since the Doctor's day. The Doctor, who boasted that he was too busy to read the newspapers, in the spring of 1940 suddenly discovered that England was in peril and that his post was not here but in the firing line. He sold out and went home, and one after the other his masters followed him. Today the school is run by natives of the country who have made it unrecognizable. In my time the walls of the dining hall were lined with minute pictures of Admirals of the Red and Admirals of the Blue, interspersed with the heads of wild beasts. Now they contain a portrait gallery of Canadian prime ministers and the trio of leopard heads which used to snarl at us over the headmaster's chair has been replaced by a group photograph of the new board of governors. Waterloo, quite a few old boys complain, is no longer the place it was, and in these days of conformity I confess there are moments when I regret it.

Chapter III

BUT during my actual time at Waterloo I saw nothing humorous about the place, and it was the weekends that kept me sane. Every fourth weekend I was on duty, sometimes I was down with a cold and often I was broke, but whenever I had a chance and could afford it, I fled from the place on Friday afternoon and went to Montreal.

Never before was Montreal as it was in the Thirties and it will never be like that again. The unemployed used to flow in two rivers along St. Catherine Street, and I used to see eddies of them stopping in front of shop windows to stare at the goods they could not buy. There was a restaurant that used to roast chickens in its window over electrically-operated spits, and there were always slavering men outside staring at the crinkling skin of the chickens and the sputtering fat. I remember how silent the unemployed were when they emerged after a snowfall to clean the streets, often without mittens on their hands, and how pitiful their cheap worn shoes looked as the snow wet them and turned the unpolished leather gray. And above all do I remember my own guilt as I saw them, for I had work and they had none.

In those days the streets of Montreal were a kind of truth to me and I roamed them. I learned them block by block from their smells and the types I saw, I came to love the shape of the city itself, its bold masses bulging hard against the sky and the purple semi-darkness of the lower town at evening when Mount Royal was still high and clear against bright sunsets. I loved the noise of the ships booming in the harbor and along the canal to the Lakes, and the quiet little areas some said were like London but which were actually indigenous to this wise, experienced, amiably cynical town.

Though I slept in my parents' flat in Nôtre Dame de Grace, I seldom went there until after midnight when they were asleep; Sunday was the day I reserved for my parents, Sunday when I was tired. On Friday evenings when I arrived in town I checked my bag in the station and roamed. The streets were so candid and unashamed that they made everyone who walked them seem equal: housewives and office clerks and the thousands of unemployed, threadbare boys and girls in love with each other and whoremasters sliding around corners after silent girls and the hideous olive-green street cars of that period with their graying conductors half-sitting, half-standing in their cages at the back while the crowds read the bad news in the papers—all these people seemed part of a collective sameness which had a character entirely its own. In winter the city was more than ever itself.

In winter when the snow slanted like black wires against the lights, or creaked under foot when the stars were hard overhead, I would see the young people in hundreds in their ski-clothes going down to the cheap special trains that took them north. And in those days you could see the hockey for fifty cents.

In my first year at Waterloo I spent nearly all my Montreal weekends alone, and it was the autumn of 1934 before I began to make friends in town. The first ones I met were through Adam Blore, the young sculptor who had been expelled from Waterloo and now sold carpets at Eaton's, the man who had told me I would get beri-beri from the Waterloo food. With him began a chain which eventually led me to Jerome Martell and back to Catherine after all those years.

I have heard Adam Blore described as typical of his time, but he was probably typical of nothing. His father was a Superior Court judge and his mother came from one of the old business families, but Adam himself was a sport. After spending thousands of dollars of his father's money pretending to take advanced courses in Cambridge, Berlin and the Sorbonne, he had finally announced that he was a genius and his father had finally got tired of paying his bills. Now he worked at Eaton's and sculpted in his spare time and his rooms in a disintegrated district of downtown Montreal had become the focus of a group of angry and discontented young people who met to drink beer, make assignations with each other and talk about politics and art, their villains being every conventional politician and artist and their heroes Picasso, Soutine, Eliot, Pound, Joyce, Kafka and Gide. Among them was Adam himself, who came closer to being a genuine nihilist than anyone I ever knew.

But I owe Adam something. He taught me to look at pictures and he introduced me to one of the kindest people I ever knew.

Her name was Caroline Hall, and I often wondered what chance of taste had led her to Adam's group. She was a buxom, brown-haired physiotherapist excellent in her work, and she made every man feel that she liked him. She was cheerful, buoyant, healthy-minded and absolutely amoral so far as her sex life went. Her attitude to sex was simply this: "It's good fun so long as you like the fellow."

It was Caroline who kept me returning to those long evenings of beer and cigarette smoke where the young artists and poets wrangled and intoxicated one another with talk. It was also from Caroline that I first heard mention of Jerome Martell. She worked in the hospital where he served on the staff, and she described him ruefully—ruefully because he had failed to notice her existence—as the most attractive male animal in Montreal.

Adam also knew Jerome, and I was anxious to discover what sort of man he was.

Adam gave a sardonic laugh. "Martell? Underneath he's pure rhumba."

"Isn't he supposed to be a great surgeon?"

Adam shrugged and made a face. "Perhaps. But don't you think being a surgeon is rather obvious? Not *quite* as obvious as climbing a Himalaya. But obvious, George, obvious."

I knew—I had known for some time—that Catherine and Jerome were married, and now I realized that if I saw more of Adam's friends I would be bound to meet them. I was afraid. For the Catherine I knew was a girl on the Lakeshore and the Catherine married to Jerome Martell was a mature woman far beyond me. I was a failure and knew it. I honestly believed I had found my true level in jobs at Waterloo and in women in Caroline Hall.

Bless her wherever she is. She took me in the second time we met, and whenever I came up to town I tried to see her. She became for me what Shatwell's widow was for him: something to look forward to in the dry weeks at Waterloo, something to keep the chalk dust from hardening into my blood.

And yet I never loved her nor she me, for she liked many men with an equally disinterested affection. Her big, smooth, purring body was the comfort of a dozen lonelinesses. She mothered us all and she even made some of us laugh in the night. Everyone liked her, even those who said frightful things of her. Old ladies with arthritis asked especially for Caroline when they went to the hospital for treatment and she listened with a real loving kindness as they talked indirectly of their fear of death. She was born, I have often thought, to be at the disposal of others, and yet she was always herself and in the long run she always did what she liked.

Her best friend was the most unlikely person imaginable for

someone like her. She was a surgical nurse, also in Jerome's hospital, who lived with her husband across the hall from Caroline in a rooming house not far from Adam Blore. If I talk about her and her husband now it is because they were to become far more important to this story than Caroline or Adam or anyone else I knew in those days before I met Catherine again.

I knew little of Norah's background, for she seldom mentioned anything about it beyond the fact that she had been raised in an Ontario puritan town. She must have got a fair education there, for she had read all over the shop in poetry and when I knew her she seemed to have read most of the books on the social revolution which were popular in the Thirties. Her voice will always haunt me, and so will her face. Her voice was Cordelia's: soft, low and musical, a romantic man's idea of what every woman's voice should be. Her face was slim, delicate, flushed easily and movingly, and her mouth, full and wide, was a surprise in it. Her brown eyes were enormous and fey, her slim figure was classically formed but so fragile-looking, so innocently sensuous in its movements, that it made you feel you wanted to hold that body in your arms in order to shelter it.

Yet this girl who seemed like a Victorian survival, almost but not quite Dresden china, was an exceedingly competent surgical nurse. Her slim, small hands were strong and deft, and in her work she thought like lightning. She could look unmoved on the grimmest of operations, and when she talked about her work she was as professionally objective as a surgeon. It was when she talked about the workers and the sufferings of humanity that she sounded like a pre-Raphaelite poetess who had wandered into the pulpit by mistake.

Strangest thing of all about Norah was her choice of a husband. I am no beauty myself, but poor Harry Blackwell must have been preposterous from birth. His head was too large for a body shaped like a pear, his legs were bowed and so short that he always seemed to be trotting. If I say that his face reminded me of a Dutch cheese I don't mean that it had the complexion of a Dutch cheese; it simply made you think of one. At thirty-two, Harry was becoming bald in the unfortunate way he did everything, for his hair, instead of falling out, looked as though it were wearing out. He was also unemployed.

But strong passions can exist in men like that, and Harry adored his wife. Norah was his religion, his refuge, his dreams come true, his reason for being. I used to see him tagging along after her, coming into a roomful of people with a desperate smile and then making himself small in a corner and never opening his mouth while the rest of us talked. His little eyes would move from face to face, never critically—he professed liking for everybody—but in sheer delight as he searched for the admiration he was sure everyone felt for this wonderful creature who was his wife. He had gladly made himself her servant in the days when he was out of work, and even if he had been working twelve hours a day he would still have loved to serve her. It was Harry who kept the apartment, and their cramped rooms were as spotless as the kitchen of a good French-Canadian housewife. It was Harry who mended their clothes, cooked their meals and washed their dishes. And it was Harry who did most of the loving in that home and was pathetically grateful for the little he got in return.

The months and the years blurred past punctuated by international disasters which exploded like the cannon salvos which, in some countries, were used in the old days to herald an execution. Dolfuss turned his artillery on the socialist apartments in Vienna while his henchmen in Styria hanged Wallisch a foot from the ground. Mussolini invaded Ethiopia and Hoare and Laval connived at it. Hitler marched into the Rhineland and the British compelled the French to accept it. Murder exploded out of the soil of Spain and the British and the French washed their hands of it. And unemployment became no less.

I tell you, there are few people who passed through the Thirties who even dare or can recall what that time was really like or what it did to human beings. Of course the sun shone and the rain fell. I was young and there were many days when I was happy. There were nights when I was gay. There were times when, being young, I allowed myself the luxury of hope. But there was poison in the air then, and I think it spread from the rotting corpses of the first war. The Thirties lie behind us like the memory of guilt and shame.

The months and the years blurred past and I lost them. I seemed to be fenced in with invisible walls. I was without love. I worked at Waterloo and did the best I could, but honestly I don't think it was possible for anyone to teach very well in a school dominated by Dr. Bigbee unless he believed we were still in the nineteenth century. In the summers I got by with various mean little jobs I counted myself extremely lucky to get. Once I tutored a juvenile delinquent whose father was a rich manufacturer. Another year I sailed to the West Indies on a fruit ship. I learned the bitter language and thoughts of the period, as any sensitive man was bound to in a time when his elders and leaders betrayed him. I learned to profess a blanket hatred for whole human groups, to talk wildly about politics and to encourage others to do the same. It is not a time of my life of which I am in any way proud, and least of all am I proud of my on-and-off affair with Caroline Hall, for she deserved someone better than the man I was then. I still cannot understand why she was so generous, so genuinely fond of a man who so obstinately refused to allow himself to be loved by a whole woman. For the truth was that Catherine was still with me, she was lodged deep in my being; even in the days when I deliberately avoided meeting her, Catherine was there.

Caroline guessed at her existence though I never mentioned her name.

For once she said: "George, I'd want to marry you except for one thing. I'll never marry any man unless I believe I can be good for him. You're carrying such a torch for somebody you'll never let any woman be good for you. Is she married to somebody else?"

"Yes," I said, and flushed.

Her voice became tender and kind: "Then all I can say is that your whole attitude is unhealthy. You men are all such hopeless dreamers. Why can't you live like we do? Why can't you be tough like we are? George"—and the sudden appearance of tears in her eyes touched me—"I wish you'd let me love you. But since you can't"—a smile and a shrug of her buxom shoulders—"I guess I'll have to face that fact. Whatever happens, though, don't blame yourself or worry about me."

She said this and I was afraid inside. But I did not understand how deeply she had meant it till the Friday night in late October when I came to town to take her out to dinner and got no answer when I pushed her bell.

I crossed the hall and rang the bell by the Blackwell's door and when Norah opened I asked if I could come in and wait.

"Of course," she said, and her eyes were disconcertingly wide.

"Where's Harry?" I said as I sat down and lit a cigarette.

"He's out. It so happens that he's got a job at last."

"That's wonderful."

Norah sat opposite me with her slim thighs pressed together and pain in those large brown eyes.

"He's an usher in the Capitol!" she said in the tone a wife might use if she said, "He's dead," or "He's just been arrested."

"Well, at least it's a job."

"But he wants to *work*, George. He wants a real job, not to show stupid people to their seats at escapist movies. Harry's a wonderful electrical engineer. Everyone under-rates him because he hasn't had a job lately and has never had a chance."

This was news to me and I said so.

"He's so modest he never talks about himself," said Norah, "but he had two years in Engineering and he had to leave college because there was no money. In Russia a man like Harry would be appreciated. Technicians are given a chance in Russia."

I was bored with Harry, so we talked about Russia and for half an hour we agreed that it was wonderful. I knew little about Russia beyond what I had picked up from the panegyrics I heard on Saturday nights from others who knew no more about it than I did, but Norah had read *Das Kapital* and several books by Lenin and some tracts by the Webbs.

"Where the hell is Caroline?" I said after a while. "She's at least an hour late. Do you know where she is?"

Norah's slim face tightened and she looked at me tragically.

"George—I don't think you know!"

"Know what?"

"You mean she didn't even tell *you*?"

"I don't know what you're talking about."

"Oh George!" She gave a little gasp. "George dear! George— Caroline's got married."

"Good God!" I said and stared. Then I flushed as a wave of anger mounted to my head.

"She didn't tell me, either," said Norah. "She just got married and never told a soul till it was over. It was five days ago."

I sat in silence and anger and frustration. "Well," I said after a while, "who was it?"

"Jim Lawson, George."

With a slight effort I recalled a blousy man of indeterminate age who had an untidy mouth and a loose body, and had recently appeared in some of the Saturday night gatherings Caroline and I had attended.

"For Christ's sake!" was my comment.

"Were you in love with her, George?"

I looked out the window and watched a prostitute pick up a man under the corner light.

"I swear I knew nothing," Norah said behind me, "till last Monday night when Caroline burst in and told me she and Jim were married and were going away and would I keep a few things she didn't have room for in her bags. It so happens that she only rented by the month and her lease was up at the end of this week. There's a queer man moving in over there."

I came back and lit another cigarette. "Where did she go?"

"New York. Jim has a job there."

"I never knew he was an American."

"She just came to see me and ran. Did you want to marry her, George?"

I gave a short laugh: "Marriage is a luxury one doesn't contemplate these days."

Her large brown eyes stared into mine, her full soft mouth quivered, and then suddenly her fists clenched and her face set and her voice hardened with exultation.

"George—stop running away. Become one of us!"

"What do you mean—one of us?"

"There's only one place for people like you and me—the Communist Party."

"I didn't know you were a communist. How long has this been going on?"

"I've been one for a month. Before that I was nothing. Nothing, nothing, *nothing!* Now I belong to the most wonderful thing in the world. Caroline used to laugh at me, but I don't think she does now. And you won't either. You and she should have married but—"

"Look Norah, what has communism got to do with Caroline and me not getting married?"

"Under a decent system you would have been able to. When the marrying time comes, people should marry. But look at this —this bourgeois filth! Look at yourself, George. You go crawling around corners after sex and—"

"I'm not that bad."

"It all should be open, honest and above board. Oh George!"

I don't know how I felt, really. Partly lost and rejected, partly relieved because Caroline was no longer my responsibility, but mostly I felt disintegrated, and so I was.

Norah's eyes were hypnotic: "You know I've always been fond of you, George?"

"I've been fond of you, Norah."

"Have you been terribly hurt?"

I shrugged.

"If I wasn't married I'd take you into my arms."

I looked at her, startled, then looked away.

"Do you mind if I talk a little?" she said. "Sometimes I feel I'll die if I can't talk to somebody who understands. Harry's so sweet, and he's so devoted I feel unworthy of him. He's such a wonderful man if you know him. I love him, George. You must believe that. I really do love him so much. I couldn't live with him if I didn't love him, could I?"

"I believe you."

"It's just that sometimes I wonder if I'm going crazy. The things Harry accepts. Just everything. Just everything, George."

"Maybe he's sensible."

"He's like a sacrificial lamb. When I think of what the system's done to him! Harry in that insulting bellhop's uniform showing moronic bourgeoisie to their seats with his flashlight. It so happens that he even has to pay for that monkey jacket out of his wages. How long before everyone starts screaming? We're trapped, George. Harry's been trapped all his life. His mother died when he was fourteen and then his father married a sloven. Now in the depression he couldn't get work. And he's so good and kind, George. He ought to have children. He'd make such a wonderful father if he had children."

"Well," I said, feeling selfishly angry and totally uninterested in whether Harry Blackwell would make a wonderful father or not, "you're both married. So if you want children at least they won't be bastards. At least you won't have to get an abortion if you become pregnant."

Tears filled those wide brown eyes.

"I had an abortion once, George. What else could I do? I had to go on working. And I wanted children desperately, and I still do."

Then she flushed and changed the subject. She told me about a workman who had been brought into the hospital that afternoon with a broken back and a shattered skull. He was dead before Dr. Martell had been able to reach him.

"I gather you think a lot of this Dr. Martell?" I said.

"He's the most wonderful man I ever met in my life."

"I knew his wife once. Do you know her?"

"Well of course I'm not important enough to know Dr. Martell socially. But I think he respects my work, for he often asks for me specially for his operations. Of course I've *seen* his wife. Sometimes she comes to the hospital and waits in the sunroom if she and the Doctor are going out somewhere afterwards."

"She was only a kid when I knew her," I said with deliberate carelessness. "What's she like now?"

"She's a very wonderful woman," said Norah.

Suddenly I wanted to get away from there. The feeling came over me that I had reached an absolute dead-end and I wanted to be alone and above all I wanted to be alone with music, and I remembered that Adam Blore had a fine collection of Bach recordings. It was strange that he should like Bach but he did, and I wanted to hear some Bach now.

At the door Norah put her slim arms about me and kissed me gently, I kissed her back and suddenly she surged against me and I held her.

"No, George, we mustn't."

"No," I said, and stepped away.

Then I said good-night and walked down to the street.

Chapter IV

THE pattern of that curious evening continued to unfold. There was no answer when I pressed Adam's bell, but I remembered that he often left his room unlocked when he went out for food or cigarettes, so I turned the handle and went in. Newspapers littered the floor, the bed was unmade and the unwashed dishes of several meals were stacked on a table containing Pound's *Cantos* and a little magazine called *Scrutiny*. In the middle of the room was a sizable statue looking vaguely like a seal with holes in it. I walked around it, stumbled over a pair of shoes, and got to the phonograph. Finding it was broken I decided to go out and eat, and a few minutes later I found Adam himself sitting in a booth in a neighboring cafe eating spaghetti and reading a novel by Céline in the original French.

"Sit down," he said, and brandished the book at me. "Have you read this? Tell me how I've managed to miss Céline all these years."

I ordered scrambled eggs, toast and coffee and looked around. The atmosphere was thick with the smells of over-used cooking fat, dishwater, cigarette smoke and humanity. The booths and the counter were crowded with students and Adam's saturnine face was veiled by cigarette smoke as he leaned back and looked me over.

"Yes, you must really read Céline. Have you gone into the public lavatory of a New York subway lately? One of those places where the unemployed sleep on the ledges above the urinals? That's what Céline's work smells like. By God, but he's got integrity!"

Having so pronounced himself, Adam inhaled his cigarette and let the smoke reek out of his nostrils. I told him I had been around to his room and he asked me if I had liked his figure. I told him I had not been able to understand it.

"Good!" he said. "If you had, I'd have smashed it. I'm calling it *Negress Awaiting Unsuccessful Abortion*. Of course it's not a negress, it's just pure form annihilating itself. But speaking of abortions, did you know our Caroline's pregnant?"

I started: "Is that why she got married in such a hurry?"

"I suppose so. Who knocked her up—you?"

My hair prickled as I denied the possibility and Adam laughed. "The question wasn't serious. You'd have been too careful. What a white hulk of a greedy female organism that girl is! All shapes and sizes for Caroline with more to come. You know this bastard she's married?"

"I met him once or twice at your place."

"I'll lay five to one he's not Oscar's real father. How could anyone who rolls over the way she does know who was technically responsible for the biochemistry?" Adam scratched his beak and made a face. "Lawson smells like an undertaker's hands. I suppose you know he's a commie?"

"I don't know the first thing about him."

"Neither does Caroline." Adam hunched over the table. "Listen, George. This Lawson's no local puritan hot-shot who joins the party for sex. He was probably born in the baggage room of the Smolensk railway station. I know a thing or two, George, and I happen to know that son of a bitch is in a commie *apparat*."

Adam bent over his coffee, which he said was getting cold, wiped his mouth and surveyed me with another sardonic grin. "You know what's the matter with you? You just won't admit that we all live in the *merde*. History sloshes through it like a truck with broken brakes and splashes it over everyone. Relax, George, relax and decay. Look at Caroline. What the hell is she but a normal woman and what's a normal woman but a biology factory? In normal times she'd have married the local druggist and had a baby a year till the druggist ran out of gas. But now look at her. She's so dumb she doesn't even know what an *apparat* is. What a sweet cover for an *apparat* man that big, white, mothering piece of womanflesh is going to make!"

My eggs arrived and I began to eat. Adam called for more coffee and lit another cigarette.

"Have you been seeing Norah Blackwell tonight?" he asked with a sharp look.

"I ran into her when I was looking for Caroline."

"A little piece of advice, George. Since you're obviously looking for a new lay, don't touch *that* little piece of puritanical nymphomania."

"What gave you the idea I intended to?"

His eyes with the premature pouches regarded me with cynical amusement.

"This is Father Adam you're talking to. Watch your step, she's a mink."

"She's just a poor kid who happens to be a good nurse and she also happens to be married to a friend of mine."

Adam laughed loudly and took another sip of his coffee.

After a while he said: "I used to wonder why Norah took up nursing, but after I thought about it I realized it was exactly what she *would* take up. She's deep in D. H. Lawrence at the moment. Watch out, boy, watch out."

"What's D. H. Lawrence got to with all this?"

"Hell, they all start on him. All these puritans cut their sexual teeth on that ignorant English peasant. Lawrence a genius! He's a semi-literate romantic with a guilt-complex the size of the Empire State."

I surveyed the restaurant while Adam stared with distaste at the bulging backside of a female student who was eating a sundae at the counter.

After a while he said: "Did Norah Blackwell ever happen to mention Jerome Martell to you? I mean, during the various opportunities she's doubtless taken to explain to you how noble she is, and how much she loves her husband whom nobody but she understands, did she by any chance talk about Dr. Martell?"

"Why shouldn't she? She's a nurse in his hospital."

Adam looked at me sharply, then laughed. "Why go on the defensive, George? We're all in the *merde* together, aren't we? Why didn't you tell Father Adam that Martell's wife's an old pal of yours?"

"How did you find that out?"

"From the lady herself. She told me. By the way, did Norah ever happen to mention Catherine Martell as well as him?"

With my eyes on my plate I nodded.

"And did she offer it as her considered opinion that Mrs. Martell is a very wonderful woman?"

My expression must have betrayed me, for Adam laughed again.

"She says that to everyone she meets," he said. " 'Mrs. Martell is a wonderful woman'—just like that. Can you beat it?"

I finished my eggs and leaned back: "What are you getting at, Adam?"

He scratched his nose and then he blew it.

"You know, George, you're that very rare thing, a perfect specimen. You're middle class to the bone. You're a nice guy. All you want is a nice little wife and a nice little apartment and a nice little job, and yet you hang around with these hot-shots that hang around me. You're about as revolutionary as Stanley Baldwin. Ah well—the middle-classes have driven you out, and by driving out people like you, they're exterminating themselves. When old George howls like a wolf, what do the real wolves sound like?" He savored his own rhetoric in a moment of silence, and then went on. "Now take this old girl friend of yours, Catherine. When but in a time like this would a girl like her have married a primitive like Martell?"

"What's the matter with him anyway?"

"Nothing. Nothing." Adam grinned. "Pure rhumba, that's all that's the matter with him. Incidentally he's one more proof of my thesis. The middle classes are driving him out too, and he's the sort they absolutely should never drive out. He's dumb, but he's dangerous. He's an idealist, and he has five times more energy than any normal man. Push a man like him outside your camp and what does he do? Nine times out of ten he tries to break in and capture it."

"He's not a communist, is he?"

"No, not yet." Adam grinned. "He works too hard to be one —yet. Eighteen hours a day, they tell me. It's plainly compulsive. Everything he does is compulsive. His wife's a partial invalid and that may be one reason why he works so hard, for you only have to look at the man to know he's a stallion." The most sardonic grin of all. "This little Blackwell bitch has been heard to mention how noble he is to put up with his domestic situation without a murmur. It's one of the remarks she makes before she tells you that Mrs. Martell is a wonderful woman. You think you're still in love with her, don't you, George?"

Adam Blore was the only man I knew who talked to me like this. He knew I disliked it, and my dislike gave him an obscure pleasure. I shrugged and suddenly he became serious and genuinely bitter.

"You know, George, talking about Catherine Martell makes me think. She's a lady. Actually, she's a real lady, and I confess that when we met I felt rather down at heel in character. Why do I go on like this anyhow? These puritans with their hot pants and their little affairs in the name of art—my God, if I'd known enough in time, I'd have got some doctor to feed me the necessary hormones and turn me into a homosexual. The pansies are the boys today. The commies make me laugh with their big talk about their great, big beautiful revolution—bah!" His sneer was so loud that several students turned and stared. "The real revolution has nothing to do with them. It's sexual. No? Just wait and see. Fifty years from now this country of sod-breakers and salesmen is going to be a third-rate Rome. Can't you hear the pansies titter behind their hands at the rest of us poor saps? They're right, too. They're the best artists because they're clear of women. They're not romantics. And they hang together. If I was a homosexual in good standing, I'd get shows in London right now. I might even get a show in Paris. I'd certainly get one in New York." A loud sniff. "That bastard D. H. Lawrence. Just another of those damned romantics. *Das ewig weibliche zieht uns heran.* Art for the sake of a bitch with hot pants, for Christ's sake! Goethe, Hugo, Shelley, the rest of those obscenities—name me one who could tell the difference between his soul and his balls."

I finished my coffee and decided to get away. Adam asked me to come to his room around midnight and bring a bottle, but I said I was going early to bed. He nodded and went back to Céline and I left him.

There was a hunter's moon over the city and the air was clean, northerly and almost intoxicating after the fog and talk in the restaurant. People were moving about in the early part of a Friday night and most of the ones I passed seemed young and a few were gay. On the corner of St. Catherine Street I put a quarter into the palm of an unemployed man, bought a *Star* and boarded a tram running west. Sitting on one of the straw-yellow seats in the bright lights I read in the paper that Stanley Baldwin believed that the situation was improving, that a man just escaped from Dachau believed that Ernst Thaelmann was still alive, that a visiting Catholic bishop believed that Franco was a Christian hero, that a visiting English journalist believed that unless Franco was destroyed our civilization would perish and that a visiting American mayor believed that Montreal was one of the four most fascinating cities in North America.

I got out of the car at Guy Street and stood in the corner lights wondering what to do next. Half a block up the street Sir Cedric Hardwick was playing at His Majesty's and that was where I had intended to be now, for I had planned to take Caroline. Now there was no Caroline and the play had already begun, so I had nothing to do but walk back along St. Catherine Street the way I had come.

St. Catherine Street on a Friday night in the depression: the news vendors closing their stalls, the unemployed slouching along, the shop windows lit like altars, the trams jangling their bells, the boys and girls going into the movies. I stopped at a tavern and drank a beer. I crawled to another and had two beers in the company of a hairy truck driver who informed me there was no work in Saskatoon, Winnipeg, Port Arthur, North Bay, Ottawa or Montreal. In a third tavern I was told by an Englishman that everything would have been fine for him if it had not been for his wife, and on my way to the fourth tavern I was accosted by a prostitute who asked me if I wanted a good time and said the price was three dollars, and when I told her I didn't have it she asked if I expected a girl to work for nothing. My next beer was political with a Belgian sailor who knew what Goering had said to Hitler the last time they had talked, and for half an hour he spoke learnedly about the coming war until suddenly his digestive tract gave a whoop and he was sick on the floor, and while a disgusted waiter tried to get him out of the place, he moaned that he loved his wife who had left him. Then I walked, was accosted by a gray-haired whore who asked if I wanted a good time, and after a while I found myself on a corner leaning against a light standard wondering whether I was going to be sick myself. The long street with its department stores, movies, little shops, taverns, empty banks and crowded trams wavered in and out. The moon had sunk and a rising wind was blowing scraps of paper and dust. The crowds were

thinning out but there were still plenty of people and I saw
a solitary whoremaster slink around a corner after the shadow
of a woman. A tram crashed to a stop, I stepped out to board it
but there were too many people so I turned away and walked
the streets for nearly an hour until I felt steadier. Now it was
past midnight. Now I was alone in St. Catherine Street at the
hour when everyone is alone, and I stood on a corner and
stared.

It was the bottom hole of my life up to that time. I saw then—
and it is one of the most terrible things anyone can see—my
own worthlessness. I told myself that if my luck had been better
I too might have been better; that if I had had an opportunity
for work I enjoyed and believed in it would have made the
difference. But the unemployed still drifted down St. Catherine
Street as the whole world drifted into the war. I heard a scratch-
ing noise and looked down and saw the front page of a news-
paper dragging eastward along the pavement in the wind. Then
I stared all the way down that bleak, empty street and seemed
to be staring into the recesses of my own soul.

Chapter V

THE next evening after an early supper in town I decided to
escape from myself, to escape from the only kind of people
I knew in Montreal, to escape from talking about politics, simply
to escape. So I bought a ticket for the show at His Majesty's
to which I had intended taking Caroline the night before, and
I actually enjoyed the first act. Sir Cedric Hardwick was play-
ing the role of an Irish canon miserable in his native land because
he had been spoiled by a long sojourn in Spain, where priests
had been austere and learned and not the pair of soccer-playing
hobbledehoys he had for curates here. The play moved well
and I was engrossed in it when the curtain fell on the first act.
Thereafter I have no idea what happened on the stage that night.

For in the intermission I saw her at last; after a dozen years
I saw Catherine. I saw that sable hair, the Picasso sweep of
her fine shoulders, the opulence of her small figure. I trembled

and my knees went loose and my throat felt like dry sand. Nor was this all. Suddenly I felt bitterly angry at her, resentful be-cause of the bondage in which my love for her had held me, and I almost turned and went back upstairs.

I did not do so because of my fascination with the man beside her, who I knew must be Jerome Martell. He looked very different from the image I had formed of him. For one thing he was shorter than I had imagined, for another he was burlier even than Adam's description had suggested. He looked much older than Catherine and much, much older than I fancied myself to be. There was a small blaze of gray on his temple before an ear shaped like a faun's. He was in profile and his nose seemed to have been flattened by an old break. His fore-head was corrugated with wrinkles and hooded against the irri-tation of the smoke spiralling up from the cigarette he held between the thumb and forefinger of a square, powerful hand. He dropped his cigarette and turned to crush it with his heel, and under the close fit of his dinner jacket a pack of shoulder-muscle shifted and I remembered that Adam Blore had called him a stallion.

Physically ruthless—that was my first thought. But an instant later this impression disappeared. For an usher approached Jerome with a message, and when he turned to read it I saw his face full front and the eyes were wide, intelligent and young. The mouth was sensual but it was also broad and strong; the cheekbones were high and forceful and the features were dis-ciplined. In any crowd I would have recognized that for a doc-tor's face.

He crumpled the message and looked at Catherine with a rueful smile that was completely charming. When he walked away to the cloakroom I saw that his powerful body moved with a limp.

I waited. Then Catherine turned. She saw me and her whole face opened up. An instant later we were together.

"I've so often wanted to write," she was saying. "I've so often wanted to see you."

The anger I had felt an instant ago went out and I was with her again and her voice vibrated through me.

"It was my fault," I mumbled. "I was afraid even to let you know where I was."

"Oh George—why?"

"I was afraid I wouldn't be able to stand how things have turned out for me."

In spite of a defensive habit of depreciating myself, I am a proud man and it was not easy for me to say this to her. But I thought it must be obvious to her that I had not fulfilled myself, and also I had forgotten her kindness. Ruthless her mind could be at times, demanding her nature could me, but I had forgotten her wonderful kindness, and now there seemed much more of it than there had ever been before, and as I stood looking down at her I felt it enfold me, and I felt something like a vast weight, a cloudy weight under which I had labored for years, a Sinbad-weight, melt away and leave me light.

Somebody jostled us, apologized and passed.

"When you didn't even acknowledge my wedding invitation, I gave up finally. I wondered what I'd done to offend you. George, dear!"

Then she reached up and in front of all the people she kissed me.

"Catherine!"

Her eyes twinkled and the intensity disappeared behind the mask of a happily smiling woman at ease with herself and the world.

"There's so much to tell you I don't know where to begin. Oh yes I do, though. I've got a family. Can you believe it? Not a big family, but one very nice, vigorous, impish little girl. Her name's Sally and I'm very proud of her and me."

"That's wonderful."

"You didn't even know?"

"No Catherine. Nobody told me."

"You see—" a little droop of the eyelid, a recall to the old defiant impishness which was also so deeply serious with her —"you see, I fooled them again."

Over my shoulder I saw Jerome emerging from the inner vestibule with his hat crushed sideways on his head and a navy blue gabardine over his dinner jacket. He came slowly through the press with his forehead wrinkled against the smoke that filled the foyer with a blue haze, and I wondered how old he was. Thirty-four? Thirty-nine? Perhaps even older than that.

"Jerome dear, here is somebody I've wanted you to meet always. This is George Stewart."

At first he did not seem to hear my name. Then he took it in and as he lifted his bulldog jaw I felt his personality strike me with an almost physical impact. His face broke open in a welcoming smile. His hand closed on mine so hard I winced, but I liked it and I liked him.

"Well!" he said. "*Well!* I certainly have wanted to meet you. Aren't you the first man Kate fell in love with? Why the devil didn't you marry her when you had the chance?"

I mumbled something incoherent and Jerome gave a frank laugh.

"I suppose I shouldn't say things like this to a man I've only just met, but I'm going to just the same. You know," he said with another laugh, "there's nothing worse this side of hell than to be married to a woman who thinks herself unattractive. Kate would have been that kind of woman if it hadn't been for you. You were the only person in that god-awful place where you were raised who gave her any self-confidence. I've been drawing interest on it ever since. Thanks, George, thanks very much." He put his arm about her waist and smiled at me like a boy. "How do you think she looks?"

She looked like a woman well and truly loved, but all I said was that she looked grand.

"The things you boys talk about together!" Catherine said, but she was pleased because Jerome had liked me.

"Here," said Jerome, and handed me two ticket stubs. "Take these and sit with Kate for the rest of the show. I've got to go to the hospital. If I don't have to operate I'll be back before it's over, but I probably will have to operate. So you go along with Kate after the show gets out and we'll have a talk later."

He left us and I saw a tall, dark woman who had been staring at Jerome shift her glance to Catherine and appraise her with the candor some women use on each other and her expression seemed to say; "What has *she* got that I haven't?" I was amused to notice that Catherine was aware of the inspection, and that

I was conscious that she was, for her gray eyes twinkled, and *her* expression said to me: "I have a lot more than some people would guess."

The buzzer sounded for the second act and people began moving toward the doors, but Catherine and I stayed where we were.

"Is he always like that?" I asked her.

"Pretty often. Is it any wonder his patients love him?"

"First I thought he'd be so old he'd not notice me, and then he seemed as young as myself. Do you always dress for dinner?"

"Hardly ever. We had to go to a medical banquet where Jerome had to make a speech. I wish he'd let me edit his speeches. Sometimes he does, too. But when he gets excited he throws the script away and just talks. He was excited tonight, I'm afraid."

"What about?"

"It was Sir Rupert Irons, really. He's the president of Jerome's board and he was there tonight, and Jerome contrived to say about everything he could think of to raise Irons' blood pressure. Of course Irons thinks he's a communist."

"Is he?"

"He's just Jerome."

We went in and found our seats, the lights went down and the play resumed, but I have no recollection of it. Catherine was beside me, her full white arm and her breathing presence in the tide of her life, and I still felt like a man come home. When the curtain fell and the people went out for their smokes and their inspections of each other, Catherine and I remained in our seats and talked.

"Oh," I said in answer to her question, "after Father went broke it was bed-sitting rooms and odd jobs till finally I got a degree out of Toronto. Since then I've been at Waterloo. It's a lousy job but I'm lucky to have it."

"Teaching isn't a job to be ashamed of."

"I wasn't talking about teaching, I was talking about Waterloo. And I'm not complaining, Catherine. I couldn't get anything else. I suppose a war will change things."

"Are you another of the ones who expect war?"

"Of course."

"Jerome thinks it's here already."

"He's right."

"If only there weren't so many people who want it."

"It's coming, wanting or not."

"Yes," she said quietly, "I know it's coming."

Her excitement had made her talkative as she seldom is.

"One consolation," she went on, "is that when the war comes, Jerome is in the one profession where a man is allowed to do some good. When I first met him he called himself a pacifist, but I'm afraid I never took *that* seriously." She gave me a rueful smile. "It's a warrior I married, George. In his more obstreperous moments he says Ha-ha in the midst of the trumpets."

"He's made you very happy, hasn't he, Catherine?"

She looked at me calmly. "Yes, George, he has."

"Do you see any of our old friends any more?"

She shook her head.

"I don't suppose Jerome would have any time for them. I don't see any of them, either."

"You're one old friend I'm going to see. Jerome likes you. I hope you like him."

I rose to make room for a returning couple to stumble past, and when I sat down Catherine's eyes met mine and our hands touched and joined. The third act played itself out and when the curtain fell the people gave Sir Cedric an ovation. But there was no sign of Jerome when we reached the foyer.

"Obviously he's had to operate," she said. "Do come with me now."

"Where are you going?"

"Most weekends lately we've been meeting in various people's houses for talk. Sometimes I'm not up to it and sometimes I leave before the party breaks up. They're all used to me, so it doesn't matter. But Jerome has to work so hard and read so many medical journals that it's his only way of keeping up with things, talking with people who have the time to know about politics He's a wonderful doctor but he's always dreaded the narrowness of the medical profession. There's going to be a famous English journalist there tonight. I think he writes for *The New Statesman*."

"Is his name Clifford?"

"That's it. He's back from Spain and Jerome wants to meet

anyone who's been in Spain. Professor John David is giving the party."

"I read about Clifford in the paper."

My old shyness returned and I hesitated, for in the teaching profession the university professor is an officer and the schoolmaster an N.C.O.

"Please come, George," she begged me. "These are the kind of people you belong with. You don't belong in that crowd around Adam Blore."

"They're all right," I said.

"They're not all right. Jerome pretends to find them stimulating, but I wish he didn't."

"They've been the only friends I've had lately, Catherine."

"Do you really like them?"

"Some of them. How's your heart these days?"

"Now you're changing the subject on me. My heart is in the same old place making the some old sounds, but I'm not afraid of it any more. Now dear, please call us a cab."

A few minutes later we were rolling east along Sherbrooke Street and I saw moonlight flicker off the darkened windows of a church, then the dew-covered campus of the university looking like a sheet of hoarfrost and finally we stopped in a dark street before a line of graystone houses where professors lived.

Chapter VI

THOSE Saturday evenings of the 1930s—they seem so remote in these days when we drink the better brands while the satellites flash around a planet governed by propagandists and advertising agencies. There were six professors and four laymen crowded into John David's living room and eight women including Catherine, most of them faculty wives, and they talked of the things people talked of then. Clifford, the English journalist who wrote for *The New Statesman,* seemed acquainted with everyone in England who had written a book or made a speech, and to me it was exciting to hear the famous names drop from a man who knew their owners, and to know what G.B.S. had said to H.G.

the night Clifford had sat between them at a dinner, and what Harold really thought of the Webbs. Clifford stood with his back to the empty hearth with his hands in his pockets, his well-bred head on one side and his loose hair cut long and brushed back along his temples, his face distinguished and diffuse as he talked about violent things.

The conversation went round and round, rising and falling in a sequence of arias and duets. In the middle of the room was a low coffee table with biscuits and Oka cheese. We drank beer, and a young man called Arthur Lazenby was the bartender for the night and kept our glasses filled. I sat on the floor with my back against several rows of books which reposed on plain pine boards resting on loose stacks of bricks. Over the fireplace was a large painting of an Ontario forest in an autumn storm, on the walls were etchings of the Oxford college where John David had lived as a Rhodes Scholar and on the mantel were souvenir beer mugs from the Bavarian town where he had learned to speak German. The names and phrases of the time cascaded learnedly through the room: Laski, Keynes, Marx, Selassie, Lenin, Ras Desta, Trotsky, Hitler, Mussolini, Blum, Azaña, Hitler, Mussolini, Litvinov, Goebbels, Suñer, Samuel Hoare, Hitler, Mussolini, Baldwin, Stavisky, Chamberlain, Lansbury, Franco, Mussolini, Hitler, Van Paassen, Wallisch, Fey Miaja, Duranty, Roosevelt, Cabellero, Dos Passos, Hemingway, cadres, fifth column, new deal, technician, trade index, putsch, kulak, liquidation, the Ukraine, and would Hitler get it, Abysinnia and would Mussolini keep it, Cagoulard, Stormovik, the Manzanares—hands kept reaching out to the table for biscuits and cheese and Arthur Lazenby kept replenishing glasses with beer which still cost only fifteen cents a quart and Catherine sat under an etching of Tom Quad looking over-dressed among the faculty wives in their blouses and dirndls and the men in their gray flannels and tweed jackets. The 1930s was the last time for so many things; it was certainly the last time in which college professors could believe themselves capable of planning the future of humanity.

It was past midnight when the room stirred and Jerome entered, and when I stood up my eyes popped, for Norah Blackwell was with him.

"The best surgical nurse in Montreal," he introduced her while Norah blushed. "She wants a beer and so do I. Catherine, you know Norah Blackwell, don't you?"

The two women greeted each other formally, but behind Catherine's easy courtesy was an alertness which made Norah uncomfortable. Lazenby appeared with foaming glasses and Jerome, after shaking hands with Clifford, began talking as though he had been present all evening.

"I don't know why operations make me thirsty, but they do. Maybe it's self-indulgence, maybe it's the heat and the ether, but tonight it could be remorse."

He found a seat on the sofa and drained half his glass.

"Remorse," he repeated. "With Norah's help I performed a crime tonight. If it hadn't been for us, one of the biggest bastards in Montreal would now be dead."

Lazenby refilled his glass, he lifted it in thanks, then drank half of it.

"There's no doubt the man's going to recover," he went on. "I give him five more years at least." Then he caught sight of me: "Hullo, George, so you came after all. I'm glad. You and Norah know each other. She told me."

Clifford, the English journalist, was showing signs of annoyance for which I did not blame him, for he had been in the middle of an explanation when Jerome had entered and broken it up. He eyed Jerome appraisingly and I could see him disliking him.

Norah, shy and fey as she usually was with strangers, found a place beside me against the books, and when Clifford got going again I began talking to her in whispers.

"Does he always talk like this about his cases outside the hospital?"

"No, no, of course not. He's just tired and worked up."

"What were you doing at the hospital at this late hour?"

Dr. Martell had this emergency and Miss Elliott, she's the senior O.R. nurse, she suddenly had a gall bladder attack and Dr. Martell phoned me to come over."

She was obviously pleased and proud and I asked her who the important man was whose life they had saved.

"It wasn't me that had anything to do with it, it was Dr. Martell. He's so wonderful. Don't pay any attention to him when he talks like this. That old man he operated on was scared to death, and Dr. Martell treated him so gently. That's the way he operates—gently."

"How can you operate gently?"

Her large eyes stared at me as though I had asked a foolish question.

"If you don't, the patient will suffer shock. Dr. Martell understands about things like that. He's not like Dr. Rodgers at all. If he wanted to, he could operate twice as fast as Dr. Rodgers, but he's so gentle with the patient's organs."

"He doesn't look a gentle type to me," I said. "But I must say, he does look tired."

"Why shouldn't he be? He's been on his feet since six this morning and he's done seven major operations in addition to everything else."

Jerome relaxed on the sofa like a resting animal, smoking and drinking beer, the glass solid in his hand, his eyes hooded against the smoke.

"Some surgeons are such prima donnas," Norah whispered to me. "The way some of them talk to a nurse, she wants to crawl off somewhere and die. That's what Dr. Rodgers is like. And of course he's so jealous of Dr. Martell everyone knows it."

I wondered if she ought to be talking this way about the hospital, but there was such innocence in her expression and manner that people never seemed to notice it when she said things like this.

"Of course Dr. Rodgers is in with the capitalists," she went on. "And that's another reason why he hates Dr. Martell."

Her eyes on Jerome, I suddenly noticed, were adoring. She knew I was there, but I was only somebody she could talk to. Her eyes never left Jerome's face. I noticed that at least half the other women in the room were also turning their eyes to him. He himself seemed unconscious of their admiration. He leaned forward and cut himself a hunk of cheese, and I watched that square, powerful hand stuff the cheese into his mouth. It looked more like the hand of an able seaman than of a surgeon, except that it was clean and the fingers were supple and quick.

He swallowed the cheese, took another sip of his beer, then leaned forward and entered the conversation with a crash.

"Clifford, will the Spanish people still be fighting by spring?"

"There can't be the slightest doubt of that," said Clifford.

"How do you know there can't be the slightest doubt?"

"Well you see, I've just come from Spain."

"Were you in the last war?"

Clifford flushed slightly. "Not really. I was turned down by you doctor chaps."

"The only reason I asked," said Jerome, "was to get some idea of how you'd look at a war. A civilian usually misses the signs that count—you know, the things you notice if you've lived for years with troops." He paused and frowned. "I don't like one damned bit what I read about Spain in the papers."

"I'd presume anybody'd know that the capitalist press is lying," Clifford's clipped voice said sharply. He pronounced "capitalist" with the accent on the second syllable, "capit'alist."

Jerome reached for more cheese, and while he munched it Clifford resumed his monologue. But the moment Jerome had swallowed the cheese, he interrupted him again.

"You can't dodge it, Clifford. Those poor bloody Loyalists are taking one hell of a beating. Their generals are obviously useless and their troops are obviously untrained. On the other hand this Franco seems a reasonably good general."

Clifford flared angrily. "You really believe that? My information is that Franco's nothing but a routine Spanish army officer."

"I don't know what your information is. Probably it's right. If so, so much the worse. For he's winning."

"There's such a thing as morale," said Clifford, now thoroughly annoyed. "You see, the Loyalists happen to know what they're fighting for."

"You found the morale of Franco's Moors bad? Or the morale of those fascists who held out in the Alcazar?" Jerome heaved himself forward. "Do you really believe it when you tell me the fascists don't know what they're fighting for? They're fighting for their lives, that's what they're fighting for."

"If you saw Spain," said Clifford, now pale with suppressed anger, "you couldn't compare the morale of the fascists to the morale of the Loyalists."

Jerome shrugged: "I only hope you're right."

Then he leaned back and drank some more beer, and it took the frustrated conversation several minutes to get going again. I looked at him in fascination. Never in my life had I seen a man who had this singular capacity to set a room on fire. That was the only word for it—he set that room on fire because somehow he struck right through to people's underselves. I looked at Catherine's calm, heart-shaped face, at her small, beautifully formed body outlined by her evening dress and wondered how she could stand the exhaustion of living with a personality like this. Rude? In one sense as rude as anyone I had ever met. Yet underneath I did not think he was rude at all, for he was not seeking to humiliate Clifford. He simply lost himself in whatever interested him. Clifford did not interest him now but the beer and cheese did and he gave to both the attention he had given to the argument a moment before. Then he interrupted again.

"I got a letter from Norman Bethune today." For Clifford's benefit he explained that Bethune was another Montreal surgeon. "He's over on the other side and he's gone to Spain. He asked me what I thought of a new idea of his. He wants to organize a blood transfusion service for the front lines. He also wants to know if I'd be interested in joining in."

Catherine's face paled slightly but she did not move or speak. Norah sucked in her breath and stared at Jerome as though he were a god.

"Beth's one of those impetuous men who says what he thinks and does what he likes and relies on his energy to get by. He's also a terrific surgeon. I wish he wasn't so impetuous, though."

What do you think you are? I thought when I heard Jerome say this.

"I believe in going more carefully and scouting the ground. What's the use of people like Beth and me in Spain if the Loyalists are going to collapse?"

"There's not the slightest possibility of that," Clifford said sharply. "Almost with their bare hands they've—"

"Wars aren't won with bare hands, Clifford."

"May I ask," Clifford said, straining to be polite, "just what is the purpose of a blood transfusion unit?"

"The purpose of a blood transfusion unit is to keep people from dying of shock. It's never been used on a battlefield before. In the last war, at a rough estimate, about a third of the men who died of wounds actually died of shock. However, to get back to Beth and myself, what's the point of two busy men throwing up their work if mismanagement and incompetence wrecks the whole Loyalist resistance before we get there? I don't see how they're going to win. How can they, with this non-intervention?"

"If you don't mind an interruption," said Clifford, "it's my impression that I'd been talking about that subject for some time."

"I heard you," said Jerome, "and while I listened I couldn't help wondering why you're a member of the Labour Party."

Clifford's pallor now changed to a brick-red flush. He was accustomed to being listened to with respect and without interruption, for in addition to being a journalist, he was also a professor of political science at the University of London. He believed that Jerome was deliberately needling him. Jerome was certainly needling him, but not deliberately; when I knew him better I learned that he almost never talked like this deliberately.

"My dear sir," said Clifford in the most formidable Winchester accent he had yet produced, "the Labour Party, as I'd presume you might have known, does not at the moment, thanks to the bankers' ramp of 1931, happens to be ensconced on the Treasury Bench. Non-intervention is a Tory policy."

"If you guys were in power it would be a Labour policy, too."

"Really? Might I ask for your evidence?"

"Of course it would be. Your crowd are pacifists. You're pure. You're still trying to stop fascism by passing resolutions."

"Our crowd—as you put it—cannot possibly be held responsible for any aspect of this present mess. If the 1931 election had been honest we'd have got in, and this situation would never have arisen."

"You mean, if you'd got in you'd have stopped Hitler by passing resolutions against him?"

"If we'd got in, Hitler would never have got into power in Germany. A socialist victory in Britain would have confirmed the socialists on the continent. Socialism would have nipped this situation in the bud."

"The hell it would have. The Germans are hungry and the Germans like wars."

I looked at Catherine to see how she took this. It was not so much what Jerome said that was so rude; it was the physical force with which his words came out of him.

"You see what I mean about Dr. Martell?" Norah whispered to me. "He's real, and this Englishman is just a Social Democrat."

Jerome, apparently forgetting Clifford, began thinking aloud. "Somebody's got to walk out to the bull and the Spaniards are the only ones who are doing it. God knows how they can win this war, but what's that to do with us? Maybe the time to go to Spain is now, when you know they haven't got a chance?"

"But I insist they have every chance," said Clifford.

Jerome put down his empty glass and stared at his feet, and after a while he breathed heavily and stood up and looked at Clifford with a sheepish smile.

"It's just occurred to me I've been rude to you tonight," he said.

"Has it really?" said Clifford at last giving himself away.

"I didn't mean it. I get like that when I'm tired. I had two cases today I didn't like. Tonight I wasted a good operation on a bad man who ought to be dead, but this afternoon a good man who ought to be alive died on me." He looked across the room at Norah, who also had got to her feet. "He fell off a girder a hundred feet from the ground in a structure being built by the company tonight's patient is the president of. He left a wife and five children and it looks as if there's going to be an argument about compensation." Jerome closed his eyes an instant. "By Christ, if the widow doesn't receive compensation, that man is going to receive the biggest bill anyone ever got from a surgeon in this city."

Jerome swayed on his feet and Catherine stood beside him and took his arm. It was the first time I had seen him like this, but I was often to see him like this later when suddenly the energy went out of him and left a void.

"We'd better go home now, John," Catherine was saying to our host. "Jerome has been on his feet since dawn." She turned to the Englishman. "It's been lovely meeting you, Mr. Clifford."

Clifford murmured something polite, but he did not say it had been lovely meeting her or Jerome.

I noticed a flutter in Catherine's carotid artery, and saw that Jerome had also noticed it, and that their eyes were meeting with the understanding of a husband and wife. He put his fingers on her forearm and gave another sheepish smile to the company.

"I'm sorry I talked too much, everybody."

Outside in the dark street, while Jerome unlocked the door of his Pontiac, Norah spoke to Catherine.

"I think Dr. Martell was absolutely correct in every single thing he said tonight, Mrs. Martell. Don't you think he was, too? I don't believe he was rude to that English Social Democrat. I think everyone should speak out the way Dr. Martell does. He was so upset by the accident case this afternoon it's a wonder he was able to operate at all tonight."

Catherine looked at her calmly and said: "I know he was upset by the accident case, Mrs. Blackwell. Could we drive you home now?"

Chapter VII

AFTER that night my life changed. I still worked at Waterloo and five days of every week were still spent in those nerve-grinding classrooms with noisy boys, and one week in four on duty. Shatwell, McNish and the others were still my colleagues, but from then on my life ceased to be empty, for Catherine and Jerome took me in, and they restored my soul. They let me become a kind of uncle to Sally, then in her sixth year; they introduced me to their friends and to their friends' interests and slowly I began to believe I might be more than an usher in that school of Dr. Bigbee's. Jerome's apartment in the little half-moon street near the university became the place I thought of whenever I thought of the meaning of the word "home."

Whenever I came up to town they insisted that I see them, and I realized that Jerome was especially glad that I should.

"Kate's lonely," he told me. "Any doctor's wife is bound to be left with the pickings of her husband's time, but Kate gets a worse deal than most. It makes me feel better to know you're around and can take her out occasionally when I'm tied up."

Sometimes I did take her out: to concerts or shows and once to a hockey game, for during the first year there were several weekends when I never saw Jerome at all and when Catherine never saw him either. Sometimes she would be asleep when he came to bed and still be asleep when he got up, and she would see the bed had been used and would wonder when she would see him next. We worked long hours at Waterloo, but compared to Jerome we were loafers, for on the average he slept no more than five hours a night and sometimes only two or three. His daily routine called for about six operations in addition to his calls, he lectured in the university, he spent two hours every day in a free clinic he had established for the unemployed, and he was involved in various public causes. Besides all this he managed to find time to read, to help people in trouble and even to play with his child. The one thing he almost always did: he came home for dinner and reserved the half-hour before it for Sally.

Weeks passed and my life came close to theirs. Catherine I thought I knew, for she was in my bones, and in some ways she could talk to me more easily than to Jerome; I really think I was able to lessen the loneliness that came to her from loving strongly a person very different. But Jerome I liked without even pretending to understand him, for in those days he seemed to me more like a force of nature than a man. Also he was so much older and abler, and he had under him what I and all my other friends lacked, a real career.

It eased Catherine to talk about Jerome and their life together.

"When Jerome likes a person he goes all the way and tends to take it for granted the other person does the same. He's so reckless. At the same time he can sometimes be incredibly aware. But he won't calculate except in his work. In his work they tell me he's bold—the boldest surgeon in Montreal, they say—and he's never reckless in that. But in his life he's so reckless he makes me shiver sometimes. That way he has of jumping out at people like electricity jumping a spark gap—have you ever seen anything like it?"

I hadn't, and to me this quality had seemed wonderful, for I was shy in those days and in any case I was unaccustomed to people taking me in like that. Already, without my knowing it, I had come to think of Jerome as a protector, almost as a substitute for the father I never had except in the biological sense.

I was aware of Catherine regarding me with critical amusement.

"I disliked him intensely the first time I met him," she said.

I laughed: "Did he dislike you, too?"

"He never even saw me. That may have been why I disliked him. I used to go to far too many parties in those days. I was so insecure and afraid of being unpopular and left out of things. I made a fool of myself pretty often and got myself talked about and more than once I did things that shocked me. I could be reckless too—or did you know that already?"

There was a fond little twinkle in her eyes and I said: "Yes dear, I've not forgotten."

"I wanted men to like me in the most outrageous way, and I used to get so annoyed with myself for wanting that."

She seemed so calm now and sure of herself in her own home, the tea cups on a tray in front of her.

"Those first times I saw Jerome," she said ruefully, "were probably the last times I'll ever be able to see him as others do. I had no idea where he came from. I thought he talked too much. I thought he was abominably opinionated. You know how we are in Montreal—the way we keep our opinions to ourselves if we think people will disagree with them. I knew he was a Canadian but he was almost a foreigner to me. Then suddenly we met. I mean we really met."

Her gray eyes looked frankly into mine.

"George dear, I'm not blind and I know how you feel. I'm being very bad for you."

"You're being very wonderful for me."

"If I weren't so selfish and fond of you I'd be mean and horrible so you'd run away and forget me. You're much too fond of me for your own good. And I love it too much for the good of either of us."

I laughed: "I thought you were talking about the time you met Jerome."

She gave me a small twinkle. "So I was to be sure. It was at a cocktail party in July and there he was again. He wasn't a party-goer, at least not in those days. It just happened that over the past six months I'd met him a few times. Well, this time he actually saw me. We'd been introduced before but I knew he'd forgotten all about that. But this time he saw me and came shouldering across the room and said: 'Why haven't we met before?'

"That was really too much, so I said, 'Dr. Martell, we've actually met six times and I think it's simply marvellous that you never even noticed it.' "

She gave me another ruefully pleased smile: "He was perfect then, George. Just perfect. Do you know what he said? 'Let's get out of here,' he said. 'I don't see any particular reason why we should get out of here,' I said to him. So naturally, five minutes later both of us were on our way to Chez Stien in his car. In the middle of dinner he left to call up the hospital and came back to say he'd got another doctor to take an operation. I never knew him to do such a thing since. 'It's just a simple appendectomy,' he said, and I was too ignorant to know what it meant, him doing a thing like that.

"Does he seem terribly direct to you, George?"

"I don't know about terribly. But direct—yes."

"He explodes. Do you realize that, George—Jerome explodes. It scares me. Sometime he's bound to explode wrong."

"But this time he exploded right."

A beatific smile: "Oh, but beautifully right. He took me up to the Lookout on Westmount Mountain and we stood staring down for hours like a single person. And then, try to guess what he said. 'What's your other name besides Kate?' he said. Now try to guess what I said."

"I couldn't."

" 'If I didn't adore you I'd want to kill you for that,' I said. Then I said: 'In case you're not interested, I come from a very old and obscure family in these parts. And in case you're interested any further, nobody but you has ever called me Kate.' And then I told the man my name and he said he liked it. 'Your name means Hammer,' I said next. 'Where did you get it from?'

"Then he told me his father was an Englishman and that the name was of Huguenot origin. He told me he had grown up in Halifax and he didn't understand Montreal.

" 'All I knew was the Maritime Provinces before I went to the war,' he said. 'After the war I did my basic medicine here at McGill and after I qualified I did the usual rounds in Scotland and England and got my F.R.C.S. I've been practicing here about four years, but I haven't had a chance to meet many people except doctors.'

" 'You had six chances to meet me and you didn't take them,' I said."

Catherine gave me another of her charmingly helpless smiles: "George, how can any woman feel safe married to a man who behaves like that? But let me go on. He didn't even hear what I said, for while I was waiting for him to answer he said: 'I suppose you're worried about that heart of yours?'

"Now that was the last straw, for I'd never mentioned my heart and of course I supposed somebody'd told him about it. I was so mad when he said that. Here was developing a lovely, surprising, exciting evening and the man had to begin talking about my confounded heart. I got flustered and said something idiotic like did my heart show on my face.

"And then he looked at me, George, the way he does sometimes, with that wonderful, gentle expression which makes you forget everything else: 'No Kate,' he said, 'your heart doesn't show on your face, but I'm afraid it does in your wrist. I've been taking your pulse. Rheumatic, isn't it?'

"Then I tried to tease him—I'd no idea that he can't be teased —and asked him if it was a new line with doctors to diagnose a girl's ailments the first time they met her. And do you know what he did? He just turned and took me and kissed me, and George— from that minute I was a gone goose."

Catherine was so queen-like in her appearance that when she said things like this they always sounded odd and incongruous. Yet they were perfectly natural to her, for the little girl in Catherine never died.

She continued: "Later when we were driving back down the slope of the mountain, he began talking about my heart again.

" 'I suppose you've been told the usual thing?' he said. 'I suppose some bright member of my profession has put on his best bedside manner and shaken his head in the solidest way and said it's too bad, Miss Carey, but it's my duty to inform you that with a heart condition like yours you must never contemplate child-bearing? Well,' he said, 'am I right or wrong?'

"I told him he was more or less right and he let out that snort of his.

" 'To hell with him whoever he was! He said it to protect himself, not you. Mind you, I'm not pretending that heart of yours won't bear watching. I'm going to see a cardiogram of it in a day or two. But I think you're going to be all right. You want children very much, don't you?'

"I asked him how he could tell, and I said there were plenty of women who didn't choose to bring children into a world like ours, but he cut me short.

" 'You mean there are plenty of women who say that to plenty of men when they want to marry some guy who doesn't see how he can swing it.'

"By this time we'd reached the upper streets of the town and Jerome kept the car ambling along through the traffic.

" 'You know,' he said, 'the purpose of medicine is supposed to be the preservation of life. But that's not *my* idea of the purpose of medicine. My idea is to help people get the most out of what life they have.' "

Catherine stopped and gave me a rueful smile. "George, it's wonderful for me to be able to tell someone this. I've never told anyone. I haven't many close friends, you know. Do you mind?"

I told her I didn't, even though her recital was making me ache, for I remembered how I had feared to take her when she had offered herself, and I knew I could never have accepted the kind of responsibility Jerome had accepted. She looked at me shyly and flushed.

"Do you mind if I tell you something else? What he said to me then?"

I said, "Of course not," and her flush deepened. She looked away and her eyes misted with tears which came from joy and pride, not from sadness.

"Jerome suddenly stopped the car and turned to me and said; 'Catherine, you're going to marry me and I'm going to make you pregnant and you're going to have at least one child and you're not going to die for a long time. At least you're not going to die till you've had a chance to use a lot of that life of yours.' "

So that night they became lovers and three weeks afterwards they got married, and Sally was born so soon that Catherine believed she had been conceived before they went to the church. Sally's birth came close to killing Catherine, but her vast will to live combined with Jerome's force pulled her through. After Sally there could be no more children.

"I don't have to ask anyone what Jerome means to his patients," she told me, "because twice I've been his patient myself. I'd never believed it possible for a doctor to take away a patient's fear as he does."

That was her story and she told me I was the only person who knew all of it. She had not told many of the details to her parents, and indeed she saw her parents seldom, for Mrs. Carey disliked Jerome and disapproved of him, and Mr. Carey had retired from business and had become absorbed in his garden and scholarship as though he were trying to forget that he was alive. Catherine now lived with Jerome in what to me is the most interesting part of the whole of Montreal, the no man's land between the English and French blocs, almost unknown to both of them, which contains international people with interests all over the world.

I was not particularly observant in those days, and I was slow to recognize something which an experienced man, or any normal woman, would have seen immediately. It was this. No matter how much Catherine might love Jerome, she was lonely with him: nor was the loneliness caused entirely by the fact that his practice absorbed so much of his time. Maybe Adam Blore had been right to call him a primitive, for the little coddlings a woman likes to bestow on a man were wasted on Jerome. He never noticed them except when he was exhausted.

But these two had known their honeymoon happiness just the same, and the glow of it still was with them. Catherine told me that the first few years of their marriage had been heaven, and I believed her. Jerome had picked her up and whirled her as though she had never been sick in her life. In those early days he, too, was relaxing from a hard-driving life of constant struggle and emulation. He had qualified, he was establishing himself, he was getting rapidly better in his work; at the same time, for a few years, he was free of care and lived in the present. Every summer in those years he had taken a full month off, and the third autmn of their marriage he had taken Catherine to Europe for three months of travel and high living. Jerome loved sailing, and in his Halifax boyhood he had not only owned a sailboat; twice he had gone out to the Grand Banks for the fishing season with the great black schooners of Lunenburg. Living high, at times even past his means, he had rented a sixty-foot ketch one year for a month's cruising in the Carribean, and if his money had not run out he would have taken the craft through the Panama Canal.

It was this gaiety of Jerome's early life which had won him the initial regard of the man who now had become his enemy, Dr. Stamford Rodgers, the chief surgeon of his hospital. For Rodgers was an aristocrat and he liked to see his young protégés living large so long as they did their work. Jerome's life might have been easy had it not been for the change that came over the whole world in the early Thirties. When the depression struck, suddenly the sun went down for him, he remembered his childhood and the war, he closed the book on fun and good times, he began working twelve and sometimes eighteen hours a day, and Catherine saw less and less of him.

But the halcyon years of love, excitement and fun were still marked on Catherine's face and showed in the manner of her carriage. A woman well and truly loved, had been the phrase which struck my mind the night we met in the lobby of His Majesty's. More even than that: a woman who had known real glory and was aware of it, for it still shone out of her. I hope I don't sound sentimental if I say that to me there is no finer sight in the world than a young mother in the full tide of joy with her husband and child. That was how Catherine had been and still was.

My own position with the Martells was at once peculiar and simple. Jerome was unconscious of jealousy and he liked me, as I liked him, yet I doubt if he ever thought about me when I was not in his company. I desired Catherine in addition to loving her, but it takes two to make desire jump the spark-gap, and in those days all her desire was polarized to her husband. She used to tease me and tell me I ought to marry, and several times—for she was something of a stage-manager—she introduced me to girls she thought would make good wives, and in a motherly way she professed to feel responsible for my future. Yet I doubt if she ever hoped I would marry any of these girls of hers, for she knew I loved her. She supposed I occasionally went to bed with other women as I had gone to bed with Caroline Hall—I had told her about Caroline—but I did not tell her that I had almost become a celibate from necessity. So far as women were concerned, I discovered that I either had a one-track mind or lacked the animal vitality which makes it natural or even healthy for men to desire and make lusty love to women they merely like. Catherine engrossed my thoughts and feelings. Often I took out girls telling myself in advance that I would make love to them, but I seldom did. Catherine's image always intervened.

So I continued at Waterloo living for my weekends in town, where now I was making new friends and acquiring some self-respect. Catherine's affection for me and Jerome's interest in me were rapidly giving me a feeling that I was recovering a lost dignity. Adam Blore was right when he called me a bourgeois at heart. What else is a bourgeois but a man who wants a home, some respect from his fellows and a feeling that he has a future and belongs to a human group?

But Jerome—I really came to believe this—could never belong to any particular group of human beings; he belonged to humanity itself. This he never seemed to know. He had less ordinary social sense than anyone I ever knew, and if he met the King of England he would have been interested in him solely as a human being, and if the King bored him he would have been quite capable of changing the subject or walking away to talk to somebody else. He was utterly without a sense of class distinction, and the subtle layers of these distinctions in Montreal entirely escaped his notice. I'm sure he was snubbed dozens of times; I'm equally sure he never noticed it.

Gradually I came to learn something about his background, and I suppose his background was responsible for his indifference to the social shades one learns in Montreal without even realizing one does so. He had grown up in Nova Scotia, and this small but senior province is only a part of Canada by reason of a political agreement. When I was there in the war I met a few people who reminded me slightly of Jerome in their attitude toward us of the upper provinces. Their snobbery rested on brains, ability and the kind of courage you find in navies. Their democracy was in fact a kind of aristocracy: they talked to everyone they met as though he were at least a potential equal and they were franker than we, less subtle, but in a blunt way much more sure of themselves.

It was in the late November of that year that I discovered that Jerome was not really a Nova Scotian but had only been brought up there. He told me the story himself.

During one of those interludes of warm weather which occasionally come to Quebec just before the permanent winter snow falls, with daytime temperatures in the high fifties and the nights well above the verge of frost, Jerome suddenly decided that we should all go up to his cottage in the Laurentians. Catherine, Sally and I joined him in his Pontiac and under a dappled sky we drove north. There were glad cries from Sally when we entered a cottage that felt like a dry icebox, put wood on the hearth and got the Quebec heater burning. While the cottage warmed up, the four of us ate a picnic lunch on the veranda, and afterwards Catherine put Sally to bed for a nap and lay down to rest herself.

Jerome and I smoked for a while and then he became restless and said: "Let's go down to the lake and work up a sweat."

"Let's go down to the lake by all means. But you can work up the sweat."

"That suits me fine," he said.

The November silence was so profound that the crack of a breaking stick carried a mile. No weekenders had come up, there were no human voices but ours, and Jerome's cottage was in the wilderness anyway. There was only one other cottage on that lake and it was at the other end of it. The lake itself was shallow as most Laurentian lakes are with the spruce coming down to the water and parts of the shoreline were cemeteries of gray stumps bleached smooth and eroded to fantastic shapes and the water was the color of amber. Strangest of all was the effect of the sun that afternoon; less than a month from the winter solstice, the sun was so low that its light streamed almost parallel between the sky and the earth. The lake was a dog's leg about three miles long and half a mile wide at its widest point, and while Jerome paddled I lay in the bottom of the canoe and smoked a pipe.

"There's a loon over there," he said. "He's just come up."

Looking over my shoulder I saw the black bird humped by the mirage about a quarter of a mile away, and while I looked the loon gave its crazy laugh, tilted up its tail and dived.

"When I was a kid I used to hear the loons at night. Yes, I used to hear them when I was alone at night."

He began to paddle solidly and I felt the strokes pulsing through the length of the canoe. I had never seen anyone paddle so well, for he wasted no effort and the prow of the canoe drove forward with a real bow wave and never a flicker to port or starboard because the angle of each stroke was so firm and perfect.

"You must have done a lot of paddling when you were a kid," I said.

"I learned to paddle when I was eight. Yes, I did a lot of it."

We rounded the first bend and the lake opened up.

"It's almost as warm as early September," Jerome said, and shipped his paddle. "I love these November days when it's like this. They're like a resurrection. There was snow a month ago, and a fortnight ago there must have been seven or eight inches here. You can see a few patches at the fringe of the woods. But now it's like summer."

He pulled off his shirt and wriggled out of his trousers without even making the canoe wobble, and he sat in the stern in his jockey shorts. When he began paddling again his body was like a statue springing into life, and with each stroke those powerful shoulder and pectoral muscles tensed and relaxed. The suns of many years had left his skin permanently tanned and heavy work in his youth had muscled him so thoroughly that not even the years of medical practice without regular exercise had softened him. With the close-cropped dark hair blazed with white in front of his ears, with the prize-fighter's body surmounted by the doctor's face, he looked, stripped down like that, unlike any man I had ever seen. On his left thigh, dead center, was a livid splash and a pucker in the flesh, and when he saw me eyeing it he grinned like a boy.

"Neat, don't you think? It was so perfectly done it ought to have been from aimed fire, but it was just a browning shot from a traversing machine gun. A beautiful fracture of the left femur. I was walking straight into that bullet. By God, bullet wounds hurt."

"Does it still hurt?"

"When the weather turns damp, it does. It's my private barometer. It makes my skiing a joke, but my skiing would have been a joke anyway. Down home in Nova Scotia when I was a kid nobody did any skiing. I played a lot of hockey down there and football. We played English rugger—not this game you have up here—but the first time I was on skis I was on the top of an Alp and I rolled most of the way down."

He paddled to the far end of the lake and turning the canoe he paddled slowly back to the widest part in the center, when he rested. Around us the lake and forest and sky were silent as glass, and the silence went a thousand miles to Hudson Bay. There was not a breath of wind, not a human or animal sound, just the canoe and its shadow, the lake and forest and sky with the sun streaming pale from west to east.

"George," he said after a while, "I'm glad Kate's found you again. Believe me."

"I'm glad you don't mind."

He lit a pipe and looked up at that immense November sky and sniffed the air like an animal.

"It's going to snow tomorrow and it's going to be the real winter snow." A little later he said: "Why does a sky like that look so wise? Do you remember that scene in *War and Peace* when Prince Andrei lay wounded and looked up at the righteous sky? That was wonderful. Nothing like that ever happened to me when I was wounded."

In the uncanny stillness I heard the sound of tobacco burning in his pipe.

"George," he said shyly, "please tell me the truth. What do you think of me?"

"It's hardly a question I would answer even if I could."

"You Montreal people." He grinned. "All right, it was a stupid question. All right. But you do like me, don't you?"

"You know that."

"I like you, too. Tell me something else. Is Kate happy?"

"Don't you know she is?"

He shook his head and looked away. "I'm not sure. I'm not easy. But you'd know, and that's why I asked you."

"What she feels is bigger than happiness."

"You really mean that?" He was as grateful as a boy. "You know her much better than I do. When I see you together I recognize that. She's easy with you. She's not so easy with me, you know. She needs friends. I have my work, but a woman married to a man like me, she needs friends. She has this peculiar feeling that people are careful with her. I think she's getting over it, though. It came from being sick when she was a child. My God, George, I'd hate to hurt that woman."

He looked away into the woods, then his eyes traversed the lake and settled on the loon which had risen from a long dive and was sitting on the water a hundred yards off.

"I've never liked those birds," he said.

He shouted at the loon which rose and flew away, and the silence closed in after its departure.

A little later: "A day like this makes me believe I might be a good man."

It was such an unusual thing to say that I laughed.

"No," he said, "I'm being serious. I'm afraid of hurting Kate."

"How can you be afraid of doing that?"

"We're beginning to disagree about too many things. She wants above all to protect her home, and so she should. As for me—I wish she didn't get hurt so easily. I wish she wasn't so vulnerable. And I wish I were an easier man." He knocked out his pipe, stuffed it with more tobacco and relit it. "You know Adam Blore and that gang. What do you think of their work?"

"Not much. Some of them may be good, but who am I to say?"

"What do you think of them?"

"Some of them I like very much, but Adam is pretty hard to take."

Jerome gave me an appraising look: "For his age, that young man understands quite a lot of things."

"Such as?"

"Cruelty, for instance. Kate thinks he's just plain evil. But if he's evil because of what he knows, then I am too. Cruelty to me is the ultimate evil. Sex—that's nothing one way or the other unless it's connected with cruelty."

He began paddling again and the canoe pulsed gently onward in that amazing silence and I looked at his abstracted face and wondered what he meant by this apparent association of himself with cruelty.

"I love that woman, George, but the two of us have pretty strong personalities. She's much more sensible than I am, I know. And yet this situation in the world—to me she doesn't understand it at all. She doesn't even try to understand it. She'd be very happy if I turned my back on it. She can't see—I mean, she can't *feel*—how it's got into my bones. Meantime in these wonderful years we've had together look what have I gone and done?" He gave a boyish laugh. "I've gone and made her my judge. And sometimes these days it makes me feel damned lonely. In fact it makes me feel damned guilty, when I do some of the things my reason tells me is right to do and she disapproves. Do many people call me a Red?"

"I suppose some do."

The fighting look came over his face: "That's become the word they smear over everyone who's against them. Look at the hospital where I work. Oh sure, if I went along with the current I'd be safe and rich and they'd all say I was grand. Nearly all the medical people do that. They're conniving at the whole situation we have in this city." The bulldog jaw thrust forward. "The place to attack disease is where it starts, and where it starts—a good deal of it—is in economic conditions. Not enough to eat. Not enough of the right food. The slums. The insecurity. The whole damned nineteenth century set-up Sir Rupert Irons represents. The hospitals fawn on those millionaires for grants, and the millionaires compete to get themselves onto their boards because it proves they've arrived and amount to something. Do you know anything about the chief surgeon at my hospital?"

I shook my head: "Only that Norah Blackwell told me once that you and Dr. Rodgers don't get along any too well."

"Does she go around saying that?" His voice was sharp. "I should slap her backside for saying things like that in the city."

"I don't think she says it to other people."

A pleased look came over his face. "I like that little girl. She's a first-class nurse, though you'd never think it to look at her. She's had a hard time, and she's intelligent. Is it true that husband of hers is a moron? Adam Blore tells me he is."

"When did Adam tell you that?"

"Oh, I ran into him about a week ago and he told me."

"The bastard!" I said.

"For saying that?"

"That's what I meant. Harry's not a moron, even though he's not any too bright. And he's very fond of Norah."

With his singular imperviousness to a key personal remark, Jerome returned to the subject of his hospital.

It was a small hospital and a relatively modern one, and its name was the Beamis Memorial. Old Joshua Beamis had made a sizable fortune in my grandfather's day in the lumber business and had left the bulk of it to endow a hospital in his own memory. There had been a contest over the will and it was a long time before it was settled, with the result that the Beamis was then only twenty-one years old. From the beginning its chief surgeon had been Dr. Stamford Rodgers, who looked like William Ewart Gladstone without the whiskers and enjoyed an international reputation. According to Jerome his work was no longer what it had been. According to Jerome an excess of adulation, especially of the kind lavished on top flight medical men in a city proud of its medicine as Montreal is, had affected the old doctor's vanity.

"It's a vanity of the super-colossal kind, actually. To most people it passes for pure austerity. For instance. He hates my guts as a person now, but he's not small. The very fact that he loathes me protects me from old Rupert Irons, who'd like to have me fired from the staff. Rodgers goes to the clubs with the big business men, but in his heart he despises them. He's a kind of medical emperor in his own mind and he thinks the rest of us should be his subjects. He's also getting old."

I lay back and watched this strange man's face. He was so boyish and yet he was so competent, he was so rugged and yet so vulnerable, so intelligent in some things and yet so naive in others. The word "insecurity" was not used in those days as often as it is now, but if it had been, I would have applied it to Jerome. And if I had known as much about life then as I do now, I would have recognized that here was a man to be deeply concerned about if you loved him, for his very vitality —the thing which marked him out from everyone else—made him violently impulsive.

"Is this situation between you and Dr. Rodgers really serious?" I asked him. "Or is the question none of my business?"

"I don't mind telling you about it. Not you, George. You're one of the family."

When he said this I felt a glow of gratitude to him. He meant it just like that, for he had an enormous kindness which people who knew him only in his defiant and explosive moods never recognized.

"Well George, it's roughly like this. Sir Rupert Irons is chairman of our board. So far as I can tell, Montreal has always had a single tycoon like that who bosses it during his lifetime, and there's no doubt Irons is the boss now. Wouldn't you say?"

"Yes," I said, "I certainly would."

"The rest of them—these real old Montreal families—they never seem able to stand up to rough boys like Irons."

"They don't try," I said. "They tame the rough boys' sons instead. Just like the Chinese."

"By God"—Jerome grinned—"I never thought of that." He gave a few more thrusts with his paddle and rested again. "The funny thing is, I get rather a kick out of old Irons. He's a real fighting man, say what you will against him. He fights because he likes to fight. If his principles weren't those of a tiger, he and I would get along a hell of a lot better than either of us gets along with the respectable people you grew up with. But of course Irons is antediluvian. He's too old to belong to anything but the dying order. If he'd been a German he'd have done exactly what Thyssen did with Hitler, and find out too late just what Thyssen has found out now.

"Now get this. Irons doesn't hate me personally. Not like Rodgers does. He just thinks I'm a Red and should be fired. And here's what the Irish would call the geg of it—if it wasn't for old Rodgers vanity, I *would* be fired. I wouldn't give five cents for my position on the staff of the Beamis if my chief was like some other chiefs who've nothing against me personally."

"What do you mean?"

Jerome laughed.

"I told you—Rodgers thinks of himself as a medical emperor. He's a wonderful specimen, in his way. He had a classical education to begin with. His father was a judge and his grandfather was a professor and his great-grandfather was a soldier. He's so gloriously Tory that he looks down on people who are in trade. In his own way the old man can be more imperious than Irons, for he knows how, and Irons is just an Ulster boy who came out here with one pair of pants and fought his way to the top of the financial heap. Rodgers takes it for granted that the professions are above business and that the top profession is medicine. Very well. When Irons calls him up—as he does about twice a year —and informs him he should get that communist Martell out of his hospital, Rodgers says, very bleakly, no. He'd probably get rid of me himself if Irons wasn't always telling him to do it, but as it is, I'm safe. Can you beat it?"

I knew nothing then of this world of pressure and politics and all I could do was listen.

"It's bad for the hospital," Jerome said. "It's bad all round. It's certainly bad for my character." He gave another boyish smile. "I can say this to you out here. Old Kate thinks I bring a lot of this onto myself because I like fighting. But I don't believe I really like fighting. It's just that I'm apt to explode. She's afraid of that in me, and I don't mind admitting I'm afraid of it, too."

I looked at the cool serenity of the steely lake under that amazing sky and the silence held us.

"What made you decide to become a doctor, Jerome?"

"The war." His face changed again—I never knew a man whose face changed so quickly as his—and became sad and haunted. "I was too good a soldier in the war, George. Before a battle I'd be so scared my throat was sand and my knees knocked together and I'd pray to be wounded before I went over the parapet. Anything not to have to do it. I'd walk out with the others and have no sensation in my legs from the hips down. But when we came up with them I'd go berserk. I killed eleven men with the bayonet, George."

"And that decided you to go into medicine?"

"Afterwards, yes. To kill a man with a rifle at a distance means nothing much unless you've got imagination. But the bayonet is murder. His face is right in front of you and he wants to live. His hands drop to the knife and get sliced. I <u>killed eleven men</u> that way."

He looked off into the distance and the expression on his face at that moment is with me still.

"I got one poor devil through the throat. I kicked him off it and he fell back into a shellhole. I took one step forward and the bullet smashed me in the thigh"—his right hand tapped the scar—"and I fell into the hole on top of him. He gurgled his life away before I could get off him, and then I had to spend ten hours in that hole with the body, for the machine guns were registered so close to the ground a rat couldn't have escaped. Well George, that was something. There'd be no wars if every soldier who killed a man with the bayonet had to spend ten hours immediately afterwards in a shellhole with his body. I took that kid's life away, and that's all he was—a kid. A frail blond boy who never had a chance against a man as strong as me."

Jerome stopped and looked out over the lake. "That's why this Spanish thing has got under my skin. The big war made no sense at all, but this Spanish thing does. If we can stop fascism there, we'll stop it for good and there won't be another big, senseless war."

We were silent for some time before Jerome resumed.

"I never really got over that last bayonet murder I committed. Afterwards in the hospital I was in a state of psychological shock and for weeks I couldn't speak. In the bed next to mine was a Jewish boy from Oshawa and his name was Aronson, and this boy had that funny understanding of people a lot of Jews have. 'Tell me about it,' he kept saying, 'and then maybe it will go away.' But I couldn't, because I couldn't talk. Finally, one day I did talk and I told him. 'It wasn't you who killed that soldier,' Aronson said. 'You were just an instrument. It was the system, the capitalistic system.' Then he explained to me how the system worked and for the first time I understood why every soldier who could think felt he was cheated and turned into a murderer for nothing. He changed my life, Aronson did."

Again that haunted look returned to Jerome's face, and with

singular gentleness he looked at me and said, "You're lucky, George."

"What do you mean?"

"Certain things haven't happened to you. They don't and can't happen to a man like you. Do you believe in God?"

"No," I said.

"Did you ever?"

"When I was a kid."

"So did I. I believed in God till I met Aronson. I believed in Him very much."

He frowned and looked away, and after a while he began talking again.

"There's another thing I feel like telling you. That time I killed this German boy"—his sensitive face winced—"yes, that time I killed him was doubly bad. The year before, I'd been through all the heavy battles and then came that spring of 1918 when Haig issued his 'Backs to the Wall' order and most of us expected to be sent up to the line again and get killed. Instead we were held in reserve and I got my first leave. To London for the first time, and I thought I'd be dead inside a month or two, and I was human. Some woman picked me up and I went with her and just after I got back to the line I discovered I'd contracted gonorrhea. My first woman and a dose of clap. Not pretty."

Then he gave a smile as though the sadness of that moment had never left him.

"A boy brought up like me, naturally I felt the brand of Cain was visible on my forehead. I deliberately tried to get myself killed in that attack. I went on ahead of the rest of them in spite of the fire hoping I'd be killed." He gave a grim smile. "And for doing that, I was given the M.M. For committing murder because I'd caught the clap, I was called a hero.

"The doctor laughed about it in the hospital and said it could quickly be dried up, and so it was. Of course I told Kate about it. But the scar is there, George." He tapped his head. "The scar is here."

"Meanwhile in the hospital this young Jew Aronson talked to me about Marx and socialism and the causes of war, and it all added up and made sense. Wars are the inevitable products of the capitalist system. We're all compelled by the capitalist system to become murderers. When I left that hospital I'd have refused to fight again, and I might have been shot or sent to the glass house, but the war ended before any question of fighting or not fighting came up. I decided to become a doctor then and there. I believed in nothing anymore, but I did like people, and I thought of them all with pity. My own life had been nothing but a series of accidents over which I never had any control. But medicine seemed to know what it was doing—at least so I thought in those days. And as soon as I got into the wards I loved the work." His face brightened. "I wanted to be a biochemist the very first time I looked through a microscope. Why don't some of our artist friends look at life through a microscope? Ah well, there were too many other things. I qualified, I made the usual rounds abroad, and I came home and I met Kate, and then I became sweet again inside. The first two years with her the world opened up like a rose."

Silence for many minutes while I glanced at his face and saw truth in it. Then abruptly his face changed.

"I think I'd have stayed sweet if it hadn't been for the way the world is."

"Yes?"

"Around 1933, with the depression and Hitler and everything else, all those bad days came back to me like unpaid bills. I was a doctor now. I was reasonably successful and it would have been easy to have lived a private life. But how can anyone live a private life now? All the hatred and the killing has started again and this time it's a thousand percent worse because the killers understand what they're doing. Anything to break the system that causes these things, George. Anything!"

Again the silence closed us about. The words had been spoken and there was no more to say. Jerome had thrown them out into this cool afternoon which was like the peace of the God neither of us then believed in, and he planted them inside of me as long as I shall live. But the peace of that afternoon has also remained inside of me. Jerome picked up his paddle and sent the canoe gliding, and looking past his shoulders I saw the November sun ball-round in a pastel-colored haze and there it was, the ancient marriage of good and evil, the goodness of this day and the compulsive evil people must see and know, but the sky dominated in the end. Pale and shining, it told me that our sins can be forgiven.

"Sally's nice, don't you think?" I heard him say.

"She's grand."

"I took an awful chance making old Kate pregnant. Why do I take chances like that? It's almost impossible for a woman with a genuine rheumatic heart to have a child, and nobody knew it better than I. But something told me she could have one and live. I think it's saved her as a woman. Won't Sally be a darling when she's eighteen?"

"I think she's a darling now."

"Kate thinks she's like me. Do you?"

I answered his shy, happy smile: "I don't know."

Again his expression changed and startled me. "You and Kate know who you are. Everyone I meet knows who he is. It pleases me to think that Sally will always know who she is."

"What do you mean by that, Jerome?"

"Only that I don't know who I am."

"What do you mean?"

"Just what I say—I don't know who I am. I don't know my father's name or my mother's name or even their nationality."

"Are you a foundling?"

He shook his head. "Not in the usual sense of the word. I remember my mother quite vividly. Oh well, I'd better tell you the story. I wasn't born in Halifax. I just grew up there after my father—I still think of him as my father—adopted me. Actually I was born in the middle of a New Brunswick forest. Or at least I think I was. It's the first thing I remember, anyway. Have you been in New Brunswick?"

I shook my head.

"That section where the forest comes right down to the Gulf of St. Lawrence with the rivers pouring through the trees to the salt water—I've never seen anything like it for loneliness. What makes it so particularly lonely is that the people have been there so long. People have been there nearly two centuries, but nothing ever changes. Those fishing ports on the shore and those lumber camps upstream in the woods, they never change. They just grow old without ever growing up. I lived in one of these camps till I was ten years old."

He bent forward, pulled his sweater on and wriggled into his trousers. Then for over an hour he recounted the story I am now going to tell you. Not all of it, but most of it that mattered, and the rest I learned later from Catherine. What I tell you now is true to the best of my ability, for somehow this story of Jerome's childhood wove itself into me later on, when I sought to understand what made him behave as he did. Anyway, this is his story.

PART FIVE

Chapter I

I KNOW that part of New Brunswick now. I have driven through it and flown over it and looking down from the aircraft I have seen those steely rivers winding through the somber green of the spruce and the outcroppings of rock and sometimes on a fine day, looking down from 14,000 feet in the TCA aircraft, I have seen a sort of shimmering in the green mat of the land and recognized it as sunshine reflected upward through the trees from the water of thin swamps. I also know those little fishing ports and lumber towns along the Gulf shore and in my mind I can smell them. Such ripe combination of smells they give out: balsam, lobster pots, drying fish, oakum, new lumber, bilge and the stench of fish-offal on beaches under umbrellas of screaming gulls. But inland, even four miles inland in that country, there is no sense of ocean at all, but only of this primeval forest of spruce with the tangle of deadfalls and the sound-absorbing carpet of spruce needles that have accumulated over the centuries. The rivers run through it teeming with trout and salmon, and moose, bear, deer and all the northern animals large and small are at home in the tangle of trees. So are blackflies and mosquitoes in the spring, and in winter so is the snow. In winter this whole land is like Siberia.

The camp where Jerome lived as a child was an old one; for all I know, men worked there a century and a half ago when the Royal Navy harvested this forest for masts. He grew up in a works-barracks where his mother was the cook and almost the only woman; *almost* the only woman because, so Jerome said, it is impossible for a body of men to be located anywhere without at least a few women finding them. The camp lay on the left bank of one of the larger rivers and was bordered by a branch of quieter water flowing down through the woods from the north. Around a barn-shaped cookhouse in the center of a chip-covered clearing were the log bunkhouses of the lumberjacks, a stable for horses and an unpainted shack housing a stationary engine which drove the power saws. There were corduroy roads leading off in various directions into the woods, some of them for miles, but all of them ended in forest. Between the camp and the river estuary there was no road at all in those days, though I believe there is one now. In winter the men went down on the ice and in summer in boats and canoes, and when Jerome was a boy the first motorboat appeared on the river.

Those days are gone in Canada. Now the lumbermen eat fresh meat and fare reasonably well, and in some camps they tell me they sleep between sheets. But in those days it was pork and beans, scouse and salted horse and lime juice against the scurvy, it was boils and the savagery of melancholy temper which comes when men live and eat like that. The workmen wore red and black mackinaws and caps, broad leather belts and oiled leather top boots with metal hooks for the laces, and Jerome told me that some of them could be utterly silent for days and would never talk unless there was drink in them. Then they talked violently and fought. Rum got into the camp smuggled up the river, and raw alcohol and essence of lemon, and when the liquor came the fights broke out.

"Those fights were a substitute for sex," Jerome said. "That greedy look of a crowd of sex-hungry men watching a fight. It's in us, George, it's in us. Once I saw a man flogged. He was seized up just like the fleet sailors used to be, and the man who did the flogging was a white-haired man who'd been a bosun's mate in the Royal Navy. Why the man was flogged I never knew, but he was, and the men were for it. I heard him scream. Yes, that was in this country. Not now but then. I saw it and I heard it, George."

There was no school in the camp, no store or church or any other boys for Jerome to play with, and when he was a child he thought this was how it was for all children, for he knew nothing different. Yet in a way he was privileged, not only because he was the only boy but because his mother was the principal woman.

He lived with her in the kitchen attached to the eating barn, the bedroom they shared being a narrow room back of the kitchen, and not even the foreman could enter their quarters without his mother's permission. She was absolute ruler of the kitchen, and more than once she drove men out of it by throwing boiling water at them or threatening them with a carving knife. At meals the men lined up outside in the main cookhouse with tin plates in their hands and Jerome, helping his mother inside, would watch her ladling out the food from the big pot and dispensing it to each man as he held his plate through the hole in the wall between the kitchen and the eating barn itself. It was in this posture that he best remembered her: a short, square, powerful woman with moist beefy arms and a bead of sweat around the line of her yellow hair. Behind her in the kitchen was the big, wood-burning stove, the sink with the pump that drew water from the river, and the walls of the kitchen were yellow pine stained with dark knots and festooned with black pots and pans.

"That's what I meant by saying I don't know who I am," said Jerome. "I don't know anything about my mother at all. Where did she come from? I don't know. Was she local? Somehow I don't think so. A Balt? A Norwegian or a Swede? Somehow I think she was a Balt though I don't know. Who was my father? He'd disappeared long before I could remember anything about him. I don't suppose he was ever married to my mother, but he may have been."

It haunted Jerome that he did not know her surname. The men called her "Anna" or "Mrs. Anna" and he remembered her presence in certain smells like porridge and salt codfish and the strong yellow kitchen soap they called Surprise Soap in the Maritime Provinces. She had a wide, straight mouth with thin lips, and as his own lips were rather full, and his stiff hair was dark brown while his mother's had been yellow, he had conjured up a picture of his unknown begetter as a swarthy man, Portuguese in his swarthiness, surly, haughty and sly, and probably quick with a knife. But this was pure fantasy, for nobody ever told him what his father was like and his mother never mentioned his name.

Some of the men in the camp Jerome remembered very well, better even than he remembered his mother. There was an old sailor, proud of being an Englishman, who used to tell him stories of Africa and India and China and who tried to make him promise that when he grew up he would take to the sea. Another man he particularly liked was a gigantic French-Canadian with a freckled face, a red complexion and the hairiest arms he had ever seen on anyone.

"He spoke French most of the time, but with his looks he must have been descended from one of the Highland soldiers who settled in Quebec after Wolfe. He was the strongest man in the camp and he was a seasonal worker, for he had a wife and children on a farm somewhere in Quebec. He loved children, and I was the only kid in the place and he used to look after me. On nights when the accordian man played in the cookhouse I used to sit on his knee."

This red-headed giant was also a master craftsman. He built tiny ship models inside bottles, and it was he who built Jerome's first canoe. It must have been one of the strangest canoes ever made, for it was boy-size, its strakes of varnished birch bark, its frame of thin pine, and there were air cans under the thwarts to keep it afloat if it capsized. When the river was open, Jerome used to paddle in the branch and go considerable distances into the forest, but he was never allowed to take the canoe into the main stream that poured down in front of the camp, for the current was so strong he could never have paddled back against it.

"My mother," he said to Catherine once, "I still dream about her sometimes and usually it's a nightmare. Whoever she was, she must have had character, for she was the queen of that camp and make no mistake about it. She had power over those men, and the power went far past her control of their food. It came out of something inside of her that used to frighten me. Did she love me? I'm sure she thought she did. She was as possessive as a female bear with a cub, and I never had to worry about being molested by the men with her there. With her there I didn't even know there are men who molested little boys. She'd have taken the carving knife to any man who so much as looked at me sideways. She hated men as a group and she despised them, too. 'They're no good,' she used to say I don't know how many times. 'All they want is one thing. That and drink is all they want. And they're all the same.'"

Catherine told me years later that Jerome's abnormal fear of displeasing a woman came from his mother.

Cyclically, this man-hating female required a man, and when she wanted one she took him. There would be weeks when she cooked for them and hardly noticed them, or bothered to answer them when they spoke, and then Jerome would see a certain look on her face and await the night with dread.

"The nights she had a man in were bad nights for me. I was always afraid. I'd be asleep—I used to sleep in the same bed with her—and I'd wake up with her carrying me out of the bedroom in her arms. She used to put me down on a palliasse she kept beside the stove in the kitchen and she left me there under a blanket with the dog. Sometimes when it was over and the man went away she'd take me back to bed with her, and when that happened I'd lie awake all night. But generally she left me till morning under the blanket with the dog.

"Was she a whore? I mean, did she take money for it? Somehow I don't think she did, though she may have. Maybe I just don't want to think she did. I don't know. I can't really remember what she waš like. But I'll never forget the nights when she had a man in. I think I remember every one of them in my last year in the camp."

He would lie on the palliasse listening to the lift of the lock of the kitchen door, he would hear the muttered announcement of some man that he was there. Sometimes the man's boots would creak on the boards and sometimes his thumbs would snap at his leather belt and sometimes he'd give a throaty little laugh and sometimes he'd stand in the dark like a moose in the woods. In the deep of winter when moonlight reflected from the snow brightened the kitchen, Jerome would recognize the man as he stood among the shadows cast by the table and chairs and the pots and pans hanging on the wall. After the bedroom door closed, Jerome would lie tense on the palliasse with the dog nuzzling at him, watching the thin slip of light that struck out from under the bedroom door, waiting for the sounds.

"Oh God," he said, "men are such slaves to themselves! None of them, not one of them, wanted my mother for herself any more than she wanted any of them for themselves. And all of them were better than her. Oh yes they were, because I remember some things well. They wanted a woman—yes. But more than the sex they wanted sympathy and some woman to talk to. If she'd ever given them any of that, most of them would have taken it instead of the sex if there was any choice. I used to hear some of them talking about their mothers to her. Trying to talk about them, that is, for she'd never let them do it for long. I used to hear some of them trying to tell her about their wives and children. And I remember her saying—mean and sharp—'What do I care if you love your wife or not? What's it to me?'

"All she wanted from any of them was the sex, and by God

she could be noisy about that. I'd lie there listening and driving my fingernails into my palms hoping to God the man she had that night would be able to satisfy her. Not many did, and she was cruel to them afterwards. I used to hear her sneering and mocking them. Usually she never talked unless she had to. But if she had a man, and he didn't give her what she wanted, then she talked and I knew what her face would look like. I used to see some of those men creeping out like whipped dogs and I used to hate her for what she did to them. There was only one man that last winter who satisfied her, and he was a mean-looking, wiry little foreigner who could hardly speak a word of English. No, she didn't like him, and in the daytime she never even looked at him, but he used to come in pretty often. Then without warning he went down the river and never came back."

It was Jerome's last year in the camp, the year he was a husky boy of ten with the strength and robustness of a boy of thirteen, that he remembered best. What happened before that last year he could hardly remember at all, but the last year was vivid.

"There was a man that winter," he said, "that used to frighten me the way a snake frightens me now. There was nothing snake-like about his appearance, but there was a look in his eye, the way he had of looking at everybody. He never talked at all, and when he drank he drank sullenly. We all called him the Engineer because he was in charge of the stationary engine and he was the only man in the camp who could keep the motorboat in repair. He was dark and lean and he had this queer, drawn look in his face, and he used to carry a spanner wherever he went as though it proved he wasn't an ordinary lumberjack like the rest of them. He carried it in a loop attached to his pants and he even wore it to meals. Maybe he even slept with it.

"One March morning, about three weeks after the little foreigner went down the river, the Engineer said something to me while I was watching him work on the engine. I used to be fascinated by the engine and I would have watched more if I hadn't been afraid of him. I knew all about the work the men did. I used to go out on the sleighs with them and come back on top of the cut logs. It was easy for me with most of the men. But this was the first time the Engineer had ever spoken to me. All he said was, 'I want to eat pancakes tonight. Tell your old lady I want to eat pancakes and syrup.'

"So I went back into the kitchen and told her the Engineer wanted to eat pancakes and syrup, and when she made them I knew I'd soon be seeing him in the kitchen."

But "soon" turned out to be quite a long time, for the Engineer stayed solitary all through the long spring breakup and through all of April into early May. In those days the cutting season ran from late September till April, and before the river opened the logs were piled on the banks. When the ice went out they floated the logs down in two big drives, the long, timber logs going first and the short pit-props following. As soon as the logs were in the river, most of the men left camp and went back to their farms for the spring work. Now only a handful of men remained, the permanent maintenance crew and the men who went down the river after the drives to float off the logs which had stuck on the banks or piled up on some of the little islands on the way to the sea. One of the men who remained was the Engineer, for there was still a large pile of logs to be cut into lengths for pit-props.

It began peacefully, Jerome's last night in the camp. It was one of those magic Canadian spring evenings that seem like a miracle when they arrive, one of those times in early May when a tide of southern air pours up from the United States and seems tropical over the half-frozen earth and around the sticky, unopened buds of the trees. All day long the forest had been hot. The few men remaining worked in a holiday mood stripped to the waist in spite of the blackflies and by evening some of their bodies looked like broiled lobsters wealed all over by flybites. Some of them went swimming in the water of the branch, water as cold as melted snow, and one of them took a cramp and had to be hauled out on a rope. Supper time came and there were pancakes and syrup to follow the pork and beans. After the men had eaten, in the long spring evening just six weeks from the June solstice, they sat about in the clearing and watched the sun roll down out of sight into the forest. The accordion man took his place on the cookhouse steps and played song after song, some of the men sang, and the others lounged about, fly-bitten, hot and tired, their backs propped against stumps on the forest fringe while they listened and drowsed and drank. There was liquor that night, but in the magic of the evening, the purest kind of evening we ever have in this northern country, the men sipped at their liquor without swilling it and nobody got drunk. Jerome's mother came out in her apron and leaned in the doorway of the cookhouse listening to the singing, finally it fell dark and one by one the tired men got up and drifted off to the bunkhouse to sleep. When Jerome went to bed it was much later than his usual hour and the camp was so still the only sounds were the ringing of frogs and the slow sigh of the river in flood.

He guessed it was an hour before midnight when he woke in his mother's arms, his hands about her neck and his chest against her warm, heavy breasts. His face was still hot from the sun and his ears were swollen and hot from the blackfly bites and he woke so slowly it was only when the spaniel nuzzled and licked his face that he opened his eyes. He saw moonlight pouring into the kitchen in three separate shafts through the three high windows that faced the moon, and between those shafts of light he saw the Engineer standing still. The bedroom door opened, his mother stood there, and he heard her say, 'What are you waiting for?' Then the man followed her in and the door closed.

This time the encounter was different. The Engineer he had feared so much began talking in a low, earnest stream of conversation, talking about himself and how lonely he was and how wretched was his life, and how different everything would be if she would go away with him. Jerome could only partly hear his words, and hardly any of them could he remember, but he knew that of all the lonely men in the camp this was the loneliest of all, and he yearned for some gentleness to come into his mother's voice in place of the withholding silence or the sneer he was afraid would come if the Engineer continued to talk like this. He wanted the Engineer to break through his mother's refusal to some kindness inside, to some safe kindness inside.

After a while the Engineer stopped talking and the usual noises began. They ceased almost at once and Jerome heard his mother's voice flare in a jeer of unspeakable contempt.

"So that's the best you can do! A kid could of done better!"

He heard the man groan and cry something out, and then he heard his mother mock and scorn him, and Jerome remembered thinking: Don't let her treat you like that, Engineer! Please, please, please do something to make her stop treating you like that!

The Engineer did. Suddenly his voice changed as the woman drove back his longing for tenderness into the pride and hatred Jerome had feared in him all winter. The man began to curse the woman in a stream of obscenity using every word Jerome had ever heard the men apply to the women they called whores. There was a short struggle, the pant of his mother's breath, then a loud smack as she hit him across the face and Jerome thought: Please, please don't let her do that again!

What happened next was as sudden as a bottle exploding. Jerome and the dog sprang up together at the scream of enraged fear that came from his mother. Something bumped and fell in the bedroom, there was a heave of bodies, then the crack—crack—crack of hard fists driven expertly home. This was followed by a yelp from the man, a gasp of pain, then a crunching shock more terrible than a fist blow. Then silence.

This silence, as abrupt and profound as the end of the world, was soon filled with a multitude of sweet noises. Mating frogs were singing high and happy in the night, so loud and high that the whole kitchen was filled with their joy. Then came another sound, the sobbing breath of a frightened man in agony.

Jerome put his hand on the knob of the bedroom door and pulled it open. He saw the Engineer bent double clutching his groin and he knew where his mother had hit him that last time. Beyond the Engineer's hunched body he saw his mother's legs and thighs naked in the moonlight, but the hunched man was between the boy and her face.

It was the dog who betrayed Jerome's presence. Whining into the room, the spaniel rubbed against the man's legs and made him turn. The Engineer gasped, his face came around distorted with his sick pain and was horrible with the knowledge of what he himself had just done. But he saw Jerome and recognized him, and the moment he saw him he plunged. The boy dodged back and the Engineer stumbled and hit the floor with a crash, his spanner rattling away from his right hand. Jerome saw that his pants were down about his lower legs and that it was these which had tripped him. On the floor the Engineer looked up, his mouth shut, his violence as silent as that of a fish in the sea. Jerome turned to run, escaped from the room, reached the kitchen door, felt the dog against his legs and had the presence of mind to push him back before he himself went out. He closed the door behind him and with his nightshirt fluttering and his feet bare he ran across the moonlit, chip-strewn clearing into the darkness of the forest. When he was in the trees the undergrowth began cutting his bare feet, he stopped, turned and lay flat.

Nothing moved in the clearing. The long cookhouse with the two metal pipes that served as chimneys stood silent, its sloping roof whitened by the moon, its walls dark, its windows glittering like gun metal. He heard the sigh and gurgle of the river as it poured among the tree trunks along the flooded banks, but there was no sound of men and no light in any of the bunkhouses. He could not see the bunkhouse which was still occupied, but if there had been lights in it he would have seen their glimmer through the trees.

With the instinct of an animal Jerome got up and changed his position, slinking through the shadows among the stumps at the edge of the forest-fringe to a place he knew about thirty feet away. He found it, a depression in the ground about ten feet from the edge of the moonlight, and lay down and scooped pine needles over himself to conceal the whiteness of his shirt and skin. Lying flat with his chin in his hands and his elbows in the needles, he stared at the kitchen door and listened to the pounding of his heart.

The Engineer was only ten feet away when Jerome first saw him. He was skirting the forest-fringe with the spanner in his hand, staring into the darkness of the trees and stopping to take quick looks behind him. He wore no cap, his mackinaw shirt was open and in the moonlight Jerome saw the splash of dark hair rising out of his shirt to his throat. The man stopped directly in front of him and Jerome kept his head down, pressing his face into the needles, the needles itching in his hair. Once he lifted his eyes and saw the man's feet and noticed they were small feet even in those high leather boots. There was a crunch of bracken as the man entered the woods, one of his boots came down within a yard of Jerome's head, but the engineer was staring into the total darkness of the forest and did not look down at his feet.

In the cool air of the night Jerome could hear the man pant and thought he could feel the heat of his body. The boots turned and went back out of the forest into the clearing and as they crunched farther away Jerome looked up and saw the man's shoulders go around the corner of the cookhouse and down the path to the bunkhouses.

"I knew for certain that he was after me. He was putting himself between me and the men asleep in the bunkhouse. He knew I couldn't get around through the woods without making a noise. He knew the path was the only way I could hope to go."

Jerome wondered if he ought to call out, but he knew how hard the men slept and he knew who would be the first to hear him. In any case he was too frightened to call. Except for that single jeering laugh of his mother and the man's single outburst of obscenity, what had been done that night had been done with the silence of animals killing each other in the dark.

Jerome lay still until he began to shiver and when the shivering came it was so violent it seemed to shake the ground. It was like being tied up in the cords of his own muscles shaking the earth so that everyone living on it must know where to find him.

Getting to his feet, he beat the pine needles off his nightshirt and scraped some more of them out of his hair. Others chafed the tender skin between his thighs, but these he disregarded as he stepped slowly out of the forest into the moonlight. He stopped, waiting for the man to appear and give chase, but the only sound he heard was the pounding of his own heart and the only man he saw was the man in the moon. He believed there was a man in the moon who saw everything and didn't care, who sat up there seeing and not caring and laughing to himself, and he thought he was laughing now. With his nightshirt fluttering, the boy ran across the clearing, opened the kitchen door and went in. This time he forgot about the dog, who jumped outside and ran away before Jerome could close the door.

Inside the bedroom the blind was drawn and the darkness was total. Jerome found the match box, lit the lamp and turned to look. His mother's body lay like a sack under the blankets because the engineer had covered her and pulled the blind before going out. Jerome lifted the blanket, put his hands to her face and felt the fingers of his right hand sink into a warm stickiness. He jerked them back as though he had put them into fire and stood frozen.

"The bad wound was on the left side of her head and her left eye was bruised by his fist. Her mouth was open and her clear eye was open and angry. She looked far angrier than frightened. My mother died in a rage."

Her body was not yet cold, but it had lost some of its warmth and the blood barely oozed now that the heart had ceased to pump it. Blood was dark and wet all over the pillow and wetly thick in her hair; her breasts were like chalk-white balloons when he tried to shift her body. It was only then that he knew absolutely that she was dead. He cried out to her, he beat her naked breasts with his palms to wake her and all the time he did this he understood she was dead. Knowing she was dead he called to her to come alive again and take care of him, yet all this while he was glad the Engineer had not been like the other men whom she had humiliated.

Then he froze once more, for a step creaked outside. He blew out the lamp and turned to run into the darkness of the cookhouse where there were tables to hide under, but he was too late. The kitchen door creaked open and he crawled under the bed and crouched there against the wall with the sag of the spring just over his head.

The man entered and when Jerome heard him sniff, he knew he was smelling the snuffed wick of the lamp. When the man lit a match it was like an explosion of sound and light simultaneously, but the man did not carry the match to the lamp. Jerome saw his boots standing by the bed as the light slowly died. Then darkness again. Then the Engineer let out a slow, choking sob and went away. Jerome heard his feet go away noisily, heard him bump into a chair in the kitchen, open the door and leave.

He crouched shivering with cold and fright, and he might have stayed there for hours if the dog had not returned to the room. The dog came under the bed whining and nuzzling, and Jerome felt his long, wet tongue licking his feet. The feeling of the dog's tongue horrified him and he rolled over and pushed the animal away, pressing his hands against its muzzle. The beast whined appreciatively and Jerome's hair bristled when he knew the dog was licking his mother's blood off his fingers. He hit the dog and heard him whine. He hit him as hard as he could on the muzzle and the dog let out a yelp and left him alone. Then Jerome came out from under the bed and stood up.

Years afterwards he told Catherine that this was the first of many occasions when a sudden, clear-headed coolness came to him after moments of paralyzing terror. He was only ten years old, but he knew exactly what had happened and what else would happen if his mother's murderer caught him. He knew the murderer had left the bedroom because he was in terror of what he had done there, but he also knew he would be on the watch outside. The Engineer would almost certainly be watching by the kitchen door, for that was the natural way for Jerome to get out and it would also be the shortest route to the bunk-house where the rest of the men were sleeping.

Jerome had to escape from the horror of that room where his mother lay dead. He took his clothes from the hooks where they hung: his shirt, stockings, pants, sweater and cap, and the heel-less larrigans of cowhide he wore all year round. He took them out to the kitchen and dressed beside the stove which still was warm, with the dog nuzzling and whining, and he had to push the dog away several times as he pulled on his stockings. After he was dressed he washed the remaining blood from his hands under the pump and dried them on a roller towel. Very clear in the head now, he opened the big ice chest where the food was and took out the first thing he found. It was a garland of blood sausage much too clumsy and big to carry, so he cut it into lengths and stuffed a length of sausage into each of the side pockets of his pants. He left the kitchen and entered the long eating barn where the benches and trestle tables were, heading for the door at the far end, a door rarely used, and when he reached it he found it unbarred. He guessed that the Engineer had used this door when he had first gone into the clearing to search for him.

"It must have been the dog that saved me that first time. When I ran out into the clearing, the dog must have gone into the eating barn and when the Engineer heard him moving there, he must have mistaken him for me. That was the mistake that gave me time to hide."

The dog was with Jerome now and this time Jerome made no error; he caught him by the long hairs at the back of his neck, held him while he stepped out, then pushed him inside and closed the door on him.

From this corner of the cookhouse the distance to the edge of the forest was no more than twenty yards and nobody was in sight as Jerome ran across it and disappeared into the trees. He worked his way silently through trees and deadfalls until a quick coolness touched his cheeks and he knew he was near the water on the edge of the northwest branch where his canoe was beached. In flood time the branch invaded the forest a distance of thirty yards or so, and now it was pouring through the trunks of the trees, gurgling and sighing as it strained through the scrub and deadfalls, and Jerome saw quick flashes of light as the moon struck here and there against the living water.

He worked his way along, his oiled larrigans keeping the moisture off his soles, but once his foot sank into a hole and the icy wetness poured in through the laceholes and his foot felt cold and soon went numb. After a few minutes he reached the place where the canoes and rowboats were beached, his own little canoe among them. The camp motorboat was moored to a jetty about a hundred yards downstream in the main river, but the canoes and rowboats were moored where the current was weak, and now he saw their snouts projecting out of the blackness of the woods into the moonlight. He stepped out, looked up to see the sky a wide open dome with a moon in the middle of it and a vast circle of light shining around it.

"I knew I was going to make it. Every time afterwards when I was older, every time when I've been in danger and everything seemed hopeless, some moment like this always came. Suddenly I'd hear myself saying, 'You're going to make it. You're going to make it after all.' "

The short birch bark canoe with the air cans under the thwarts was easy to lift, he turned it over and ran it out into the water. He found his own paddle made to fit his height, and with a single movement he pushed the canoe off and swung himself over into the stern seat, then crept forward and settled down just about midships, got the paddle working and guided the canoe past a tree trunk and clear of some fallen branches. The movement of the current kept pressing him inshore, but he paddled hard on the left into a backwash that took the canoe gently out, he changed sides and gave two hard thrusts on the right, and then the canoe floated silently out into the great wash of moonlight where the branch widened into the main course of the river. The current of the branch carried him far out from the shore and when he felt himself making leeway he knew he was in the central stream at last. He gave two more thrusts and pointed the bow downstream, and at once he began to move fast on a river wide, firm, silver and alive bearing him down past the silent camp, utterly alone for the first time in his life, bearing him down under that wide open sky through the forest to the open sea which he knew was at its end.

Jerome paddled as he had been taught to paddle in a current, slowly and evenly, making long, steady sweeps of the paddle and after each stroke taking a short rest with the blade trailing behind like a steering oar. The river at this season and place was flowing at more than five miles an hour, breaking and gurgling in the shallows and sparkling in the moon, but out in the central current the flow was so satin-smooth the eddies were like whorls of polished glass. A thin mist lay patchily over water colder than the air, and the moon was enormous in the wide greenly-shining sky.

"When I grew older and learned how human organisms behave," he said, "I knew I was in that queer state of euphoria that often comes after shock. The response of the adrenal glands to danger. But that's a mechanic's way of looking at it. It's just as real for a man to say, after he's escaped a danger to his life, that he feels twice as alive as he ever felt before. All that night I never thought of my mother. I just thought about the canoe and the river and I was so alert that everything I saw and did—everything —I still remember."

Steadily the tiny canoe went down the river between the trees, following the curves almost by itself in the current. Now that he was secure in the canoe, Jerome eased further back against the air-can lodged under the stern seat and got the head up and sank the stern to give more purchase for the current to take him along. Often he passed floating logs and once he came up with a raft of them lodged on a hidden rock and damming the current, the water washing over and making the whole raft pitch and heave as though things were alive under it. He paddled around, touched logs once or twice and when he was clear he found himself in a flotilla of individual logs that had shredded out from the raft and were going down by themselves. He kept on paddling down, occasionally rubbing against a travelling log and sometimes afraid of holing his canoe, but as the logs were going in the same direction there was little danger of this. There were no lights on the shore, no cabins or houses, there was nothing but the forest, the sky, the moon, the river, the canoe and the logs floating down to the sea.

"I had no sense of time that night, but I'd guess it was about one in the morning when I first heard the motorboat. I can still hear it. It was a primitive boat, nothing but an old high-bowed fishing boat with an engine installed. Its motor was always getting out of order and the Engineer was the only man in the camp who could do anything with it. When I first heard it, the boat was still around the bend I had just rounded, and its sound came to me muffled by trees."

Jerome was abnormally strong for his age, his shoulders powerful even then, and now fear gave him its added energy. He paddled hard toward the shore, but at this point the current was so swift that when he tried to move athwart it the canoe was swept hard a-lee, he knew it would take him minutes to reach the shore and that even if he did, the backwashes would sweep him into the current again. A hundred yards ahead was a small wooded island in the middle of the stream and he brought the bow about and paddled for his life making the featherweight birch bark craft jump to his strokes. The drub-drub-drub of the motorboat struck his ears solidly and looking back he saw its dark shape with the hunched outline of the Engineer sitting at the hand-wheel in the starboard forequarter. As Jerome drew in toward the island he saw that many logs had got there first. Instead of a beach there was a mat of logs bobbing in the press of the stream and he was panic-stricken, for the log mat spread in clear moonlight about twenty yards out from the shore, and he knew he could never get through it to hide in the trees. There were all kinds of logs there, long ones and pit-props mixed, some of them piled on top of others and the whole mat creaking in the current. "I had never seen this island before but in a vague way I knew about it. There were several islands like that in the river and they caught tons of logs every year. Once the drives had gone down, work gangs used to follow to clear the islands one by one. That was one reason why men were still left in the camp."

The canoe lifted, slid smoothly up onto some half-sunken logs, stopped dead, and there was nothing for Jerome to do but lie in the bottom and wait. He peered over the side smelling the wet logs and hearing the gurgle and lap of the stream, the canoe bobbing gently with the logs while the motorboat came straight on growing larger all the time, its drub-drub-drub filling the river and the man at the wheel looming up. Jerome was sure the man was staring straight at him, but when the boat was about twenty-five yards off the island the Engineer moved and Jerome saw the bows swing sharply off and an instant later the dark length of the boat went out of sight around the left side of the island.

"Then I knew what he was doing. He was running away. All the men knew about the railway track that crossed the river at the town just inside the estuary. It was the railway a man made for when he got into trouble or just wanted to get away. Sometimes a man left after a fight and sometimes he just left. Looking back on it, I know the Engineer was numb with his own fear. He may have been drinking and that may have been why he didn't see me. Or maybe he was just exhausted by what he had done and in the state of mind when a man can't think or see anything because he can't stand thinking or seeing anything and does one thing automatically after the other. I don't know. But he was certainly getting away as fast as he could and in the only way he knew. There was no telegraph or telephone and it would be morning by the time any of the men would find my mother and a good time would pass before they missed the Engineer and put two and two together. He'd have lots of start. He'd reach the railway long before any of the men could reach it, and once he was at the tracks he'd have his choice of trains moving east or west. I knew nothing about east or west so far as the railway was concerned, not then. I didn't know that east was down to Moncton and Halifax and a dead-end, and that west was up to Quebec and

Montreal, and that he'd certainly go west. But I did know he'd be able to catch a train, for all the trains stopped in that town for water."

For a long time Jerome lay in the canoe listening to the diminishing throb of the engine. Such wind as there was came up the river and it must have been twenty minutes before the throbbing ceased. It would die away and return, die and throb up again, but at last there was no sound but the lap of the river and the slow, water-softened creak of the shifting logs.

With the passing of the motorboat Jerome's euphoria left him and he began to shiver and cry. He was chilled because at dawn the cold increased and his left foot, which he had soaked while moving through the trees, began to ache. He reached into his pocket and felt the stickiness of the blood sausage he had stored there, he took it out, washed it in the river, bit off a mouthful and ate it. The taste of blood made him feel sick but he went on eating until his shivering stopped and he felt new strength grow inside of him. He scooped water out of the river in his cupped hands and sucked it in through his teeth though it was so cold it made them ache. Meanwhile more logs from upstream were floating down and kept looming at him out of the dark water, hunching at him silently, pressing at him out of the dark as though they were the river's muscles forcing him out. The log mat was loose enough for him to get his paddle into the water and he changed position and pushed and paddled until at last the canoe gave a quick slip sideways, swerved broadside on to the stream and began to list against the mat of logs as he paddled hard to get clear toward the left-hand channel. A new log loomed at him about to ram but he fended it off, struck hard with the paddle as the canoe's bow yawed against the pressure of the stream, then the unseen hand of the current caught him, he struck with the paddle on the left, the bow shot around and again he was in the flow, passing the island so effortlessly that he was by before he knew it and now in a widening river he went on with the current pouring down through the forest to the sea.

After a time—how long he did not know for he had lost all sense of time—he became conscious that the world was lighter and opening up. Instead of seeing the forest as a dark mass on either side of him, he saw it clear and close with individual trees standing out. Now the western sky where the moon was had become darker than the east, soon there was more light in the east than there had been in the dome of moonlight under which he had sailed since leaving the camp, and looking over his shoulder he saw the moon low over the forest, its light a pallid copper-colored lane along a river that had become steel gray. Colors appeared, a flush of pink in the east broke apart until it looked like the parallel bars of a gate across the pathway of the dawn, the bars merged, the colors grew stronger, they swelled into a cool conflagration that flushed up into the wide and real sky as the entire world opened up.

Now Jerome became aware of life all around him as birds called in the forest on either side of the river, he saw the white trunks of a stand of birch, and as the current at this point swerved in toward the shore, the carolling ring of bird calls was loud and near. A crow flew out from a pine top and its cawing racketed back and forth across the river echoing from shore to shore. The hammer of a hungry woodpecker whacked against a dead trunk while a larger bird, one of the blue herons called cranes in the Maritime Provinces, flew slantwise across the rising dawn and turned slowly, its long legs folded in under its body and trailing behind, its snaky head hanging down as it quested for fish with slow flaps of its wings heading upstream along the right bank. Jerome heard a snick and saw the flash of a trout's belly. He paddled on through clear water with hardly a log in sight and within ten minutes there were snicking flashes all around him as trout broke the surface to feed on early flies, the first run of the season in from the sea, quick, slim fish with bellies as bright as silver coins, firm and fierce from a winter of cold salt water as they drove up against the current to the beds where they had been spawned. Jerome saw the lazy roll of a salmon about ten feet from the canoe, the little humping of water as the fish turned and went down; he heard a splash behind him but when he looked over his shoulder there was only a ruffle of broken water; he paddled a few minutes more, the trout still snicking, and then directly in front of the canoe the river broke open and a huge salmon slashed out shining, paused in the air with its hard muscles bending its body like a sickle and dropped with a drenching splash, the canoe crossed the broken water, and

Jerome looking over the side saw the last twisting tail-thrust as the big fish went down.

Still the tiny canoe throbbed down the stream, the boy in the stern, and around the next bend he saw a shack but no smoke from its chimney pipe. Now he was sleepy and tired and stopped paddling; he sat with the paddles across his knees and his head sunk forward.

"I must have slept like that for half a hour, when I woke the canoe was drifting slantwise and light was hurting my eyes."

It was the rising sun, a turmoil of gold like a tremendous excitement in heaven pouring its arrows into the forest and flashing them off the stream. His limbs dead and cold, Jerome straightened the bow of the canoe and let it drift in a current much slower now because here the river was deep and he felt the huge unseen pressure of the tide lower down. Close to the shore he passed a deer drinking on a sandspit and after a while he was afraid that if he fell asleep again he would lose his paddle. A small cape stood out with a sentinel pine, the canoe struck it with a soft crunch and Jerome crawled ashore and dragged half of it clear of the stream. Then he got back in and slept.

When he woke the sun was almost directly overhead, his nostrils were dry with heat and his body felt tired, hot, heavy and stiff. It was a May morning without a cloud in the sky and already the heat had made the balsam forest pungent.

"The time must have been somewhere between eight o'clock and nine. At that season of the year the sun rises about five, so I must have been asleep nearly three hours. If it hadn't been for the glare I suppose I'd have gone on sleeping all day. I was in the aftermath of shock. Even now I can't tell you how far I had come down the river, but I had been paddling with a fast current for at least four hours before I fell asleep.

"But I didn't think about distances when I woke up. I didn't even know what distances were. What I remember is how I felt. I felt black. I felt the way I felt that morning after I first killed a man in the war. I saw my mother's dead face hard and angry in front of mine. God, she was an angry woman, that mother of mine. I saw the Engineer with his spanner and when I tried to eat some of my sausage I nearly vomited it up. I had to get out of that forest and get off that river. Far away was where I wanted to go, and then I thought about the trains."

Though he did not know it, Jerome was now close to the sea and was paddling in a new kind of river. As it nears salt water that river becomes wide and is tidal for several miles. The town lies a distance inland and Jerome could not see the open water of the Gulf, but he could smell it and his cheeks felt a new salty, moisture in the air. He became conscious of settlement along the shores—not a town, but a scattering of frame houses and large breaks in the forest where there were fields and cattle. He also became aware that paddling had turned into heavy, leaden work, for the river was much wider here than it had been at the camp, and its current was stopped by the pressure of an incoming tide from the sea. Jerome ached all over his body as he forced the canoe forward, he sobbed with exhaustion and shock and was drowned in his own sweat, he was on the point of giving up when he rounded a final bend and there, right in front of him, was the black iron bridge that carried the main railway line between Halifax and Montreal. Beyond it was a small wooden bridge for road traffic and beyond that the river seemed enormously wide. There was a town on Jerome's left, a small, drab town built almost entirely of wood, and through his sweat he remembered having been in it before, last fall when he came down in the steamboat with his mother and some men, the time she bought him his first ice cream. As his canoe drifted in toward the bridge he backed water and tried to ease toward the shore. He was so tired he cried. Then he almost dropped his paddle in terror, for a train appeared out of nowhere almost on top of him as it crossed the bridge.

"It was only a small work-train—an old-fashioned engine with two olive-gray cars and a caboose on the end. It made an awful racket though, for it crossed that iron bridge with me almost underneath it. Its exhausts were crashing as it got up speed and it belched smoke from the soft Cape Breton coal all the engines burned in those days. The whole river seemed to shake as it crossed the bridge, but by the time I passed under it the roaring had stopped and I heard the singing drone that rails make when a train goes away down a track. I looked up and saw a man on the platform of the caboose looking down at me and his face was shiny black. He was the first negro I ever saw and I wondered if all the people in the world outside the camp were black like him."

Jerome forced himself into a last spurt of action and paddled the canoe across the current, making heavy leeway, toward a jetty on the left bank between the two bridges. He remembered it from the time when the steamboat had landed him there. The sight of the jetty also reminded him of the motor boat and he became terrified, for what if the Engineer were waiting for him on the wharf? But there was no sign of the motorboat either at the wharf or along the shore.

"He had either beached it above town or sank it in the river. He'd have wanted to walk quietly into town at dawn before the people were up and hide somewhere near the tracks till a train stopped."

Two men in dungarees and peaked caps were sitting on the curb of the jetty watching Jerome as he paddled in, but neither of them moved as he swung against the landing stage. He climbed out and hung onto the canoe with no plan whatever. He was just doing one thing after another and the next thing he did was to take the painter and secure it to a mooring post.

"Wheer'd yew git thet canoe from, son?"

A lean, unshaven face with a chicken throat was staring down at him from the curb of the wharf.

"It's mine."

"Littlest goddam canoe I ever seen," the man said and spat into the water.

Jerome climbed the ladder stiffly and as he reached the wharf the man made a lazy half-turn in his direction.

"Wheer'd yew come from, son?"

"I bin paddlin'."

The man spat again but did not answer and continued sitting with his legs dangling and his unshaven lantern jaws working steadily on his cud of tobacco. Jerome, afraid of everything and everyone and tired in every bone, walked shakily off the dock onto a dirt track that ran along the riverside of the little town. He reached the railway, bent down and touched one of the shiny rails and found it so hot it burned. When he reached the station he saw men unloading freight out of a solitary box car and was surprised that none of them were negroes. Jerome sat on a bench under the overhang of the station roof and ate one whole length of his blood sausage, and there he continued to sit an unknown length of time half-asleep and half-awake like the town itself, but feeling a little stronger now there was food in his stomach.

It still seems ironic to me that a man like Jerome Martell should have made his entrance into the organized world in a town like that. It seems almost as ironic as that two prime ministers, one of Canada and one of Great Britain, should have grown up or worked in their youth in that general area. Once in a fit of curiosity I drove all through that town, a feat I performed in less than twenty minutes, and it left me depressed. These semi-ghost towns of a colonial past—we have several of them in that part of the country, and when you see them now it is hard to believe that once upon a time British officers in swallow-tail coats stepped ashore into their wooden jetties from corvettes, frigates and sloops-of-war. I remember the town's main street was a hundred yards of battered macadam containing two wooden churches, half a dozen shops, a sad red brick bank, a sadder red brick post-office with a four-faced clock on the roof. I can't remember the street's name, but I would lay even money it was either Wellington Street or King Street. I remember the sawmills screamed so monotonously that the only time when you were conscious of them was when they stopped, and I remembered shirt-sleeved men leaning against store fronts whittling or chewing tobacco. In the back area of the town along the river there were a few expensive houses and one was a real period showplace, a wooden Victorian castle with a stucco front, four turrets, a lot of iron fretwork, a wooden belvedere and a sundial on what once had been a lawn. There were no curtains at the windows and a grove of dwarf spruce was creeping in through the back fence. The only thing that seemed to matter in that town, except for the sawmills, was the railway station.

It was to the station that Jerome went that morning, and the first citizen of organized society who spoke to him was the ticket agent. He bulged at Jerome, armbands on the sleeves of a striped shirt, a blue serge waistcoat protruding over a solid belly burdened by watch chains, lodge charms and indelible pencils, an eyeshade separating the gray baldness of a bullet-head from the gray baldness of a pudgy face.

"Who're yew waitin' fer, son?"

Jerome stared at him.

"What's your name, son?"

Jerome continued to stare at him, and the agent broke into a laugh like a mule's bray.

"Don't know nuthin, eh? Haw, haw, haw! Your Maw comin' in on a train?"

Still Jerome stared. The man pulled out a silver hunter, snapped it open and dangled it in front of the boy's eyes.

"Yew know what this-here is?"

The boy nodded, the ticket agent shot a squirt of tobacco juice out of the corner of his mouth and Jerome heard it smack the nearest rail.

"The Maritime, she don't get in here for a long time, son. What hev you been doin' gettin' dirtied up like thet? Yew stink like my old man's privy." A big paw shot out and grapped the boy's shoulder. "Yew come along with me."

Jerome was too tired to struggle and the ticket agent frog-marched him down the platform and into the station where he saw a potbellied stove with a dust of gray wood ashes around it, several slopped-over cuspidors and a door with a sign on it.

"Kin yew read?" said the ticket agent.

Jerome shook his head.

"Don't know nuthin, eh? Well, that sign says Gents. Git inside and clean."

He opened the door, pushed Jerome in and left him there. The boy stood trembling in the stinking place, knowing from the smell what it was used for. He heard water dripping from a leaking tap, and in a cracked mirror he saw his own face filthy and red about the eyes, some spruce needles in his hair and his ears like fans on either side of his head. There was a cake of grimy yellow soap on the edge of the basin and he washed his hands and face and the back of his neck. As there was no towel he rubbed his sweatered arm over his face and dried his hands on his pants. Although he had never seen a flush toilet in his life, he recognized the purposes of this one from the condition in which it had been left, so he used it, washed again, bent his mouth to the tap and took a long drink of water. Then he left the washroom and slunk out, crossing the waiting room on tip-toe for fear the strange man would see him. The man did see him, but he did not move or seem to care. He was sitting with his legs apart on a swivel chair beside the telegraph, his jaws working steadily on his cud, his eyes half closed.

Outside in the sunlight it was better. A shunting engine had moved in and was pushing the solitary box-car along the line onto a siding. It disconnected, puffed backwards along the track and disappeared around a bend in the line leaving the platform to bake in the open heat. A wave of sleep engulfed Jerome and his eyes closed. He slept unconscious of everything and nobody touched him or troubled to wake him up. It was noon before he woke in fright to feel the whole station shaking as a huge loco-motive crashed past hauling a long line of freight cars that blocked the sun and darkened his eyes. The train ground to a stop and Jerome heard the engine panting under the water tower.

"I had to get out of there. I remembered the way the men talked about hopping trains and here was a train right in front of me. I saw the back of the ticket agent far up front talking to the engineer and I crawled under the train and came out on the other side. There was a double track and I walked back along in the path beside the train looking at it. Most of the cars were red box-cars, but there were some flats and some black gondola cars for coal. It was a train of empties and there must have been more than forty cars, for they ran out of sight around the bend in the line."

As he was walking along wanting to climb on board but afraid to, the train itself made up his mind for him. It gave a shudder and a volley of crashes went banging down its entire length as the engine gave its first heave and the couplings cracked tight. The noise terrified him, for up front the engine was giving out the shuddering roars of an old-fashioned locomotive getting under way with a heavy weight behind it. An empty flat car moved by and Jerome caught the iron ladder at the end, climbed in and lay down on the boards until it had passed the station. Looking up he saw the town and the river recede around a bend and for the rest of the afternoon the train took him down the eastern side of New Brunswick.

"It's amazing how fast a human being can learn. Once there was a terrific crash and a different kind of train slammed by and I knew it was an express for passengers. I'd heard the men use the word and I knew what it was."

Late in the afternoon he ate the last of his sausage and slept, and when he woke the train was still and a huge eye of light was bearing down on him. He leaped up in terror to hear the crunch of feet on cinders and that enormous light made his hair prickle. He crouched back against the floor of the car as the light came on top of him and then it was suddenly dark and he looked up and saw, so close he could almost reach out and touch, the shoulders of a man in overalls sitting in the cabin of a locomotive with one elbow on the ledge of the cabin window and his right hand working the throttle. A red glare burst into Jerome's eyes and he saw the toss of the fireman's shoulders swinging a shovelful of coal into the firebox, then the engine passed, moving with no cars behind it, and looking over the edge of the flat car Jerome saw a forest of trains.

"Hey there, you kid! What the hell are you doing on that train?"

A man was standing below with one hand pointing at him and the other holding a lantern. Jerome jumped back, crossed the car, swung down the ladder on the far side and felt his feet touch ashes. He broke into a run between two stationary freight trains and fell flat on his face as his foot stumbled over a switch-block. Cinders cut his forehead and the heels of his hands, but he felt no pain because he was so frightened and got up and tried to escape from where he was. He was in a maze of box cars with his ears hearing hammer clangs in all directions as the workmen tested wheels and looked for hotboxes. The two lines of cars were sheer walls on either side and the lane between them dark and interminable. Suddenly the train on his left jerked and crashed and began to inch forward, frightening him so much he bent double and crawled underneath the train he had just left. When he came out on the far side there was a clear length of track ahead of him to a point about fifty yards away where it ended with the shunting engine whose light had awakened him.

Beyond this empty track was still another train. He crawled under it, felt a small scratching pain as his knee caught a splinter from a sleeper, and came out on the other side. Another train faced him and again he crawled under.

There were no more trains. Instead he found himself facing a sight he had never seen in his life: a large town at night. Everywhere he looked there were lights. He was on the edge of a cinder embankment and when he scrambled down he felt a cinder lodge harsh and gritty against the tender skin of his ankle, but he went sliding down in a spray of cinders and coal dust until he hit the bottom and tripped and fell. He got up and dusted himself and felt inside his larrigan with his finger and worked the cinder out. He was sobbing for breath and wet through with his own sweat, but he was too frightened to stand still even though he had no idea where to go. He was absolutely lost because he did not understand what a town is or what people in a town do. He was on a wooden sidewalk beside a dirt street and a team of horses was hauling a heavy cart up the slope of it to the station with a teamster sitting on the wagon box cracking his whip. Jerome called out to the teamster but the man merely turned his head, looked at him and spat, (this was a spitting country in those days), so Jerome walked up the slope beside the wagon and stopped abruptly on the top. He recognized a station platform, one far larger than the one he had left that noon, with a new kind of train standing beside it. This train was full of lights and there seemed to be hundreds of people.

"Out of the way, son!"

He jumped as two men pushed a cart piled high with boxes and suitcases along the platform beside the train. He looked around for a place to hide, but the platform was as bright as day and everywhere he looked there were people—people strangely dressed, women among them who did not look at all like his mother, men who did not look at all like the men in the camp.

"I had reached Moncton without knowing it. It's all very well to say now that Moncton is only a fair-sized railway town where trains come in from Montreal, Boston, St. John and Halifax and are shunted around and re-grouped. I tell you that no city I ever saw afterwards—not even London where after the first day

I fell asleep with streams of red from the buses roaring down my mind—not even London seemed as colossal and terrifying as Moncton did that night with all those trains and lights and noises and strange-looking people coming and going."

Jerome slunk through the crowd without anyone noticing him, and in the waiting room when he looked at his hands they were like raw hamburger with coal dust ground into it.

"You know, in those days this country was used to ragamuffins. Kids who looked like me were a part of the landscape."

The ticket agent in that little sawmill town had already made Jerome ashamed of being filthy and he was afraid somebody here in Moncton would see him and talk as the ticket agent had done and throw him out into the dark. He stole through the waiting room sure that everyone was staring at him until he found an empty corner in the farthest and darkest corner, and there he sat with his body crowded against the wall. He smelled coffee and frying eggs and salivated, but he was afraid to go over to the bright stall with the metal coffee boilers where all the people were eating sandwiches and drinking. A harsh voice bellowed its ritual about all aboard for some place or other and the people began crowding toward the doors. The waiting room emptied and after a while Jerome heard a train pull out. When it left the whole big waiting room was as quiet as an empty barn.

It must have been half an hour before anyone noticed the dirty-faced boy huddled in the corner. An old sweeper came slowly up the floor pushing his wide broom ahead of him, and whenever he had a big enough pile of peanut shells and candy papers and orange peels he bent down and swept the debris into a wide dustpan which he then emptied into a tin pail. When he reached Jerome's corner he stopped and looked at the boy and Jerome hung his head. Then the sweeper passed and the thought came to the boy that this old man was as lonely and wretched as himself.

"Hullo," he said to the old man.

But the old man did not turn around, and after a while he finished his job and went off with his pail and pan and broom and disappeared.

Now the station was settling down for the night. The coffee stall went dark, some of the overhead lights went out and a stout woman appeared from behind the coffee stall, walked briskly across the floor and out of the station. There were two lighted windows at the far end and Jerome could see the eyeshade of a man sitting behind one of them and was afraid the man would see him.

From watching the people he had guessed where the men's room was, so now he went into it and let out a deep breath when he found himself alone. There were half a dozen wash basins instead of the single one he had used in the little station up the line and most of them were fairly clean. He ran water and cleansed his hands and once the dirt was off they did not look so bad: they were pitted with tiny red specks but they did not bleed. He used one of the toilets, washed his hands again and made his hair as tidy as possible by using his fingers as combs, then he left the men's room and wandered about the station alone. He stared through the windows of the doors at the lights of the town and they seemed marvellous to him, the shabby buildings splendid as palaces, the street lights amazing as they shone over the empty sidewalks and against the fronts of locked stores. Soon he felt tired and returned to his corner where he sat with his back against the wall and his feet stretched out along the bench.

It was then that the wretchedness of his life finally overwhelmed him. He longed for the camp and the dog beside the stove and the warmth of his mother's body as he lay beside her in the bed. He whispered the word "Mama" over and over like a litany and his eyes were hot with tears as he sat in that dark lysol-and-cuspidor-smelling waiting room not knowing anyone, or where he was, or what would happen to him, or anything at all. His final night on the river had gone away like a ghost and with it the exhilaration of his escape. "Mama, come back!" he whimpered. And then he screamed as loudly as he could, "Mama, Mama, Mama come back!" There was no answer and not even the man in the ticket office moved. At last the boy's exhaustion was merciful to him and he fell into such a deep sleep that he was unconscious of any of the trains that passed in the night.

When Jerome awoke it was bright day and the station hummed with movement and a man and a woman were looking down at him. The man smiled and Jerome, rubbing his eyes as he came out of sleep, smiled back. He was a thin little man with the kindliest, funniest face Jerome had ever seen, with crowsfeet smiling out from the corners of his blue eyes and a gray goat's tuft on a pointed chin. His suit was of pale gray serge, his waistcoat a shiny black bib and his collar white, round and without a tie. On his head was a soft black hat and his long hands were thin, graceful and astonishingly white and clean. Beside him was a woman as short as himself, but plump, with wide apple cheeks, a smiling mouth, hair flecked with gray and a straw hat square on the top of her head.

"Now then, little man, and what may *your* name be?"

The man said this so pleasantly, the pompousness of his words sounding so fresh because Jerome had never been spoken to in such tones, that he lost all his fear and smiled back.

"Jerome," he said.

"Are you all by yourself, Jerome?" asked the woman.

"Yes."

"No mother or anything like that?" asked the man. "No father? No uncle? No brothers or sisters? Nobody at all?"

"My Mama's dead."

"So is mine," said the man. "Ah well!"

The kindly wrinkles about the clergyman's eyes never altered, but when he glanced at his wife he ceased smiling and Jerome knew with a child's intuition that this strange little person might be willing to help him. Even more certain was he that this funny little woman would be his friend. Her lips were so warm looking and soft, when she smiled she was like a gentle bird, and that hat of hers—

"You've got a dishpan on your head," the boy said suddenly.

"By Jove, but so she has!" said the man. "Jo, this is a clever boy."

"You must be hungry if you're all alone," she said. "How would you like something to eat? How would you like a nice cup of tea?"

"Cocoa, my dear," the man said. "There's so much more food in cocoa."

"What would *you* like, Jerome—cocoa or tea?"

He was afraid of offending one or the other, but the word "cocoa" sounded so nice he said he would like it.

"Then cocoa you shall have," the woman said, and her husband went up and crossed to the coffee stall to get it.

It was then that the gentle care in her voice reached down inside of him, touched the hard knot and dissolved it, and in a passion of sobbing he scrambled off the bench and buried his face against her shoulder. He threw his arms around her small, plump body and she smelled clean and fresh to him, and all the while he hid his face against her he felt her short little fingers stroking his hair and heard her voice soothing him. At last she forced him gently back and when he looked up she was bending down—she was so small she did not have far to bend—and the brim of her straw hat scratched his forehead as she dabbed his eyes with her handkerchief. She took a comb from her bag and brushed his hair, and then she stood back, smiled and said, "There now!"

The tears had ceased, leaving Jerome hungry. He scrambled back onto the bench and smiled at her. He looked around for her husband but all he could see was his narrow back at the coffee stall.

"My husband has gone to get food for us. We're hungry ourselves, you know. We've been up half the night in a train. I do so dislike railway stations. They're so dirty and noisy. You poor little boy—are you lost?"

"I don't know."

"Do you live here in Moncton?"

He shook his head and looked across to the coffee stall where the clergyman was gesticulating to a big woman behind the counter. His goat's tuft was waggling and Jerome, thinking he was quarreling with the woman, was afraid he might get hurt, for he remembered what happened to the men who had quarreled with his mother.

"What's your other name, Jerome?" the clergyman's wife asked him.

His face remained blank and she added: "All little boys have more names than one, don't they? Don't you have more names than just Jerome? Tell me."

"My name's Jerome."

"Dear me!" said the woman.

Now the little clergyman approached with a tray in his hands and a pleased look on his thin white face. He set the tray down on the bench, rubbed his hands and smiled at his wife.

"Jo, you should be proud of me. You've always told me that women take advantage of me, but this morning I have outfaced a battle-axe and come off victorious. That female standing in receipt of custom for food which is both flyblown and over-priced denied me a tray. But I insisted. I even pointed to a tray in her lair, and after a time she yielded, and here it is, so we all shall breakfast together. What's this little man's name?"

"He says it's Jerome," said the man's wife.

The clergyman beamed at Jerome. Then he removed his hat and became solemn.

"Now my boy, close your eyes while I say grace. Come now, close them tight. It won't take long."

Jerome did not understand why he should close his eyes, but he closed them and at once the clergyman began to pray.

"Most merciful God, we thank Thee for this food, such as it is. Most humbly do we beseech Thee to bless it to our use and us to Thy service. We pray Thee also to guard us against the seeds of indigestion we suspect lurk within it. And especially do we pray that we may be guided to help this lost child, who from his appearance and general plight seems to have been conceived in sin somewhat grosser than most, and we ask Thee also to tell us what to do with him, Amen. Now Jerome, open your eyes and eat."

The boy instantly closed his eyes lest the clergyman should see that he had opened them too soon, then he opened them again and took the heavy mug of cocoa and drank half of it down.

"Giles," said the woman mildly, "when you said grace, you didn't have to put all that in about Jerome."

"More cocoa, Jerome?" said the clergyman.

The sweet warmth of cocoa and the filling solidity of ham and buttered bread began to make strength in Jerome. He ached all over from his efforts of the day before and the night on the river, his hands were painful and the splinter in his knee had begun to fester, but now he could smile because he was with friends. The clergyman ate and talked simultaneously, now praising the ham, now blaming the poor quality of the bread, and when the food was consumed, he wiped his hands on a white handkerchief, crossed his short, thin legs, put his fingertips together and cleared his throat.

"Jerome, we shall now introduce ourselves. Our name is Martell—M-A-R-T-E-double-L, Martell. I'm Giles Martell and this woman is my wife whom I call Jo. Do you know what a clergyman is, Jerome?"

The boy shook his his head.

"I rather suspected that might be the case," said the clergyman. "Well, I am one of the species. It is a most unpopular calling and its chief disadvantages lies in the fact that one's parishioners have such a poor view of their Master's intelligence that they deny in their minds that he was in earnest when he performed the miracle at Cana."

"Giles!" said his wife.

"Now Jerome, if we are to help you we must know more about you. Your first name you have told us, but not your second. Don't you have a second name?"

"My name is Jerome," the boy said.

"I have heard of such cases in London," said the clergyman to his wife. He pressed his fingertips so hard that the lean fingers bent, and again he looked at the boy. "You must know where you come from, Jerome. Tell us where you come from."

"The camp."

"Ah, the camp! Now where might this camp be?"

Jerome stared and said nothing.

"Was it a lumber camp, by any chance?"

Jerome nodded.

"Now how did you get to Moncton?"

Again the boy stared.

"This place here"—the clergyman waved his arm round about him—"is Moncton. We must not be harsh in our judgments, so we will let it go at that—the place is called Moncton. But how did you get here?"

"I jumped a freight."

"You *what* a freight?"

"Giles," said the woman, "please! You know perfectly well what Jerome means."

"You did this thing alone? Not with your father or mother?" The boy nodded.

"Well, to be sure you must have come a long way." Looking into the boy's eyes, one hand stroking his goat's beard, the little man said gently: "Tell us all about it."

"I was scared." Suddenly Jerome burst into tears and began talking wildly. "He was going to kill me so I ran away from him in my canoe."

"Who was going to kill you?"

"He killed my Mama."

The two older people stared at each other and Jerome felt the woman's arm come about his shoulder and press him against herself.

"There now!" she murmured. "There now! There now!"

"He was the Engineer and I saw him."

At that moment a short, stout figure in a blue suit with a blue cap encircled with silver braid entered from the platform, cupped his hands about his mouth and brayed that the train for Halifax was ready and would depart in ten minutes. The clergyman groaned and got to his feet.

"It's the way of the world," he said, "that when nothing important is happening there is all the time possible for it to happen in, while if anything important is afoot there is none. Here we are with this—"

"Go see to our bags, Giles," the woman said, "while I stay and talk to Jerome."

The clergyman crossed the floor to the baggage room, and when he was gone, Jerome understood something in the way children do: of these two people the woman was the stronger. This seemed natural enough because in the camp his mother had been the queen, yet this woman was utterly different from his mother. She was soft, warm and gentle and still she was strong.

"Jerome dear," she said quietly, "we haven't much time. Mr. Martell and I must take that train for Halifax and it leaves in a few minutes. The thing you just told us is so terrible we must be very sure you are telling the truth. So now you must look into my eyes, Jerome, and tell it to me all over again."

He did so and saw the woman's gray eyes kind and earnest.

"You must tell me how this awful thing happened. Or—" she

smiled "—if it didn't happen, then you must also tell me that."

Jerome was terrified that she would be displeased and leave him. He felt he would have to make her believe he was telling the truth.

"He was screwing my mother and she said he was no good, so he got mad and he hit her and he killed her and there was blood."

A blush struck the woman's face like a blow and Jerome saw her mouth drop open and his terror grew, for now he had certainly displeased her and now she would certainly leave him.

"He was screwing her," he repeated desperately, "and then he hit her and he killed her."

The woman's hand came over his mouth and closed it. "Child, do you know what you're saying?"

He nodded desperately and watched her, seeing the flush change to the color of chalk. Then she took away her hand and surveyed him calmly.

"What you have just told me is the most terrible thing anyone has ever told me," she said. "It is so terrible a thing that I know you have spoken the truth, for a little boy like you would never have been able to make up a thing like that." Tears welled into her eyes. "You poor child! And I suppose there are thousands of other little children just like you in the world!"

He looked up at her dumbly.

"I must ask you a few more questions, Jerome, just to make sure. What about the other men in the camp? Where were they when this awful thing happened?"

"Asleep."

"I see." And quietly: "Was this man your father, Jerome?"

He shook his head. "I got no father."

The little clergyman was returning, his narrow shoulders bowed under the weight of the two bags he carried. As he deposited them the stout man in the blue uniform came inside and again cupped his hands about his mouth.

"Alla-booooard for Sackville, Amherst, Truro, New Glasgow, Sydney and Halifax! Alla-bo-o-oard!"

People began moving toward the doors. A man and a woman embraced and exchanged a quick kiss. Children toddled door-wards holding the hands of their parents and Mrs. Martell rose from the bench and smoothed down her skirt.

"Jerome has been telling me what happened," she whispered to her husband. "We mustn't ask him any more questions now."

The clergyman looked at his wife, then over his shoulder, then at Jerome, and seemed worried about something.

"The train is leaving." he said. "I suppose I should speak to the police or the station-master before we go."

In terror Jerome scrambled off the bench and clutched the woman's hand, pressing it against his cheek.

"Please don't leave me! Please don't leave me!"

The two older people looked at each other again, and the little woman bent down and kissed the child on the forehead.

"Jerome dear, we will never leave you unless the time comes when you may wish to leave us."

Then a feeling of joy filled the child so that he could not speak. He took the woman's hand and went out to the platform with her just like any other child who was getting onto the train wih his parents. The conductor took the clergyman's bags and hoisted them up to the platform of the car and the three of them climbed aboard. The clergyman found two empty seats in the middle of the car, swung one of the backs over to make a space for four and they sat down together, just as other families were sitting in other parts of the car. The train started and pulled out of Moncton, and looking out the window Jerome saw the station and the shunting yards and the lines of box cars slowly disappear, soon they were running smoothly through a green countryside. Jerome stayed awake until after they crossed the isthmus into Nova Scotia, where he saw the prairie-like expanse of the Tantramar Marshes with hawks and gulls flying over it and the sleek, brown mud-banks in the grass where the long tides of the Fundy came up salting the land, but after Amherst he fell asleep for several hours.

Coming out of sleep somewhere between Truro and Halifax, eyes closed and his mind half dozing, he heard the two older people talking.

"He has a good face," the little clergyman was saying. "He'll be a strong, handsome man. Isn't it strange? So long as he lives, he'll probably never know who his real parents were."

"One can hope he doesn't."

"Jerome?" the little man said reflectively. "Generally only Roman Catholics are called Jerome. I wonder if there'll be any difficulty about that? I wonder if some priest will hear his name and decide he was born a Roman Catholic and should be taken away from us? Ah well, one should always remember to stand up to the Romans, whom actually I prefer to so many of—by Jove, that boy is dirty. I think he's the dirtiest boy I've ever seen in my life. I admire your fortitude, Jo. He's been sleeping on your shoulder for hours and he smells quite fearfully. Even from here I can smell him. I think they can smell him all over the car. Do you think he's lousy as well?"

"A good bath is all he needs. And what if he does have lice? I'm not as much afraid of lice as they'll be afraid of what I'll do to them if I find them."

"He can't be bathed too soon." Jerome heard the clergyman chuckle, and lifting an eyelid he saw the little man lean forward and place a hand on his wife's knee. "A boy in the house, Jo! By Jove, after all these years! I wonder if they'll let us keep him? I suppose we must speak with the police. Ah well, I know the police chief reasonably well, but there are lawyers and things. It would be altogether too fearful if some fearful relative were to crop up and claim this child."

"If God sent him to us," said the woman, "I don't for an instant believe that God intends to take him away."

"I wish I could be as certain as you of God's intentions. He has always been a puzzle to me. Of course this whole affair is really so astonishing I don't believe anything about it but the way this child smells. He might turn out to be a liar, Jo. He's probably some ordinary boy who's run away from some ordinary brute of a father who beat him. Perhaps his father's a judge? Perhaps he's a Baptist minister? One never knows. He must be at least thirteen years old. A strong little boy, Jo. Have you felt his muscles? Much stronger than mine, but of course that says little. You know, I like his hair. When we have it cut, it will grow like spikes all over his head. I envy men with spiky hair, they're so virile. Everybody respects a man with spiky hair.

"You can cut down my old gray suit, I suppose. It's lucky I'm small for after he's grown some more we can hand my clothes down. When we heard that service Edwards was preaching in Woodstock, I confess to a little envy when I saw that family of his sitting there looking up at him, even though I wondered how he manages to feed such a flock. I know he does better than me, but seven children is quite a lot for a member of the profession. I wonder if Jerome will enjoy *my* sermons? I don't suppose he will, for I'm beginning to find them dull myself, though the one I preached last Good Friday wasn't so bad if you remember. When I was his age—I've just thought of something. Of course that boy can't even read and write. We'll have to put him to it right away. Fortunately we have the whole summer before us, and I'll tutor him every day. Do you notice the width between his eyes? Obviously a most intelligent boy."

The train rumbled on, whistling every now and then before it crossed a road, and Jerome lay half asleep and half awake.

"Jo," the little clergyman said, "have you thought of it?"

"Of what, Giles?"

"Of this little lad and me. I mean, of me when I was a lad his age. How strange it is that I should know how he feels! You see —I'm correct to believe in the miracles! Of all the people in the world, that he should have come to us—the only people who would want him and understand how he feels! One tells the Congregation that God watches everything and sometimes one wonders if He really does, but then something like this happens to prove it."

Still the train rumbled on, and after a while Jerome sensed that the little clergyman was becoming restless.

"It's nearly five o'clock and I haven't had a drop all day. I think it's time, don't you, Jo?"

"Giles—the people!"

"Pshaw! How will they guess?" He touched his dog collar. "I'm perfectly disguised. I could go to the water cooler and come back with a paper cup—with two paper cups—and who would notice? I think I'll go now."

"Please be careful, Giles."

"You know I'm careful. When am I not?"

Jerome fell asleep again and when he woke the clergyman was gently shaking his shoulder and on the clergyman's breath he smelled the sweet, familiar odor of rum.

"Wake up, Jerome, we're nearly there! Now I want you to look at something."

Opening his eyes, Jerome looked out the window and saw what seemed to him a vast spread of open water with a green shore on the far side shining in the sun.

That's Bedford Basin where all the fleets of the world could swing at their anchors without the ships even bumping each other. Over there behind that hill with the red building on it is Halifax where we live. You'll like it there. I come from England, Jerome, and when I first arrived here I liked Halifax the moment I saw it. There are big ships and small ships and we'll teach you how to sail—a real boat and not one of those Indian canoes you saw on your river. There are schools and churches and other boys to play with. You'll be proud of Halifax, for it's a fine town, a fine place to grow up in and—well, even for a grown man it's not too bad a place. I say—I told you I came from England and something just occurred to me! Do you know what England is?"

The boy shook his head.

"Fancy!" the clergyman said to his wife. "Fancy meeting *anybody*, even a child, who doesn't know what England is!" He chuckled. "By Jove, there are some people I'd enjoy telling that to!"

They all stood up while the clergyman took his bags down from the rack and Jerome nearly fell as the train lurched to the left and began its run along the eastern shore of Bedford Basin. A few minutes later it lurched in the opposite direction and suddenly the land and water closed in and they were running beside docks and a shipyard and saw a lean gray shape with flags hanging from its masts.

"A cruiser, Jerome! Do you know what a cruiser is?"

The boy shook his head.

"Oh, it's going to be wonderful, all the interesting things you're going to learn! That cruiser's the *Niobe*. She's so old they don't let her out of harbor for fear she'll sink."

The train's rumble changed into a solid, heavy roar, daylight disappeared as though a shade had been drawn and they passed under the smoke-stained, glass canopy of the station and stopped.

"It was the old North Street station," Jerome told Catherine later, "the one that was destroyed in the Halifax explosion of

1917 and nearly a hundred people were killed that day when that glass roof fell in on top of them. It seemed noisy and colossal to me, and at the end of the platform there was a line of cabbies waving whips and shouting behind an anchor chain. We came through and they closed around us and I was frightened, but Mr. Martell knew one of them and soon we were out in the street getting into one of the high black cabs they had in Halifax in those days. I reached Halifax in the last decade of the horse, and the streets smelled of horse manure as well as fishmeal and salt water and the harbor smells it still has. Coming into Halifax was like coming into a world of new smells."

The cab drove them along Barrington Street, then over a very steep hill crowded with houses and after what seemed a long time to Jerome, it came to rest in front of a house with a little lawn before it and three cannon balls making a black triangle beside the bottom step. There was an ivy-shaded porch with a hammock concealed behind the ivy and there were white curtains at the windows. The clergyman set his bags down, took out his keys and opened the door, and Jerome smelled the closeness of a shut-up house after a warm day.

"This is where we live," the little man said. "It's a small house and it's not in the best part of town by a long chalk, but we like it."

That evening Jerome was given a cold meal out of tins while kettles boiled on the stove and an ancient, spluttering, English-style geyser, heated by gas, warmed the water for his bath. He was undressed and his filthy clothes were burned. He was put into the tub, which was made of tin and painted white, and the paint felt delightfully rough against the skin of his back. The warm water soothed his skin and the fresh-smelling soap made it feel slippery and clean. He laughed as Josephine Martell bathed and dried him, then he held his arms over his head while she put a flannelette nightgown on him.

"This is one of mine," she said, "but I'm so small and you're so big it will fit you quite nicely, at least for the time being."

Soon he found himself in bed between cool sheets looking at pictures on the wall. One was a print of Joshua Reynold's *Age of Innocence* and the other was a sailing ship in a storm, and he lay in the white linen smoothness and looked up at the woman and smiled. His hand, questing under the pillow, closed on a small, rough-feeling little bag which had the cleanest scent he had ever smelled.

"That's lavendar," she said, still smiling. "We always have it under our pillows."

"What's that?"

"It's a kind of flower that grows in England where Mr. Martell comes from. I've never been to England, but it's the most beautiful and wonderful country in the world, and it's where the King lives. The roses in England are the best roses in the world and it's where the lavendar grows."

"It's nice."

"We're not rich people, Jerome, and we don't matter much to anybody, but we don't mind that because we believe we matter to God. Mr. Martell came from quite a famous family in England, but he was never happy when he was young—not as I hope you're going to be with us. Since our little girl died we've just had each other and a few friends in the church—I mean *I've* just had that, for Mr. Martell knows nearly everybody in Halifax, or at least he talks to them as if he does. I'm afraid some of the people in the church don't altogether approve of Mr. Martell, and I can well understand why they don't. But he's a good, good man, Jerome, and you'll soon find out for yourself how good he is." She took the little lavendar bag and smelled it, blushed a little and handed it back. "It's a silly thing to say, but we never had lavendar in my house when I was a little girl and I always had a craving for nice things like that. My father was a clergyman too, but he was a much sterner and plainer man than Mr. Martell." She scented the lavendar again and handed it back. "When I first met Mr. Martell he was visiting my father's house—he's quite a lot older than me, you know—and I remember smelling lavendar on his handkerchief and it seemed so nice and distinguished."

She bent and kissed the boy's forehead and was about to leave the room when she remembered something and came back.

"Jerome dear—have you ever been taught to pray?"

He shook his head, not knowing what the word meant.

"Then I think I'd better begin teaching you your first prayer tonight. Usually you pray on your knees because that shows how much you respect God, but you're so tired tonight I don't think

He will mind if you pray just where you are in bed. All you have to do is shut your eyes and repeat after me."

Jerome shut his eyes and felt the woman's hand close over his own.

"Now I lay me down to sleep, I pray the Lord my soul to keep . . ."

He repeated the words without understanding what they meant.

"If I die before I wake, I pray the Lord my soul to take."

Again he made the repetition, she laid her hand on his forehead, he felt its cool softness, he felt her lips brush his cheek and then he closed his eyes.

"There now, it doesn't matter if you don't understand what you were saying. Mr. Martell will explain all about it later on. Indeed I'm afraid the dear man will be only too eager to explain to you everything he knows himself, and that is quite a lot, even though I'm ashamed to say I don't listen carefully enough to know how much it really is. Go to sleep now, dear. God will watch over you all night long, and in the morning we shall be waiting for you."

That night while Jerome slept the little clergyman and his wife sat before their empty hearth holding hands and talking for hours. Before they went to bed they fell on their knees and thanked God and promised that they would lead this child into the paths of righteousness. They believed, they believed at last, that goodness and mercy would follow them all the days of their lives, now that they had a son.

So it was that this waif, conceived by an illiterate peasant woman heaving in the embrace of some man whose name she possibly did not even know, grew up in the old naval and garrison town of Halifax in a Christian family and became an educated man. So it happened that the name he lived under was Jerome Martell, and that he thought of Giles and Josephine Martell as his father and mother.

During the war I spent several months in Halifax working on a program with the Navy, and I met a few men who had gone to school with Jerome when he was a boy. The little clergyman had been right about his intelligence. Jerome had learned so rapidly that in six years he had made up all the lost ground and was ready for college when he went to the war, which he did at the end of his seventeenth year when he was as powerfully built as the average strong man of twenty-five. He had been well thought of in Halifax, good at games and at his work and very religious, but the war, as he told me that afternoon on the lake, had destroyed his religion and launched him into a new orbit. He had come back from the war an agnostic, so full of guilt and so shocked by his experiences that he had been unable to live any longer with his foster-parents. Instead of entering Dalhousie where a scholarship was waiting for him, he wrote examinations for McGill, won a scholarship there and supported himself by various jobs until he had got his degrees and qualified as a doctor.

Meanwhile he had almost broken the hearts of the two little people who had saved him. Catherine met Giles just before the little clergyman died. She met Josephine several times and loved her, and Josephine loved Catherine and was grateful that Jerome had found and married her. But he himself after the war could not face the gentleness and simplicity of this Christian couple, and for this he felt sorry and guilty, and after Giles died he several times went home to visit his mother and supported her and bought her a small house when the rectory fell vacant and she had to live elsewhere. He always wrote letters to her and she to him, and she died during his second visit to Spain. How lonely she was or how disappointed she never told him, but Catherine once said this of her:

"People like her are the strongest in the world. They ask so little for themselves that almost nothing can be taken away from them. And they accept so much that almost nothing can be added heavy enough to break them."

In the Bible given by Giles to Jerome when he went overseas I saw these words from *Pilgrim's Progress* written on the flyleaf:

"A man of a very stout countenance went up to the keeper of the book of life and said, 'Set down my name, sir,' and immediately he fell on the armed men and cut his way into heaven after receiving and giving many wounds."

Catherine also said to me after Jerome left her:

"Josephine told me once that I'd never understand Jerome

unless I understood that while he was with them he had really thought of himself as a soldier of God. He believed the Gospels literally, and they meant far more to him than they could mean to most people, because he had such a desperate need to belong. When you were a little boy you were religious too, weren't you?"

"Yes," I said, "but I got over it in the depression."

"Jerome never got over it," Catherine said. "He lost it, and that's different."

The evening after our long afternoon on the lake, after Sally had been put to bed and Jerome and I had cleaned up, the three of us sat for an hour and a half before the fire in the cottage, the oil lamps turned down and the only light coming from the burning logs on the hearth. Jerome was utterly relaxed and so was I, and I don't think I ever saw Catherine look so well. Happiness shone from her, and in the half-light she seemed all ages of woman in one. I was grateful. I thought of Jerome's strange story and asked myself how anyone can ever hope to plan a human life. That two such people should have met one another— it seemed to me a chance in a million.

Around nine-thirty Jerome stretched and went outside to fill his lungs with cooler air, and Catherine and I glanced at each other.

"This is wonderful," I said.

"Sometimes, like now, I'm so happy it scares me."

"Why should it."

"Because it's so intense. It scares him too, sometimes."

"This afternoon he told me about his childhood. What an incredible story."

"I thought he might have done that. It means he likes you very much, for I don't think he's told anyone that story except me. Bits and pieces to others, but not the whole thing."

"He's rather amazing, isn't he?"

She looked into the fire and was silent.

"Does it haunt him? I mean, does it come back in dreams the way the psychologists say?"

"Sometimes." Still looking into the fire, she said: "It's still part of him and it's not easy living with a man like that."

"Is it easy living with anyone?"

She smiled. "That's fair enough. But I couldn't imagine myself living with anyone else—not now."

It hurt when she said this, and I suppose she must have realized it, but she had said it and there was no point in unsaying it.

"It's not easy for him either, living with me. I try to make things simpler for him. I try to plan and arrange and I'm quite good at it. But I wish I were stronger."

"You're so much stronger than you used to be that nobody'd know you'd ever been sick."

She shook her head. "I'm not strong, George. It's the same old heart. Jerome tells me the rest of my organism has accommodated itself to the heart and made compensations, but the heart is the center of the whole thing. You know something, George?" She looked at me with a rueful, wondering smile. "It's been wonderful, living with Jerome. I've never been bored once—not for a single day. But I've never been able to relax, either."

"You're relaxed now."

"Yes, perhaps I am. Perhaps it's having you here."

The door creaked open and Jerome entered smoking his pipe, square and rugged in a turtle-necked homespun jersey, his hands in his pockets, a contented look on his face.

"In case anyone's interested, it's getting colder. The wind has hauled and there's some east in it. Only a few of the stars are visible." He stood in front of the hearth in silence and after a while he gave a sort of chuckle. "I guess I talked a lot this afternoon."

"I was complimented."

"Complimented, hell! I talked too much. Look George—do you like that job of yours?"

"No, but it's a job."

"You talked a little, too. I heard you, and it's given me ideas. You have a remarkable speaking voice. How would you like to work in radio?"

"Me—radio!" I laughed.

"You're in a rut in that school and I don't think it could ever be the right job for a man like you. I'm not implying you're not doing good work, but you're not the type. Only a few men are. I had a great schoolmaster once in Halifax, an absolutely wonderful man who went to the war at fifty-two because he couldn't stand the idea of his boys going into the line without him. He went through from the fall of 1915 to the end, and when it was over he returned to the job as fresh as ever. But the reason he was good was that he never stopped being a boy. He was very rare. You have stopped being a boy."

I laughed. "Dr. Bigbee hasn't stopped being a boy. Does that make him a great schoolmaster?"

"He's supposed to be one, isn't he?" Jerome grunted. "Anyway, what's that got to do with you? You're in the wrong line of work, George, and you must know it. The trouble with the capitalist system is that it harnesses everything to the profit motive. It regards a teacher as a kind of superior servant, and it won't let him teach—not really. Listen, George, the way things are now there's no future in teaching. Maybe later on when things change, but not now. And there'll never be a future for a school like Waterloo. You've got something better to do with your life than teach the sons of the rich. Think it over. You understand a lot about politics and you have the right kind of voice. Somebody like you could do well in the CBC. Think it over. Keep your mind open and I'll make a few inquiries."

After some small talk, Jerome and Catherine exchanged smiles and a little later they went upstairs to bed. My cot was in the living room of the cabin and I undressed before the fire and lay watching the shadows flicker among the rafters, and the big shadow of the Quebec heater bulging black and steady against the pine wall. I felt at once relaxed and wide awake and I lay thinking about what Jerome had told me and wondering if it was really possible that I might be more than a failure. Boards creaked overhead, there was a faint murmur of voices from Catherine and Jerome, then their door closed and silence fell. I lay happy and without jealousy and full of wonder, and suddenly I was asleep.

The next morning I woke to creaking boards and moving feet and Sally's excited voice crying "Look! Look! Look!"

I sat up and looked out the window at a white world. Snow had fallen steadily all night and now the sun was struggling out of a gauze of mist and the lake was black ink against a white land. Sally pressed her little face to the cold window pane in an ecstasy of delight and the tonic air made me want to do everything at once. From the back of the cottage came the smell of frying bacon and Jerome's voice singing as he cooked it.

"You get out of here," I said to Sally. "Get upstairs and get your clothes on so I can get mine on, too."

She rushed at me as though she wanted to make sure I loved her too, that everyone loved her in this lovely world, and we horsed around for a while until suddenly she stopped and said gravely, "Now I'm going upstairs and get dressed. I can get dressed, too."

Just after I had my clothes on, was shaved and ready to eat, Catherine appeared for the morning wearing heavy tweeds and the peaceful, inward look of a woman who has been well-loved the night before. I don't believe I ever saw Catherine as happy and as well as I saw her that morning, and when she kissed my forehead and smiled she seemed so serene that I missed the point of what she said, and only thought about it months afterwards.

"If only the world would leave us alone," she said, and stared out at the white land and the ink-black lake. "If only it would leave us alone our days would be a paradise."

PART SIX

Chapter I

THE following winter I was too engrossed in myself to think
how deeply Catherine had meant that remark to me. Through
her and Jerome my whole world had opened up; through them I
was meeting people I had previously read about only in books.
My weekends in town became series of mental explosions, and at
school after the day's work I used to sit up in bed for hours read-
ing books about politics, history and the ideas which flamed in
that peculiar time. Jerome seemed to know everyone in Montreal
whose brain was alive, and most of them came from Europe or
other parts of Canada. The old dynasty still ruled the city, as
oblivious as mandarins to new faces and new ideas, but they were
there: after a long, long time they were there at last and they
were turning Montreal, in spite of itself, into a real world city.
Coming back to Waterloo from those Montreal weekends was
like stepping back into the colonial nineteenth century.

Light can blind you more than darkness, and this sudden new
light blinded me to signs that now would have been obvious to
me.

That winter, increasingly after New Year, the atmosphere in
the Martell household changed. Several times I noticed Catherine
withdrawing herself. Often she made sharp, cutting remarks that
surprised me. At the same time I noticed that Jerome talked with
increasing obsession and violence about the political situation.
I assumed that this was the sole source of disagreement between
him and Catherine, and indeed I think it was the primary one.
Catherine would not, and could not, be interested in politics
even to the extent that I am interested in them now. She believed
that Jerome's impetuosity caused him to be used by people un-
worthy of him, nor was she the only one who believed that. But
this fixation of Jerome was real and sincere, and its very violence,
oddly connected with his own violent history, undoubtedly had
made him lonely with a wife who feared for him and for herself
and for her daughter and dreaded where his impulsiveness might
lead him. This was a time in which you were always meeting
people who caught politics just as a person catches religion. It
was probably the last time in this century when politics in our

country will be evangelical, and if a man was once intensely religious, he was bound to be wide open to a mood like that of the Thirties. By why waste time explaining the pattern? It is obvious now, and dozens of books have been written about it. Less obvious have been some of the attendant passions that went along with this neo-religious faith. Passion has a way of spilling over into all aspects of the human mind and feelings. It is the most dangerous thing in the world whether it focuses itself on love, religion, reform, politics or art. Without it the world would die of dry rot. But though it creates it also destroys. Having seldom been its victim I have only pity for those who are, and I would be a hypocrite if I judged them by the standards you can safely apply to a man at peace with himself and his circumstances.

But I was blind to all the signs, and meanwhile my ordinary routine went on. Week after week I endured the boredom of teaching boys who did not wish to learn, and in my spare time at Waterloo I made myself extremely unpopular by trying to foist on my older colleagues some of the new political theories I now regarded as gospel. Most of them had been out of England so long they had no notion of what the new England was like. Ponson still thought of England as the England he had known as a youth at the time of Queen Victoria's Diamond Jubilee when she had the ships, she had the guns and she had the money, too. McNish thought only of getting back into the Navy and the Doctor, who read about one newspaper a month, cheerfully assumed that when the time came John Bull would teach the foreigners a badly needed lesson. Meanwhile the younger men, the socialists from the provincial universities, were selfishly pleased to see their social betters humiliated by the present Tory government. Waterloo in those days was a depressing place.

The winter passed, a fateful winter for Catherine, Jerome and myself even though I did not realize it at the time, and finally on a Friday evening in early April I again found myself on the Montreal train accompanied by Shatwell. He was the only colleague with whom I felt easy. He was almost invariably cheerful in his languid way, and though he read the papers diligently, they never angered or depressed him. "I've always taken it for granted things were going from bad to worse, you understand," was Shatwell's perennial attitude toward everything, including himself.

But on this particular evening Shatwell was so depressed he could hardly talk. I knew he was tired, and I assumed his depression was caused by one of those humiliating incidents which so often happened to junior masters in Waterloo. The Doctor was so busy being the Doctor that without realizing it he undermined the authority of his assistants. That morning Shatwell's class had rioted, and Dr. Bigbee himself had exploded into the room to quell it. Now I was trying to cheer Shatwell up.

"Old Bigbee deliberately creates all this confusion," I said. "If it wasn't for him our lives would be easy. Why worry about it?"

Shatwell turned to me wearily. "George old boy, absolutely the last thing that ever worries me is that old bastard. I had his number the first time I ever met him. He's simply an older version of my company commander in my A.S.C. days in India. A krait bit that chap and put him out of commission."

Shatwell then told me the real reason for his malaise. His widow, whose name was Mrs. Moffat, had been operated on by Dr. Rodgers in the Beamis Memorial for a non-malignant growth, and all week Shatwell had been telephoning the hospital for news of her.

"Something quite fearful and drastic has obviously happened," he said. "They say she's distended, whatever that is, and isn't comfortable, which coming from a nurse or a doctor bloody well means she's bloody well in agony."

"But there's bound to be some discomfort after an abdominal operation," I said, quoting Jerome.

Shatwell shook his head and stared miserably out the window. The train was bowling along through sodden fields under a dappled sky, and the sun, flaring suddenly out of the west, illuminated standing pools of water and turned them to gold.

"You see," Shatwell explained, "everything I've ever touched has had such a way of turning out badly. It's not as though poor Martha were strong, you understand. She's quite petite, actually. She's never had much luck, and she never asks for anything, and I rather fancy with these doctor chaps, if one doesn't ask pretty firmly, it's not likely to be given."

"They're not like that at all."

"Your friend Martell may not be like that, but I've seen a thing or two, George. You see, one time when things had gone a little worse with me than usual, I was reduced to working as a hospital orderly. Bed pans, enemas, slops, cleaning up the messes they make—that sort of thing. A perfectly frightful job. But it taught me a thing or two, you understand. In hospitals they cover up for bad work just as we do in the school."

"But you have no evidence of bad work here."

"I've got rather a nose for that sort of thing, old boy."

A west-bound express crashed by, the air shock from each car slamming against the window, and when it was past Shatwell continued.

"Martha's so gentle and kind, you understand. We've had the jolliest times together. She doesn't ask a thing of a chap, I mean to say, she never nags or tries to prod one into marrying her or any of that sort of thing. I mean to say, she just takes a chap like me and we have a jolly time. You can't guess what that means to me, old boy. I haven't had too much of that sort of thing in my life. Mum was rather a dear, but Dad was the military type, and the British military can be pretty bloody. He was always trying to keep Mum and me up to scratch, as he put it, and he might just as well have saved his time. Of course the only reason he did it was because he liked it. They're all like that, those chaps, and most women nag one so. I had a wife once and she nagged.

"You never told me you were married, Randolph."

"What was the use? It didn't work out at all and it was ages ago. She's married to some engineer chap in India now. But poor little Martha, she just took me as I am, you understand. She never had children, poor thing."

"When did her husband die?"

"I rather fancy about a dozen years ago. He was much older and I gather he was one of those chaps who gets married and sits. He was in some sort of trade. I don't think he was much good, but I rather fancy he thought he was, or perhaps he thought he ought to be. He never had any appreciation. Poor Martha's so appreciative of everything it quite wrings the heart."

I told Shatwell he was worrying unnecessarily, that people always recovered from operations these days, but he was not comforted.

"If she were fond of somebody else instead of me," he said, "I can't help thinking she might have a better chance."

"Oh come on, Randolph. What's that got to do with it?"

He shook his head miserably. "There was a girl in Smyrna I brought a packet of bad luck to. And there was that consul's daughter in Kuala Lumpur—but I told you about her. And there was the one in Calcutta who was married to that bloody gunner. And then there was the nicest one of them all in Brisbane—but I don't expect I told you about her."

"Not that I remember."

"The fact is, old boy, I was too ashamed. You see, I went to the very best medico in the place, and he assured me, he positively staked his reputation on it, that I was a complete cure. But I wasn't, you understand."

He looked at me with his soft calf's eyes and I was sluggish in getting the point.

"George old boy, if a chap gives a girl the clap, especially if he's fond of her, there simply aren't any words. So you understand my point about the doctors. Just because they tell you there's nothing to worry about, that doesn't mean there isn't a packet."

When the train reached town, Shatwell jumped into a taxi and rushed to the Beamis Memorial. I checked my bags and took my time walking up the slope of the city to Jerome's apartment.

It was one of those delicious afternoons which sometimes happen in Montreal between the break-up and the opening of the leaves, robins calling in Dominion square while there was still a grit of left-over winter sand on the pavements. I stopped in a flower shop and bought tulips for Catherine, then walked leisurely upward and through the university campus where boys and girls were sauntering hand in hand, and all about me was the feeling that comes when windows are opened after a long winter. The sky was dappled and some of the clouds reminded me of the underwings of doves.

Catherine's living room window was open when I entered and Sally was playing on the floor.

"Uncle George!" she cried, and rushed at me to be appreciated.

I tousled her ash-blonde hair and rubbed her nose and she gurgled with pleasure, but when I asked her what she had been doing she turned grave and placed a finger on my lips.

"Listen!" she commanded.

I did so and heard the happy noise of a barrel organ, and going to the window we saw the wonderful old Italian who looked like Toscanini and had been playing his barrel organ around the town as long as I could remember. Toselli's *Serenade* was making windows pop open all along the curve of that little half-moon street and people leaned out smiling, while over the roofs the cloud-cover was sliding off to the east with the sky around the sun shining like a field of daffodils, and Sally looked so happy I wished I were her father.

The doorbell interrupted us, and while Sally clamored to be let out to play with the barrel-organ man, Catherine called downstairs and asked me to answer the bell.

It was Jack Christopher, the other dinner guest, and he had come over from the hospital where he was a senior interne. He was, and still is, a handsome man in a punctilious way, tall and serious with lines like a pair of parentheses framing a shrewd, disciplined mouth. We were the same age but I thought of him as older than myself and I still do. He was one of Jerome's various protegés. He came from an old Montreal family with some financial backing, and his people had wished him to go into business. But somewhere along the line, when he was hesitating between business and medicine, he had encountered Jerome and Jerome's enthusiasm had fired him. Now he was hesitating between entering practice in internal medicine and doing specialized work in endocrinology. It was typical of Jerome that he had advised him to try both for a while.

"Mummy, can I go out and play with the barrel-organ man?"

From upstairs came Catherine's voice: "So long as you're sure to put on your coat."

"I'll put it on, Mummy."

I watched Sally go out the door and behind me the phone rang. Jack was nearest and he picked it up, and after half a minute and a few monosyllables he turned to me.

"That was Jerome. He says he's been held up but will be here in a few minutes. He tells us to get our own drinks. Do you want one?"

I did, and after thinking it over Jack decided he wanted one too.

"Has Jerome been busier than usual?" I asked him.

Jack gave a slight shrug but made no comment. We sipped our drinks silently, after a while the barrel organ stopped playing and a little later Sally came in again. I asked her to get a vase for Catherine's tulips but she preferred to play with Jack, so I got one myself and brought it into the living room with the tulips arranged. Jack was down on the floor with Sally looking as much at ease as an elder statesman playing with a child at election time and Sally was demanding to know why her father was not here.

"I haven't seen Daddy all week!" she said. "Not all week!"

Then she ran upstairs to talk to her mother and Jack resumed his seat with an expressionless face.

After a while he said in his abrupt way: "Out of the mouths of babes. I don't like it."

"What don't you like?"

"Of course it's none of my business what he does."

"What who does?"

"Jerome, naturally. Tell me something—is he, or is he not, a communist?"

"I don't think he's one."

"Are you one?"

"No."

Jack made an impatient gesture: "But the whole lot of you talk like a pack of Reds all the time. Girls and boys together. That little O.R. nurse, that Blackwell girl—she's a pal of yours too, isn't she?"

"I wouldn't call her that. I've known her a while, but—look here, what are you driving at?"

"Jerome sees too much of her. He has no sense of form and I don't like it. Apart from being bad for the hospital, it's bad for him. Now *that* girl's certainly a communist, and the two of them have been seen at too many meetings not to get themselves talked about. I don't like it. Mind you, I'm not saying anything more than that."

"You seem to be hinting at a hell of a lot more than that, Jack."

"Am I? Perhaps so. Other people are, if I'm not."

I finished my drink and poured myself another.

"What's got into everyone these days I don't know. This damned Spanish War, you'd think it was happening here. All these meetings where the same people tell each other the same old things. What do they know about Spain? How the hell do they know whether what they say is true or not? At best they're guessing, at worst they're saying what they like to hear. Those Spanish War meetings are like revivals in a Methodist tent. What's Spain to a man like Jerome? He's never been there. That country's always been an impossible country. What's Spain to any of these people except an excuse for them to give free play to their neuroticism?"

I became irritated. "Don't be so stuffy, Jack."

"You think I really am?" He looked like a scientist faced with new evidence it was his duty to assess. "Perhaps you're right and I am stuffy. But I was talking about Jerome, not myself. Some of the things he's doing and saying at the hospital are getting past a joke. We've had a new bequest, a considerable one, and with no strings attached. Before there was the slightest mention of how the money was to be used, he was saying around the corridors, so that everyone heard him, 'Well, now I suppose we'll be building a new pleasure dome for our rich patients.' He knew as well as the rest of us that the Beamis is short of beds, but he made it sound like a dirty deal. Of course what he wants is an extension of the out-patient's facilities, and I'm not saying he's wrong in that—at least not at the moment. It was his work in that clinic for the unemployed that got him started in all this. I'm not saying it was a wrong thing to do, but all sorts of people have got around him on account of that."

Jack was seldom so talkative and I looked at him in surprise.

"Of course," he went on, "every word he said reached Dr. Rodgers. Why does he have to behave that way? Why do all you people talk as though everyone in authority is a crook? Medicine should be above this propaganda."

"According to Jerome, a good deal of medicine in this town is on the side of the big battalions."

Jack's cheeks showed a faint flush. "He's too suggestible. He used to be a medical man, and that's what he still is. Politics disgust me."

"Can you keep politics out of anything these days?"

"You people rot your minds with all this stuff you read and repeat it to each other. I suppose you think I'm a reactionary."

"Since you ask me, I do. This country happens to have about one million unemployed in it. The States must have about twelve million. Meanwhile Hitler's on the rampage, and you want to live in an ivory tower."

Christopher shrugged. "It so happens I have a scientific mind, George. You haven't, and neither has Jerome. He's a good bio-chemist—it amazes me how much science he actually does know. But that's because he has an incredible memory and was well trained. He's quicker to learn than anyone I've ever met. But he's *not* a scientist."

"Okay. He's not a member of the priesthood. So what?"

"So this. Outside his profession, he's as gullible as anyone I've ever met."

"Which no scientist ever is—outside his profession?"

Jack gave me a coldly level glance. "It so happens, George, that I owe a great deal to Jerome and I care what happens to my friends. He's rotting his mind with this stuff. He's a wonderful surgeon. You can't possibly know how good he is. Don't ask me why. Surgeons like him are born, not made. In time he could become the greatest abdominal man on the continent. Besides that he's got a mysterious power very few doctors possess. I can't describe it, exactly, and I don't want to sound sentimental or give you any of the guff you read about doctors in novels and maga-zines. But it's an empirically observed fact that some medical men have more powers of healing than others. In that respect Jerome's unique. I've never seen his equal."

"Well?"

"This is very rare, George. A man like him is worth ten dozen politicians. But if he keeps on the way he's going now—" he gave an exasperated shrug. "He's letting these neurotics and trouble-makers use him. There's not one in that whole crowd of socialists and communists and talkers who'd be acting like that if they were personally successful."

"Jack," I said, "tell that to your friends in St. James Street, where you probably heard it the first time."

"Did I?" He flushed in anger, a rare thing for him to do. "Let me tell *you* something. They're using a man better than themselves. They flatter him and he laps it up. If I didn't love the damned fool I'd be disgusted. I don't like seeing a first-class man used by a third-class one, and above all I don't like seeing him used by that bitch of a nurse. Maybe I'm stuffy, but there are a lot of people who look up to Jerome. Whether he likes it or not, he's expected to set an example of discipline in the hospital."

Never had I heard so much conversation from Jack Christopher, who could be silent for hours. If I had been more observant I would have realized that such an outburst from a man like him was actually an understatement, but I was not observant, I was blinded by my own feelings, I was determined to permit in myself no jealousy of Jerome and I was hostile to Jack's entire point of view outside of his work. I became angry, and would have soon become offensive if Jerome had not at that moment entered the house.

We heard his voice loud in the hall: "Well everybody, here I am!"

Sally came tumbling down the stairs to meet him, he picked her up and swung her almost to the ceiling as she squealed with delight, and while still playing with her he called to me to pour him a drink, and to make it a stiff one. He continued to play with Sally who gurgled with joyous laughter while Jack contemplated the scene as though he were trying to figure out its hidden mechanisms. Jerome roughed her up and she loved it, and he was still doing it when Catherine came down. He tossed the child onto a sofa and turned to his wife, kissed her, put his arm about her waist and fondled her, slapped Sally's backside, swallowed half of his drink and told Jack he wanted to speak to him in his study. Jack rose and went with him, Sally ran upstairs to find something she wanted to show her father, and Catherine and I were left alone.

"Well," I said, "this seems one of his manic days."

"Every day would be like this if he didn't wear so many people out they begin to wear him out in turn. Come, help me set the table."

We made small talk between dining room and kitchen and a feeling of desire came to me, so sharp it hurt, as I saw the curve of her hips.

"Jack tells me Jerome's been doing too many things," I said.

"That's how the man is made. Sometimes I wonder if he can think of anything else besides Spain. Do you think about Spain all the time?"

"I suppose I do."

"I'm sure he thinks about Spain in the middle of his operations. What's the matter with me, George? I can't think about Spain when I'm cooking a dinner. I could spend a week doing nothing and never think about Spain at all."

"It's a pretty important subject these days, Catherine."

"I suppose it is. But do you really believe that's why all you people think about nothing else?"

She looked at me with a frown line between her eyes, her heart-shaped face not at all serene.

"It's not so easy being a good wife to Jerome," she said.

I laughed: "It must be tiring sometimes."

"Tiring!" she turned away.

"Jack believes he's doing too much outside his work."

"Jack's right. He's the only one of our friends who's not completely blind." She turned to me again. "He changes so fast, George. Can't you see the change in him since last fall? What causes it? I wish I knew. He's so exposed and he doesn't know it." She lifted her hands and let them fall. "Oh, let's not talk about us. How was your own week?"

"My weeks are always the same."

It was seven-thirty before we sat down at table and Jerome, not noticing Catherine's mood, talked with manic excitement about a Spanish tank officer he was going to introduce to a public meeting the next night.

"When the war began he was a garage mechanic and now he's a full colonel. How's that for proof of what a man can do in a good system? For the first time I'm beginning to think that Norman Bethune was dead right about Spain. Even that Englishman Clifford was right. Now that the Soviets are helping them, the Loyalists are going to win. But they do need doctors. Beth's over already. They need all the outside help they can get."

When we went into the living room for our coffee, Jerome's excitement spread itself as it so often did. He put his arm about Catherine's waist and gave her a glance that caused Jack to turn aside in embarrassment. He was certainly obvious; when he felt sexual desire it showed as though an electric light had been ignited in his face. With a quiet smile Catherine slipped away to an armchair, and I guessed this was one of her bad days.

The phone stabbed into the middle of Jerome's monologue, he answered it and said it was for me. Wondering who beside my parents could know I was here, I picked up the instrument and heard Shatwell's voice hysterical with anxiety.

"George, Martha is dying. They wouldn't let me see her at first, but I made them and it's pitiful and they're doing damn all."

He poured out details about her symptoms until I stopped him and asked why he did not consult her doctor.

"How can I? The chap who cut her up, the surgeon, you understand, is in Detroit or Buffalo or some such bloody place reading some bloody paper to some bloody other doctors."

"I meant her own physician."

"Oh, he's absolutely not of the slightest use whatever."

"Come on, Randolph, how do you know that?"

"This physician chap who turned her over to the sawbones who botched her, he's conked out himself. He's a patient here too." He hesitated. "For God's sake help me, George. Speak to Dr. Martell, will you please, George?"

I had seen this coming. "That's asking quite a lot, Randolph. It's not Dr. Martell's case."

"But he works in this bloody hospital, doesn't he?"

"Who is her physician?"

"I think the name of the chap is Crawford. Listen, old boy, this isn't merely serious, it's desperate. I've spoken to all the housemen or internes or whatever it is they call them over here, and it's quite obvious not one of them is giving me anything but a cover-up. If Martha has to wait for this chap to come back from Detroit she'll have to wait till Monday, and by Monday she'll be dead."

"Come on, Randolph! They don't take cases into hospitals and just leave them."

"Don't they, though! Don't they! George, please help us!"

"I'll ask the doctor, but I can't promise anything. Where can I reach you if I have to call you back?"

"Here at the hospital. I'm sticking, George. They'd like to get rid of me but they bloody well can't."

After hanging up I spoke to Jerome, who frowned and asked Jack and me to join him in his study. Sitting in a swivel chair with a cigarette between thumb and forefinger, his eyes hooded against the smoke, he listened in silence while I repeated Shatwell's story. Christopher gave me a glance suggesting he wished I'd dropped dead.

"Crawford's laid out, all right," Jerome grunted when I had finished. "The poor devil's passing a kidney stone."

I had never seen Jerome involved in a case, and the change in him was dramatically impressive. His gaiety disappeared and so did the youthfulness of his manner. He became intense, concentrated and grave, and he looked like my idea of a general pondering a tough decision. Christopher responded to the change and reverted to a correct interne in the presence of a senior.

"Do you know anything about this patient?" Jerome asked him.

"I was with Dr. Crawford when he made his rounds this morning."

"And?"

"I'd rather you asked Dr. Crawford himself."

Jerome shot him a bleak glance and Jack stopped hedging.

"There've been complications. Dr. Crawford said if her temperature continued to rise it would be necessary to go in once more."

They exchanged some medical language and Jerome abruptly picked up the telephone extension from his desk and dialed the hospital.

"Who's on her floor tonight?" he said over his shoulder to Jack.

"I think it's Sawyer."

When the interne came onto the line I felt sorry for him. Jerome shot a series of questions at him, interrupted most of the replies, and finally exploded.

"Has it occurred to you that you're being trained to think for yourself? Even to act for yourself? You tell me her temperature was 101 at eleven-thirty, 102½ at three and you tell me it's now 103. And while this goes on you've dutifully observed what you've read on her chart. What's that you say? *I* know Dr. Crawford's passing a kidney stone. The whole hospital knows about that damned stone. Aren't there any other doctors? You say Dr. McGregor's up north and Dr. Smith can't be found? Damn it, you knew where *I* could be found. Why didn't you call me?"

He slammed down the phone and looked at Christopher as though it were Jack's fault.

"Dr. North is in town," Christopher said quietly. "And I know where I can locate Dr. Adamson and Dr. Simpson."

"Yes," said Jerome, "I know where I can locate them, too."

We followed him out and heard him tell Catherine he had to go to the hospital. Before leaving he asked her to make his apologies to the guests who had been invited for the rest of the evening.

"Perhaps I'd better go along with you?" suggested Christopher.

"No, you stay here."

"I'd really prefer to go."

"And I'd really prefer you here."

Jack went slightly white as the door closed behind Jerome and we heard his feet running down the steps. We heard his car start and drive away.

"Damn him!" Jack said between closed lips.

He came into the room and looked at Catherine, she looked back and they seemed to understand each other. Catherine was tired and anxious, and I hardly knew what to say, for I did not understand something which she and Jack, without having mentioned it to one another, clearly did understand.

Then steps sounded and the first guests arrived, followed by more, and soon the familiar chorus filled the living room: Spain, Chamberlain, Blum, Hitler, Mussolini, Franco, Roosevelt, the Soviets, capital, unemployment and all the rest of it. I found my way to Catherine, sat on the floor beside her chair and our eyes met.

"I wish I were in bed," she said.

"Why don't you go to bed?"

"Not till Jerome comes back."

"Is anything serious the matter?"

"With Jerome? Yes, I'm afraid there is."

"I meant with you."

"Oh me! I'm just weary of being half of a person. Help Arthur Lazenby with the drinks and forget about me."

"Wherever Arthur is, he's always serving the drinks."

"Wherever there's an evening like this, there's always Arthur."

"Except that he doesn't talk."

"You talk, George. It's good for you. Talk all you like."

But that night I did not feel like talking at all; or rather, I wanted only to talk to Catherine, and not about politics. Jack Christopher, who was spending his first and only evening in this kind of a crowd, sat in a corner chair with his fingertips pressed together and his eyes on the ceiling. For an hour nobody paid him the slightest attention and he paid none to anyone else. Lazenby crossed and tried to interest him in a beer, then in some broken conversation, but he failed and presently found himself another place. Around eleven-thirty Jack left the room and I guessed his destination was the phone in Jerome's study. Soon afterwards I was conscious of him tall and aloof in the doorway looking with exasperated contempt at the cluster of intellectuals bent forward to argue and agree, and when he caught my eye, I joined him in the hall.

"Well," he said coldly, "he's done it. He's operated on your friend's mistress."

"How do you know she's Shatwell's mistress?"

He disregarded the question and said: "I suppose it might have been worse."

"For Mrs. Moffat?"

"Frankly, I don't give a damn about Mrs. Moffat."

"Is it your idea that he should have let her die for the sake of medical ethics?"

Jack gave me a glance of withering contempt, then his anger disappeared almost instantly behind the facade of his professional manner. But he look at me very coldly.

"You'd never have made that remark if you hadn't heard him make similar ones. And he'd not make them if it wasn't for these new friends and ideas of his. He shouldn't do it, George. What's more, he knows he shouldn't do it. Maybe it's true that in one case in a thousand a patient's neglected because he's not important, but—"

"It occurred to Shatwell that this might be the one case in the thousand."

"Which is not an original thought. About one family in ten gets the idea sooner or later that it's not getting all it deserves from the medical profession."

"I'm sorry, Jack. I heard Jerome's conversation with that interne."

"You heard only his half of it, and you aren't in a position to understand it. You political people are always on the lookout for something crooked. I don't know what's the matter with you." Jack gave an exasperated shrug. "At least he telephoned Detroit, but of course Dr. Rodgers wasn't in his hotel room and he didn't locate him. He did talk to Dr. Crawford, but Crawford's blind with pain and apparently did nothing more than tell him to use his own judgment. Oh, I suppose in the technical sense Jerome's been correct enough."

"Then what are you beefing about?"

"Simply this. For the last two or three years Jerome has been inviting this competition with Dr. Rodgers in the hospital. I don't think he realizes the extent to which he's done it. That man's always trying to prove something—God only knows why. Maybe just to himself.

"Now look at this from Dr. Rodgers' point of view. He's old enough to be Jerome's father. He's taught Jerome a great deal. He once regarded him as his protegé. And in case you've picked up from Jerome the wrong idea about Dr. Rodgers, let me tell you an absolute fact. Ten years ago Rodgers was regarded one of the greatest surgeons in the world. Now how do you think a proud old man is going to like it when he discovers that on one of the few occasions when he's made a mistake, the one man he especially dislikes sees the details of the mistake and puts it right?"

"Then Rodgers did botch the job?"

Christopher turned away in exasperation, then back again.

"I'd appreciate it very much, George, if you'd suggest to this friend of yours with the funny name that he can be grateful for what's been done for him, and that if he wants to show his gratitude the best way he can do it is to keep his mouth shut. I saw this fellow at the hospital and I didn't care for the look of him. He looks like a remittance man to me."

"Do you think he enjoys knowing that everyone thinks that about him?" I said.

Jack went over to Catherine, said he was leaving and thanked her. The conversation went on in the room as though he had never been there and had never departed, and a little later I joined Catherine in the corner. I knew from her face that she was not listening to a word anyone said.

When I sat down her hand closed on mine, pressed it slightly, dropped it. She looked away.

"You should be safely married to somebody nice," she surprised me by saying. "You shouldn't be involved with me."

I laughed and said something non-committal. Then I saw the pain in her face, I saw her deep inner seriousness transparent.

"I suppose you know all about it?" she said calmly.

"All about what?"

"Our trouble. Has nobody told you?"

"What is it, Catherine? Jack was talking in a vague kind of way, but—what trouble, Catherine? What trouble?"

She lifted her hands and dropped them: "It would be so easy if the question could be easily answered. What trouble? Oh George, it must have been easy fifty years ago when everyone knew who was to blame for what."

I looked at her baffled.

"How can I blame anyone? Even that girl. I don't like her, but how can I blame her. She's not responsible. How can I blame Jerome? He can't help this thing inside of himself. How can I blame myself? I can't believe this war in Spain is a crusade. But he does. You see— oh George, you ask me what the trouble is? Do I know anyone who can tell me what the trouble is? Life, perhaps. Life in this time." Her pale, smooth face remained calm. "Or perhaps it's the vacuum left by his lost religion. I tried to fill it. I thought I'd filled it, but now I know I didn't."

I looked over my shoulder, but none of the others were paying any attention to us. I saw Arthur Lazenby's profile intent on some argument and turned to Catherine again.

"Everyone takes it for granted he's having an affair with this Blackwell girl," she said calmly.

"I'm sure he isn't."

She smiled elliptically: "I wouldn't care if he was so long as he didn't feel responsible for her. You see, George, he doesn't understand women. The way some of them scheme and rationalize, the way some of them play on a man's better nature and make him feel responsible for situations they've engineered themselves—Jerome didn't grow up with girls, and he's worked so hard he's never had time to find out what some of us are like. Even if he did understand them, I'm not sure he'd understand Norah Blackwell."

Catherine sat small and erect, hurt and proud, yet her heart-shaped face was serene.

"I'm worried about Norah Blackwell," she said, "and not for any of the reasons people believe. I'm not going to pretend I like her. I'm not going to pretend he hasn't hurt me horribly on account of her. No, I'm not noble at all. But George, none of this matters compared to one thing. That girl is mentally unbalanced."

"I think she's unhappy and intense, but would you say that—"

Again she looked at me calmly: "She's lethally attractive, George."

"I don't think she is at all."

Catherine smiled; she smiled almost pityingly at me.

"To a man like Jerome she's one of the most fatal women I could possibly imagine. She looks so soft and gentle, and at the same time she's apparently very good at her work—which is almost his work. She's unfortunate. She wants to better herself —indeed she does! She hero-worships him, and he's so terribly insecure."

"Jerome insecure!"

"More than you'll ever be. And he doesn't even know it. He's too proud. Or—no, it's not even that. Underneath he's too desperate." Catherine took a deep breath and sighed. "If only Norah Blackwell was not so noble-minded!"

"I could think of nothing to say and just looked at her.

"I don't under-rate her, George. Not for a minute. Quite possibly she may love him, though I know he'll never be able to love her for long. I don't think he ever did, really. I don't think he does now. But one thing I do know—she'll cling. She'll make him feel responsible. He's not a light man, George. He's still religious underneath. He's never done anything like this before, that I know. If he had, he'd have told me. He can't stand anything undercover. He has a compulsion to confess. Oh George, what a winter this has been, what a winter!"

"Catherine!"

"Don't feel sorry for me like that! Don't let me do things to you!"

"All right. I won't."

"This girl—if only she schemed *consciously*. But I don't think she does. I'm not even sure she arranged a situation for him. Perhaps it just happened. He was tired, I was sick, with flu, they looked at each other, they happened to be alone, and he exploded. But that look in her eyes—she'll cling, George. With the best motives in the world she could ruin him. And on top of it all she's a communist who's all in favor of him going to Spain, and I'm not a communist and that makes him feel alone with me at the very time when he shouldn't. I could help him with Norah. I could help him and save his pride, too. But this other thing is too much. And one thing more, George—I believe that at bottom Norah Blackwell is a suicidal type, and I believe Jerome knows it and is scared to death."

Again we were silent and the rest of the room with its political talk might not have existed for us.

"Conscience is such an awful thing, and he has such an awful conscience," she said. "I've failed him so badly. I've battened on him too much."

"How can you say that?"

"Because it's true. I made him my whole life."

"There's also Sally."

"Yes, bless her and thank God." She smiled with rueful bravery. "I've said such hateful things in my own mind about Norah Blackwell and I loathe myself for it. About Jerome, too, and of course he senses it. So Spain becomes an escape for him."

"I'm sure it's more than that."

"Yes." Her face suddenly looked older. "Yes, it *is* more than that. What he told you about killing Germans in the war was all too real. He has that terribly on his conscience. He thinks that in this Spanish war he has a chance to make recompense by saving life. Oh conscience—it really does make cowards of us all! George, George, I'm so frightened for him! If he goes to Spain the communists will capture him for good. His home means more to him that most people will ever guess. This girl can't begin to understand that. She sees me only as a partial invalid holding him down. Yes, but I also keep his home. This foolish girl! How I wish she'd never been born!"

Suddenly I couldn't stand it and got to my feet.

"I think I'd better go," I said. "I think I'd better go up to the hospital and see how Shatwell's doing."

The April air tasted delicious as I walked up the steep slope of the city, the starlight filtering down through the bare trees, and reached the hospital where Jerome worked. It was late for visitors, but nobody paid any attention when I went up in the automatic elevator to the floor where the sunroom was. The convalescent patients were all in their beds and the hospital was very quiet. Windows were open in the sunroom and the cool air stole in sweet and clean. The lights were turned low and in the far corner I saw the shadows of two men, one lying back in a chair and the other hunched forward talking to him. I recognized them as Shatwell and Jerome, and Jerome was talking.

"She's going to be all right." Jerome was saying, "and so are you."

Shatwell had apparently broken down, for I heard him sobbing.

"This does you no discredit, old man," I heard Jerome say, and his voice would have healed almost anyone. "You've had a hard life—the hardest any man could have—and of course it's not been easy to bear."

"Hard!" I heard Shatwell, his Englishness entirely collapsed, almost sob. "I've been worthless. I'm not fit to live. I've failed at everything."

"No," said Jerome, "you have not."

"You don't know about me, Doctor."

"I know the only thing that matters about you. You're a kind man, Mr. Shatwell."

"Does that matter?"

"It matters far more than you can ever guess. Oh, it's not easy for anyone not to be able to do what his society expects. It's to your credit you failed in the English colonies. A man like you was bound to, for a simple reason. You were too kind. Now"—Jerome stood up—"come with me and I'll give you a sedative, and then you'll sleep and wake up a new man."

Jerome saw me as they passed on the way out, but Shatwell did not. He walked unsteadily, and smelling whisky I guessed he had been drinking pretty heavily to deaden the pain of his anxiety. I waited, for Jerome had made a gesture indicating that he would return, which he did after ten minutes.

"Well," he said, and his voice sounded tired, "it was the only thing to do. There were indications of septicemia and if we'd waited there wouldn't have been much chance."

"Is everything all right now?"

"Yes, everything is fine so far as she's concerned. How are things at home?"

I made no answer and was aware of him searching my face in the shadows.

"Has Kate been talking to you?" he asked in that abrupt way he sometimes had of striking through to a main point.

"I don't suppose it matters if I say that she has."

He put his hand on my forearm and pressed it: "I'm sorry, George. I'm so sorry I—"

I said nothing because there was nothing to say.

"The weakest excuse a man can give is that he can't help himself. But what else can I say but that? For sometimes I can't."

There was a kind of despair in his voice; not self-loathing but despair at his own helplessness against inner forces.

"Are you in love with Norah Blackwell?" I forced myself to say.

"In love?" He shrugged. "It all started with my trying to help her. She was confused. She's never had much of a chance."

"She's also an attractive girl."

"Yes. Especially to a man of imagination."

"I think Catherine understands that."

His voice changed. "But she doesn't understand the meaning of Spain and I can't make her see my side of it at all. If I didn't adore Kate—if I didn't worship her—" He turned away and then back again. "These people"—a sweep of his hand toward Montreal—"these people think I'm a Red because I want to help the Spanish Loyalists. My God, how stupid can they be! I'm not a

revolutionary. I see a thing that has to be done—like tonight—
and I do it. It gets damned lonely bucking the current all the
time." His eyes stared into mine. "Have you the slightest idea
how lucky you are, not being born with my temperament?"

Below us the city shimmered in its lights, around us the hospital
was still. The sweet, gentle air of the April evening kept coming
in.

Jerome, motionless and massive in the shadows, was silent for
nearly a minute.

Then he said: "If I'd been raised like you and Kate maybe I
wouldn't feel the way I do about all this. But do you know,
George—it's always seemed to me an incredible privilege to
belong to civilization."

I said nothing.

"You people take it for granted. I don't. One more big war
and it can go so fast. A life can go so fast. And when it's gone?"

He lifted his hand and shrugged. A moment later he began
talking again in a soft, gentle voice.

"In my work I often have to see old men die. They could live
if—if they were younger. It's as simple as that. Old men are run-
ning our civilization now. Men like Rodgers. Well-meaning
men, but old and tired. They want to be left in peace. They hope
if they look the other way the tiger will eat somebody else."
He hesitated. "I understand Kate better than she knows. I under-
stand how hard it's been for her. With that heart of hers, of
course she wants to be left in peace." Another pause. "But unless
fascism is stopped in Spain, she won't be. There'll be a war we'll
probably lose. I know that's what fascism is. It's not political
at all, it's simply the organization of every murderous impulse
in the human being."

He got up and I rose with him, and for a moment longer he
brooded out over the city.

"George, I'm not clever. Maybe I'm wrong in this, but I really
believe it. The old countries which gave us our civilization are
tired of being civilized. But people like me, people born on the
fringes, we really care. When I grew up in Halifax"—he turned
and looked at me with a shy small smile—"do you know what I
used to dream about? I used to dream of a city on top of a hill
—Athens perhaps. It was white and it was beautiful, and it was

a great privilege to enter it. I used to dream that if I worked hard all my life, and tried hard all my life, maybe some day I'd be allowed within its gates. And now I see the fascists besieging that city and a handful of Spanish peasants holding out inside. They're dying for lack of medical care. So what is my duty? Tell me that—what is my duty?"

Chapter II

IN MY years of work as a political commentator I have come to a conclusion which shocks some of my friends who think of politics as a rational occupation. I believe that most international crises are like gigantic mystery plays in which obscure and absolutely irrational passions are handled by politicians, and viewed by the public, in a form of ritual akin to primitive religious rites. Hardly anything anyone says or thinks in a time of political crisis is likely to be rational or a representation of the facts. The crisis is almost never about the outward things with which it professes to concern itself. Also no political crisis ever blows up quickly. It matures underground for years and months, the chemical ingredients are various and many. So it is within a nation, a human group or a city, and it often happens that the fulminate which fires the explosion is something nobody notices. We forget how in those days Spain was the stage on which a multitude of passions met. The big war which followed—very possibly because the powers refused to face what Spain meant— has made most of us forget what the very mention of the Spanish Civil War used to do to people's minds. It was the fulminate to so many conflicting fears and hopes that it caused explosions thousands of miles away from Madrid and Barcelona.

The night after Jerome operated on Shatwell's widow it caused an explosion in Montreal, and when it was over the newspapers pretended to be astonished that such an affair could happen in the city. But there was no reason why they should have been astonished, for the ingredients to make that particular explosion had been there for years.

My own part in the affair began quietly enough. Around noon

the phone in my parents' flat rang and I discovered Arthur
Lazenby on the other end of the line.

"I suppose you know tonight's the night when Jerome intro-
duces this Spanish tank officer?" Arthur said. "Are you going?"

"I'd been thinking of it."

"Then let's eat some spaghetti first and go together."

Over our supper Lazenby talked with more excitement than I
had ever heard from him. He looked lean, hungry and fanatical,
something was on fire in him, but in a singular way he seemed
happy and fulfilled. The successful, middle-aged Lazenby I know
now has a dead face, but not the young one of that evening.

"There's going to be trouble tonight," he said over our coffee.

"What kind of trouble?"

"You remember that priest who stopped the Loyalist priest
from speaking this winter?"

"I know who he is. Isn't that the time they had to hire a hotel
suite and then the management was unable to get them out
legally and turned out the lights to stop the meeting?"

"No, that was another meeting and another Spaniard. This
priest orders his students to break up all meetings in favor of
the Loyalists. He tells the priest-ridden fools the Loyalists are
anti-Christ. You wait—there'll be trouble tonight."

The Mayor had evidently come to the same conclusion, for
when we reached the hall we found police all over the place. They
were stolidly good-natured in the way of most Montreal cops, but
as we went in we had to pass between two men in plain clothes
whose eyes were very sharp indeed.

"The R.C.M.P.," said Lazenby.

Inside the hall the atmosphere was electric because the com-
munists had packed the house. There was a solid bloc of them
in the middle, and they were ominously silent and disciplined.
The hall filled up and there was no hint of trouble except for
this unaccountable air of tension. Then half a dozen extra-large
cops came in and posted themselves at the doors, where they stood
impassively surveying the house.

Suddenly there was a loud, organized hissing and the cry: "The
Cossacks!"

It sounded so foreign I was startled, and yet I should not have
been. Most of the communists that night were Jewish; some had

been born in Poland and Russia, and those who had not were the sons of parents who had emigrated to escape the pogroms. A considerable Jewish quarter had slowly emerged between the French and English sections of the city, and the depression had hit the Jews—at least in their minds—harder than it had hit any other racial group in the city.

I want to be clear about this. To me the Jews are the senior people of civilization and it annoys me that I am unable to say that some of my best friends are Jews without being accused of sneering at a people whose tradition I reverence. However, some of my best friends are, and one of them tells me that it is very easy for a Jew who leaves the synagogue, especially for one who left it in the 1930s, to become a communist. In Montreal quite a few had done this and had broken their parents' hearts, and the guilt they felt for having done so had made them all the more bitter. By no means all the communists in Montreal in those days were Jews, but I think it a fact that it was the Jews who provided the passion. Who could blame them? For they knew, while the French and English blocs did not, exactly what Hitler was preparing for all of us.

"The Cossacks!" the cry rang out again. "The Cossacks!"

When the platform party came out the hissing changed to applause, the applause to foot-stamping and the foot-stamping to cheers. The first man out looked like a middle-aged shoe clerk, the second like a tallyman on the docks, the third was the Spanish tank officer and the fourth was Jerome. The Spaniard had a long scar down a swarthy cheek, he was lean and fanatic and as proud as a matador. The central bloc in the hall broke into the *Internationale* and looking down the aisle I saw the mild faces of a pair of Presbyterian ministers staring in surprise. The platform party stood at attention to the workers' hymn and all but Jerome raised their clenched fists. Then Jerome, seeing the others doing it, did the same. The hymn ended and silence fell with a crash.

The shoe-clerk in a toneless voice introduced Jerome as a great doctor, a great scientist, a great friend of the working class. He spoke as though Jerome was already a member of the Communist party, and as I listened I thought of what Jack Christopher had said about Jerome allowing himself to be used, and I felt cold and guilty. For that Jerome was being used now was obvious. The excitement of the crowd had worked on him. His own impetuosity, his own generous, reckless way of throwing himself into a moment and responding to the emotions of others—all this sucked him out of any restraint he might otherwise have had. He said things that night he would not have uttered had he kept his head. He sounded to an untrained ear more like a communist than the shoe-clerk had done, and at every point he made the crowd barked like dogs.

The Spaniard rose and for three-quarters of an hour he spoke in halting French all the more moving because of a certain grim naiveté in his manner and choice of words. He told us about horrors he had seen in Spain. He spoke of the murder of his parents by the fascists, of the hope of the Spanish people had had before the Moors came in under Franco, and the passion of the Spanish war reached us even through the communist jargon he employed. He was arrogant, but in a way he was noble. I could not like him; I had the impression that if he ever achieved power he would be merciless. But he was obviously brave, he was fanatical, and he was literal. It was my impression that he had not been a communist for a long time and had become one only because the communists seemed to offer him hope. He ended his speech, raised his clenched fist and received a standing ovation. Then the central bloc, as though on a word of command, broke into the marching song of the German detachment of the International Brigade. It was called *Freiheit* and when they sang it in German it sounded like a Teutonic paean. They were still singing when the riot began.

The riot started with a ripe fruit which sailed over the heads of the crowd and squelched on the wall just behind Jerome's head. Jerome came to his feet with his bulldog jaw outthrust. Excited and stirred by the Spaniard, he had reverted to the primitive and if I ever saw a man thirsting for a fight it was Jerome at that moment. The Spaniard stood immobile and stately with folded arms, the shoe-clerk smirked and looked well pleased, but Jerome stepped forward to the edge of the platform and his very aspect was a challenge announcing that if there was anyone who wanted trouble, he was ready to oblige him. I turned and saw the black berets of French-Canadian students crowding in and the surge of the people in the back. Then I saw berets running down the central aisle toward the platform.

"The Cossacks have let the fascists in!" one of the communists screamed.

Fists began swinging and I heard French voices crying *"Sales Juifs"* while others responded with *"sauvage"*, "fascist" and "peasoup." The flash bulbs of newspaper reporters began popping and a body of cops following the students down the aisle began to take control of the spectators. Three black berets climbed the platform and made for the speakers and Jerome, his eyes glittering, his body moving craftily despite his limp, slipped a punch and landed a solid right on a student's jaw. The student was knocked clean off the platform and disappeared and Jerome's eyes gleamed with joy. More students milled up and Jerome was in the center of a tangle of them, doing all right for himself, and then the police went up to the platform and began pulling the fighters apart.

"Let's get out of here!"

It was Lazenby talking and pointing to the cops with one hand and to a side door with another. He disappeared while I stood where I was, wondering what to do. By now the police had the riot under control and solid blue uniforms were marshalling the crowd from the center aisle to the side doors. I was pushed out in the mêlée and found myself next to Professor John David, who said excitedly that it was quite a night. In the street there were several paddy wagons, a crowd of loafers and about twenty cops, and everyone looked quiet and orderly except for one character who was being pushed by a pair of enormous cops into the back of a paddy wagon. His mouth was opening and closing very fast and I heard him scream that if they didn't let him go he would sue them for false arrest. The cops threw him in, closed the door on him and left him there.

I waited around thinking about Catherine and feeling shocked and rotten and wondering what to do. Now that the communists had made their demonstration, they were quiet and orderly. A few of them stood around, but most of them moved off singly or in small groups in an easterly direction. I saw no sign of Lazenby and forgot about him, and after a while I went to a cop and asked him what had happened to the platform party. He gave me a stolid look and did not answer. Then I walked around to the back of the building and saw a police automobile drawn up before the back door with one cop behind the wheel, and two more standing outside talking to a trio of students in black berets. I asked one of them in French what had happened to the platform party, but he did not answer. I waited about four minutes and then the door opened and they all came out: the shoe clerk, the tallyman, the Spaniard and Jerome, and directly behind them was a woman I recognized as Norah Blackwell. Jerome had a mouse under his left eye and was laughing as though he had enjoyed himself. Norah came up to him and took his arm, Jerome gave her a quick kiss, then all of them piled into the police car and were driven off. This happened in less than thirty seconds.

"What are you doing?" I asked the sergeant in French. "Arresting the speakers?"

He evidently thought I was a reporter, for he replied with courtesy.

"No, monsieur, we are protecting the speakers."

There was nothing more to see or do at this hall, so I walked away, and as I came around the corner I saw a familiar figure ahead of me, quickened my step and overtook Adam Blore.

"Were you at that goddamned meeting?" he asked me.

"I certainly was."

"Did you ever hear such crap in your life?" He let out a sneering laugh. "Well, was I right or wasn't I about Martell and that little Blackwell bitch? He's fallen for her like a tree in a swamp. Where are you going?"

"Home, I guess."

"I'm looking for a woman. There's nothing like a show like tonight's to serve as an aphrodisiac for some of these little puritan girls. Down on Dorchester Street it would cost me two bucks, but with them all I have to do is say I hate Franco."

We parted company and I turned in the direction of the university and walked until I ended in the little street where Jerome and Catherine lived. There was no light in the living room, but knowing Catherine was home I went up the steps and rang the bell. When nothing happened I walked through the tradesmen's lane to the back and looked up at the bedroom windows. They were all dark. Catherine might be asleep or she might be lying awake, but with all of those windows dark it was certain Jerome had not come home.

Leaving the quiet area of the university under a rising last-quarter moon, I walked down to St. Catherine and saw by a clock that it was only ten minutes after ten. I walked slowly along in the streaming crowds of St. Catherine Street on a Saturday night: the unemployed shuffling with the noise of a river, the young couples with petty jobs emerging arm in arm from the movie houses, the trams clanging, the lights glaring, the popcorn smell on the corner of Peel, the vendors selling the bulldog edition of the *Gazette,* the grit and the torn scraps of newspaper and the throb of downtown Montreal after dark. I boarded a westbound tram and when I reached my parents' flat in N.D.G. they were both up and surprised to see me home so soon. My mother inquired about dear Catherine and my father, happy in his shirt-sleeves after several hours at his work bench, produced a telegram he had received that morning.

"They're going to take my can opener," he said, and his sheep dog's face beamed.

"Isn't it wonderful?" said my mother.

"Who's going to take what can opener?" I asked, and both their faces fell.

"But George, you know all about it. Father showed you his can opener months ago."

"Here, George, read this." And Father handed me the telegram.

I read it and learned that the Acme Home Industrial Development Corporation of Buffalo, N.Y., was at least interested in Father's can opener.

"This time I decided to make something simple and indispensable—something everyone wants," said Father, smiling. "I got the idea from reading about King C. Gillette in a magazine. You know, the razor man. He had a theory. Invent something which becomes indispensable to a man the moment he has it, but something which wears out quickly and has to be replaced. Now take this can opener. Think of the number of times you've been on a picnic and used the old fashioned thing that jigs and jags, and you end up by cutting yourself and leaving the top of the can like the edge of a saw. Wait—I'll show you the thing itself."

Father darted into his bedroom and returned with a gadget

that looked like an old-fashioned, medium-sized jack-knife. He opened it up and it turned into the kind of can opener you now see screwed into kitchen walls, but with a difference: this one was anchored to a tripod which could be held onto the ground.

"If you don't mind me saying so, Father, this thing seems a little flimsy."

"But that's the point. It's meant to be flimsy. It will break somewhere, or bend somewhere, after a month or two. But during that time it will work, and it will carve the tops off cans as neatly as King C. Gillette's blue blade shaves off beards, and once a family has owned one, it will never be without one again."

Suddenly I felt exhausted. I looked up from the sofa, handed the gadget back and said: "That's wonderful, Father."

"You really think so, George? I value your opinion, old man. You're not pretending?"

"Of course I think it's wonderful."

"I've always known your father was wonderful," Mother said. "And I've always known he'd be recognized."

"What happened to that crossbow?" I asked him.

Father laughed. "Oh, that! When I became a man I put away childish things."

He embraced his wife and kissed her as though he had just married her; I said good-night and made ready for bed.

The next day was Sunday and I went to the Martell's apartment just before noon and found Catherine in a housecoat. She sent Sally upstairs on some pretext so that we could be alone.

"I suppose you were there last night?"

I nodded.

"I wasn't, of course. I haven't gone to one of his meetings in months. Perhaps I should have gone to them all. Perhaps that's been the trouble."

"How is Jerome today?"

"I wouldn't know. I haven't seen him."

"You mean, he didn't come home?"

"He called up around midnight to say he was all right and that he had to look after this Spaniard. He told me to sleep and get my rest. I hardly slept all night."

"I came here after the meeting," I said.

"I thought it might have been you who rang the doorbell."

She got up and rearranged some glass objects on her mantel-piece and spoke to me with her back turned.

"My father was a great reader, and when I was a girl I remember one of his favorite poems was by an ancient Greek. Something about the turn of a dragonfly's wing."

"Like the turn of a dragonfly's wing, so rapid the change," I said.

"So you know it, too."

"Is there anything I can do, Catherine?"

Still with her back to me, she said: "Only give me a normal heart. Only give me enough strength to be a normal woman."

I said nothing and stared at the floor.

"I've been reading the Bible lately," she said. "Do you know the Ninetieth Psalm?"

"No."

"Nobody ever reads it any more, I suppose. They should. 'Thou turnest man to destruction and sayest: return, ye children of men.' Yes indeed all our days now are consumed in somebody's anger. Well, George—" she turned and faced me and her whole face was pain, and at the same time beautiful. "I think you'd better go now."

"Catherine!" But I got to my feet.

"Yes, I think you'd better go, for he may be home any time now." Her large eyes looked into mine. "Was the Blackwell girl there last night?"

I would have liked to lie, but it was useless to lie to Catherine, so I nodded.

"Was she there in her capacity as a communist, or as a woman?"

"As both, I'd say."

I told her briefly about the scene on the stage and about seeing Jerome and the platform party drive away.

"She could be very attractive and appealing," Catherine said, "especially to a man like Jerome who always wants to help people. He's spoken to me about her quite frankly. He'd like me to like her. Of course he would, poor dear." An elliptical smile. "Men seem so strange to me sometimes. Probably we seem equally strange to them. However—from the way she's behaving and from what he's told me—I'm afraid he'll rue the day he looked at her, for she can't be judged normally. I tell you, she's an unbalanced personality, and I think Jerome must have been tired of her a few minutes after he first made love to her. If only he wouldn't feel responsible for her! But she'll see to it that he does."

I lit a cigarette and looked out the window and for a while neither of us spoke.

"Well," she said finally, "if he must go to Spain, then he must go to Spain. I know he's sincere in that, and I wish this girl were out of the picture for the sake of our dignity. People will say he's going on account of her. He tells me a personal life doesn't matter in a time when millions are going to be killed. I suppose he's right, but I'm a woman and a personal life is all I can understand."

Then she said very simply: "Jerome and I loved each other too much. I haven't been able to rest him. He needs rest and this winter I failed. One gets so tired of hurting and being hurt. One gets so tired of thinking."

I looked out the window at a street empty save for a cat washing its face on the curb.

"I loathe that girl for what she's done to our dignity," Catherine said. Then she shrugged: "But Jerome is unconscious of this, so why should I be? He's put me into an impossible position, and he doesn't seem to realize it. He's put me into a position where I can't help him. If I tell him the truth about that girl—at least what I think is the truth—what else will I seem to be but a jealous woman? How can I tell him to stop feeling guilty to her when he also feels guilty to me?"

"Is he as mixed up as that?"

"I've been badly mixed up myself, so how can I blame anyone for being the same? I feel useless. I seem to be one of the few people you know who distrusts everything about the communists. Lots of people join them because they're idealists, but the real communists hate too much. I can't accept Jerome's view of them. Now—on account of this girl, who is also a communist—I can't even talk to him about *that*. Women can be frightful deliberately, but men can be frightful out of sheer chivalry."

She got up and with her head held so high that for all her small stature she seemed tall, she said: "In spite of all this I'm going to make one more attempt to talk to the silly man. But

I'm not going to pretend I see anything good in the communists."

She went to the door and turned: "Now George, you'd better go, for he'll be back soon."

Bumblingly I said: "I'm sure he didn't spend the night with Norah. I'm sure he just went off with the speakers and got talking and didn't come home."

Her smile made me feel like a child: "I know the difference between love and sex, George. And I know that what he feels for Norah Blackwell—apart from a normal desire—is pity and not love."

The following Monday morning, eating breakfast beside McNish in the Waterloo dining hall with my back to the admirals of the Red and my face to the admirals of the Blue, I learned from the morning paper that Saturday night's riot had outraged opinion in Montreal, and that the real cause of the outrage had not been the Spaniard, the students or the communists in the audience, but the presence of Jerome and the role he had played.

It is a curious city, Montreal, and in this story I keep returning to the fact that it is. Strangers never understand its inner nature, and immigrant families, even from other parts of Canada, can live here two generations without coming to know it in their bones. I am absolutely certain that Montreal is the subtlest and most intricate city in North America. With her history she could not have been otherwise and survived, for here the French, the Scotch and the English, over two centuries, have been divided on issues which ruin nations and civilizations, yet have contrived to live in outward harmony. This is no accident. They understand certain rules in their bones.

As a born Montrealer, I had been startled and shocked the night of Jerome's meeting even though I had gone to it in sympathy with its apparent aims. Now when I read the account of it in the Monday morning paper I trembled for Jerome and Catherine. This newspaper account could not possibly make a difference to the shoe clerk, the tallyman or the mob which had shouted "Here come the Cossacks!" They were outsiders. But Jerome, no matter how much an outsider he might have felt himself to be, could not be dismissed as one because he was involved in the most respected institution the city has, the medical profession which has been great here since the days of Osler. By virtue of his position at the Beamis Memorial, Jerome had been at least half-way inside the Montreal Thing whether he wanted to be or not. Had he been a born Montrealer he would have realized what he had done, but he was not a born Montrealer and I was sure that even now he did not.

The press that morning had done something it seldom does here: it had featured a local riot. This I knew to be the result of a deliberate editorial decision to declare war on Jerome personally. Not only did they make a front page story of the riot; most of page three was covered with pictures of it, and the pictures made me feel cold all over. The caption under one of them was: "Dr. Martell Gives the Clenched Fist Salute." A lot of people at the meeting had given the clenched fist salute, and Jerome himself had given it too, but I remembered the instant when this particular picture was taken and the reason why Jerome's fist was up and clenched was that a rioter was making for him and he was making to hit the rioter on the jaw. In another picture the stage was a confusion of policemen, students and speakers, and in the middle of that mêlée was Jerome again. This picture was even more damning than the first, for there was something absolutely sordid and undignified about it. Jerome's eyes shone with the joy of battle, beside him the morose face of the Spanish tank officer looked sinister, and the last straw was Norah Blackwell. This picture, taken after I had left the hall, showed Norah clinging to Jerome's arm with a face rapt and staring at his. How she had got there I could not know, but I guessed she must have listened to the speeches from the wings and come out to stand by her hero when the fighting began.

Worse still was the story on the front page. It was under the by-line of a man called Irving Dublin, whom I knew to be a crypto-communist, and Dublin had worded his piece to make it appear to everyone that Jerome was not merely a humanitarian doctor with an interest in the Spanish Loyalists, but an actual member of the communist party. I realized that Dublin had done this deliberately in order still further to isolate Jerome and drive him all the way over into the arms of the communists.

I turned to the editorial page and found what I expected: a

scandalized sermon asking how it was possible for a man with the educational advantages and public position of Dr. Martell to associate himself with such a disgraceful affair. And when I read all this I felt guilty and lacking, for I had known Montreal and I should have warned him of the danger he was entering. I should have listened to Jack Christopher, who also understood Montreal, and I should have recognized my own responsibility in even tacitly encouraging Jerome to behave as he did.

I had to wait a fortnight before I learned the details of the aftermath, for I was held at Waterloo on weekend duty. Every day I searched the papers, but they told me nothing. Their silence was also typical of the Montreal technique in an affair of this sort: having fired their broadside the editors let the matter sleep. They printed a few letters expressing horror at Jerome's behavior, but none in support of him, and then they let the whole thing drop.

When I finally reached town, the first person I called was Jack Christopher, who was at home and asked me to drop around. Somehow the details of his story don't seem to matter, but here they are.

Dr. Rodgers, returning to the city from Detroit on the Monday morning after the riot, read about it while eating his breakfast on the train. It would be presumptuous of me to guess what the old man felt, but I can't believe that his feelings were simple. He may have felt a bitter pleasure because Jerome had finally delivered himself into his hands, but he came from an old Montreal family, he was the son of a judge, in his youth he had worked under Sir William Osler and he was a patrician by nature and training. It is impossible for me to believe that a man like Dr. Rodgers could ever have felt it necessary to prove his worth to Jerome or to anyone else in Canada. He was certainly outraged, and he may even have reproached himself for not having taken steps about Jerome long before.

But this is guess work; I never knew Dr. Rodgers and what I have is hearsay.

According to Jack Christopher, the old man did not reach the hospital until mid-morning, and by then Sir Rupert Irons, the chairman of the board, had twice called to speak to him. Rodgers knew what Irons wanted, and it was typical of him that even at this moment he ignored Irons' request that he get in touch with him the moment he arrived. In Rodgers' book a man like Irons, for all his wealth, was a parvenu. The old surgeon went to his office, read his correspondence, dictated a few letters and then made his customary rounds.

It was in the course of these that he discovered that on the night before the riot Jerome had operated on Mrs. Moffat. He at once consulted with Dr. Crawford, who had passed his kidney stone but was still resting in one of the hospital beds. After learning the details from Crawford, he returned to his office, read a report of the case and passed out the word that he would be pleased to see Dr. Martell at the Doctor's earliest convenience. As Jerome was then in the operating room, the two men did not meet until nearly noon.

With his capacity for sensing the hurt in another person, Jerome immediately understood that the old surgeon had been deeply humiliated by the Moffat case. What he had done or failed to do in the first operation I don't know, but it was obvious that he had slipped up somewhere.

Jerome, with the quick kindness which was the other side of his quick pugnacity, made the first move.

"Please don't concern yourself about this case," he said. "It's a thing that could have happened to anybody. I've had a thing like that happen to me once."

This remark, Jack told me, was the most unfortunate he could have made under the circumstances to an older and more experienced man.

The old doctor looked at the younger one, hated him, and said: "Since this case has been taken out of my hands, we will please not discuss it any further."

"But it's not been taken out of your hands." Jerome gave his gentlest and most sincere smile. "I just filled in because there was an emergency."

"We will not discuss it."

Then Dr. Rodgers picked up the morning paper, jogged it across the desk to Jerome and examined the younger man's face.

"Yes," Jerome said, "I've read it, too."

Rodgers continued to regard him, and Jerome, sensing implacable hostility, flared out.

"What I do outside the hospital is my own business, Dr. Rodgers. I don't happen to believe that the medical profession is a priesthood. That meeting was concerned with the most important subject in the world today. Look what happened in Germany. The men of science, the professors, the medical men —they were all so correctly professional they did nothing at all. They left what resistance there was to a handful of workers and unemployed. And now look what's happened to them."

The old man raised his eyebrows. "This is not Germany, this is Montreal. We have no Nazis here."

"No?"

"The name of this hospital, according to my count, appears five times in this morning's paper. I'm afraid that what you do in your spare time has a great deal of connection with this hospital."

"It wasn't us who started the riot." Suddenly Jerome began talking like a schoolboy. "It was a crowd of students duped by that fascist priest. It was a perfectly orderly meeting till they came in and started fighting."

After a moment's appraising silence, the old man put his finger down on the account of Jerome's speech.

"Did you actually say the things reported here?"

"I can't remember every word I said, but what's the matter with what's reported here? If you'd take your blinders off, you'd see it's true."

"You say it was an orderly meeting when you admit you made these statements? These are generalizations of the wildest kind. These are seditious accusations. These are statements no man of science should ever make anywhere. I shouldn't be surprised if they bring you within range of the courts."

Jerome looked at him and said: "Do you think you can stop fascism by closing your eyes and pretending it's not there?"

The old man looked back at him: "We will not argue, please. There have been quite enough generalizations. We will confine ourselves to some facts." His finger came down on one of the pictures. "Is it a fact that this young woman has been a nurse in this hospital?"

"Yes, she's Mrs. Blackwell."

"May I ask what she was doing in the middle of all this?"

"Isn't that her business?"

The old man leaned back in his chair and surveyed Jerome.

"What's come over you? You have often been rude and aggressive, but I put that down to your temperament and possibly to your background. You were a promising surgeon, and that was enough for me." A pause. "I have great respect for your wife and I have known her family for years." Another pause. "I am an old fashioned man, as you have been heard to point out more than once in the corridors of this establishment, even to some of the housemen. I don't believe in washing dirty linen in public. I am even prepared to close my eyes to behavior I deplore so long as it does not expose the parties concerned to vulgar gossip. But"—again his finger came down on the photograph—"you have not only displayed your dirty linen in public, you have actually flaunted it in front of a newspaper camera." He stared at Jerome with his ascetic face, and Jerome flushed. "This particular sample of dirty linen, Dr. Martell, will no longer be associated with this hospital."

Jerome jumped to his feet: "Take that back, Dr. Rodgers."

The old man regarded him calmly and said: "No, I will not take it back. It was a considered statement. I will be even more explicit. I will inform you that Mrs. Blackwell has been discharged from the nursing staff of this hospital. She will probably find it very difficult to attach herself to the staff of any other."

"It's not her fault. You're unjust to her. She needs the job to live. She got mixed up in this riot the same way I did. What has she done wrong?"

The old man looked at Jerome and said: "I have received word that Sir Rupert Irons wishes me to get in touch with him immediately. I can guess what he wishes to talk about and what he will demand. So far I have not got in touch with him." A pause. "I am an old-fashioned man, Dr. Martell, as I have already mentioned. It is contrary to my principles that any hospital, school or university should have its policies and actions dictated by business men in any matter which lies outside a business man's competence." Another pause. "I dislike you, Doctor Martell, and for a reason which has not occurred to you. People like you place men of responsibility in an intolerable position. I have protected you for two years—not for your sake but **for**

the sake of the principle. But you continue to make it intoler-
able for me. Moreover, you do this wilfully. You do it because
you enjoy making trouble."

"That's absurd!" said Jerome.

"Is it? Please examine the situation more closely. If I discharge
you from the staff, I will be vilified by you and by all your com-
munist friends. You will say I am part of the capitalist conspiracy.
You will say—and you will be right—that your work here has
been satisfactory, and you will add that your private life is your
own. But this propaganda"—again the finger tapped the news-
paper—"aims at the destruction of the entire social order. Do
you deny it?"

"Of course I deny it. Do you think—"

The old man waved his hand: "Medicine and science are
sacred to me. They should be to you. No medical man or man
of science ought to touch this—this vulgar filth."

Jerome sat in silence and after a while he said: "I will not
vilify you if you demand my resignation. Instead I offer you
my resignation. I'm sorry, for I was happy here. I think I did
good work. I'm grateful for many things you've done for me.
I never wanted to be your enemy, but you live in another world
from mine, and I think mine is the real one."

The old man sat still, then shrugged: "We might have been
friends. But as we are not friends, I will not shake hands with
you now. I deplore your character and your behavior and your
principles—or lack of them. As a surgeon you might have had
a great career, but you will never have one now. I accept your
resignation and I will inform the board it was given by you
freely without my asking for it. You have ruined yourself."

That was the story told me by Jack Christopher, and when he
ended I asked: "Has he really ruined himself?"

"He certainly has in Montreal. He'll never get another hos-
pital appointment here after this. He's a surgeon, and a surgeon
without a hospital—he's ruined himself all over the country."

"What will he do?"

"I can only guess, and I don't like what I'm guessing."

"What do you mean by that?"

"Do I have to spell it out? Where else can be go but to the

people who've captured him? That damned girl! I could poison her, for she's poisoned him."

"Jack," I said, "I don't think that girl has anything important to do with it. He'd have been mixed up in this anyway."

He said wearily: "I suppose you're right. But that's not what people will say. And he did let himself get mixed up with her. I don't think anything like that happened before, but it might have. There's a lot of animal in him."

"There's a lot of animal in any normal man, isn't there?"

Jack said bitterly: "All right, to hell with Norah Blackwell. But this thing that people like you are feeling is like a disease. Jerome's sick with it. What's the matter with you all?" He stopped. "Have you seen Catherine?"

"Not for over a fortnight."

"Neither have I. I hadn't the courage. Do you know where Jerome is?"

"I was going to ask you that."

"I don't know where he is. Catherine went up north to the lake with Sally. She's there now."

"I'll go up tomorrow and see her."

"You'd better borrow my car, then. I have to run down to New York for the weekend and I won't be needing it."

Chapter III

APRIL had turned into May and the world was bright and clear: cool air and warm sun, a powder of buds on the hardwoods, fields skunk-cabbage green against the heavy viridian of spruce and fir, the muscles and bones of the land visible as an athlete's under the light dust of its first verdure. All the waters were cold, and crossing the bridge at Sainte-Rose I saw the wash of the river coming around the northern curve of Montreal Island with eddies as smooth as the backs of enormous jellyfish. It was almost hot under the mid-morning sun and yet the air was cool, only the striking of the sun hot, and further north when I crossed a freshet the white water from the hills had a breath like snow. I drove up into the Laurentians and after a while turned off into a valley, then up over a hairpin bend into a trail embraced by firs and maples until I descended in a pair of brown ruts to the cottage. When I got out of the car there was a sough in the firs and I wished I had been here at dawn when the birds sang. Little waves danced on the lake, ferns had sprung in fiddleheads, trilliums were white stars under the trees and the daffodils Catherine had planted five years ago swayed in the breeze like golden dancers. Looking down the bluff to the shore I saw the red flank of Jerome's beached canoe.

Catherine was alone on the porch in a deck chair staring into the distance.

"George!" she said, and without rising she took my hand and indicated the empty chair beside her.

I sat down and for a long while neither of us tried to talk.

Then she said: "I've been losing myself in this. Look and look. I'm going to start painting in a week or two. I'm going to learn how."

"How do you feel?"

"If I could paint, I feel as if it would never matter how I felt about anything. Jerome is so fond of saying that you must belong to something larger than yourself. So look at all this in front of us. Look at it, George."

Silence, and after a while I murmured the line about one generation passing away, another coming and the earth remaining.

"I don't know about all these big things. Only about the little human specks passing through what I'm looking at now. I never knew before that the earth has bones."

"How are you?" I asked again.

"I'm fine, I think. I lifted too many things yesterday and got too tired, but the Stephensons from down the lake drove Sally and me up and helped us unpack. They were so kind. Jerome used to like them, but they're conservatives, so now of course he doesn't like them. He's still in town. I think he's coming out this afternoon. You know he's resigned from the hospital, I suppose?"

"Jack told me about it last night."

"Poor Jack, he's so upset by all this. He's so perfectly organized, and he's going to be such a good doctor, but he'll never be a Jerome. He just can't spend himself the way Jerome does. He doesn't know how."

There was another long silence and again it was I who broke it.

"Will you be leaving Montreal now?"

"*I* won't be leaving. No, Sally and I will stay in the same old place."

"But Jerome?"

"Well you see, after that meeting he won't be able to practice here any more. The girl played such a charming part in that meeting, didn't she? It was so dignified, that picture of her in the paper. I suppose he'd have gone to Spain anyway, but after that meeting there was no more question about it. He's going all right."

She said it just like that, but the emotion underneath her words was the more ominous because superficially her voice was brittle and bright.

She smiled in a way I cannot describe: "I'm not sure when he leaves, but it will be just as soon as he can complete his arrangements. That includes turning over his old patients to other men."

"Catherine dear—I hate all this."

"So do I. I just loathe all this. But it's what's happening, and if I married a man as impulsive as Jerome, don't you think I should have known all along that something of the kind would happen?"

"He'll come back."

"He says so, of course. This week he's been excited and quite manic. The last time I saw him he reminded me of somebody I knew who joined the Oxford Group. The light on the road to Damascus. For a few days after his scene with Dr. Rodgers he was very depressed, but you know Jerome. The moment he made up his mind what to do next, he bounced up again."

I stared at the bright wilderness and tried to force myself to accept that what I was hearing was real.

"Anyway," I said, "it's just Spain, and the girl has nothing to do with that. She's not going with him, is she?"

"Apparently not," she said. "But she does have a talent for

the undignified, don't you think?" Calmly she went on: "I wish the coming week or fortnight or however long it's going to be were over and done with. Jerome and I have had such wonderful years, and we love each other so much that the time between now and when he goes will be horrid. After that?" A smile. "Sally and I will manage somehow after that. I only hope he'll manage half as well."

Forcing myself to be factual, I asked how she was fixed for money.

"There'll be enough for a while. Jerome says this mess at the hospital means nothing in the long run. He thinks it's cleared the air, as a matter of fact. He calls it a godsend because it's fixed things for him so there is no choice. So off he goes to the Spanish crusade. He's sure the big war will start next year or the year after, and then this mess at the hospital will be forgotten by everyone."

I sat in silence staring at the landscape which stared back: form and color and light and shade, useless to farmers, some of the oldest rock in the world cropping out of it, dark green and light green, ancient, mindless, from everlasting to everlasting without any purpose anyone could possibly understand, but there.

"I don't know what to believe about anything any more," I said.

"Neither do I. It's strange, not knowing what to believe about anything any more. A lot of us will have to get used to it, though."

"He loves you. Of that I'm sure."

"But of course he does. And I love him more than you can understand, for you've never been married. In these years we've signed ourselves on each other, and we both know that. Of course I don't understand him. I suppose I know him better than he knows me, but the more we've lived together, the greater mysteries we've become to each other. He knows me perfectly as a woman, and I know him perfectly as a man, but what is that? Perhaps that's why he's panicked, for panicked he has. At the moment he's not really thinking. He's just moving ahead like a sleepwalker."

"Jack Christopher says it's a disease, this thing he's caught. I know what he means. I nearly caught it myself."

"What fools we've all been, all us clever people. We were so sure we understood. We were so positive we knew all the answers. We're not like the man who built his house on the sand. We're like the man who tore down all the walls of his house in November and then had to face the winter naked. It's so hard to be married. It's so hard to keep on going. It's so hard just to live. Now I suppose we've got to make up the rules as we go along, and one gets so tired doing that. It would have been so much simpler and safer to have kept the old rules."

Sally's voice broke out from under the porch saying she was hungry and Catherine was glad to stop talking and go inside to prepare a lunch. I left the porch and let Sally show me some daffodils swaying in a tiny bed around the corner of the house.

"They're mine," she said. "I planted them last year and Daddy says they're better than Mummy's."

"Well dear, they're certainly lovely daffodils."

"Daddy knows everything. He's coming out this afternoon to be with us. It's such fun being with Daddy."

Jerome did come, arriving in his Pontiac at five-thirty with bright eyes and a strained expression on his tough face. He was surprised to see me and also relieved, for this weekend could hardly have been one he looked forward to. What words had passed between him and Catherine I did not know, but I did know that this tough-looking man was very sensitive and that his antennae were acute.

Catherine was resting upstairs when Jerome arrived and Sally, fresh from her afternoon nap, was playing alone in the woods. Jerome stretched out in the long chair and I sat in the one beside it.

"Did Kate tell you I've decided to go to Spain?"

"Yes."

"All the arrangements are made. My ship sails next Friday. Southampton first, a fortnight in London getting things organized, then a freighter from the London docks to Barcelona."

"Are you joining Bethune's unit?"

He shook his head. "It's probably just as well I'm not, for Beth and me in the same outfit—no, this team will be all British except me. Surgical entirely. For front line service wherever they send us."

In profile he looked very tired, but this bright, tense excitement made his face more arresting than I had ever seen it.

"How long do you plan to be in Spain?"

"For the duration, I suppose. Now, how about a drink?"

He went inside and came out with two glasses.

"The water up here in May is so delicious it's a shame to put whisky into it. But the whisky's good too, and by God, it's become a necessity."

Sipping our drinks we looked out over the lake which now was heavily shadowed along the length of its western shore with the promontories thrusting their outlines far out and deep down, the sun still bright but westerly over the hills. The wind had dropped and in the total silence of the empty north land we heard the musical sigh of a tiny stream coursing through the trees into the lake. Apart from the sound of the stream this stillness in which we sat went all the way north to the Arctic and all the way west to Hudson Bay. A robin swooped down to settle on a patch of manured ground and stood listening for worms.

"I'd like to plant tomorrow," Jerome said. "It always used to make me feel good getting my hands into the dirt in the spring. But what's the use now? Kate loves gardening, she's far better at it than I am, and if I plant she'll try to keep the damned thing up. What a woman. Did you know she's studied botany? But she's too much of a perfectionist, and if I plant that garden —that was part of the trouble, her perfectionism. My God, George, it's not so easy being me."

We were silent for a while and I said: "You're going to miss this place."

He looked sharply around and his eyes misted: "You think I'm a bastard, don't you?"

I shook my head.

"You're in love with Kate and you think I'm deserting her and Sally, don't you?"

"I didn't use that word."

"But you thought it. Like the rest of them, you're enslaved by words. Desert. It sounds very bad. But nobody owns anyone else, and who the hell do you think you are to keep your nose so clean? It's not easy being me. Kate and I have had some good years. Who are you to judge?"

"I'm not judging, Jerome."

"Oh yes, you are. All of you are. Did you ever read a book called *Foxe's Book of Martyrs?*"

I could not follow this jump of his mind and shook my head.

"My father, I mean my foster-father, was the gentlest man I ever knew. He was probably the only genuine Christian I'll ever meet in my life. He used to drink a lot of rum. Some old smuggler down in Halifax, some old man he'd done something for, this old man used to deliver the rum to the rectory in a cask at dead of night. There was always a cask in our basement, and Father used to sneak down at all hours for a nip.

"Now my mother, who was a lovely, gentle, kind woman, deplored this. Father was never exactly drunk, but he was never precisely sober, either. Mother deplored his drinking, but she understood why he had to have his rum. Quite literally that man drank rum for the love of God, for it was only when the rum was in him that he felt close to his God and was sure his God loved him. It wasn't easy being Father, for his own father had given him a hell of a time when he was a boy. Now Mother wasn't a perfectionist. She understood that, and she loved him, and she didn't expect the man she loved to be perfect. She accepted his rum because it was a part of his necessity, and she never nagged or tried to change him, even though the doctor told her he'd probably die of cirrhosis of the liver, which he did, and even though she knew perfectly well that people snickered at him and criticized him because they were narrow-minded bastards who thought it a terrible thing for a clergyman to drink, and even though we were dirt poor in a poor parish, and she knew he'd never get out of it or be preferred on account of his habit, she never tried to change him. She took it, George, she took it."

"And Catherine isn't taking what's in you now—is that what you mean?"

A spasm of pain crossed his face and he looked down at his feet. Then he went on:

"I began by talking about *Foxe's Book of Martyrs*. My father

—this gentle Christian—gave it to me to read when I was thirteen. It's practically a handbook on torture. But it was right that it was written, and it was right that he should have given it to me, because it happens to be true, and to contain a lot of truth about human nature. Those savage priests of the Reformation time pretended that if Christ had died a horrible death on the cross, it was necessary to invent even worse tortures for sinners. As a doctor I know how fiendishly ingenious they were. Well, I used to wake up nights with my hair on end on account of that book. I saw it all. I wondered how any man, knowing what it would cost, could stand up for what he believed. Then came the war, and I saw this absolutely depersonalized butchery for absolutely nothing."

Jerome stopped and stared at me with incandescent eyes.

"Try and understand this—the fascists have brought back torture, and torture calls for martyrs. And what else is fascism but the logical product of the capitalist system?"

"What do you mean—torture calls for martyrs?"

"Simply this. Unless a man is able to stand up and look the torturer in the eye and say, 'I'm not afraid,' torture becomes the way of the world. It's as simple as that."

"Is it really as simple as that?"

"No." He shook his head impatiently. "No, because underneath it all is the plain economic exploitation of a rotten world. The communists are the only people who understand that. How can you pretend they're not one hundred percent right when they say that at a time like this the life of a single individual isn't worth a snap of the fingers? Wasn't Debs right when he said that so long as there was a soul in prison he wasn't free? What does a single marriage count in a balance like that? It isn't easy being me. I *know* what all this means. This evil inside the human animal—the fascists are charming it out like a cobra out of its hole and the capitalists let them do it because they think its good for business. You think I'm abandoning Sally by leaving for Spain. I tell you, if I don't leave for Spain then I really do abandon her to a future of fascism and concentration camps."

These words poured out of Jerome like a torrent of lava, and I thought of Catherine with her fragile heart having to live with a force like that, and of a force like that having to live with her fragile heart.

"Jerome," I stammered, "you're only a single man, and what can a single man do unless the governments act? Is this reasonable?"

He stared at me and for an instant I felt I was being annihilated. I had felt his force before, but never anything like this. Then he smiled with a surprising new sweetness and touched my knee.

"George, you're a very nice fellow, and I'm going to say something you may think is an insult. Just because you're nice, you don't know what you're up against. People like you—left to your own devices—you'll be crushed like nuts in the jaws. You don't want to fight. Neither do I. But you don't know *how* to fight. And I do. I wish I were like you. I really do wish it. I don't want to fight, George—I tell you, I don't want to fight. I hate this thing in myself that makes me. But at the same time" —he stared out over the lake—"at the same time let me tell you this. No civilization has a chance unless it has civilized men in it who can and will fight when they have to."

"All I've been thinking about—" I began.

"You *think* all you're thinking about is Kate. But I wonder?" His eyes burned against mine, and then they misted. "That wonderful woman, she loves me. She's a fighter, too. But against her fate, George. And she's a woman all the way through, and that means she's a private person. Do I betray her?" A shrug. "I'm honest, George, and honestly I don't know."

A long silence fell and his profile brooded over the lake. Jerome loved the stark grandeur of the Laurentian Shield which evoked a response in him it has never called out of me, for I prefer a gentler land where flowers and fruits grow. But now with the sun sloping westward and the shadows of the hills thrusting easterly over the lake, with the clean, innocent smell of the sun-warmed spruce and the utter stillness of this empty land, now I thought it must be unbearable for him to leave this place where he had been happy.

He said slowly and heavily: "A man must belong to something larger than himself. He must surrender to it. God was so convenient for that purpose when people could believe in Him. He was so safe and so remote." A wistful smile. "Now there is nothing but people. In Russia our generation is deliberately sacrificing itself for the future of their children. That's why the Russians are alive. That's why they're happy. They're not trying to live on dead myths."

I said nothing and my thoughts wandered back to Norah Blackwell, and Jerome—one of the most animal-like things about him was his on-and-off capacity to be a medium—suddenly startled me.

"You think I'm a hypocrite, don't you?"

"I said nothing of the kind, Jerome."

"But you're thinking Norah is back of this?"

"Since you ask me, I don't think she's helped."

He passed a hand over his eyes and breathed heavily: "I wish to God I'd never laid eyes on her."

I said nothing.

"As the world understands the word, I'm not a lecher. I make no excuses. But perhaps you can tell me what there is to protect a man like me against his own impulses?"

For a while I said nothing, but after a time I said: "Do you feel responsible for her?"

"In a way, yes, I do. I suppose you think this thing with her— it's over now and it never amounted to much—you think it sullies my motives?"

I said nothing.

"Norah is very gentle and kind and troubled. Oh well! I'd have gone to Spain in any case. But has she affected my motives? Does this thing with her have anything to do with them?"

I said nothing, he scrutinized my expression and shrugged.

"I suppose it does. Can I help my own vitality? But the motives were there anyway, and they have nothing to do with Norah."

"I was thinking of Catherine."

He stared at me with deep pain in his face: "Do you think I don't, too? She tried to use her will against me this winter, and she's got a strong one."

"I was thinking of her health."

"Are *you* a doctor? Are *you* her husband? She and I—we've set our seals on each other."

I had a vision of Jerome in his tiny canoe going down the

New Brunswick river and of Catherine on the shore trying to beckon him in.

"We're both casualties," he said. "She and I."

"But you're leaving her."

"The only way I could do that is to write my own life off. I married her knowing what her heart is. You didn't marry her. You didn't take—what's life and death anyway? When I operate on a serious case I don't think of saving a life. I think of saving a few years. If the patient's young, perhaps quite a few years. But in a lot of cases I bargain for five, or three, or even for one."

I sat without answering and he said: "The only immortality is mankind."

"Can anyone love a thing as big as that?"

"What's love to do with what I'm saying?"

"Is Norah going to Spain with you?"

"Not if I know it. My God, but you've got a middle-class mind! Do you think this thing is as vulgar as that?"

Had I been older or more experienced I might have been able to stand up against him, but in those days I had no inner authority against a man I had installed as a substitute father in my own mind. In any case I was up against the whole climate of the period, some of which was within myself. To people who had exiled themselves from the establishment, as most of us had at least partially done, the volunteer for Spain had a special aura about him. I rose from my chair and stood by the railing with my back to Jerome looking down the shadowed slope to the lake and again I asked myself how he could bear to leave all this. I remembered Adam Blore's remark that I was a middle-class man. Jerome had just said the same thing. I knew then better than ever before how greatly I had longed for a home and a family, and how much I would surrender to have them if the chance ever came.

I heard Catherine's step descending the stair inside the cottage and expected her to appear, but the step receded toward the kitchen at the back.

"I think I'd better leave and go back to town," I said.

"Don't go, George. Stay the night."

"I don't belong here tonight, Jerome."

"Yes you do. You'll always belong here." A moment later he said quietly: "Look after Kate when I'm gone, will you?"

I faced him: "She's not my wife. She's your wife. She doesn't want me to look after her. She wants her husband to look after her. She wants her home."

For the first time that day his face became confused; he breathed noisily and I thought that at last I might have reached him. I was totally unprepared for what he said next.

"I said 'yes' to Kate when it was her marrying time. If I hadn't, she'd have disintegrated. Norah had this moronic husband and she thought she was going crazy. I said 'yes' to her and perhaps I gave her some respect as a woman. Perhaps I didn't. It's so easy to be correct. Perhaps I did wrong. Yes, I was disturbed. Yes, I feel guilty. Yes, yes, yes to all of that. But let me tell you something—everyone takes from somebody else and gives what he's taken to another. What Kate took from you years ago she gave to me. What she took from me all these years—if I'm killed or if she's through with me—she'll give to some other man. And what I took from her"—he stopped and stared out over the lake.

"What about yourself?"

"I've written myself off."

"Why? Kate hasn't written you off."

Staring over the lake, he said: "I'm tired."

I swallowed the last drops in my glass and rose, intending to say good-bye to Catherine, but he called me back.

"Before you go, listen to this—I forgot to tell you earlier. In town I talked to Tom Storey about you. He's with the CBC. He's interested and I think he'll make a job for you. Call him up tomorrow. It's stupid for you to go on working in that school."

He reached for his wallet, took out a piece of paper with Storey's telephone number and I slipped it into my pocket without even thinking about it, much less that this simple action was going to change my life.

In the kitchen I found Catherine standing in front of some dish she was preparing, but her eyes were staring at the wall.

"Is there a thing I can do?"

She shook her head.

"Let me take Sally back to town so you and Jerome can be alone?"

Again she shook her head.

"Jerome tells me he sails next Friday. I'll be in town early next Friday. I'll come out by bus and see you."

She did not turn around. She lifted her head in pride, but she looked fragile as I had never seen her look; she looked beaten.

Chapter IV

DRIVING down that evening from the Laurentian highlands with the sun behind me orange and red, the shadows deep on the road and presently the lights coming on, driving down through Saint-Jerome, Sainte-Rose, onto the island of Montreal and thence into the city itself, I saw virtually nothing around me. I had never before witnessed the break-up of a marriage, and something told me that this was what was happening here. It might be mended, it might grow again, but both of them felt inwardly that they had failed the other. I cursed Norah Blackwell for her part in it even though I knew in my heart it was not basic. Yet she sullied Jerome, she added that nasty touch of sordidness and equivocation to a situation I frankly could not understand. What he said about civilization and defending it was probably true, but I could not believe it was the whole truth. What he said about the fascists charming out evil like a cobra out of its hole sounded truer. But I was not like him and I could not know what his pressures were. I had not seen my mother murdered, I had not escaped in childhood down a forest river to the sea, I had not fought in the war and killed men hand to hand with a bayonet. Nor was I married to Catherine even though I wished that I were. Nor was I a brilliant professional man with revolutionary ideas which the established men in my profession dismissed. But that night as I drove back to Montreal I at least discovered this: that there is no simple explanation for anything important any of us do, and that the human tragedy, or the human irony, consists in the necessity of living with the consequences of actions performed under the pressure of compulsions so obscure we do not and cannot understand them. Morality? Duty? It was easy to talk of these things once, but surely it is no accident that in our time the best of men hesitate inwardly before they utter these words? As Jerome said, "What is my duty?" Did not the generals who sent millions to their death in the war feel certain they understood their duty? The time was the 1930s. Everyone I knew remembered what had been done in the name of duty only a decade and a half ago.

In the massed traffic I slowed to a crawl, and it was a long time before I reached Jack Christopher's place and put his car into the garage. It was nine-thirty and one of those spring nights in Montreal which pull the heart out of you. After the long winter the air was alive with tiny life and billions of insects swarmed about the street lamps. Girls and boys sauntered arm in arm and the air was soft enough to corrupt a saint. I walked past a tavern, smelled its malty breath and went in for a beer, and when I came out it was dark. I walked some more and at ten-fifteen I was mounting the stairway of the musty lodging house I had known so well in my time with Caroline Hall. I rang the bell by the Blackwells' door and Norah opened.

"Come in, George," she said.

I had come there hating her. I had come remembering Catherine and prepared to say anything to make her leave Jerome alone. And now as I looked at her in that mean little apartment, her eyes enormous, her face with the inward expression of a woman who at last has known love, her voice gentle as it had always been, her body at once frail and strong, her whole being like a flower which had opened after a long frost—when I saw all this I knew how much wiser than I Catherine was, and how right she was to be terrified for Jerome. For Norah Blackwell really was lethally attractive, and I was attracted to her myself, and under the circumstances I hated myself for being so.

I sat down and said: "I've been up north. I've just spent an afternoon with Catherine and Sally and an hour with Jerome."

"How is he?"

That look on her face! Not even guarded but open, offering herself—to what?

"Norah," I said, "I came here to—" I hesitated and looked down at the floor.

"I know why you came, George. You love Kate."

I felt a spasm of anger when I heard her use Jerome's name for his wife, but it passed.

"She's a very wonderful woman, George. I know Jerome loves her. I've always known that. I've never wanted to hurt his love for her. All I want is his good. That's all I've ever wanted."

I looked at her and knew she was sincere, and I remembered what else Catherine had said about her, and my world rocked, for this was the first time—I had always been slow on the uptake —when I realized that under certain circumstances sincerity is the most dangerous thing in the world.

"What are you going to do?" I asked her. "Jerome's going to Spain, he says, What are *you* going to do?"

"I don't know. The capitalists have turned us both out of the hospital. When Jerome learned what Dr. Rodgers did to me he resigned at once."

I searched her face for a sign of pride, but found none. Oh, but Catherine had been right about this girl! Norah—God help her—really didn't know any better.

"*You're* not thinking of going to Spain, are you?" I asked.

She looked at me mournfully; she looked so sad and lost that despite my feelings about this situation I had to force myself to sit still and not to take her into my arms and comfort her. She was everyman's daughter who might, given the circumstances, become everyman's loved one. Catherine had known it; possibly she had known it immediately she had seen her.

"No," she said, "not now. But I'm a surgical nurse and they need nurses in Spain. I don't think I can stand it here. But it's for the Party to decide."

"For the Party, and not for Jerome?"

"Oh George, how do I know?"

"I wish I could hate you."

"I know you do, but you can't, any more than Harry can."

Harry! I had forgotten about him.

"What's *he* going to do?"

"He'll be all right, I think."

"Norah, how can you continue in this mess? You have Harry and he needs you. Catherine used to have Jerome and she needs him. Cut your losses, Norah. This situation is hopeless."

"Everything seems to be but one thing. The Revolution will come and then everything will be different. That's why I can't blame myself for Kate, George. You see, she doesn't understand it any more than you do."

"Oh, to hell with that! She understands better than any of us."

"Don't you believe in symbolism? I do. Oh, I don't blame her, George. It's not her fault. But she's not well, and Jerome is so strong and can do anything. She's a—a symbol of our sick civilization."

I was glad she said that, for it enabled me to become angry at last, and in that condition I left her.

Chapter V

THE next Friday I asked Dr. Bigbee if I might leave Waterloo after morning classes and was somewhat chagrined by his response.

"By all means, my dear Stewart. I'll take your classes myself. I've been wondering lately whether you've been keeping them up to the mark."

I reached town by bus about three o'clock in the afternoon and took a taxi from the terminal to Jerome's apartment, but just as I was about to mount the steps I hesitated. Suddenly it occurred to me that this was their last afternoon and what business had I to intrude? So I walked away and at the nearest phone booth I called the shipping company and learned that Jerome's vessel was not due to sail until eight o'clock that evening. Then I walked the central city which rested me as it always does on a fine day neither too warm nor too cold.

After fifteen minutes I remembered Tom Storey and the CBC, went into a phone booth and found him in his office; he told me to come around right away and as soon as I met him I liked him. He was a man only two years older than myself, but he had taken a Ph.D. in philosophy in Yale, and unable to find a teaching job he had ended with the CBC. In talking about the organization he insisted that its men had more leeway under the government than the broadcasters had in the States under the control of commercial advertisers. He also explained that they earned much less money. Then he took me into an empty studio, introduced me to the engineer on duty, put a script before me and asked me to study it, and ten minutes later I was in the middle of my first audition.

When it was over, Storey smiled: "Now listen while I play it back and try not to be too startled at the sound of your own voice."

The disk revolved and when I heard my voice I was more than startled; I was incredulous.

"Jerome told me I had a voice a little like Roosevelt's," I said. "I thought he was kidding."

Storey smiled. "He's an amazing man. I've never known anyone like him for discovering a flair in a person the person doesn't know he has. I met him as a patient when I didn't have a job, and he told me I'd make a lousy philosopher but would be good in radio work. I don't know whether the latter part of the statement is true, but anyway I'm in radio earning a living."

After thanking the engineer, Storey took me back to his office. Then, while the noise of St. Catherine Street traffic drummed through the open window, he talked.

"Jerome tells me you have a history degree and a remarkable feeling for politics?" he began.

I was about to disclaim the compliment, but all I said was: "At least I have a history degree."

Storey said: "As you know, the Americans have made a very big thing out of news commentaries over the air. For my taste most of their men exaggerate and are too hyperthyroid, but that needn't concern us. We have a quieter public here and we don't have to worry about the commercial sponsor." He paused and looked out the window. "I'm not in a position to promise you anything definite now, but I have an idea I'd like you to consider. That audition was excellent and your voice is perfect for what I have in mind."

He outlined an idea that amazed me. There was a travel agency in town which wanted a courier to lead a summer tour to the Soviet Union and Storey asked me to take the job. There would be no salary, but there would be full expenses. I would be out of the country from June until Labor Day and only a handful of people would be on the tour. My duties would consist in taking care of tickets and baggage, and making arrangements from city to city.

"Jerome tells me your French is perfect and that you have a smattering of German," Storey said.

"My French is passable, but smattering is a compliment to my German. I suppose I could order a beer, but that's about all."

"It won't matter. With French and English you'll manage without trouble. Now this is why I want you to take this job."

It was Storey's notion that I use the tour as a means of getting into radio as a commentator. He wanted me to go to Russia with an open mind, to observe what I saw and record what I thought, and he was sure a series of scripts would come out of it. If they were successful, the organization might then hire me on a permanent basis.

"It's a gamble like anything else," he said, "but your way will be paid to Russia and you've got nothing to lose. How about it?"

I protested that the whole thing sounded much too ambitious for an unknown person like me, but he cut me short.

"This damned depression has made everyone our age think too small. I was just as bad before Jerome picked me up by the scruff of the neck and shook some sense into me."

I proposed as another objection my job at Waterloo, telling him that I would be unable to broadcast these trial scripts because I would not be in Montreal.

"That won't matter. When you come in over the weekends we can put them on wax. And anyhow, why not look at the bright side? If this idea works out, you'll be able to leave Waterloo forever."

I left Tom Storey full of elation, but the moment I reached the street all I could think about was that this was Catherine's last afternoon with Jerome and that I might never again see Jerome himself. I walked for a while and around six I stopped in a cafeteria for something to eat. Coming out at six-thirty I jumped into a cab and drove to their street just in time. Another cab was parked by the curb and the driver, his door open, was picking his teeth in the attitude of a waiting man. I paid off my own driver and got out and then the house door opened and the whole little family emerged. Sally was holding her father's hand and Catherine was ahead of them, and the instant I saw her face I knew that an important change had happened. She was serene, pale and beautiful.

"George!" Jerome called. "George, I'm so glad you've come. Everything is fine now, everything is fine. Get in and come down to the ship with us."

We drove down the long slope of the city toward the river, bumped over some railway tracks and got out in front of a huge shed surmounted by the twin funnels of a C.P.R. liner. We walked through the dock, and afterwards Catherine said she would never forget the sight of a pair of gulls perched high on one of the metal rafters. After talking with some officials, Jerome went up the gangplank with Sally on his shoulder and disappeared into the ship. Catherine and I were alone and she looked at me with this new, intense, pale calm.

"I'm grateful for last week, George."

"I'm glad."

"We came close to each other again. Now it will be easier. Now no matter what happens. . . ." A proud little smile: "I might have got sick, you know. I might have held him back by getting sick, but I didn't. It was hard not to, but I didn't."

"Are you tired now?"

Another smile: "Frankly, I'm so exhausted I wouldn't be surprised if I fainted, but I feel better than I've felt in a long time in spite of that."

"You'd better sit down on something, though."

There was an empty baggage truck, and as I had a folded newspaper in my pocket, I spread it out on the truck and helped Catherine up. She sat like a little girl with dangling legs and wide gray eyes staring in surprise out the huge open gate of the shed toward the high white flank of the ship. The falls squealed on the fo'c's'lehead, the last baggage went up the slide and was lowered into the hold, some late passengers made their adieus and went up the plank and disappeared. A chorus of happy voices rang bibulously through the shed and a twenty year old girl and a boy no older, covered with confetti and pursued by a gang of youths in morning coats and girls in bridesmaids' dresses, rushed up the plank and disappeared.

"Yes," Catherine said quietly, "this week has at least saved something. It's saved my soul. Please God it saves his, too."

"I'm so glad."

"Since he must go to Spain, then he must go. I'm not the first wife who's seen her husband off to the wars and I won't be the last."

Then we saw Jerome's head and shoulders coming down the plank with Sally walking cautiously in front of him. They stepped out onto the dock and came up to us.

"Well Kate, it's time."

"Daddy says that if we go up to the bow he'll come out and wave to us."

I rose to move away in order to preserve what remained of their privacy, but neither had eyes for me at that moment. She sat as she was with her whole soul in her pale, calm, eloquent face while he stood before her and looked into her. I never saw a pair of human beings look at each other as they did then. In their eyes was a hurt amazement that they were parting, an incredulity that, loving each other so much, they had made each other suffer. There was shock and pain, there was a terrible, almost despairing tenderness.

"Kate," he said hoarsely, "I don't want to go."

With calm, pale pride she said: "I know, dear. But you must."

Suddenly the dock shook as the steamer's horn roared, and the thunder of it broke the tension. Jerome stepped forward, Catherine melted into his arms as he lifted her off the baggage truck, then he set her down, turned to Sally and swept her off her feet, kissed her, set her down, and then in spite of his limp he ran fast up the plank and disappeared into the ship.

I turned to Catherine: "Now let me take you home."

"No," Sally cried, "Daddy promised to wave to us."

Looking down at Sally I knew that she had sensed with a child's intuition the pain and the tragedy and was trying to deny it.

"Daddy is going to wave to us. He promised."

Catherine was weak, but she rallied and smiled down at Sally and together we walked along the dock under the huge white flank of the liner until we came to the hawsers. Looking up we saw the heads of a few passengers along the rail but on the concrete apron of the dock Catherine, Sally and I were the only people. We waited. Twilight had dimmed the river, had covered St. Helen's Island with a transparent purple shroud, the air was cool and the gulls had not begun to scream. We looked, there was the flash of a white handkerchief and we saw Jerome's head and shoulders at the railing.

"Daddy! Daddy!" screamed the child, and began to cry.

Jerome cupped his hands to his mouth and called down to us, but at that instant the steamer's horn roared again and shook the air and his words were lost. Looking down the length of the dock I saw that the gangplank had been lowered. There was a swirling hiss of dirty water between the dock and the ship, the stern lines were cast off and she began to swing out rapidly, and still that tiny white handkerchief fluttered, and Sally waved back and Catherine stood like a statue.

"Catherine, please let me take you home!"

But I was too late. For at that instant something happened which I had dreaded all along yet could not really believe would happen. Beside Jerome's shoulder, high and small above the railing of the fo'c's'lehead, very close to him but not close enough to touch, appeared a woman's head. That woman's head had come by stealth, had come under the terrible compulsion of that destructive power within her of which she was utterly unaware, and all three of us saw her before Jerome did, who clearly did not know she was on board the ship. Catherine went white as chalk, she lurched and I took her arm and stared up.

"Please let's go! Please!" I cried. "Please come with me now!"

Walking as though she were unconscious, her whole body trembling, Catherine went beside me along the enormous white flank of the ship. A swirl of gulls screamed at the stern, tugs pushed and pulled, but Catherine saw nothing. At the entrance to the dock we paused and I looked back and saw Sally, tiny in that colossal setting, waving frantically to her father on the ship. Then even Sally seemed to understand, for she dropped her handkerchief and turned and ran to her mother as fast as she could. The three of us walked silently thought the shed to the space of cobbles on the other side, where we got into a cab. We drove across the tracks, up past the sailors' boarding houses, up through the ancient part of the city, through an empty Place d'Armes, up Beaver Hall Hill into the traffic, the noise, the shining lights, the river-like crowds of central Montreal on a warm spring night.

Two hours later Sally was in bed and Catherine and I were

alone downstairs. She looked so exhausted that I asked if I might call Jack Christopher, but she would not let me.

"Jerome knew nothing about her," I said. "I know that. I absolutely know he didn't know she'd be on that ship."

Calmly she said: "It doesn't matter any more."

"That girl—she doesn't know what she's doing!"

"Yes she does," Catherine said. "In one part of her mind she knows perfectly well. But not even she matters now." She turned her face away. "I don't know where I am. I don't know who I am. I don't know anything."

Through the open window I heard the faint hum of the night city and the sound of footsteps passing below, and I think it was then that I became consciously afraid of life itself. This is what happens, I thought, when the leaders close their doors and the walls of custom collapse. This is what happens when people try to play a game making the rules as they go along. I saw Catherine, Jerome, myself and everyone I knew like lost shadows moving perilously over a crust covering a void.

"I tried so hard, George. I tried so hard. And now I'm exhausted, and I feel so ugly."

"You're not ugly. You're beautiful."

"I'd like to fall asleep forever."

"Catherine dear—just fall asleep now. Take a sedative and sleep."

"I begged him to stay with me. I went down on my knees. I threw all my pride away."

"He loves you. Didn't you hear him say he didn't want to go?"

"I know." Her calmness returned. "He will always love me, and that makes me grieve for him, for I failed him. He was born in— what? Naked he came into the world, and now naked he goes out into—what? He's naked now. He's in agony now and I grieve for him, alone on that ship with that girl."

"He probably hates her now."

"Yes, he probably wants to murder her now, and that will make him hate himself the more."

"She doesn't matter, Catherine."

"That's what's so terrible. She doesn't matter—in herself she never did—and yet she's done this."

"He'd have gone to Spain whether he met her or not."

"Yes. Yes, he'd have gone. But cleanly, and not like this. Not hating himself. He'd have gone and perhaps he'd have found himself. Perhaps he'd have found what he lost in the trenches in the war."

"You mean his religion?"

"I mean something that would protect him at three o'clock in the morning. He thought he'd found it in me. He did find it in me for a while. Then everything went bad. Not our life together —no, not that. But his war experience regurgitated when everything went to pieces and the fascists started this new war. And of course he tried to do too many things. He has this awful vitality, and everyone sucked it out of him, and he got himself involved. Oh, why talk? Everything's gone out of control and I want to sleep forever."

"He'll come back."

"Now I don't think I can stand it if he does. Love can be such a terrible torment, George. It's so powerful it exhausted me. What is it? God knows what it is, but it's cruel. People break loose into sex because it's so direct and simple. Oh, I feel so ugly and tired."

A long silence and the city's hum coming in through the window.

"I was too frightened. We were all too frightened. He seemed so brave and strong and everyone sucked from him. Me too. And he got tired—tired inside, tired in his soul, and this communistic thing seemed an escape. And yet he wants to do good. I don't know. I don't understand. All I know is that I failed him."

"Catherine dear, please take a sedative and rest."

She made a movement to rise, but stayed where she was.

"What's going to become of him, George?"

I shrugged my shoulders; I was wondering what was going to become of her.

"All right, I'll take that sedative and I'll try to sleep." She rose, small and I thought beautiful, and haunted. "It's so awful for a woman to learn that human love isn't sufficient. We need God, and He doesn't care. Perhaps because we don't let Him care. But where is He? Where has He gone?"

She went upstairs and when I guessed she was in bed I followed and she called me into the double room she had shared with Jerome. She looked tiny lying there in that huge double bed all alone, but her eyes were enormous. Her body lay still under the sheets and I sat by her bedside and we looked at each other.

I took her hand and found myself saying: "The Lord is my shepherd, I shall not want. . . ."

But the familiar words had lost their potency for both of us because the Lord who had shepherded Israel and our fathers had gone away and we had lost the habit of searching for Him.

Chapter VI

Was it only a month and a fortnight ago?

Standing on the balcony of the Europa Hotel in Leningrad I had forgotten, for the time being, the intense little tragedy in which I had been involved the previous spring in Montreal. Now I was out in this huge, news-making, future-making—what? Who could understand Europe in 1937, or Russia then or ever? The provincial walls in which I had lived had crumbled and I was out in this alone. With me was a young American I had met on the train out of Helsinki the night before, and he had come all the way from Nebraska to see with his own eyes the shape of things to come. By noon of his first day in Russia he had seen enough to daze him, to terrify him with its unknown quantities, to smash to pieces the neat little walls of theory with which he had armored himself. Now we were together, close and intimate in Russia though we barely knew each other's names.

The *nuit blanche* of Leningrad in late June made eerie the perpetual rustling of thousands of shoeless feet on the pavements below, the pavements laid out by the Czars which the communists had captured along with this hotel and the marble palaces nearby. We could just distinguish the human swarm in the *nuit blanche*, not the faces of individuals but the smock-wearing, shuffling swarm which flowed hour after hour without ceasing because, apparently, they had nothing else to do and no place to go.

"*Byprizorni,*" the American kept muttering. "*Byprizorni.*"

In the weird white night they swarmed like creatures mysteriously risen out of a Sargasso Sea, ourselves on the ship's bridge looking down, and after a day in the Leningrad streets we knew that every face, to us, was a variant of the same face we had stared at since leaving the Finland Station that morning: a face wrinkled, prematurely old, unsmiling, unblinking, the face of Tolstoy's peasant in a world he could not understand, scarred by years of cold and hunger, knowing a totality of unwantedness, the face of the millions too old, slow, ignorant and stupid for this new Soviet world.

"See Russia," said the American, "and let your theories die."

The thousands of feet shuffled with the sound of a restless sea that would never be still and never know a storm, and they shuffled like that because each one of them was wrapped in bandages and hemp, and they were wrapped in bandages and hemp because there were not enough shoes in Russia, and because the price of a pair of cheap shoes cost more than double the monthly pay of the average Soviet worker that year.

"Where do they come from? Where are they going?"

A voice with an English accent answered behind us: "They come from the land and they are going no place. These, my friends, are counter-revolutionaries. They are, or were, kulkas. They are the sons of serfs, and the Bolsheviks liberated them in 1917."

This elderly, ironical Englishman had eaten a seven-course dinner with us a couple of hours earlier, and it was he who had told us that hemp was the basic footwear of this crowd. He was in the hemp business himself and every year his firm shipped thousands of tons of the stuff into the ports of Leningrad and Odessa. He claimed to know Russia well, both before and after the revolution, and we had seen what diabolical pleasure he had taken in baiting visiting Americans in the hotel, and a few English trade unionists as well, who were fellow-travellers and spoke the jargon, and already were noting down the wonderful things they would report to their little cliques in Brooklyn, Chicago and Manchester when they got home. The moment this Englishman heard an English voice in the lobby utter one of those key words of the period (cadre, stakhanovite, the masses—any one of the key words would suffice) he would pick a conversation with the man. Pretending to seek instruction, he would lead the man into one absurdity after another, and then with a perfect innocence of expression he would agree that Russia was absolutely wonderful because she was the only country in the world which had solved her unemployment problem, providing work camps for some eighteen million, forbidding socialists to tamper with the productive powers of labor, accustoming labor to work for a quarter the pay they got in England and America, maintaining by conscription an army of twenty-one million men and tolerating no soft-headed nonsense about giving consumer goods priority over guns. With a gleam in his eye the Englishman would watch the angry flush mount to the fellow-traveller's face until the moment came, as it inevitably did, when he would be called a fascist or a reactionary.

To us he had been more gentle, deciding after a while that though we knew nothing we were at least not true believers. But he delighted in shocking us.

"Those people down there," he said calmly, "will not be entirely useless to the state. When the war comes, their hour will strike. They will be sent ahead of the tanks to blow up the enemy minefields."

"It can't be as bad as that?"

"Perhaps not. Time will tell. But if you had any sense, you'd say it can't be as good as that, for whether they like it or not, the Russians are going to be our allies." He chuckled and said to the American: "At this moment in our hotel seventeen of your countrymen are living better than they ever did in their lives. Caviar three times a day. I find them charming. Here they are, coming all the way from America to teach Russia how to out-produce America. Oh, don't think she won't, given the time. There aren't any trade unions here, you see. And now let me tell you the most wonderful thing of all about Russia. These people don't understand themselves. They haven't reached that fatal watershed in a nation's history when they think they should."

The American raised some objection to this, and the Englishman laughed.

Hadn't we read Russian literature? It was a wonderful literature, the truest there was, and if truth was what you wanted out of a literature, Tolstoy and Dostoievsky were worth a dozen Shakespeares. But it was not a literature of understanding. You couldn't pin it down. That was why it broke all the limits and was true, because the truth couldn't be pinned down. Oh yes, this was a great country and the fact that it was dreadful had nothing to do with its greatness. It was big enough to do what it liked with anything. Look what it had done to communism in twenty years. It had taken the Romans three centuries to take care of the Church, but the Russians had taken care of Marx in two decades. This was all right because the Russian never cared about understanding himself. That was why the future was Russia's. We doubted that? Look at France, the only country in the world which even tried to understand herself. Yes, look how she had castrated herself with understanding. We doubted it? Wait a few years and see how that French army of critics would fight when the war came. England? Well, England had certainly had a fine run for her money, but she was finished now. For centuries the English had contrived to avoid thinking about themselves, but they were doing it now and that meant only one thing. Chamberlain knew they were finished. He was stupid, of course, he had seen better days. But he wasn't as stupid as everyone said he was.

"Listen, my dear boys, Mr. Chamberlain understands one thing most of you refuse to accept. He knows that Hitler is the last ace Europe has to play. If Hitler can't knock Russia out, Europe is doomed. But he won't knock her out because he's a lunatic, and I don't think he could do it even if he was sane."

Then he went on to say that the war was going to be so terrible that only the Russians could win it because only the Russians could suffer enough. Generalship? Forget it. Suffering was what was going to win the war, and Stalin would make it as terrible as he could, just as Hitler would, but the Russians could suffer more than the Huns. We doubted it? Wait and see, wait and see.

At dawn the Englishman yawned and left us, and the American and I stayed a little longer watching the old Czarist palaces emerging out of the brief *nuit blanche* into full daylight. A bird perched on the parapet near us and called, then flew away, and we smelled the indefinable smell of a Russian city which travellers say is the smell of the doorway of Asia.

"Well," said the American, "I guess I'm about ready for the sack."

When we went downstairs a band was playing corny American jazz for the Russian officers and bureaucrats who had come into the restaurant after the fellow-travelling tourists had listened to the program of folksongs and gone to bed. I entered the huge room the Intourist had given me, undressed and lay down and tried to sleep, but I was still wide awake when the sun stared in and found me reflecting that this was the first time in my life when I had felt like nothing. I had often felt small, I had often felt weak and afraid and inadequate, but now I felt like nothing at all.

"This," I had heard a fellow-traveller say at dinner, "is the future."

The fool had believed that reason was in control of it.

Before falling asleep I remembered Jerome. The canoe in which he had issued from the forest had now taken him out into the ocean. A canoe in an ocean, at night, with a hurricane rising. Jerome, Myself, Everyone.

Chapter VII

As THE liner moved into the estuary of the St. Lawrence and I looked across miles of cold water to the barren mountains of northeastern Quebec, I felt old. But at least I was coming home. It was strange, but before this sight of that barren land I had never thought of Canada as home. It had been where I was born and lived. I had never thought of Canada as having a future with a future role to play. Now I knew better. "I will work here," I thought. "I will try to understand this country. It's all there's left for me now, for the rest is beyond me."

By arranging that summer trip for me, Tom Storey had changed the whole pattern of my life and thought. Never again would I be able to believe that there is a simple explanation for anything. Never again would I trust a politician with a theory. Now I knew that the two subjects about which we talk the most are the two about which we actually know the least: politics and the weather. There are so many factors conspiring to make politics and the weather that no human mind, not even a calculating machine, can assess them.

Why was there going to be a war? Why, unless the very people who professed to want peace wanted war?

Staring across the water at the mountains I recalled a conversation with a Polish travel agent on the Warsaw platform just before I boarded the train for Berlin.

"Well, you have seen Warsaw. Inside a few years there will be no Warsaw. You've met me. In a year or two I will be dead." And then he grinned and said: "But one very good thing comes out of all this. In a year or two there will not be a single Jew alive in the whole of Europe."

Yes, there was going to be a war.

The ship steamed up the enormous cleft in the Laurentian rock where people lived knowing nothing of the emotions I had felt all that past summer. Was this what had haunted Jerome—their ignorance, their innocence? Had it haunted him to the extent that he found life here intolerable? I did not know the answer to that, either.

Steadily the river narrowed, and in the late afternoon we rounded the Ile d'Orleans and stopped to let off passengers at Quebec. As we cast off an hour later the evening Angelus tolled over the stream and we sailed into the sunset toward Montreal. After dinner I walked the decks till midnight, the parish lights very close on either side most of the time, moving off occasionally as the river widened, closing in again, and the sudden thought came to me that about this country, this Canada where I had been born and lived all my life, I knew almost nothing. My forebears had been here six or seven generations, and still I knew nothing important about it. I thought of Waterloo and despised myself for having squandered so many years there. The fault, dear Brutus, is not in our stars if we allow the Bigbees to bluff us. Walking the deck, smelling the balsam in the moist night air, I swore I would trudge St. Catherine Street rather than spend another year in Waterloo. And I thought of the half dozen scripts I had already written for Tom Storey and wondered if they would open the door at last.

The next morning in town I took the scripts to Storey and he promised to read them at once and to talk with me in his office about them early in the afternoon.

After leaving him, I phoned Catherine's apartment and waited while the instrument buzzed ten times. Then I phoned the Beamis Memorial and learned that Dr. Christopher was now in private practice and that I should be able to reach him in his office. At noon I did reach him, and he told me that Catherine had sublet her apartment and taken Sally out to the Lakeshore to live with her parents.

"I'm sick about the whole thing," Jack told me. "After you went away her nerves went all to pot. She was in a state of shock and didn't know it until the middle of July, when she collapsed with a fair-sized nervous breakdown." He hesitated—he was her physician now—but decided to tell me the rest: "Unfortunately that's not the most serious of her symptoms. Her heart has begun to fibrillate."

"What does that mean?"

"Omitting the details, it means that it can't carry a normal load. In turn that means that she has aged—so far as her lifespan is concerned—approximately twenty years in the last six months. Of course she's taking digitalis and her organism will make certain accommodations, but there can be only one long-range prognosis, and that's progressive heart failure."

I felt as if the bottom had fallen out of me and asked if I might see her.

"I'm sorry, but I must say no, George. She's—no, I can't advise that just now."

Feeling cold and queer, I tried to steady my voice: "Tell me one thing—did Jerome anticipate this when he went away?"

Jack answered quietly: "He's an experienced medical man."

"You mean, he went away *knowing* this would happen?"

"I didn't say that. But he knew it was bound to happen ultimately. He married her knowing that."

"But to go away knowing it was possible!"

Jack, whom I had always assumed to be rigid and correct, surprised me.

"Don't judge him by yourself, George. You—if you'll pardon my saying this—may be in love with Catherine, but you were never married to her, and you're not a man who can do about a dozen different things and wants to do them all. Jerome saw the sick all day and had to go home each night to a wife who was becoming an invalid."

"But she was his wife! And I know he loved her."

"Oh for God's sake, George, what do I know? I'm getting to the place where all I know is my own plumber's work."

"Has Jerome written to Catherine?"

"I believe quite often. He's even written to me asking about her health. But Catherine's been shaken. There's just so much a person can stand; she stood very much and she was frailer than I thought. I only knew how much she drew out of Jerome after he left and she collapsed. But don't ask me about all this. I'm a doctor. I'm not a psychologist."

After saying good-bye to Jack, I went out to my parents' flat and found them delighted to see me. My trip to Russia, however, was not real to Father who had no interest in politics and had omitted Russia from his reading list. He soon began talking about the new can opener he had invented and said it was going to make money. There was a stream of correspondence about it between him and Buffalo, he said. He also spoke of another invention, but I forget what it was.

That afternoon I went to see Tom Storey, and this extraordinarily kind, modest man was as pleased with my scripts as though he had written them himself.

"But there's nothing here that isn't obvious," I said. "It's just ordinary reportage. I don't really know anything about Russia."

"That's just why I like them. Everyone else is sure he knows *everything* about Russia. Everything I see about Russia is slanted. This stuff rings true and fresh." He smiled. "I'm afraid it's going to lose you any left-wing friends you may have. Now let's go to the studio and record the first of them."

In the studio he rehearsed me several times for emphasis and timing, then he gave the word to the engineer and we put the script onto wax.

"Now," Storey said, "I have a proposition to make you. There's a vacancy in our organization in Vancouver, and these scripts might just as well emanate from there as from here. I don't want to hold out false hopes, but I'm going to Toronto tonight and I'm taking along both the scripts and this disk we've made. I'm going to make some of the big boys consider them, and inside a day or two I'll have a decision one way or the other. That will give you time to resign from the school before term begins, and if you don't come in with us—well, you can go back to the school."

Late the following afternoon he telephoned me from Toronto to say the job was mine if I wished it. I said I did.

The next morning I took the train to Waterloo to pick up some clothes and books I had left there and to inform Dr. Bigbee I would not be returning. I was stiff with anxiety on the train, for I expected the old man to throw a tantrum or even to threaten to take measures against me if I walked out a week before the beginning of term. He never drew up a contract with any of his masters, but I had the idea he must have some hold over us and was afraid, because he made everyone feel like a child.

I need not have worried. When I gave the Doctor my news he blew his nose, looked out the window and after a while spoke.

"Well, I fancy we'll not have any trouble filling your place. I've just had a cablegram from a man at home who wants to come out here. I don't know much about him, but I fancy he'll stop the gap."

That was the extent of my final conversation with the Doctor after five years in his service. He did not even ask me what I intended doing, where I had been in the summer or why I had decided to leave.

Twelve days later I got off the train in Vancouver.

Chapter VIII

THAT year I began to grow up. The depression was over at last so far as I was concerned, and I came out of its deep freeze retarded by some ten years suddenly eager to live and amount to something.

By New Year's I had established myself in the CBC organization. The series of Russian scripts were so successful that for a short while I enjoyed the mild notoriety of a new radio personality in a small country. When the original series ended, I was given a regular spot for news interpretations and began a systematic study of newspapers, journals of opinion and European and Asiatic diplomatic history. For the first time in my life I had a real job. For the first time in my life I became more than a cipher. I began to get used to knowing that all over the country people said occasionally: "Did you hear George Stewart last night?" Or, "Do you think George Stewart is right or do you think he is crazy?"

It was one of the various ironies in my life that I owed my reputation to no less a personage than Adolf Hitler. On my return from Russia I had spent a week in Berlin, and nobody with eyes or ears could have spent even a day in Berlin at that time without knowing Hitler's intentions. Most people I knew were emotionally unable to believe—really to believe—that Hitler intended war. I found it impossible to believe anything else, and in an odd way my own involvement with Jerome and Catherine, my witness to their break-up, had prepared me emotionally for this colossal break-up which now was under way.

That year of Munich—it has always seemed marvelous to me that people did not throw away their radios, considering what that instrument did to their nervous systems in the Munich year—I used to receive frantic letters from people abusing me for being pessimistic when I called Munich a surrender. A week after Munich, when Hitler made a truculent speech at Saarbrücken which even Chamberlain must have trembled to hear, I predicted that within six months he would gobble up the rest of Czechoslovakia. I had noticed that Hitler in those days, like a python who eats an enormous meal periodically, got starving hungry every six months. Late in the winter of 1939 Sir Samuel Hoare made the statement that a golden age for Europe was about to begin. I used this as the basis for a broadcast in which I said, without hedging, that Sir Samuel's golden age would be ushered in before summer by still another German outrage. A fortnight later Hitler entered Prague.

I had been so consistently right—I take no credit for this, because surely all I said was obvious—that the organization decided to move me east where I would be closer to the capitals. I returned to Montreal in the late spring of 1939 and rented my first apartment, a two-room affair with a kitchenette three blocks from the little half-moon street where Jerome and Catherine had lived.

It was a strange spring, a haunted spring, and outwardly a lovely one. In late May the university campus was shadowed by elms in full leaf and empty of the students who soon would fight and die. In this fine weather the news I had to study seemed all the more atrocious. I began to become personally afraid. Raised on the novels of the old war, I could not imagine myself enduring the life of a soldier in this coming one. I often thought of Jerome, and missed his courage.

Meanwhile there was Catherine. During the winter we had corresponded, and in her letters she had told me she was picking up. I got in touch with Jack Christopher as soon as I returned to town. "Well," I began with Jack, "what price Jerome's opinions now?"

"It looks pretty bad," Jack admitted. "But when the war starts, perhaps that will bring him out of Spain."

Then I asked him about Catherine.

"Thank God she's picked up. Her mental attitude has definitely returned to normal. She and Sally are at the lake now. She's accommodated herself to the digitalis and she's determined to live a new and interesting life."

"You mean, she's sure she and Jerome will never come together again?"

"I don't know, George. I don't think she does, either. Did you know he was back in town last winter?"

This startled me, for Catherine had not mentioned it in any of her letters.

"Yes, he was back for about a fortnight. He'd been slightly wounded—his left arm was in a cast, I remember. I didn't meet him. He came home to raise funds for this surgical unit of his, but I don't think he was successful. Spain's become a dead issue now that so many people think we'll be at war ourselves. The communists used him for propaganda purposes, but the papers didn't even mention the speech he made."

"But he did see Catherine?"

"Yes, briefly."

"And then he went back to Spain?"

"He did. Don't ask me why, but he did."

"What passed between them?"

"You must ask Catherine that. I didn't ask her, and she didn't tell me."

There was no phone in Catherine's Laurentian cottage and the second-hand car I had bought two days ago had not yet been overhauled. I was very busy in the office anyway, so I put off visiting Catherine until the weekend. But I wanted to talk to somebody who had seen Jerome, and the first person who came to my mind was Arthur Lazenby. I called him up and around eight-thirty that night he came to my apartment.

The change in Lazenby's appearance startled me. He looked like a man who had seen his own ghost and had not got over it yet, he smoked constantly, he was nervous and figeted, there was a temporary tick in his left cheek. But what startled me most was the change in his mental attitude.

"I listened to every one of your Russian talks over the air," he said, "and by God, they were good."

"I'm surprised to hear that from you."

Lazenby winced: "This last year I've been on the verge of going out of my mind. It started with Jerome Martell."

"What do you mean?"

"I met him when he was back from Spain and he let down the boom on me. Do you know why I went to see him? I wanted him to help me get into the International Brigade. In case you're interested, I've been a communist. All the time the rest of you talked, you may remember I said very little. But I was a communist and you weren't. I won't go into the details of why the Party didn't want me to go to fight in Spain. Let's say they didn't. But Jerome had influence—or at least so I thought— and I went to him. And do you know what he told me?"

"Go on, tell me."

"He just looked at me in that way he has and shook his head: 'I wouldn't help my worst enemy get into Spain now,' he said. I was so taken aback by this I could only stutter.

"'This whole miserable tragic business,' Jerome said, 'inside a couple of months it will be over. Stalin's murdered the Revolution in his own country and to him Spain is nothing but an embarrassment. He'll never risk a war with Hitler for the sake of Spain. With him it's been political from the start. Look what he's done. He's sent a few advisers. He's let thousands of non-Russian communists commit suicide in the Brigade. He's spread the myth that the communists are the only people on the Loyalist side who are fighting, and all the time he's been using Spain as a slaughterhouse to get rid of every element in the workers' movement that doesn't follow him the way the Germans follow Hitler.'"

I listened to this and much more and said: "Then why in God's name did he go back to Spain himself?"

Lazenby stared at me as though he had been asking himself that same question for months.

"Don't ask me. He beats me, that man. He's a divine fool, I guess. Or maybe he's just one of those who sticks when the rats run out—the rats like me. He had this surgical unit and maybe he went back to that because he felt it was his duty. But what he told me about Spain"—Lazenby winced and his cheek ticked—"it was terrible for me, it was terrible, George. But it was the truth."

"You're a communist and you say that?"

"*Was* a communist. *Was* a communist. Of course I refused to believe him. Of course I used all the commie words of insult." Lazenby winced again. "All right, maybe I'd better give you the whole of it."

Apparently Jerome, as he often did when somebody attacked him, had struck back. He told Lazenby that the real underlying reason why he, Lazenby, wanted to go to Spain was to get in on the ground floor of the Revolution. He told him he'd been mesmerized by the very propaganda he disseminated.

Lazenby looked at me with an expression I shall never forget. He looked humiliated, still hostile to Jerome, yet stubborn and defiant. He was the first person I knew who had been a communist and had left the party, and I was unfamiliar with the utter desiccation of soul that this experience caused in people who had accepted communism as a religion.

"Three days after I talked to Jerome," Lazenby said, "I remembered something he'd said to me—something I'd forgotten because I was so scared and sore. He'd told me that the place for a man like me was External Affairs, and that he'd write Dr. Scrimgeour in my behalf. He said Dr. Scrimgeour was an old patient of his."

Lazenby lit another cigarette, and with his whole personality seeming to twitch, he said: "Two months ago I sat my exams for External."

"Did you get in?"

"I don't know yet. But I admitted to Dr. Scrimgeour in my interview that I'd been a communist and had got out. I told him I thought a man like me would be useful just because I'd been a communist. And it's a good thing I did, for they knew anyway. Scrimgeour talked about Jerome to me privately. He thinks he's a great man, but he thinks he's a tragic one. And there's one more thing, George." Lazenby gave me a bitter, sardonic look. "Do you think the big war will start this year?"

"Yes."

"Do you know how it will start?"

"I suppose by Hitler invading Poland."

"But before that?" Lazenby shook his head. "Before that— you watch—Stalin and Hitler are going to get together. It'll be us against the fascists with Russia sitting pretty on the side."

The same idea had occurred to me, but I could not believe it; I could not see how it could be worked.

"You wait," Lazenby said. "I told that to the people in External and they smiled. But you wait." And then he added: "It was Jerome who told me, and three days later I knew he was right. You wait and see."

Another day passed. I worked in the office, I bought a few more necessities for my flat, I wrote the first draft of a new script and I picked up my second-hand Ford from the dealer. It was my first car and I spent several hours driving around town in it, climbing and descending the Westmount hills looking at the tulips in the gardens and occasionally staring off over the downward sweep of the city to the distant, blue bend of the St. Lawrence. Around seven I came home and made myself supper, and I was just sitting down before my typewriter when the phone rang and a familiar voice spoke.

"Hullo George, this is Caroline. Caroline Hall, and if you say you've forgotten me, I'll hate you."

"For God's sake, where are you now?"

"I got off a ship yesterday and I've just found a room for a few days." She gave me the name of a tourist home near where I lived. "I've simply got to see you, George. Can you come over now?"

I had a script to re-write, it was a long time since I had even thought of Caroline, and I hesitated.

"I'm just back from Paris," she said, "and I've got to have

help. I was the last person to see poor Norah and I've got—"

"What do you mean, the last person to see Norah? You mean Norah Blackwell? Is she—"

"Hasn't anybody told you?"

I remembered the night when Norah had used almost the same words about Caroline's marriage.

"Are you telling me she's dead?"

Caroline's voice was warm with pity when she said: "She was run over in a Paris street a month ago and I've brought her baby home. She's an adorable baby girl and I have her here now."

These telephone conversations in my life!

"Is the child Jerome's?"

"What difference does it make whose it is? I'm taking her to Harry and I'm afraid to go all by myself. I just can't face that little lost soul all by myself, and you've just got to come and help me."

After this I knew I would do no more work the rest of the night, so I said "All right," hung up and went out. A spring sunset had sent a flush of clouds over the roofs and on a corner I saw an old Jewish man, poorly dressed but serene, staring up at the clouds sailing over the mountain. Five minutes later I rang the doorbell in Caroline's lodging house.

She looked older, and with brown eyes gentler even than I remembered them, she kissed me like a sister. The passion we once had shared might have been felt by two different people: we had become friends who knew each other's loneliness and still were fond.

"Let's go for a walk," she said. "The baby's asleep and I want to talk to you."

We strolled westward through the gray streets to the university campus, where we ended like a pair of students on the stone steps looking down the avenue of elms to the first lights shining in the city.

"Is Jim with you?"

She shook her head and smiled.

"Are you still married to him?"

"Technically. Norah said she'd told you I was pregnant when I went away. But there wasn't a child. I had a miscarriage in Paris."

"I thought you'd gone to New York?"

"We went there first, but since then we've been almost every-where."

"Where is Jim now?"

"I don't know," she said simply.

"Did you know he was in the Party when you married him?"

"Yes, but I didn't know what being in the Party means." An-other smile. "It's all over between us, of course. With them, the Party's everything. I'm going west to someplace where nobody knows me and find a job. I'm still fairly young, and I miss that baby almost as much as if the poor thing had never been born. I want to meet some nice man and have another."

We smoked in the twilight while the city lights grew sharper.

"Well George, I suppose you know Jerome's in Spain. Norah tried to follow after him, but she couldn't. We kept running into them separately in various places."

"In other words, they've not been living together?"

"Does it matter? Jerome's in the Spanish War and that's everything with him. Jim met him in Madrid, but when he talked about him—which was precious little—there was a tone in his voice that gave me the creeps. Those people aren't human, George. I don't know whether Jerome knows or cares, but he's in danger, and I don't mean just from the fascists."

"Is this child you've got Jerome's?" I asked her again.

Again Caroline smiled. "I don't know. Does it matter? She's an adorable baby."

"Did Jerome abandon Norah, too?"

"Well, he never expected she'd follow him to Europe. She was a member of the Party. He wasn't, incidentally. I think for a time he intended to join, but he never did. But Norah was in deep and they got her a job in a *crèche* for Spanish refugee children in Paris."

"Did she commit suicide?"

Caroline sighed: "The French police called it an accident. But earlier that year she'd had to take shock treatments. It must be terrible to have been Norah. Don't judge her, George."

"It doesn't make much sense to judge a lunatic."

"Don't use that word, either. She was just—oh, why talk?

Things were too much for her. If she'd had any luck, maybe this trouble wouldn't have come out. If Jerome had married her—"

"He'd never have done that," I said.

"I think she knew it all along." Her brown eyes looked into mine. "Does any of this matter? The poor girl isn't here any more, and she tried so hard and she was so nice."

I stared down the avenue to the city and after a while I asked her if she knew why Jerome had gone back to Spain.

"I never did understand that man, but what else could he do? Maybe he went back for the same reason that Norah walked out into the traffic of the Rue de Rivoli. I'm so lucky not being brainy like you people. I just go on from day to day. I kept telling Norah to throw it up and go home to Harry, and she did come home for a while. Last year I think. But she couldn't stand it."

"Did she see Harry when she was back?"

"Certainly she did. Poor little Harry wanted her to go back to him as though nothing had happened, but when she saw him he was repulsive to her and she wouldn't even stay in his flat. I think the Party told her to go back to Paris."

"I see."

Caroline rose and smoothed down her flannel skirt. "Now," she said briskly, "you and I have a job and the sooner we do it the better. We're taking that baby to Harry."

I looked at her incredulously. "Are you suggesting that the child is his?"

"I think the baby will be very good for Harry now. I love the little thing and I'd gladly look after her if he refuses, but I think she'll be wonderful for Harry."

"I thought babies were supposed to need mothers?"

"But that's just the point. Harry's a motherly type."

"Why do you want me to go along with you in this?"

She gave me one of those mysterious female smiles which women interpret better than men.

"Well, Harry always liked you, and if you come along I just think everything will work out better."

"Just what gives you that idea?"

"But George, isn't it obvious? If he thinks you take it for granted the baby's his, then he'll think others take it for granted too, and everything will seem much easier and more natural for Harry."

We walked back to her lodgings and found the child asleep in the middle of a huge brass bed. While Caroline picked the baby up and made cooing sounds at it, I listened to the soft rumble of distant traffic and smelled the smell of downtown Montreal in a warm night.

"She's such a darling," Caroline said. "Hold her, George. Isn't she a love?" She rubbed the baby's cheeks with the backs of her fingers and the baby made some smilingly gurgling noises for which Caroline praised her. "She's going to be a raving beauty when she grows up."

"In that case, how can you believe that Harry will think he's the father?"

Caroline smiled at me mischievously.

"Harry may be dumb, but he can't be that dumb," I said.

"George, you're being much too clever for all of us. Just you wait and see." Another mischievous smile. "Now let's go."

So we walked out into the night, the baby in Caroline's arms and I beside her as though I were the father. I hailed a cab and on the short run to those familiar lodgings, Caroline kept up a stream of endearments to the baby while I looked out the window at passersby. The cab stopped, I paid the fare and we went up the steps.

"How do you know he's in?" I said.

"I called to make sure and the minute I heard his voice I hung up. He'd think I was French and that I knew from the English voice I'd got the wrong number."

"That doesn't mean he's in now."

"We'll soon find out. I didn't tell him it was me because I didn't think he ought to have time to think before he sees the baby. Harry's so sweet."

"So are you."

"I'm not sure I liked the tone you said that in."

"I suppose Harry knows Norah's dead?"

"Oh yes, he knows that. All her old friends here know that."

Soon we were in the apartment I remembered so well and it was unchanged. The cheap prints were still on the walls, the floors were as spotless as ever and the old photograph of Norah in her nurse's cap stood on the table.

At first Harry seemed amiably glad to see us, confused but no more so than usual, and oblivious of the presence of the baby.

"It's been a long time," he said.

"Hasn't it?" said Caroline.

Harry's pear-shaped body and oversized head, his short little legs and shopworn hair were familiar enough, but his eyes had changed.

"I've kept the place pretty nice, don't you think?" he said. "Norah would like it, I think."

"Of course she would," said Caroline. "Norah'd be proud of you."

She sat down with the baby on her knees, and it occurred to me that Harry assumed it was hers, even that I might be its father. I lit a cigarette, the idea coming to me that this was one of the most bizarre situations I had ever found myself in.

"Harry," said Caroline, "I don't know how to begin." But as I looked at her I thought she knew exactly how to begin and was doing it. "Did Norah write that she and I saw a lot of one another in Paris?"

"Oh yes, she wrote all the time. She never missed a week writing me."

"She loved your letters so much, Harry. And when the baby came she wanted you there so much."

Harry's underlip trembled, his adam's apple went up and down, but he managed to swallow and speak: "But of course she had to stay because she had all that nursing to do in Paris."

"She was wonderful in Paris. You'd have been proud of her."

"Yes, she was certainly wonderful. We used to have such good times. You know, the way we always understood each other without talking, kind of, we had some good times."

He and Caroline exchanged glances and slowly a new expression emerged on Harry's cheese-shaped face. He looked at me and I managed to nod and smile, and he muttered, "Gee I'm glad to see you again, George." Then his face turned pink and I wondered if he was going to cry, but before he could make up his mind what to do, Caroline rose and laid the baby on the couch and put her little finger between its lips while the baby smiled and wriggled its toes.

"Harry, isn't she a darling, and aren't you lucky!"

Then she looked straight into his eyes, he looked straight back, and they stood still. There followed a quick sob and an expression on his face quite indescribable and again I wondered if he was going to cry. But instead he grinned like an idiot and went down on his knees to play with the baby.

"She's Norah's image," he said, "isn't she?"

"Yes," said Caroline critically, "but there's some of you in her, too. Look at her nose. Your nose isn't too terrific in a man, if you don't mind my saying so, but for a girl your nose would be just about perfect. It won't be this ski-jump I've got to carry around with me. Isn't it a pretty nose for a girl?"

"Gosh, yes!"

I stared down at the baby, and to me she was not Norah's image and she did not have Harry's nose. To me she was just an infant with pink cheeks and plump limbs fully aware that she was being appreciated. I puffed on my cigarette and stepped back.

"Norah and I—" Harry began. Then he stopped, uttered a little choking cry, picked up the baby and carried her to the open window. I saw the muscles of his back straining, his suit wrinkling, as he clasped the baby to his chest and rocked it making strange sounds.

"Norah and I had so many wonderful times together," he whispered in that choked voice. "You'll never know, you'll never know. She was so happy the night she told me she was—"

"Yes, that's what she said to me in Paris. She was so happy when she knew the baby was coming and that you knew."

"I'm going to call her Joan," Harry said, still staring blindly out the window with the infant in his arms. "Joan! Don't you think Norah would like that?"

"I know she would."

He turned and laid the baby on the couch and began playing with her, and the child liked him.

"She's laughing!" Harry looked up with an astonishment of happiness on his face. "Don't you hear her laughing?"

"She knows her father," said Caroline.

"Gosh, how can a baby know that?"

"I brought her to you the moment I could, Harry. You see, after Norah—well, after she had that accident, it was lucky I was in Paris then. It was luckier still I was just going to leave, for I was able to bring her to you."

I sat frozen at what I was witness to.

"You'll have to learn a lot about caring for babies, Harry," Caroline said sharply. "But there are books and nurseries and things, and I'll be around for a week or two to show you."

"I'll learn," Harry said. "Just watch me learn."

"Of course you will, but don't go around boasting about being able to take care of babies better than women can."

"I'll learn. You watch and see. I'll bring her up just the way Norah would have liked it."

He was full of pride. Or was it pride? No. For in that instant I saw his eyes and knew he was not fooling himself or even trying to fool us. Suddenly he had found a reason for living, something to cling to in a life which had become meaningless and horrible, and it was as simple as that. He had recovered a continuance with the only thing that had ever mattered to him, and glancing at Caroline's wise smile I wondered how I could possibly have under-rated her intelligence.

"I've got my job back," Harry said. "I didn't tell you, but I got it."

"In the radio shop? But that's wonderful!"

"From now on things are going to be fine," he said. "I've just got to succeed from now on."

"And you will. You'll make Norah and everyone else very proud of you. She's watching you, you know."

Again I stared at Caroline in astonishment.

"Yes," she went on, "before she died Norah became religious again and she knew there's an after-life."

I knew that Caroline did not believe a word of this, but Harry believed it. His eyes shone. His pathetically shaped body straightened and he nodded.

"Yes," he said. "Yes."

Soon after we left him, as we walked back to her lodgings, I said: "Does Jerome know about this baby?"

"Of course."

"Is it his?"

"Honestly I don't know, but I don't think there's much likelihood. He'd be much happier if it were."

"What do you mean?"

"Well George, I suppose I might as well tell you. When Norah went to England on the ship with him, of course she thought that would settle things and they'd be together. Jerome was kind to her, but no—he wouldn't do that. She must have made life hell for him. She had breakdowns and everything like that. She threw scenes. But when he went to Spain she became sort of awfully calm and she just slept with everyone who wanted her. This baby could have had any one of several dozen fathers. Norah'd been faithful to Harry until this thing with Jerome, you see. It had been building up inside of her all the time and once she started she just went hog wild. They often do that, you know."

"Who often does that?"

"People who are sick like that. One part of their mind is pure and the other—you see, they don't know who they are any more. Poor Jerome, it was awful for him. He blames himself for destroying her."

"She'd have destroyed herself anyway."

"I suppose so. Actually if anyone's to blame in this it's Harry, for he never satisfied her. Could you imagine Harry satisfying a woman like Norah? He's such a nice little man, but—well, I hope for everyone's sake that his next wife's not over-sexed. I'm sure he'll marry again."

"Do you really believe that?"

"Oh, men always seem able to find wives if they want them badly enough."

We said good-night and I walked homeward in the warm air, but when I reached my door I was too restless to go in and walked up the slope of the mountain until I found myself among the trees. A couple passed hand in hand talking quietly in French, starlight filtered down through the trees and the city shimmered far below. I sat on a granite boulder for half an hour feeling myself involved, and, thinking about Jerome, I knew why I was no longer shocked by his behavior. He, too, had become involved. As Caroline had, as all of us did if we lived long enough. I wondered if I would ever see Caroline again, and something told me I never would. Nor did I.

Nor, for that matter, did I see Harry Blackwell again for many years. He and his newly-found baby disappeared into the ocean of Montreal and soon I forgot all about them. But one day in the first year after the war I happened to be walking down a side-street between Sherbrooke and St. Catherine—my orbit in Montreal had narrowed to the city's heart—and suddenly I saw his name on the front of a store fluorescently lit, remodelled and extremely modern. I looked in through the window and saw Harry himself, quite bald and as absurdly pear-shaped as ever, but well-dressed and with a new manner. He was talking to a tall woman in a black Persian lamb coat, and she looked the kind of woman who would only talk to the owner or the manager. That afternoon I called up a man I knew in a St. James Street insurance office and asked him if he knew anything about Harry's business. He told me that Blackwell's Radios and Record Players was not only doing exceedingly well, but that it had captured a sizable piece of the carriage trade business in his field, and that Harry himself had become a prosperous man.

Chapter IX

A FEW days after meeting Caroline, I drove up to the Laurentians in my second-hand car to see Catherine and Sally. I felt tense and unnatural, and half-way up I even began to feel hostile. This fixation I had on Catherine had endured so long it had become a part of my life. There was no sense in pretending it had not frustrated me. There was no sense in pretending that there had not been moments when I had felt angry with Catherine for not having dismissed me outright. On that journey to the Laurentians I came as close as I ever did to criticizing her. Why this acceptance and non-acceptance of me? Had she, perhaps without knowing it, thought of me as a kind of insurance policy? It was no use my remembering that she had introduced me to other girls in her time with Jerome, or that she had urged me to regard her as a friend and live my own life. With her in my mind I had been unable to love any other girl I met, even though I had desired several.

These feelings melted away the moment I saw her, for what I saw was a small woman with an older face, a withdrawn face, a small, plumpish body still beautifully formed, a woman who had once lived a full rich life now living a circumscribed one, a woman who once had loved a lusty husband now living only for her child. I thought: once again she has gone over a frontier ahead of me.

Sitting on the porch we talked quietly of various things, and her initial coolness, her initial factualness, made me feel rejected. She told me Jerome had left her with a small annuity, that she intended to put this cottage on the market, and that she hoped to get a job in the fall.

"I probably won't be strong enough to work whole-time at anything," she said. "But I must make some extra money. Daddy and Mummy took us in when I broke down, but Daddy's health is failing and he can't live much longer, and it's impossible to try living with Mummy. She bosses Sally and she still resents me even though she doesn't know it. When Daddy goes she'll want to be free. In her heart that's what she's always wanted."

Looking down the lake where Jerome had paddled and talked of his childhood, knowing that this would be the last summer either of us would see this panorama, I had to resist the impulse to ask Catherine to marry me. I was not earning a big salary, but it was more than twice what I had ever expected at Waterloo, and it would be just enough to support us at present prices. But of course there was still Jerome.

"I suppose you saw him when he came home?" I said casually.

"Yes."

"How was he?"

Her face was a mask. "That's an impossible question for me to answer."

"Jack Christopher told me he'd been wounded."

"That's true, but he didn't take it seriously. You know Jerome in things like that."

"I was talking to Arthur Lazenby," I said, "and Arthur told me Jerome was disgusted with the communists."

Catherine breathed heavily and I thought I saw a little flutter in her chest.

"I always knew he'd be disgusted with them when he got to know them," she said. Then a moment later: "But—I don't know what to say, George. He's involved. That's the only way I can put it—he's involved so deeply nobody can touch him. It wasn't like two strangers meeting. It was"—she lifted her hands and dropped them—"it was frightening, and yet it wasn't frightening. Both of us seemed to be hypnotized."

"Lenin used to talk about dead men on furlough."

"Did he?" she said. "*Did* he?" She gave a soft laugh. "I don't suppose he spoke of dead women on furlough, too?"

I felt blasted, isolated, cut off and almost annihilated by this sentence, and for a time neither of us spoke.

Then, forcing myself to sound factual, I said: "This Spanish war will soon be over. Will Jerome come home then?"

"How do I know? Somehow I doubt if he will."

"Do you want him to?"

"How can I answer that, George?"

I looked at that small figure reclining in the chair, the face older not because it was lined but because it reflected now an inner discipline that made it almost formidable.

"Some things seem clearer now," she said. "I think I told you once that the trouble with Jerome and me was that we loved each other too much. It was something I said when my emotions were so confused I could hardly think. But now I've found out it's true—we loved each other so much we exhausted each other. Everyone wants to be happy, and so much of happiness depends on not being tired. We both demanded from each other more than was possible. Do you know that line of Rilke? 'Love consists in this, that two solitudes protect and touch and greet each other?' A marriage based on that kind of love could last. But one like Jerome's and mine—"

We talked of other things for a while, and finally I asked her if she knew that Norah Blackwell was dead.

"The poor, crazed girl," Catherine said. "I can pity her now, but not because she's dead. No, I don't pity her for being dead."

I remembered what Jack Christopher had said about Catherine's heart beginning to fibrillate, but she looked so well it was unreal to me that her life should be in danger. I had noticed her movements, and certainly they were slower and more deliberate than

I recalled them. I had noticed that she kept off her feet more than she used to, but her figure was as beautifully curved as ever, her skin was still soft and creamy, her hair still sable with that suggestion of lightness. To me she had never been more attractive as a woman than she was then. There seemed a greater depth in her, a greater—long ago I spoke of that singular force which I called, for lack of a better word, spiritual. I felt more of it in her now than ever before, I felt it emerge from her and reach me.

"George," she said simply, "since Jerome went away and since I broke down, I've had to ask myself some hard questions. While Jerome was here and we were happy I pretended the future didn't exist. I lived in the moment—from day to day. I drew on his strength. Now—" she smiled as though to protect me—"you mustn't mind this, George, but I must say it. Now my problem is a very simple one. Somehow I must contrive to live long enough to enable Sally to grow up."

This shocked me so much that I felt my color change, and Catherine laid her fingers over the back of my hand.

"You mustn't mind me putting it like that. I don't expect to die for a long time yet, but I do know that my reserves have been reduced. Sally is what I must live for now. Poor little girl, she's the bigger thing that gives her mother a reason for existing." Then her face changed, she smiled and was beautiful: "Now don't think I go around in the glooms because I don't. I'm getting a lot of fun out of hundreds of things. I've begun painting and I love it. Soon—who knows? Perhaps I'll stop worrying about Jerome."

That night after Sally went to bed, Catherine came to me with a letter.

"I'd like you to read this, George. I got it over a year ago, and it's from Jerome's foster-mother, Mrs. Martell. I met her only twice, for he was afraid or ashamed to visit them, but I wish she'd been my mother and not his."

I picked up the letter, which was bulky but written in a very fine script with an old-fashioned pen, and this is what I read:

> *Dear Catherine,* I know that what he has done to you is cruel, and I do not understand how God will easily forgive a man who deliberately leaves his wife and child, but that

Jerome himself is cruel, that I do *not* believe. He was a good boy always, and when he grew up in our house we thanked God for him every day of our lives. If you had seen the poor little thing the morning we found him and the look in his eyes you could never be bitter against him for anything he did. Grieved you could be, but bitter, no.

It was the war, Catherine dear, coming on top of that awful thing that happened to him as a little boy. The day he came home from the war was the most awful day Mr. Martell and I ever spent, and it was the day we were sure would be our gladdest. We went down to meet the troopship and I, big fool, had my arms full of daffodils because his first poem had been about daffodils and it wasn't a bad poem either, *much* nicer than the poems which are so famous today and nobody reads for beauty or gladness, but Jerome was hardly back in our little house before he turned on us and told us we had raised him on myths and old wives' tales and by that he meant our religion, and he told my poor husband that the reason he drank was that it was only when he was drunk that he could believe that everything he lived for was not a fake. My husband was *never* drunk, Catherine! Jerome's language that day was so awful I shudder to remember it, but what right had I to complain, and what could I say, for what did I know of war? He was only *nineteen* years old and he had been through those awful things, and poor Mr. Martell and I could not even imagine how fearful they were. That night we wept bitterly.

Mr. Martell was wiser than I, and he said to me the next day, "Goodness and mercy we thought would follow us all the days of our lives, but it cannot follow anyone if he tries to live his life through somebody else. Jerome must find his own path now." This was too deep for me, Catherine, for wise though Mr. Martell was, I *know* we never tried to live our lives through Jerome, we were just proud of him, and later on when he was a doctor we were so proud and happy to think that the little boy we had found in a railway station, *our* little boy, was a wonderful doctor helping all kinds of people in a great city. No, I do *not* think we tried to live our lives in Jerome, I think we just loved him and wanted him to be happy, and dear Catherine, when he married you we were so happy we thanked God once more for his goodness, for you were the perfect wife.

Some day he will return to you, Catherine dear. That I know. To you he will come back, but not of course to me, for now that Mr. Martell is gone, I hope and pray that I will soon follow him. I am Scotch as you know, and we Scotch are lonely, sentimental folk, and I love that old Scotch song Mr. Martell enjoyed so much, *The Land O' the Leal*, and sometimes I sing to myself those lines about wearin' awa like snaw when it's thaw, because that is what I am doing now, just wearin' awa as though all were a dream. Since my husband's death nothing seems real, only the times I remember and the great hope I have that soon we will meet in perfection, and sometimes I think Mr. Martell may even be lonely in heaven, though of course I know that is silly, for he won't need his socks darned there, and he won't need somebody to clean the spots off his Sunday clothes, and all the little things I so liked doing for him, he won't need them at all.

Pray for him, Catherine dear, and do not be too proud to pray for *yourself*. Pray that your belief in him will endure, for I know you must believe in your heart that in *his* heart he is a good man still. Pray that he may discover the peace he seeks, and that he will find God before it is too late because that is what he *really* seeks, for if he finds God he will find himself, and then he will find *you*. One of these days this dream will end and we will all meet in the bosom of God. You must not mind if I talk like this, for it is an old woman's weakness and some day you yourself will be an old woman and will know what it is like. It is like talking to yourself so much of the time.

I hope I am not just talking to myself now, Catherine dear, when I repeat to you a sentence from one of my husband's sermons which has helped me many a time. My husband was not a very good preacher because he had a weak voice and never believed people would be interested in what he had to say, but I always loved his sermons because usually he would say something in them I had been thinking myself, and then it would be said and I would know it was true.

This thing he said was one of the most familiar sentences in the Bible, simply this—"It comes to pass." That was his text. But the way my husband spoke it the old words sounded quite new and different, for he spoke them like this—"It comes —to pass!" That is, it comes, *in order* to pass.

I put the letter down and was unconscious of my own body as I stared over the lake to the empty hills. I heard Catherine's voice beside me.

"That was the last word I had from her. Six weeks later she died."

Catherine went inside with the letter and left me staring across the lake to a wilderness half-obscured by a purple twilight. I thought of those two gentle, loving little people I had never known. Had the ocean rolled over them as though they had never been?

Catherine returned, and sensing my thoughts, she said: "I envy those two people. They were born knowing that nobody can be equal to his destiny if he's alone. But they believed in God, so they weren't alone. I envy them, George, I envy them. I wish I could believe in God."

"I've often wondered if you did."

"I do and I don't. I think it's this wretched heart of mine that makes it so hard for me to believe in Him. I used to pray and pray when I was a child, pray to God to make me better and like everyone else. And yet there are times when I'm aware of Him."

For a long while neither of us spoke and it grew dark. Stars looked very bright in the silence, the total silence, of that northern night. I sat and thought; I sat and desired Catherine so intensely I could hardly endure it. Never had I loved her as I did then, and I did not understand until much later—though she did—that this feeling of being able to love her properly was to some extent connected with the change in her condition. Circumstances of many kinds had reduced her. Now at last—for I, too, was growing up—I could believe within myself that I was her equal.

Suddenly I heard myself say: "Catherine, please marry me."

She was so calm that I'm sure she had anticipated my question. I felt her hand close over mine, her small, soft hand with the long, lovely fingers.

"Oh George!" And then: "Dear George, it would be better if you hated me."

"Don't say such things."

"Even if I were in a fit mental state to marry anyone, I wouldn't dream of letting you marry me. You're still young."

"We're the same age, practically."

She smiled: "Yes, in the actual number of years we've lived. No dear, you must find yourself a real wife who'll be able to give you children and take care of you properly."

Overwhelmed by emotion I took her into my arms, the first time I had done so since we were children, and for an instant she melted against me and I cried out with emotion. Then she stiffened, she turned away her head, she pressed her cheek against my breast, she withdrew and sat down in silence.

"Catherine, I love you! I can't love anyone else but you. I've tried. I've tried and I can't."

I saw her breast lift and fall, her hands came up and covered her face, then she dropped her hands and sat still.

She said very quietly: "I'm sorry, I'm so terribly sorry. I've done to you what Norah Blackwell did to Jerome. Almost what he's done to me. I knew better and yet—oh George, how can people hurt each other like this?"

"Is it Jerome? Is it still him?"

"Perhaps. How do I know? Oh George, I—this has been like a bereavement. More than that, it's—I can't make decisions. I've made so many and I can't make any more. Living with Jerome I let him make them and then I was left—just Sally and me and my bad health and—I can't make another decision, I can't." Then she said more quietly: "I'm going to say something I hope you'll never find the necessity of saying."

I had been kneeling by her chair and now I got up and sat in my own.

"I'm tired of love," I heard her say. "I'm exhausted by it. All of me, body and soul. Now I'm beginning to be free of it, and how can I face it again?"

I looked dumbly at the shadow of her form in the chair in the dark and she knew what was in my mind.

"George dear, I know what you want and I want it too. Don't think I don't. But I wasn't talking of sex a while ago, I was talking of love. Sex is so easy. It's so very, very easy. But you love me and I love you. And I'm not equal to love."

"I don't understand."

"I hope you never do, dear. Now I'm going to say something which will probably shock you. A year ago I went to bed with a lonely man I didn't love. I thought it might help but it didn't. I came home and thought of the verse in the psalm: 'Deliver my soul from the sword; my darling from the power of the dog.' I knew then there is no easy escape from loneliness. I've been wounded, George. Perhaps I'll heal. If my health were normal— yes, I'm sure I'd heal. But I'm not equal to love now, and you are, so you must find somebody else."

And a little later she said: "It's funny, not really believing in a God who cares and yet believing in the soul. Yet it's all each of us is left with, finally. If I were stronger I could forget that, but I must live for that, too. For that besides Sally. For that until I get so tired I can't. Does this make any sense? Can't you see, George? I'm still a fairly young woman. I know from the way men look at me I'm still a desirable one. I know from the way I feel I'm still full of desire myself. But—" She stopped, and then she said with complete calm—"I also know that I haven't long to live."

I think I wept but I'm not sure, nor does it matter. A little later I drove back to town with the image of her face haunting me, with the feeling of her body melted into mine so warm and close that the night throbbed. I remembered Jerome in his canoe going down the river to the sea, and my thought that at last he had reached the sea and was out of sight of land in his canoe. Now I, too, was at sea and I thought of that vast reservoir of emotions and memories on which every fragile human life floats until the depth becomes a Mindinao Deep so profound he cannot plumb it. And I realized something else: that Catherine had been trying to tell me that love, sought as an escape from the burden of the self, turns rapidly into a captivity. "Very well," I said aloud, "very well." And I knew then—or thought I knew, since nobody can know in advance how he will actually feel—that perhaps I had at last grown up. If loving Catherine meant captivity, then I wanted it.

Chapter X

THAT summer and the years immediately following, my private life almost drowned in what seemed to be the disintegration of the world itself. As pigeon after pigeon came home to roost, as all the fearful prophecies we had made with angry defiance in the Thirties became living realities, my own life and that of everyone I knew shrank to insignificance.

The summer after I revisited Catherine was a sweltering one. Montreal steamed in a humid heat worse than Singapore's, the garbage smelled high in back alleys, tenement dwellers gasped for breath on their steps and porches after sunsets; even the calls from the belfries rang like dull bronze in the dead air. Thunder-weather.

Working day after day, often night after night in that humid heat I felt like a herald of death. Strangers used to call me in the radio building and say: "Mr. Stewart, can't you really see a ray of hope?" Or: "Mr. Stewart, please stop telling us there's going to be a war." Or: "Mr. Stewart, my husband was killed at Ypres and my boy is eighteen and why do you insist there's going to be a war?"

We entered it in September, 1939, in a trance. Catastrophe after catastrophe, the queer lull during the first winter, then Norway, Holland, Belgium and France: Narvik, Rotterdam, Eben Emael, Forges-les-Eaux and Hitler in the Forest of Compiègne. The bands played *There'll Always Be an England,* the airmen signed the Kentish skies with their honor and the unemployed vanished from St. Catherine Street into the army.

The week France fell I was in Washington on business for the organization, and while listening to a scared debate in the Senate Chamber of that neutral country I remembered Jerome. Where was he now? When last heard of, he had been seen crossing the

Pyrenees into France with a beaten remnant of the Loyalist army. I believed he had been interned by the French, which indicated that his passport had been lost or stolen. The previous winter I had made enquiries in Ottawa about him, but External was far too busy with the war to spend time tracing a single citizen who had left his country to join a Spanish tragedy. Where was he now? Dead, I thought, as dead as my own past, as dead as I myself will be a year or two hence.

When I returned to Montreal I went to a recruiting station to volunteer. The doctors looked me over, thanked me for coming, and rejected me on two counts. So I went back to my work in CBC and stayed with the organization throughout the war.

Strange years which now have become a blur. While the war thundered on, Canada unnoticed grew into a nation at last. This cautious country which had always done more than she had promised, had always endured in silence while others reaped the glory—now she became alive and to us within her excitingly so. My work brought me close to the heart of this changing land. And sometimes, thinking with shame of the Thirties when nothing in Canada had seemed interesting unless it resembled something in England or the States, I even persuaded myself that here I had found the thing larger than myself to which I could belong.

The war thundered on and the Thirties became a memory. I spent a winter in Halifax directing a series of scripts describing some aspects of the navy which then, without anyone seeming to be aware of it, was carrying on sixty percent of the convoy duty on the Atlantic. I crossed to England on a convoy and visited some of our army camps. I returned to Canada for more routine work. The war thundered on with the tide turned. I went out to the Alaska Highway, came back again and was sent to England just after the Normandy landings. I was back in Canada when the war ended, having spent all of it chairborne and out of uniform.

It was during the war, of course, that Catherine and I finally came together.

Late in the summer of 1939 she found a buyer for her Laurentian cottage, and a few weeks after war began she got a job with an interior decorator in the city. Yes, even then there was some business in interior decorating. She sent Sally to her own old school in the city and rapidly her confidence returned to her. In 1940 she left the interior decorator's for war work which she was able to do in the mornings and she stayed with this for the duration. In such spare time as she had, she began learning how to paint.

Then, early in 1941, came the news that Jerome had been tortured to death by the Nazis.

I heard this news before Catherine did, for it reached me in my office in the CBC building. I at once got in touch with the French aviator, Captain Lajoie, and he seemed an entirely responsible man. He was in Canada organizing a fighter wing of Free Frenchmen who were training under the Empire Air Training Plan, and before the war he had been a professional officer in the French Army. There seemed no reason to doubt his word. He told me that Jerome, after being released by the French from the concentration camp for the defeated Spanish, had tried to escape to England. But the Nazis had over-run the country and he had joined the French underground. Captain Lajoie had not seen his body impaled on the meathook in that French market town, but he himself had been in the operation in which Jerome had been captured. He said an attempt had been made to rescue him from the Gestapo and that afterwards he had been told about the torture and execution by one of his own men, who swore he had seen the body.

It seemed final and conclusive, and I left Lajoie feeling sick. But I remembered Catherine almost at once, and immediately I telephoned friends on the newspapers and asked them to repress the details of the story. Once again I was grateful to that Montreal clannishness which can be so exasperating to outsiders. The men I talked to on the papers had already heard Lajoie's story and had decided themselves to repress the details for Catherine's sake. And the *Gazette,* as I was to tell Jerome years later, wrote him an obituary notice becoming a former Montreal surgeon who had died bravely in the war.

But the details got out just the same; they always do. One day a woman Catherine barely knew telephoned her to ask if the story about the torture was true. Catherine was shocked enough anyway, but now this woman gave her the details and nearly killed her. She had to rest in bed for nearly a week, and when I visited her she looked as though she were under the torture herself.

She recovered. Once again she crossed a frontier and grew strong on the other side. I visited her more and more often, we became more and more essential to one another and at last she ceased holding me off. By the end of that summer she had persuaded herself that I would never marry anyone else. Also by the end of that summer she received from the Canadian government a formal confirmation of Jerome's death.

It was on the weekend of our Thanksgiving in 1941 that I drove Catherine down to a friend's cottage beside a lake south of the city and there we spent three days in the cathedral silence of a land which in that season is surely the loveliest on earth. For this was hardwood country with deep, clear lakes. Maples of three species, birches, oaks, beech and butternut trees flamed all the way from southern Quebec to the New England sea, mirrored in lakes while flocking birds flew south.

"Yes, George," she said, "yes!"

Three weeks later we were married.

Chapter XI

HAPPINESS is one of the hardest things to write about, and the difficulty of doing so makes me long to be a musician or a painter, for painters and musicians are at ease with the supreme emotion, which is not grief but joy abounding. To be able to make a joyful noise to the Lord or a praise of colors and forms would seem to me to equate any man with gods or little children. Happiness annihilates time. We measure history by its catastrophes, we recall the weather by its storms, but the periods of peace and joy —who can describe them?

"Many a green isle needs must be. . . ." But is it not also true that years later it is the green isles of happiness that we remember best, even if we cannot tell about them? Is it not also true that though we can describe pain, we cannot remember what it was like? Jerome once said to me that nature's greatest mercy could be found in the singular fact that nobody can *remember* pain.

You can remember that you felt pain and you can dread its return, but pain itself, the surgeon's saw across the unanaesthetized bone—that you cannot remember. But moments of joy you can, even the feelings of it. The feelings of making love in peace and excitement can return years later and live.

Happiness did not come to Catherine and me in a rush; rather it grew like summer weather after a cool spring in a northern land. I heard her laughing again, I watched her face shed some of its lines and grow younger again, I saw a new ease with the growing Sally. Happiness revealed its presence in the faces of new friends, and to me its fairest aspect was my own witness of the world's beauty once again establishing itself upon Catherine. She had been lost and now she was found. As I, lost for years, had also been found. As the world, apparently lost for more than a decade, now seemed to be finding itself, too.

Now Catherine understood what beauty was; now in her painting she was learning to capture some of it; now in the acceptance of her own infirmity she had no need to resist the knowledge that beauty's most exquisite property is its evanescence.

The war ended and still the country grew, and now I had a small but established reputation. Now we lived a quiet life and the Thirties seemed to have sunk back into the past. Good years, rich years, wonderful years. Many a green isle needs must be. . . . We lived, and we lived well, in those years before the first of the harsh inevitable commands came from her damaged heart. We lived and it was real and I remember nearly all of it. Even now on a spring morning in the country I can see again the joy in Catherine's face when she used to come out to greet a morning similar. Or on an evening of mists in the country I can still see living the serene happiness in her eyes. Or across a dinner table in candlelight, sometimes I see a handsome woman in early middle-age smile at the man beside her and remember how Catherine too had smiled at some man, hitherto a stranger, who had become her dinner companion and in whom she had discovered something she liked. Good years and full ones. I could not count all the lives that crossed and touched our own during them, each contributing to the other some atom of experience. Now when the first snow falls in the city and the apartment is suddenly brighter owing to the sun's reflection on the snow, I see again the look in her eyes which says: "How good to see this again!" Her painting became joyful: such riots of color I had seldom seen in the work of a painter in this land which so many painters see as somber except in the fall. In our country place we planted a garden and there was a spring of water beside it where warblers fanned themselves on hot days. Together we grew intimate with the seasons, and we planted our lives in one another without trying to annul the past. She, who had said 'yes' with all her might to Jerome, now said 'yes' to me.

The odd thing about this period was that we both were young in years yet felt all ages within our imaginations. In terms of a normal life-span we should have been standing at high noon. Yet, though we never used such terms to one another, we knew that our actual time was early evening. We knew, and never mentioned, that it was sure to be limited. Fortunately the evening was the part of the day we both loved the best, for the early evening of a good day holds within itself the dawn and the morning no less than the promise of the night.

Sally grew and entered college and the first touch of gray appeared in Catherine's sable hair. The country grew and became rich, and a generation to whom Hitler and the depression were mere names now stood six feet tall. Good and wonderful years when the voice of the turtle was truly heard in the spring. For Catherine's soul seemed healed. Her love for Jerome had gone down like a wounded living thing to the floor of the sea and time had covered it, the deep time which enfolds and exposes to chemical change all living things, time full of new friends and interests and life and love, and of the quiet joy of watching her child grow into a woman.

Chapter XII

THE last line uttered by the Devil in the first part of Goethe's *Faust* is the abrupt command, *Her zu mir!* Faust's adventure is over, his dream of eternal happiness gone. The Devil, who had been waiting ironically, says "Come to me!" and it is over. I think of that line whenever I hear the first movement of Beethoven's

Ninth where, time and again with a compulsive beauty, the key changes to that ominous note of pity and terror against which all but courage and art quails. From the statement of the opening theme this key-change has been inevitable. One senses, even if one does not know, that it is sure to come, and it does. So came the change in our lives with Catherine's first embolism.

It struck like a sword, it threatened her life, it paralyzed her entire left side for days. And for days I was terrified not only for her but also for myself. I learned to hate sickness as Jews learned to hate Hitler.

But Catherine recovered from this. That enormous life-force in her, after being nearly extinguished, gathered a mysterious strength not even the doctors professed to understand. After a long convalescence she got better, and a season in the country restored her. The lid of her left eye drooped from the damage done to her nervous system, but this droop gave her features a singular charm. By the fall of that year she was almost normal again.

Almost, I said. For in our minds neither of us could ever be quite like other people again. The inevitable had now happened. It did lie ahead of us, a beyond-this-nothing, as the war had lain ahead of us in the Thirties. Now it was here, as the war was here in the Forties. Previously she had known that she lived with the sword dangling over her head by a horsehair. Now she had felt its point; now she looked up and saw it there.

A year passed and the sword fell again. Once more that astonishing life-force in Catherine rallied and after paralysis she again got better.

I make these statements factually and coldly because it is the only thing I can do. Each of these attacks was an assault on her life by an enemy who had aimed at her. Suddenly it seemed to me that we were almost isolated by her fate. I became aware that some of our friends regarded Catherine's plight with awe. They spoke of her courage and outward cheerfulness, they were kind and thoughtful, but it must have been painful at times for them to think about us. They, too, were nearing early middle age. They were reaching the place where the final enemy ceases to be a mere word. They had seen his tracks in the forest, they had heard his horns in the night, they had come upon the traces of his fires.

They knew he was planting his little fifth columns in their arteries and valves and organs and the cigarettes they smoked and the tensions under which they lived. A few of them looked at Catherine, I sometimes thought, as I myself had looked at some small, defenseless country near to Hitler's Germany in the years when Hitler seemed as omnipotent as fate. She would get it first. She, still so young in years, was a preview of what lay in wait for all.

The change of key, the turn of the dragonfly's wing—was it only to us that the whole mood and tenor of life seemed so suddenly different in the last two years of the 1940s? I don't think so. For surely the whole world went over a frontier in that time and since has been compelled to live very strangely.

In the Thirties all of us who were young had been united by anger and the obviousness of our plight; in the war we had been united by fear and the obviousness of the danger. But now, prosperous under the bomb, we all seemed to have become atomized. Wherever I looked I saw people trying to live private lives for themselves and their families. Nobody asked the big questions any more. Why think, when the thing to be thought about is so huge it is impossible to think about it? Why ask where you are going, when you know you can't stop even if you wish? Why ask why, when it does no good to know why?

In the Thirties old John Donne had spoken for all of us when he declared that no man is an island entire of itself, that every man is a piece of the continent, a part of the main. In the bleak years we at least were not alone. In these prosperous years we were. The gods, false or true, had vanished. The bell which only a few years ago had tolled for all, now tolled for each family in its prosperous solitude. So with us; so with so many. How private my life with Catherine had become! How outmoded so many of my friends felt! How different was this new key!

But of course for Catherine there was the knowledge that most of her life was lived, that the best was inevitably over. Now in her final phase what I used to think of as her character ceased to matter in Catherine; her character almost disappeared into her spirit. The Catherine I knew and loved was still present and visible, was even fun to be with. But the essential Catherine—

what now was the essential Catherine—sometimes seemed to me like the container of a life-force resisting extinction.

Yet she was often gay. In public she never let out a word of how she felt except by way of excuse when there was some place people wanted her to go to and she was not well enough. Sally seemed almost unconscious of her mother's struggle, so well did Catherine conceal it from her. And does it make any sense to say that she was inwardly sad when she painted such pictures? Every fortnight or so she changed the picture which hung on the wall facing the foot of my bed, and when I woke in the dawn there this thing was, this expression—not of Catherine but of a love of life itself which in her had become so intense as to be almost impersonal.

Finally we reached this winter which I described at the beginning of the story, when I, too, almost persuaded myself that I was equal to my destiny of living under the sword with her until at last the sword fell. When I, too, almost believed I was at peace. When I, too, flattered myself that my courage was equal to hers.

Few fighters are knocked out by a single blow. One after the other in combination is the way a trained man strikes down his enemy. And after each blow the situation changes, and so do the reflexes and capacities of the person hit.

Little did I know—though I believed I knew all about it—how little I actually knew of the enormous and terrible implications of absolute finality.

The shark in the ocean may be invisible, but he is there. So also is fear in the ocean of the subconscious.

A man standing on a rock may believe himself strong enough to stand there forever. But if an earthquake comes, where is he? *What* is he?

I can say now in retrospect that I did not know what my true position was when Jerome returned from the dead. But I was soon to find it out. I was also to discover what I, and I believe every man, requires to know and feel if he is to live with a sense of how utterly tremendous is the mystery our ancestors confidently called God.

PART SEVEN

Chapter I

THIS story opened the day I went to Ottawa to meet the Minister and talk with Arthur Lazenby, Jerome was seen by nobody he knew. He checked out of that wretched hotel where he had spent his first night in Montreal and found a room in a quiet, clean place and after that he walked the streets in spite of the cold. He did not telephone Catherine or try to get in touch with me. He walked until he was exhausted and half-frozen, and then he returned to his room and lay down and slept.

The reason for this behavior was simple enough. For twelve fearful years he had lived with the thought of Catherine and Sally in his mind; he had lived to come home to them both. This was his goal, the thing that kept him alive, just as the hope of freedom in old age keeps breath in the lifer in the penitentiary to which he has become so accustomed that freedom, if finally it comes, is terrible to him.

Also during those twelve years Jerome had been haunted by the fear that when he did come home Catherine would be dead. Now he had discovered that she was not dead, but that she was married to me.

So he passed that day alone, and with thoughts I think I can imagine. The next morning he telephoned our apartment, heard Catherine's voice, and asked if he might see her that afternoon. He arrived about two o'clock when Catherine was alone.

I must tell you now what he looked like, and it is not easy.

His hair was still vigorous and closely cropped, but all of it had turned a uniform shade of dark gray. There was a small, deep triangular scar on his left cheek, two fingers of his right hand and one of his left looked splayed, for after tearing out the nails the Nazis had pounded his finger bones with hammers. Physically he was slimmer than we remembered him, wiry rather than robust, and he moved more slowly and with a heavier limp. In the old days he had looked explosive. Now he had acquired the capacity to sit still for hours.

These physical details were secondary to the effect produced by his presence on everyone he met now. Though his features had aged somewhat, they had not altered. It was his expression that was different, that announced an altered personality to the world. He was entirely recognizable. When you got used to him again you could still see in his face something of the boy who had grown up in Halifax dreaming of the white city on its hill overlooking the sea. But now—there is only one word for it—there was in his face a kind of transparency.

You see, Jerome—like Catherine—had returned from the dead.

She let him in and this was the man she saw. But what he saw was not the woman I saw because I, living with Catherine, still saw her with the eye of memory. He, returning with his memory of her as she had been, saw a small woman whose figure seemed much as it had always been but a face much older, the gray in the hair, and the changes worked in her expression by what she knew now. Each seeing the other saw in a flash that what they had believed was their past no longer existed. For a few moments they were almost like husband and wife meeting after death in the next world.

I know only some of what they said, though more I can infer. They uttered a few banalities while their spirits communicated behind the mask of their words. They saw the changes in each others' faces fade back until each became familiar to the other. Then Jerome saw her pictures on the wall.

He got to his feet and stared at them, then back at her, and she at him.

"*You've* done these! You!"

"Yes."

He had seen no pictures all the time he was away. Seldom had he heard any music. He saw these pictures and wept.

It was then that Catherine's reserve broke and she crossed to him and put her hand on his shoulder. A moment later those two who had loved one another were in each others' arms, and they held each other's remembered body, swaying as people do, their minds almost obliterated, both in tears. Then she thrust him away and sat down in silence, and he sat down on the opposite side of the hearth and minutes passed before either could speak.

She was looking at his hands, his splayed fingers, and he became conscious of this.

"I didn't break," he said simply. "I wanted to live to tell you that."

"I knew you didn't," she said, "because you never could."

"Afterwards in the cell I saw your face and slept."

"I saw your face in the cell and did not sleep."

Outside the February sun slanted across the snow and shone on the boles of the bare elms. Outside the eternal squirrels searched the snow for scraps of food and found little on this bitter day. Outside the outline of a scalloped moon was cirrus-white in the deep blue of a cold sky, and the exhaust of a North Star outward bound from Dorval made four white feathers.

"I hoped I could make love to you," he said simply, "and now you're married to George."

She looked at him, nodded and said nothing.

"Kate!" he said hoarsely. "Kate!"

Then he controlled himself, he looked for minutes at one of her pictures, and at last his face—so Catherine told me later—became peaceful as she had never seen it. After a long silence he told her a singular story.

While in China he had believed he had reached the end. Often before he had told himself that he had reached it, but never had he truly believed it within himself. Always that fighting instinct had reasserted itself: against torture, against danger, against disappointment, against apparent hopelessness. Always he had been driven on just as he had been driven down the river in his canoe that night in his boyhood. But in China he contracted amoebic dysentery, there were no anti-biotics and he was left to die. He was also a virtual prisoner of the communists. Now—neglected, weak, his whole past life regurgitating—he said that if he believed in God his only prayer would have been for death.

But his constitution resisted death, and his mind after virtually dying became active again. He longed for something to read, but there was nothing. And then the strange thing happened.

Jerome had always had a prodigious memory, and in his Halifax boyhood he had memorized the Gospels and many of the psalms. Now in an effort to retain his sanity he set himself deliberately to recall them. Day after day he would try to remember the story in its regular sequence. Weeks passed in this occupation, and in the process he changed.

"One day I woke up and Jesus himself seemed to be in the cell with me and I wasn't alone. He wasn't anyone I had ever known before. He wasn't the Jesus of the churches. He wasn't the Jesus who had died for our sins. He was simply a man who had died and risen again. Who had died outwardly as I had died inwardly."

And a while later he said to Catherine: "You've done that yourself, haven't you?"

"Yes," she said, "more than once."

"Does George understand it?"

"George doesn't know anything about it, Jerome."

Then he said in that direct way I can imagine: "Is he equal to letting you live your death?"

"I don't know. I wish he didn't have to be."

Another long silence during which again he studied the painting over the fireplace. It was as close to being a self-portrait as Catherine had ever done. It was a picture of a fourteen year old girl in a swing lost in a joy of colors that sang like trumpets, the colors exuberantly gay. Yet the picture itself was inexpressibly poignant, for the girl had no recognizable features. She was simply all the young girls there ever were lost in a spectrum of spring and knowing themselves alone. The head drooped like a flower on a stalk. Even in beauty's very heart, even in the heart of life itself, this solitude.

Catherine, seeing his eyes on her picture, said: "I keep painting because it's all I have left. It's useless, and yet it's all I have left. I know I'll never have time to be good enough to be remembered."

He looked at her and said: "By whom? Strangers?"

"I suppose so."

"Does it matter if you are?"

Ruefully she said: "I wish I could say it doesn't."

After a while he said: "Kate, I still know you, and you still know me, and we both know each other as no others ever did or ever can. About some things I was as wrong as a man can be, but about some I was always right."

"Yes," she said, "I've never forgotten that. And I've been lonely for that ever since."

"In time it will come to you, Kate. Soon it will come to you. Believe me, I know that."

"Can you tell me what it is?"

"No, but you will know what it is when it comes."

"It shows in your face," she said. "Whatever it is."

After a time he said: "And in spite of that—in spite of that—I'm still a man, and I still long to make love to you at least once again."

She raised her head: "It's too late for that, Jerome."

"Kate!"

That power in them both was exhausting to them both, even to Jerome. He became conscious of his own exhaustion, I suppose, for he suddenly remembered her heart. He crossed to her, a doctor now, and held his ear against her breast. And there, with a doctor's understanding, he heard what I had heard so often—for his ear was almost as sensitive as a stethescope—and then they looked into each others' eyes and no words were necessary, for he knew what she knew.

"Oh Kate, if I hadn't gone mad we might have had all those years."

"Or if I hadn't failed you."

Then she smiled shyly. Then not smiling, but calm and natural as I also knew her, she opened her housecoat so that his lips might touch her breasts. He kissed her and she murmured his name, and he hers, and then she lay on the chesterfield small in his arms, and he was so still she thought him asleep. For an hour they lay there and he at least was in a private peace. At last he got up and then there was twilight in the room, for it had a north light.

"Will George be equal to what's ahead?" he said very simply.

"I don't know, Jerome. He's been very good to me. I always loved him and I never pretended otherwise. It was not what you and I have had."

"Does he resent it?"

She looked away and said nothing.

"Does he resent you for being like this?"

"He doesn't think he does."

Catherine lay on the chesterfield looking up at him, knowing the great change that had come to him, knowing his need for her but knowing also that now he was a man who had gone before her the way she herself was bound to go.

"God bless you," he said, and I can imagine his face when he said it. "Thank God for letting me see you again."

"Thank Him for letting me see you."

"In a few days I'll leave Montreal, Kate. I'll not come back. I can still do my work, though I'm not as good as I used to be. There'll be some place for me out west. I'll never trouble you again."

She looked away without speaking.

"May I see Sally sometime before I go?"

"I think you should."

"Does she resent me?"

"Yes, but she won't when she sees you. You're her father, Jerome."

"Are you glad I came back?"

"You know I am." Then she gave that strange smile. "I don't know whether *I* know it, but you do."

He bent and kissed her: "It's worthwhile, Kate. In spite of everything, the struggle's worthwhile."

She heard him go to the door, the door open and close, and at last she was alone.

Minutes passed into an hour during which she lay in a trance. Then slowly, inexorably, panic grew as she became aware of a tumultuous, hostile commotion within her body, and she realized it was the palpitation of her heart. She rose to get water from the bathroom, but while it was running a wave of dizziness struck her, she went to her bed and lay cold and quaking with chattering teeth. She took her own pulse, reached for the digitalis tablets and swallowed one, then she lay quiet while the room turned dark.

Chapter II

A STRANGE feeling of apprehension, even of guilt, filled me when I came home from Ottawa and entered the apartment. I found it dark. I called out and heard nothing. I went to Catherine's room and turned on the light and saw her lying very small on the bed with her eyes open. She saw me but with no intimacy. She saw me in such a way as to exclude me entirely from herself, and inwardly I felt a surprising surge of anger.

Then I noticed something else about her: a jerky movement in the carotid artery. I laid my ear against her chest as Jerome had done and the rasping, uneven stroke of her heart sounded like a death rattle. I had never heard it so bad.

Still her expression excluded me. I had never felt like this with her before. I had made her my rock and my salvation, and now she was not my rock and not my salvation. Nor was it simply her health that had changed it.

I heard her say: "George, some day forgive me?"

"For what?"

"For what I've done to your life since you were seventeen."

I rose and looked out the slats of the blind at a glimmer of light on the snow.

"Have you seen Jerome?" I asked her.

"He left a few hours ago. I'll tell you sometime. I can't now."

"That's all right."

"Don't hate me. I can't stand it if you do."

"Hate you?"

Turning, I saw her small, curved face pale, calm and wet with tears. I sat on the edge of her bed and took her hand. She looked away.

"It's been too much," she said. "I've tried so hard and now I'm so tired."

I felt her pulse and it alarmed me: "Let me call Jack."

"Get yourself some supper first. I'll soon be better. It's just that"—she almost sobbed—"Oh George, to need to be strong and to be so weak! All my strength has been bled away."

I went to eat and the apartment was silent for half an hour. Then, just as I was finishing, I heard her call out very sharp and loud and entering her room again I saw the expression I had come to loathe, the expression that came with the change of key, the command *Her zu mir!* But it changed immediately to that look of serenity I had also come to dread, for never was her face more serene than when her life was threatened.

"Pray for me, George."

Her calmness almost annihilated me; her beauty—believe it— was suddenly that of an angel.

"What's happened?"

"Something strange."

"I'll call Jack."

And yet as I went to the phone, her life in danger, I wondered about her and Jerome and about what might have passed between them. Yes, I wondered that. For I remembered also her look when I had come in, and knew that she had gone far away from me. She had belonged to the both of us; really belonged. Did she still belong to us both in spirit if not in body?

Jack's answering service informed me that it would trace him and that I would hear from him inside a quarter of an hour.

Back in the bedroom that accepting face stared white from the pillows, and I sat beside her. I needed her more than she needed me then. I realized that in her previous two illnesses the same thing had happened: she had been stricken and I had needed her more than she had needed me.

"You don't know what it's like," I heard her whisper. "Please God you'll never know what it's like."

I did not know what she meant by this and I don't know now; I merely record what she said, and my belief is that she meant I did not know what it is like to be chained by her own body.

Suddenly she gasped, sat up and clutched her abdomen.

"It's come. It's another embolism."

"No!" I cried. "No! Your eyes and face are the same."

"This time it's not in the brain," she whispered. "It's here."

I saw her hands clutching her abdomen, her face tense with fear and pain. Then the Catherine I knew, the woman I loved, disappeared into a force I knew to be nothing but an impersonal spirit fighting for existence.

I saw her lips move, her head nod, and knew what she needed. An embolism is always followed by nausea. I rushed for a basin, brought it, held it while her body humiliated her, wiped the sweat from her face, rested her head back on the pillows, sat and waited for what seemed to be hours until the doorbell rang.

Jack Christopher came in. Another examination, another familiar routine, and after twenty minutes he joined me in the living room, his face grave.

"It looks like an embolus in the small bowel," he said. "At the same time it doesn't."

After phoning for an ambulance he sat down and stared. He

was tense and deeply disturbed, for in his own austere way he loved Catherine.

"There's something I'd better tell you," I said. "Jerome is alive." His eyes opened wide at me. "Yes, he's alive. He's in town and he saw her this afternoon while I was in Ottawa."

I had always envied Jack his self-control, but I never saw anything to equal his performance at that moment. His eyes stared only for a second, then his lips tightened and behind a masked face I sensed a cataract of thoughts and possibilities he would never utter.

"Well!" he said. Then he gave a short, wondering laugh. "Did you see him, too?"

"I talked to him over the phone a couple of days ago, but I didn't see him."

"You shouldn't have let him see Catherine." I shrugged and he went on. "Well, where has he been?"

"In concentration camps in Poland, Russia and China."

"You shouldn't have let him see her."

I said nothing and stared at the floor. What did Jack want me to say? That I was so much weaker than Catherine that I could not bring myself to decide her business for her?

"On the other hand," Jack said, "probably it was the only thing to do. She'd have found out sooner or later."

"Yes, I thought it was the only thing to do."

"I suppose you think this embolism—well it may not be an embolism—this whatever it is—I suppose you think it wouldn't have happened without him?"

"I had been thinking that," I said.

"It could have happened anyway. At any time and at any place these last half dozen years."

"Is it going to mean an operation?"

"It might," Jack said.

He went to the phone, dialed, and I heard him say to somebody in the hospital: "Put out a call for Dr. Andrews. I wish to see him as soon as possible."

I stared numbly at the floor, for Dr. Andrews was now the chief surgeon at the Beamis Memorial. I stared numbly because Catherine and I had assumed for years that she could never sustain a major operation.

Going into the bedroom I saw her small and resigned on the bed. She said nothing while I packed her bag or even when the doorbell rang and a pair of orderlies and an interne entered with a stretcher. But once we were in the ambulance, she lying on the stretcher and I sitting beside her with an interne opposite, the ambulance rushing up Côte des Neiges with its siren hooting, her gallantry returned and she smiled a little girl's smile and pressed my fingers.

"Fun!" she said. "This is the next best thing to a ride on a fire engine."

Chapter III

A MAN can carry a specific fear for years and believe he is sustaining it well. He can school himself so that he thinks he knows exactly what the fear is. But when the moment comes, he may find it larger, different and more mysterious than he had guessed. He may discover that its burden has changed his very nature. The moment comes, the fear explodes through him like poison, and he becomes a stranger to himself. *Her zu mir!* Who knows in advance how he will feel when he hears that command?

I waited two hours at the hospital with nothing to do while the doctors consulted, made more examinations, took x-rays. Then the surgeon, followed by Jack, came out to the sunroom to see me. He said they must wait for a temperature to show before they decided what to do. An operation was possible—from the surgeon's expression I guessed he believed it was necessary—but they would have to wait.

"Let me drive you home?" Jack said.

"Thanks, I prefer to walk."

Outside it was cold, clear and strange, the city a fleet at anchor under a cold sky greenish to the north. The cold searched for me, found me, and I wanted warmth, a drink and another identity. That was it—another identity. "Before I married her, I was I," I heard myself mutter. "Now I am her. And she is dying." Had there been a bar on the mountain crest I would have got drunk right then because I wanted to forget I was alive. If she must die, let her die now. The process of dying is awful. Have it over with. Have it over with.

I was not noble as I walked home in the cold.

But I did walk home, and when I entered our building the heat struck with such a shock I became dizzy and waited several minutes before unlocking our door. I supposed Sally would be home and I recorded the thought that I should have telephoned her from the hospital, but I had not done so. Instead I had sat by myself in the sunroom feeling myself turning into something strange, new and unpleasant.

The apartment was almost dark when I entered, and I remembered I had left all the lights burning. Was Sally asleep? Then I saw two shadowy forms move and spring apart and realized that she had brought Alan Royce home with her, had found her mother's door closed and had assumed her asleep, had seen no sign of me and supposed me out, and that the two had been necking on the chesterfield.

"Sir!" said Alan.

I was too tired to answer and hung up my coat and hat in the cupboard. My ears were almost frozen because I had not worn my fur cap and the cold had found them while I was walking home. Lights came on in the room behind me and I saw Sally's back as she stared ostentatiously out the window at nothing.

Alan said with a mock bow: "*I* have been surprised, sir. You, I trust, have been merely astonished. May I get you a glass of your own whisky, sir?"

"No, thanks."

"It's the least a man in my position can do, sir."

Sally, her back turned, said: "Alan, stop sounding like an oaf."

I sat down and took out a cigarette, which Alan lit for me with a flourish. I leaned back in my chair and made an effort to think. Life about to begin. Life about to depart. At the moment I was resentful of both these common events.

"Alan," I said, "I think it's time for you to go home. There's something I want to talk to Sally about."

"Is it as bad as all that, sir?"

"Strange though it may seem to you, Alan, I don't intend to talk to Sally about you."

He realized from my face that something serious had occurred, and at once his voice changed and revealed the subtle courtesy I found so charming in his generation.

"It's none of my business, sir, but if something's the matter, I'm awfully sorry."

Sally flashed around and said: "Is it Mummy?"

I nodded: "I've just left the hospital."

And when I said this Alan almost ceased to exist for this girl who had been thinking of nobody else for days.

"Yes, Alan," she said, "you'd better go."

She got his poncho or whatever that naval garment of his was called and held it for him, and he looked like a huge shaggy dog as he bent his knees, his hair flopping, and thrust his arms into it.

"Good-night, sir," he said.

"Good-night, Alan."

When Sally and I were alone I told her what the doctors had said and spared her nothing, for at that moment I was weaker than she. She asked me some probing questions and I felt still more inadequate, for I knew she was a competent young biologist and had boned up on her mother's case from the medical books. When I told her the embolus seemed to be in the small bowel, Sally went pale. She knew that if it turned out to be an embolism, an operation would follow.

"I'm going up to the hospital," she said, and went to the cupboard for her coat.

"No, you're going to do nothing of the kind. Your mother's under sedatives. If there's a change, they'll call us here."

She sat down and lit a cigarette, the frown-line deep between her eyes. Only a few nights ago she had sat on this sofa radiantly in love, and now her dream had vanished.

"Was my father here today?" she asked.

"Yes."

"Is he responsible for this?"

Wearily I looked away. Wearily I said: "How do I know anything? Let's blame it on God, for He fixed that heart for her long before you were born."

"George, you look tired. Go to bed."

"I will, at that."

I was so tired I was lurching, and after I got to bed the room throbbed like an engine and I saw nightmares and knew I could never sleep in that condition. I felt like a drunk even though I had drunk only one whisky all day. I saw, incongruously, Arthur Lazenby's face over lunch in the cafeteria of the Chateau Laurier. My God, was it only twelve hours ago since we'd talked about Jerome?

Then I felt something cool on my forehead and it was Sally's fingers and I envied Alan his good fortune. My subconscious was taking charge of me. Sally was a woman, Sally was a lovely young girl, and my subconscious wished she was my wife.

"Nobody will ever ask 'How is Sally?' " I heard my own voice say. "Everyone will always know that Sally's fine. God, I'm so sick of that eternal greeting, 'How is Catherine? How is Catherine?' From now on let's call her Kate. When she was Kate she was never sick. She was wonderfully well when she was Kate."

Sally's fingers continued to soothe me and after a while she said: "Please don't be hurt like this."

But my maturity had gone and my subconscious had taken over. I was Everyman and every frightened boy and everything and everyone but myself.

"I can't bear the thought of her looking at the sun," I heard myself say.

"What, George? what do you mean?"

"When they wheel her out to the operating room if the sun is shining and she knows she's looking at it for the last time."

"Please relax, George. Please!"

And her fingers continued to stroke my forehead while my subconscious, my identity almost gone, wished I were twenty years younger with none of my life lived and that she was my wife.

"It's going to scream like a pterodactyl," I heard myself say.

"What are you talking about?"

"The Russo-American Moon Express."

Then things blurred and I suppose I slept. I woke alone in the dawn, had an instant of happiness as I saw one of Catherine's pictures joyous on the wall, then remembered where I was and where she was. The illuminated dial of my bedside clock showed six-thirty and it was too early to call the hospital. But I could not sleep because I kept waiting to hear the phone ring. For an hour

I lay waiting for the phone to ring and the apartment was utterly still.

"This is destruction!" I heard myself say. "Of her. Of me because of her. Yes, she has destroyed me. Jerome has destroyed me. Life has destroyed us all. All for nothing. For nothing, for nothing, for nothing!"

At seven-thirty I got up and peered through the slats of the Venetian blind at a rose-fingered dawn reflected from the icicles of the nearest roof. Oh, what a beautiful morning! A beautiful, cold skier's morning in the innocent northland. A beautiful morning with no shaming horrors produced by the subconscious of Everyman. To be healthy on such a morning, to be young on such a morning, to be innocent of life on such a morning, oh, to be young in that morning were very heaven!

I put on my slippers and dressing gown and went to the phone.

"There's been no change, Mr. Stewart," the floor nurse said.

"How was her night?"

"She was under sedation."

In other words her night had been full of pain, of fear, of tumbling down unknown tunnels in the endless dark.

I turned from the phone and saw Sally's blonde head as fresh as the dawn outside, as golden as the sun on the single cloud in the sky, and I told her what the nurse had told me. A few minutes later I lay inert in a tubful of hot water.

Oh, pity every man who comes hard to the knowledge that underneath his bright, sure consciousness he is not himself but Everyman.

Fate, I thought. Who is equal to it? For to be equal to fate is to be equal to the knowledge that everything we have done, achieved, endured and been proud and ashamed of is nothing. So I thought, alone as I had never been alone, on that beautiful morning.

Chapter IV

I CAN continue with this story and make sense of what follows only if I succeed in explaining something very difficult.

The desperate sickness of a loved one, especially if the loved one is still young, does strange things to those involved. It causes them, as the old Greeks used to say, "to escape their own notice" doing and thinking and saying things. It makes them more familiar with their underselves than they choose to be, and strangers to their own notions of their own characters. It can shake their basic security in existence.

There is a savage truth in Somerset Maugham's declaration that suffering, so far from enobling people, actually degrades them. A savage truth, yes. But not the whole truth. This, I repeat, is a very difficult matter.

An illness such as Catherine's is fate palpable. Her character was not responsible for this fate. At the beginning of this story I said that some people have within themselves a room so small that only a minuscule amount of the mysterious thing we call the spirit can find a home in them, while others have so much of it that what the world calls their spirit explodes from the pressure. I say again that this mysterious thing, which creates, destroys and recreates, is the sole force which equals the merciless fate binding a human being to his mortality.

Catherine's spirit, as her fate became more obvious and unavoidable, grew larger and larger. Her courage made me feel awe; it even made the doctors feel awe. To go on like this, to struggle like this—for what? Merely to have to go through it all again at a later date. She did not seem to me like a boxer rising again and again to be punished by an invincible opponent, but more like a bird in the claws of a cat who wanted to prolong the fun. The cat was God.

Without daring to utter the thought, this is what I believed when her ordeal began. The previous embolisms had not been like this, nor on those other occasions had I understood how serious they were. Nor had she, not entirely. I had been like a recruit in the first battles of a war: frightened, none too competent, but still believing that somebody else would be the one killed. Now I knew there was no discharge from this war. Now I knew how unavoidable—sooner or later—was her defeat. And this brought me face to face with what I truly think is the great terror of hundreds of millions of people.

The terror is simply this. God, whom we have been taught to regard as a loving Father, appears indifferent. God, whom we have been taught to regard as all-just, is manifestly unconcerned with justice as men understand the meaning of that word. Why should Catherine have to suffer like this? Why should a scoundrel have health and she none?

You may think I make too much of this. I don't think I do, because these considerations lie very deep in all of us, even in atheists.

All of us are children at heart. What gives the child the desire to grow and acquit himself well is his hope of winning his parents' love. Without this hope, why struggle? Why care?

But the child becomes middle-aged, and who then can fulfill the father's role? Reason can't do it for long. Ability and success are makeshifts. A man may install his wife or children in the role of his god, as the sanction for his existence and his reason for being. A woman, more naturally integrated into the scheme of nature than modern men seem to be, may find no difficulty at all. But a man, apparently, needs a god. So in the Thirties we tried to make gods out of political systems, and worship and serve them.

But the trouble is that none of these substitutes abides. The time comes when the wife dies, and then what is there? The time comes when children go away. The time comes when the state is seen for what it is—an organization of job-holders.

Then, though we may deny it, comes the Great Fear. For if a man cannot believe that he serves more than himself, if he cannot believe there is meaning in the human struggle, what are his chances of emotional survival? We may assert that as flies to wanton boys, so are we to the gods who kill us for their sport. But we can't live long believing this. Human dignity forbids it.

I know the world is full of people who have had thoughts like mine during Catherine's ordeal, and I know they have been shocked and ashamed by many of them. There she was—so brave, so frail, her beauty being destroyed, her life chewed away. Why? There was I, torn by pity and grief, and loathing what her plight did to me. There was she, knowing that even if she recovered she would never recover as a whole woman. There was I, knowing how she dreaded being a burden. Meanwhile there was no discharge in the war. There was only endurance. There lay ahead only the fearful tunnel with nothing at the end. Could I or could I not—could she or could she not—believe that this struggle had any value in itself?

At first I couldn't, and, my humanity revolting against it, something happened to me that can happen to anyone under similar circumstances.

My subconscious rose. The subconscious—the greedy, lustful, infantile subconscious, indiscriminate and uncritical discoverer of truths, half-truths and chimaeras which are obscene fusions of foetal truths, this source of hate, love, murder and salvation, of poetry and destruction, this Everything in Everyman, how quickly, if it swamps him, can it obliterate the character a man has spent a lifetime creating!

Then a man discovers in dismay that what he believed to be his identity is no more than a tiny canoe at the mercy of an ocean. Sharkfilled, plankton-filled, refractor of light, terrible and mysterious, for years this ocean has seemed to slumber beneath the tiny identity it received from the dark river.

Now the ocean rises and the things within it become visible. Little man, what now? The ocean rises, all frames disappear from around the pictures, there is no form, no sense, nothing but chaos in the darkness of the ocean storm. Little man, what now?

. . . And the earth was without form, and void; and darkness was on the face of the deep.

. . . And the spirit of God moved upon the face of the waters. And God said: *let there be light:* and there was light.

Here, I found at last, is the nature of the final human struggle. Within, not without. Without there is nothing to be done. But within. Nobody has ever described such a struggle truly in words. Nobody can. But others have described it and I can tell you who they are.

Go to the musicians. In the work of a few musicians you can hear every aspect of this conflict between light and dark within the soul. You can hear all the contradictory fears, hopes, desires and passions of Everyman fissioning and fusing into new harmonies out of the dead ones. You can hear—you can almost see —the inward process of destruction, creation, destruction again and re-creation into the last possible harmony, the only one there can be, which is a will to live, love, grow and be grateful, the determination to endure all things, suffer all things, hope all things, believe all things necessary for what our ancestors called the glory of God. To struggle and work for that, at the end, is all there is left.

In music you can hear this kind of struggle translated into diapasons so universal that they wash like the light of the world over the little external truths of science. You can hear the spirit of Bach and the spirit of Beethoven explode from one vast chamber into another so enormous it fills, for an instant, the universe.

In the end, the new harmonies resolved, nothing outward seems to have changed. The little man is still a little man. But within he has been changed.

For within him has happened what the musicians alone seem able to record: the resolution of fear and courage, love and hate, terror and defiance, shame and honor, despair and hope—all of Everyman in the ocean of which the identity was temporarily lost —into an acceptance of humanity's supreme invention, his concept of the Unknowable which at that instant makes available His power, and for that instant existing, becomes known. The musicians can show this happen; oddly enough, they can show it specifically. One musical idea uttered in the minor in a certain tempo is surrender, despair and suicide. The same idea restated in the major with horns and woods becomes an exultant call to life. This, which is darkness, also is light. This, which is no, also is yes. This, which is hatred, also is love. This, which is fear, also is courage. This, which is defeat, also is victory. Who knows the things of the spirit except the spirit of man which is within him? said St. Paul.

So the final justification of the human plight—the final vindication of God himself, for that matter—is revealed in a mystery of the feelings which understand, in an instant of revelation, that it is of no importance that God appears indifferent to justice as men understand it. He gave life. He gave it. Life for a year, a month, a day or an hour is still a gift. The warmth of the sun or the caress of the air, the sight of a flower or a cloud on the wind, the possibility even for one day more to see things grow—the human bondage is also the human liberty.

Where wast thou when I laid the foundations of the earth? Declare, if thou hast understanding.

So, for an instant, you may have that understanding.

To have it, to feel the movement of light flood the darkness of the self—even for an instant—is the most beautiful experience anyone can ever know. And millions have known it.

Chapter V

MEANWHILE darkness and inner chaos. For days Catherine was in pain and danger, and I was unequal to the pity I felt for her. My love for her was as helpless to help her as hers, years previously, had been helpless to help Jerome. My subconscious began to scream at me: Let her die. Let her go. End this.

The doctors thought there was an excellent chance that she would die, and for professional reasons they were disturbed. They could not form an exact diagnosis. They thought it was an embolism, but they could not be sure. She seemed to me masking her symptoms. Dr. Andrewes wished to operate, believing an operation was inevitable. Jack Christopher refused to permit it until a temperature showed, because she was a bad surgical risk. So she had to wait.

Meanwhile other things crowded in. Somehow I contrived to give another lecture at the university and prepare another script for the radio. I went over my accounts and knew I would be in debt if this illness were a long one. Sally, finding no help in me, turned to Alan Royce, who was with her constantly. I became more and more frightened, more and more angry and desperate. If everything we had done and endured led to this, then everything we had done and endured led to nothing.

Still things kept crowding in.

On the second day Harry Blackwell telephoned, and inwardly I cursed at the sound of his voice, for I had totally forgotten him.

"You promised to get in touch with me," he accused.

I told him I had been out of town and that my wife was dangerously sick, and hoped that would get him off the line. It didn't.

"I'm sorry about your trouble," he said, "but I've had trouble for years. Where is Martell?"

"I haven't the slightest idea."

"Why do you lie to me? Look, I'm serious. It's not going to do you any good, this lying to me."

"I'm not lying, and I don't like your tone. I told you—I don't know where he is."

Harry's subconscious had evidently taken hold of him too, for he burst into an invective against Jerome. And then I suddenly felt he was putting into words buried feelings of my own. Up to that moment, I truly had believed, I had never disliked Jerome. Now I suddenly found myself hating him and wishing to harm him, and I felt as though I did not know precisely who I was. I felt scared, and being scared I felt angry. And then, with Harry's hatred coming to me over the line, something screamed in my brain: "No, it's not true. You love her! You love her!"

I said to Harry: "Let me alone for God's sake, I'm going nuts. I don't know where he is."

"I warn you, I'm bringing detectives into this."

"What's it to me if you bring in the whole police force? Just stop bothering me, that's all."

"Oh," I heard him say, "I know you're trying to protect your wife from scandal."

"My wife from scandal? Are you crazy?"

"It was all her fault to begin with," he said in a strange, hard voice. "Women like her, they never ought to get married to men like him." He paused and then he said something that made my hair prickle. "All they do, women like her with men like him, they give them a taste for blood."

"God damn you!" I shouted at him, "Get off the line!"

And I hung up. And I went away hearing his hard voice: "It was all her fault."

There was work to do; with me there was always work to do. So I went back to my desk and tried to work but could not, for I heard Harry Blackwell's astounding voice repeating over and over: "It was all her fault!" And looking out the window at the snow I heard my own voice say: "Can you imagine what *you* would have been like if it hadn't been for her? How do you know what you would have been like? All those years you loved her and she was married to Jerome. Now Jerome comes back and now she's sick again. *You* have her sickness. *He* had her health. And now you have her death and nothing beyond because you've spent yourself out."

The phone rang and it was Sally. She was in the hospital, and when she spoke, her voice was as calm as Jack Christopher's talking to a patient.

"George, I think you'd better eat something and come up. A temperature is showing at last."

I let out my breath and clutched the phone hard. "I see."

"The O.R. has been reserved for three o'clock."

"I'll be up right away."

"No," Sally said firmly, "eat something first. I'm going back to her now, and then I'll have to get out while they prepare her. She's in marvellous spirits and she tells me not to worry and to tell you not to worry. She's marvellous." There was a catch in Sally's voice and I heard her swallow to keep herself from crying. "How can anyone be so marvellous as Mummy?"

I drank two ounces of whisky, boiled myself an egg, made tea and two slices of toast, was bolting the food down and drinking the tea when the phone stabbed me again. This time it was Jerome. And this time I absolutely broke open.

"So you'd like to speak to Catherine?" I said. "Well, this time you've fixed things so that it's highly unlikely you'll ever be able to speak to her again. Just after you left she had another embolus in the small bowel, and your judgment is better than mine about her chances of surviving an operation for *that*."

"No," I heard him whisper. "No!"

"Yes," I heard myself say very hard. "Yes."

There was silence and then he said: "Is she in the Beamis?"

"Yes, and you keep out of it. You nearly ruined her once, and now you've come back and now it looks as if you've finished her. I've read about destructive personalities, but you beat anything I've ever known. Dead men don't bite, Jerome, and dead women don't reproach."

"George—wait a minute. Please, I've got to—"

Agony and remorse were in his voice then, and a desperate eagerness to know the facts, but I hung up before he could finish his sentence and went back to the table to my tea. The phone began stabbing again and I let it ring eight times, knowing it was Jerome. Then I put on my coat and fur cap and walked out into the cold and picked up a taxi at the stand on the end of our street.

The driver was an old acquaintance, his name according to the photo in the cab being Romeo Pronovost, and he gave it as his opinion that sickness was a terrible thing for sure. He knew Catherine and he liked her, and he knew she had been taken to the Beamis in an ambulance several days before. *"Le bon Dieu a des idées très singulières,"* was Pronovost's considered judgment, his reason being that Mrs. Stewart, who had trouble, was a nice woman, while Mrs. Allison, who lived on the same street and also used his taxi, had no trouble and was not a nice woman.

When I paid him off he gave me a probing look and said: "This one is real bad, eh?"

"I'm afraid it's real bad."

"There is some thing I could get? Maybe some thing I could do?"

I thought of Catherine on the verge of the dark and pity scalded the backs of my eyes. I thought of Catherine as a child crying out how good it was to see the squirrels return to her window, and rage at the nature of things burned my stomach. I thought of Catherine as a beautiful young girl crying: "I want to live! I want to live!" And then I cried out inside. All her struggle, all her beauty, all her love, all her art, all her trying—all had come to this moment of extinction. Why struggle like that? Why strive so hard in such a hard existence if this was all there is?

I said to Pronovost in French: "If you feel like it, say an *ave* for us."

"Ouais! Certainement. Pour sûr."

His eyes looked into mine, and for an instant the man's goodness reached me and made me feel, for an instant, pure.

I left him and went into the hospital and as I went up in the elevator, an interne in white silent beside me, out of the turbulent ocean of myself flashed a sentence from Schweitzer's life of Bach:

"Figured bass," said Bach in something he wrote for his pupils, "is the most perfect foundation of music. It is executed with both hands in such a manner that the left hand plays the notes that are written, while the right adds consonances and dissonances thereto, making an agreeable harmony to the glory of God and the justifiable gratification of the soul."

Did God value those paintings which I knew—suddenly I knew—she lived for the sake of? Did her struggle contribute to His glory? What kind of a monster-god wants that kind of service? The image we invent in our own need? "Bah!" I said aloud, and the interne stared.

I walked down the corridor to the sunroom where I found Sally, who told me they were still preparing Catherine for the operation.

"Is Jack with her?"

Sally, covering up her fear, said: "I thought I saw his states-manlike profile towering over a herd of lesser men."

We waited for half an hour, all the time staring down the corridor for a sign of Jack, or of a nurse coming to tell us we could see the patient. About two-thirty Jack's long, lean form appeared.

"Hullo!" he said to Sally and rubbed her blonde head. "Hullo, George! Sit down and I'll tell you what I know."

He told us nothing we did not know anyway, and I asked him how she was in her mind.

"Magnificent," he said. "She's the best patient I ever had."

"Can we see her now?"

"*You* may see her, George, But this young lady"—he glanced across at Sally and made one of those ponderous medical jokes— "I'll keep her company a few minutes and bone up on my biology."

In her previous crises Catherine had been half-stunned by brain embolisms. Now her mind was clear, and when I entered her room she was lying small on the bed and her expression astonished me. She was gay. She smiled. She looked at least ten years younger than she had the night before, and she even seemed to be enjoying herself.

"There's one thing I seem to be good at," she said, "and it's this. That's probably why I like to get sick. I like to show off how good I am when I'm sick. I've not been so flattered in years as I've been by the doctors. Isn't it nice to be good at something?"

I took her hand and her small fingers squeezed so hard that I winced.

"You see?" she said. "I'm as strong as a lion. Dr. Andrewes tells me I'm as brave as one. What a bore to have to be as brave as a lion."

Her smile turned into a little girl's, a small droop of the left eyelid, something *méchant* in the curve of her lips.

"The internes are fascinated with me. I hope they're betting on me. Maybe they've made a pool. I hope they have, for I'm going to fool them, George, I really am."

She was so much stronger than me that I felt like nothing. And this gaiety on the verge of extinction—oh no, you're going to live, you're going to live, you must!

"Promise me something, George?"

"What is it?"

"Get drunk tonight and have some fun for a change. I won't be able to talk to you and I'm going to look absolutely revolting when this is over."

An interne entered, saw us together, gave a professional smile and left. Catherine winked at me.

"Now there goes a really charming boy. He came all the way from California to study here and work under Dr. Andrewes and he's told me all about La Jolla. What's it like outside?"

"Bloody."

"Then this isn't too bad a day to have all this nonsense. And there's something else I've thought of—do you know, by the time I'm well again, winter will be over? I can't wait to see those tulips you planted last autumn."

She was artificially gay because of the drugs they had given her, but not entirely because of them. That mysterious thing in her, that amazing power, had taken her over as it always did in a crisis. In its presence I felt like nothing at all. I looked out the window and Montreal was obliterated by snow. When Pronovost had driven me up there had been white flecks in the air but now gray snow seethed angrily around the corners of the roofs, whorls of snow swirled like pillars of salt: no sky, no city, no traffic, no people, only the snow. Well, I thought, at least you don't have to look at the sun.

I turned back to her and the face I loved had ceased to smile. Infinitely tender, infinitely wise, so gentle I believed I would despair if I never saw such an expression again, she looked at me and lightly touched my hand.

"George dear, please don't blame any of this on Jerome."

"As you say."

"Not as I say. No. I *had* to see him. When this is over I'll tell you all about it. If he phones, just tell him I'm here and am all right. You've always been so kind." Her eyes searched mine and read through them. "Please—*for your own sake, dear*—please keep on being kind."

"All right."

She pressed my hand against her cheek and I felt the warmth of her fever.

"I've been so incredibly lucky."

I went down on my knees to her, her head turned on the pillow and her large eyes, full of love, looked into mine.

"We've had such a wonderful life together, you and I. I've been so amazingly lucky, and I'm so grateful I could sing."

"Catherine!"

"Compared to most people's, my life has been so wonderful."

"Catherine!"

"George, dear?"

"Yes?"

"Nothing is going to happen—not this time, anyway. But if it does"—never had I felt more love come out of her to me— "George, if it does, promise me something so I won't have to worry about you?"

"What is it?"

Her eyes smiled into mine: "If anything happens—marry again."

"Catherine!"

"You must. Marriage is such fun, and you're not like Jerome. You're made to be a husband."

"Catherine! Dear Catherine!"

"Oh, not yet. Not for a long while, I hope. But just bear it in mind." Another gay, little girl's smile. "I'm going to get over this and I'm going to keep on leading you a hard life. Besides all that, the pictures I've still got to paint! They're all inside me, and one of them feels like Sally did the first time I felt her kick. I'm going to make you proud of me yet, George. You wait and see.

When this is over I'll paint and paint. The Sherbrooke Street galleries will rue the day when they said I was just a Sunday painter."

"Of course they will."

Her lips brushed my hand, her eyes were clear and serene, she gave me a final smile.

"Now darling, go back to Sally. They'll be coming for me any minute."

Her head turned away, her smile vanished, her face became inscrutable. Once again the Catherine I knew vanished into this force of hers which now was mobilized for the supreme contest. I looked at her and her face was a warning, a command, to leave her. I left her almost annihilated.

Chapter VI

IT STOPPED snowing an hour before they wheeled her back from the operating room. Before they were done with her, the day itself was done and night was here. Sally and I stared out the windows and saw the whole of Montreal shimmering with the exceptional clarity of a northern city after dark on a day when a snowstorm has cleansed the air. The whole world was white and clean with a skier's snow.

Alan Royce had joined us, entering the sunroom looking shaggy and huge in his poncho and heavy snow boots, and now he and Sally were talking behind a potted palm. This trouble had brought them closer together than ordinary young love-making would ever have done. I studied Alan's profile: a some-what snubbed nose but a good jaw, a firm mouth and I liked the wrinkles around his eyes. He said something that made her laugh in spite of her fear and misery. He said something else. He seemed much older than me, she seemed much closer to him than to me. She was going to be his wife, but my wife—I looked up and was aware of Jack Christopher in the doorway with Dr. Andrewes behind him, and I rose to meet them on dead legs.

The surgeon motioned me down again; motioned Sally down as she also rose to meet the news. I saw the surgeon's gown stained with sweat and I saw his face and I thought that a general's face might look like this after a hard battle.

"Well," he began, and gave me a succinct, professional summary of the operation.

It sounded terrible. It had been an embolism in the intestines just as they had suspected, and they could not understand why a temperature had been so late in showing. I sensed a tension between the doctors. The surgeon, as I knew, had desired to operate sooner. The physician had forbidden the operation until a temperature showed. Catherine would have been in better shape if the operation had been performed two days ago, and Jack looked wretched. Anyway it was done now, and Dr. Andrewes had removed two and a half feet of her small intestine. He said he would have removed another foot if he had believed her capable of surviving it.

"The chances are fair that things will right themselves inside the next few days," he said. "We'll have to wait and see. Meanwhile I must tell you that she's very sick."

It sounded like a death sentence, and Jack Christopher's face looked like the judge's who had pronounced it, even though he had not said a word.

"Go home, Mr. Stewart," the surgeon said. "Take a sedative and get some sleep. You're in for a few bad days, I'm afraid. But I think she'll pull through. She has a marvelous constitution."

I got to my feet feeling an obscure indignation. "My God, if *she* has a marvelous constitution, how do you define a constitution?"

He gave me a fighting look: "The capacity to survive," he said, nodded brusquely and left us.

Jack stayed a few minutes longer, but he sensed that his presence troubled us and said he had to see another patient and left. Alan Royce gave me a cigarette which I smoked in silence. I went to the pocket of my overcoat and took out the flask I had brought up with me, drank heavily from it, and sat down. Alan sat in the dog-like silence of youth on such occasions, Sally was tense and still and her face looked at least thirty-five years old. After a while a nurse appeared and told me I could see Catherine, but only for a moment.

If you are familiar with the aftermaths of major surgery you know what I saw when I entered the room: a tiny form on a white bed, two splinted arms with an intravenous needle in one and a transfusion needle in the other, a gaping mouth through which the breath rasped and a tube protruded, another tube draining the wound hidden by the dressings. An unnatural warmth, the warmth of a snakehouse, pervaded the room. Five hours ago she had been gay, brave and full of love. Now she looked destroyed.

I returned to the children numb with horror.

"Let's get out of here. Let's go out and get something to eat."

Sally stared in tense enquiry: "You heard what Dr. Andrewes said." I said harshly. "You heard it, didn't you? Why ask me?"

Her underlip trembled but she did not cry. Sally too, I thought, had much room for that mysterious thing. Then Alan Royce, that great bear of a boy, put his arm about her and held her slim, tight form against his own enormous flank, he grinned at me and made a bad joke, and I was grateful. We put on our coats, went downstairs and stepped outside into the cold.

It was a lovely night, so lovely I can see it still. It was one of those Montreal winter nights after snow when a dozen stars look like stars of Bethlehem. For a short while it was so beautiful it uplifted me.

But two hours later, alone in my bed, the darkness descended and the ocean rose.

Chapter VII

ON THE third day the weather changed in the manner it so often does in Montreal. The hard, brilliant cold of the past week yielded to softer airs from the south and over the mountain was a golden light as the thermometer climbed rapidly toward the melting point. The ice on the streets had the look of ice in the first breath of a Canadian spring, blue and purple in spots, its surface spongily firm like the flesh of a fish. The taxi driver Romeo Pronovost, taking me up to the hospital in the early morning, informed me that winter was almost over and that spring, she was coming for sure.

But there was no spring in my step and no light in my mind when I entered the corridors and trudged to her room. In the nurse's face I read one thing only: the belief that it was a matter of hours or at most of a day or two before she would die. In the room that small form lay unconscious with the tubes coming out of it. There was nothing I could do.

Leaving the hospital I trudged the city on dead legs. There was nothing I could do. I stopped in the bar of a hotel around noon and had two drinks and all they did was to act like a reagent on my subconscious. I came out to a beautiful day, the streets full of people looking happy because the first breath of spring was in the air, but I saw them all as they would appear in the hour of their death. A lovely, laughing girl I saw as a rotted corpse filled with writhing, white worms. Then I saw Catherine like that. Then pity and terror and horror followed, for I kept seeing her in a series of kaleidoscopic flashes from the past. That little girl's look which said: "Here I am and please nobody mind!" Then I saw myself loving her all those years when she was married to Jerome and when I was a failure. And then I saw Jerome and hated him and wanted to kill him. I trudged the city and trudged, I wished I were somebody else, I drank more liquor, came home in mid-afternoon and shocked Sally by my appearance, went to my room and dropped into bed. The darkness roared around me.

I was not the only person who behaved badly that day, as I later learned. Harry Blackwell was also drawn into the depths of his underself.

The little man with the absurd appearance and the pear-shaped body, now prosperous and able to afford it, had hired two private detectives to track down Jerome, and one of them had located Jerome entering our apartment building. The man had then called Harry, whose store was not far away, and Harry had come around as fast as he could in a taxi. Finding nobody in our apartment, Jerome had talked a while to the superintendent, and when he came out Harry was waiting for him. Jerome came out, did not recognize Harry, and the first knowledge he had of his presence was a not too competent punch in the face.

Jerome did not reel; nor, considering how he had spent the

last dozen years, was it a particular shock to him to be hit in the face by a stranger.

"It's you!" Harry gasped at him. "You're back. It's you, you bastard."

Jerome reached out both hands and took Harry's ineffectual wrists, looked into his face and recognized him. Harry struggled like a child in that grasp, and a moment later he found himself struggling with something much more formidable than Jerome's physical strength.

"I'm glad you've found me," Jerome said quietly, "because I've been trying to find you."

Incoherent with hatred, Harry tried to spit at him.

"Harry," Jerome said in the same quiet voice, "this isn't doing any good."

"You're alive!" Harry struggled to get free and Jerome released him. But now that his wrists were free, his hands dropped helplessly to his sides. "You're alive!" he repeated in a whisper. "And she's dead."

"Yes," Jerome said.

The two men looked at each other, and I know how Jerome's eyes must have seemed to Harry Blackwell.

Mumbling now, half-weeping, Harry said: "She was all I had. She was the only woman who ever loved me. Now she's dead and you're alive. You could have had any woman you wanted, but you had to take her, and she was all I ever had."

"No," Jerome said quietly, "she was not all you ever had."

Harry tried to lift his hand, but it rose no higher than his waist.

"She's dead, Harry. None of this can bring her back."

"You ought to be dead, too."

"I've often thought so. But I'm not, and you can't alter that fact, either." Then he looked into Harry's eyes and said: "I tried to reach you because there's something I've got to say. You were the only man who ever loved Norah truly. You did everything for her a man could have done. You were the only man she ever respected. And she respected you, Harry. She did."

For a few seconds Harry stared at Jerome, then he began to shake and then he was sick. A delivery boy came out of the apartment and passed them without looking, as in downtown Montreal people so frequently pass human spectacles without looking at them. Harry quivered and discharged himself, and Jerome supported his weakness when he recovered and wiped his lips with his own handkerchief. There was a car parked by the curb, and Jerome opened its door and helped Harry inside, and the two men sat in that strange car while Harry recovered.

After a while, like a wondering little boy, Harry said: "Something has happened to me."

Jerome did not answer.

Then Harry said: "All these years I thought I loved her and now I don't. She always seemed to be around and now she doesn't. When I saw you I . . ." His voice trailed off.

"When you saw me," Jerome said calmly, "you discovered that after all these years you really hated her. I don't mean while she lived with you and you loved her. I mean all these years."

Harry started, trembled and cried: "Don't go near my daughter or I'll . . ." Then, seeing the look on Jerome's face, he stopped. Then he began to sob and his shoulders shook and at last he said: "Help me!"

Jerome said: "You've helped yourself, Harry."

Harry cried: "Did you hate her, too?"

"I hated myself on account of her."

With staring eyes, Harry screamed: "She was a tramp. She never valued anything I ever did for her. I lived like a woman for her and kept the house and she just took everything I did for her and what thanks did I ever get from her? I'd have died for her and she knew it. Yes, I would. I kept our place so nice and clean everybody talked about how nice it was. She never thought I was any good for anything, and nobody else did either while she was around. She saw to that, all right. But I proved they were wrong. I've made a lot of money. I'd have made it for her, but she never thought I was any good and she went away after something better, so she thought."

Jerome said nothing; he just looked at Harry Blackwell with those new eyes. And for about ten minutes, sitting beside each other in that stranger's car, both were silent.

Then Harry looked up and said: "You know something? I feel pretty good."

"You had to say those things, even though some of them aren't true."

"They're all true. All of them are true."

"In a few days it won't matter so much whether they're true or not, Harry. Poor little Norah is gone. She never meant anyone any harm. It wasn't your fault, and I don't think it was her fault. It was how things happened. You were strong enough to get well afterwards."

After a while Harry said: "Jerome, would you like to see my daughter?"

"Yes, but I don't think I should."

Harry took out his wallet, fumbled in it and removed the photograph of a young girl.

"She's lovely," Jerome said.

"She's going to have a wonderful life, Jerome. She's at the best school. She's good at music. She's good at pretty near everything, I guess."

"She's a very beautiful girl, Harry. You must be proud of her."

"You know Norah . . . Joan's so beautiful Norah would . . ."

"Why don't you say it?"

Harry whispered: "Norah was very jealous. She . . ." He stopped and stared at Jerome: "You got no right making me talk like this."

Jerome opened the door of the car and stepped out: "I'll go now, Harry. I'm glad you found me."

"Can I see you again?"

"Perhaps."

Harry sat in the strange car watching Jerome's back go away. Jerome's limp was more pronounced than he remembered it.

Chapter VIII

THAT day passed and I remember nothing much about it but the blackness. The next day began the same: up and down to the hospital, two scrappy meals I did not taste, too many drinks intended to deaden the pain, Catherine unconscious and apparently remaining the same. I slept in the afternoon and it was twilight when I came out of the apartment again so tired, so nothing, I hardly knew where I was or what I was doing. I got into the back of Romeo Pronovost's cab, heard him asking questions about Madame and saw far off a blink of green in the twilight over the mountain. I heard Pronovost assuring me that it was real warm weather, and that spring was almost here. All you got to do is smell, he said, and you smell the spring in the air.

In the hospital at the downstairs desk I asked if Sally was there, and they told me she had been up after lunch time and had left, because Dr. Christopher had forbidden her to enter her mother's room.

Fear brought all my senses to the alert: "Why? Is there a change?"

"We have no report of a change, Mr. Stewart."

Damn them, I thought, they never tell you anything.

I went up in the elevator and was about to enter Catherine's room when the special nurse appeared, laid a finger to her lips and beckoned me to follow her to the sunroom. I went in blackness expecting, dreading and hoping all at once that I would be told that Catherine had died. I sat down and the nurse sat opposite me and I observed her. Even at that moment I took in her appearance. She was a woman of fifty, I remembered she was married with a family, she had been on one of Catherine's earlier cases and I had liked her then very much. She looked my idea of a perfect nurse trained in the days when nursing was the most respected woman's profession in Canada and Canadian nurses were supposed to be the best in the world.

She gave me a good nurse's smile and said: "Things seem a little better now."

"Is there any consciousness?"

"No, but I'm hopeful now. Last night I had no hope at all, but now I do."

"Why don't you let me into her room?"

She answered calmly: "Mr. Stewart, you must not mind this, but Dr. Martell is with her now."

I jumped to my feet with pounding temples.

"He is there on Dr. Christopher's suggestion." Another sweet smile. "He's the finest doctor I ever knew."

I felt like murder with the blood pounding in my head: "What business has Dr. Christopher bringing him into this case? I didn't ask him to be our doctor, I asked Dr. Christopher to be our doctor."

Still calm and nursely, she said: "Dr. Martell consulted with Dr. Christopher this afternoon after lunch. I was so glad they did." A smile all-womanly. "You see, I used to be chief floor nurse on this very floor when Dr. Martell was on the staff. There was never anyone else like him. It's so wonderful having him back."

I looked at her and thought savagely: My God, did he ever make love to you once and are you remembering it? But in her smile there was nothing but this assured sweetness, this feeling of absolute confidence I remembered so many had felt when Jerome was working.

"Is he here as a doctor, or what?" I said.

"Let's say he's here."

"Have you any objections to my seeing my wife now, or must I wait until Dr. Martell decides to leave her?"

"By all means see your wife, Mr. Stewart."

The last time I had been in that room, death had been in it. I know my language is not good, it is not scientifically accurate, but it will have to do. And more than death had been there: the fear of death had been in the room, too.

Now, walking down the corridor, I was bringing into it the spirit of murder. I hated them both—Catherine no less than Jerome. I hated myself and I hated life. I went in and saw Jerome's form on the far side of her bed, the usual post-surgical apparatus and Jerome's hunched form. His shoulders were bent forward, his face in shadow leaned close to hers, the fingers of his right hand lightly touched her right wrist. I hated him and wanted to kill him. He had enjoyed her few good years and he had flung her away leaving me with the residue. He had condemned me—they both had condemned me—to feeling what I felt now, to thinking what I felt now. And there he was, back again with her to see the end. Vividly—like a human figure caught in the act by a flash of lightning—I saw Jerome with a rifle and bayonet in his hands and a fiendish look on his face driving his bayonet into the belly of a blond German boy. Now he was back. Years of concentration camps, of beatings and starvings and hatings and killings and torturings—there he was like the memory of the human race back beside her for the end, and I thought he looked like a vulture.

Jerome's face lifted, he saw me, he rose, I stepped forward, I looked into his eyes. Suddenly I went numb and strange.

I had never in my life seen an expression like his. His face seemed white, very lined but the lines finely drawn, the eyes very large. His whole face seemed transparent. And in his eyes was an expression new and uncanny. They seemed to have seen everything, known everything, suffered everything. But what came out of them into me was light, not darkness. A cool, sweet light came out of them into me then. It entered me, and the murderous feeling went out, and I was not afraid any more. Without a waver in his glance, Jerome put out his hand and I took it, and so after all those years we two met again with Catherine's small, silent body between us.

He said quietly: "Let's go outside."

We walked together into the sunroom and sat for several minutes before either of us spoke, and I continued to feel this strange mysterious power of his, and the light growing inside of me. Then I heard him say in his soft voice: "She's going to get better, George."

There was sweat on his forehead and a wet patch on his shirt. His clothes, which for some reason I had expected to look like a D.P.'s, were correctly English and I remembered that he had spent a year in Hong Kong before coming home. I stared out the window at the city lights and lay back in my chair feeling tired as a child feels, as a child feels tired and a man so seldom does, a purity of fatigue, the kind that comes before a perfect sleep.

"How do you know she's going to get better?" I said at last.

"I'm a veteran at this kind of thing, George. Believe me."

"Have you done anything new?"

"Of course not. Jack and Dr. Andrewes have done everything possible in the medical sense."

Again I marvelled at the transparency of his face. This was how he had aged. His body was lighter than I remembered it, but it was a younger body than most men's of fifty-two. It was still active and strong. But his face had the eyes of Rembrandt.

"Just before you came in," I heard him say, "just before you came in I was sitting there. And I felt death brush me as it went out of the room."

I shook my head and stared at him. I got to my feet and stared at him and there was nothing dramatic in his expression. I saw nothing in his face but an absolute serenity, a total sureness.

"You're a doctor," I said, "and you make a statement like that! What kind of a statement is that for a doctor to make?"

He smiled: "Go back and see her, George. Stay with her as long as you like. I'll be here when you return."

When I entered the room the nurse rose with a rustle of starched linen and I bent over the body alone. Her heart-shaped face was as white as paper, and moist; her body seemed to have shrunk until it was smaller than a child's. If she was alive she was barely so, for she lay as though dead, as though dead for hours. Yet—I saw it—there was still life, a flicker of it in her throat. I touched her wrist as Jerome had touched it, and then—I was surprised because I was not surprised—her eyes opened and for an instant she recognized me. They closed at once and I thought I saw the ghost of a smile.

Behind me the nurse said quietly: "She's not unconscious now, Mr. Stewart. She's sleeping."

So sleep had come, and with it, life.

I went to the window, saw Montreal as a sea of light, closed my eyes and remembered the many times I had looked down on the city from this same hospital. So many thousands had looked down from here and seen that sea of light.

Returning to Jerome I sat down and was silent for a long time before I spoke.

"How long were you with her?"

"Most of the afternoon."

"And you say you did nothing?"

"There was nothing to be done. I was just there."

"Did she know it?"

"I don't see how that could have been possible."

Through the windows I kept staring at that ocean of light that was Montreal. Then fear came back to me, and a sense of utter hopelessness all the harder to bear because, for an instant there had been hope.

"What's the use of this?" I leaned forward to Jerome. "What's the point of this? She'll have to go through it all again. Don't tell me there's any hope of her heart getting better. Don't lie to me, Jerome. Don't pretend that to me."

He said quietly: "No, her heart will be weaker after this. Weaker than it was before the operation. But strong enough to enable her to handle the next one."

I groaned: "No! No, she can't have another operation!"

"I'm afraid another will be necessary. But not before she's picked up strength. This time she was too weak for Dr. Andrewes to finish what he started. But the next one will be much easier."

Again I groaned: "How long must this go on? What's the sense of this? Why not let the poor woman go?"

He reached forward and his fingers closed on my wrist: "George, this isn't cancer. She will recover."

"For what purpose?"

"For a few more years of life."

Again the darkness came down and roared about me and my identity as a human being almost disappeared. Out of the depths I heard my own voice say: "Do you hate her? Two more years of life! What kind of a life? Pain and fear and misery. Another embolism at any time. What kind of a life is that? Is that a life or is it a torture?"

He said nothing and neither did I for a long time. But I felt his presence, and again I felt strength come into me and I stopped being so dark.

"Everything you say is true, George," he said finally. "It's inherent in her condition. It always was, and she's always known it."

"You knew it, too," I cried at him. "You always knew it." Again I felt a spurt of hatred against him. "Is that why you ran away and left her?"

He shook his head: "I don't really think I was running away from her when I went to Spain."

"What else were you doing? Tell me that—what else?"

Again that strange smile: "Actually, I think I was doing what you're trying to do now. I was running away from myself, not from her."

Then I became conscious of him coming very close to me even though he did not move. Suddenly he seemed to be inside me, *to be me,* and I became dizzy and weak.

"It will be like the world living under the bomb," I heard my own voice say from a long distance.

"But it will be living." Again he put out his hand and touched my wrist. "You must understand this, George, because I don't believe you do. I don't believe you really want to understand it. Look at her. Look at what lies ahead of her. As you are now, you couldn't face that." He paused. "But *she* can. You see, George, Kate wants to live."

"I don't believe she does."

"Her organism certainly does." He smiled again. "I've never seen an organism fight better. No, George, she wants to live and she *must* live. Her life isn't completed yet. She knows it if you don't. She wants to paint more pictures." He paused again and said slowly, wonderingly: "If need be, she must be enabled to live her own death. She is one of the very, very few who can."

Staring out at the perpetual spectacle of Montreal at night, at the curve of light along the southern shore of the St. Lawrence, at the dark curve without light that was the river itself, at the sea of light that was the city—staring out at that I felt the last of my strength go away and a cold moisture forming on my forehead.

"Is this room too hot or is something the matter with me? I'm going to faint."

I felt his hands under my armpits and a moment later I was lying flat on a couch with him beside me.

Quietly, with almost a chuckle in his voice, Jerome said: "You must stop wanting her to die, George."

I tried to sit up in denial, but could not. "No," I whispered. "You must believe that. I never wanted her to die. Sometimes I think she thought I did, but no—I never, never wanted her to die."

He said quietly: "You're a human being, George. You must stop being so hard on yourself. *You* didn't want her to die. But what is you? What is anyone? She must live a little longer in order for you to find out who you are."

I turned away from him like a broken child and was helpless.

"You've been very good to her, George," I heard him say.

"No, not good enough."

"Now you must learn to be good to yourself."

"Oh, Jerome, I'm so tired, I'm so tired."

After a while he said: "You're too naked now. There's a limit to what anyone can stand and at last you've found out what your limit is. Don't worry about that. You'll get over it. Kate is going to get better. She'll help you."

"I should be helping her."

"You *have* helped her, and you *will* help her." Then he said: "Listen carefully to this, George. You're too unprotected. You must learn to build a shell around yourself like a snail and every now and then you must creep inside of it. Two days inside and you'll come out able to face anything. Kate knows all about that. She's known it since she was a little girl."

Slowly I turned on the couch and his face swam into focus and again I had this feeling that he was within me, that he was actually myself.

"A shell around myself? What do you mean?"

"Think how Kate does it. You recognize the symptoms, don't you? She's always done it. She crawls away inside of herself for a few days and you feel as if you don't exist. You've resented that, haven't you? I know I did. You panic. You feel rejected. You resent her. And then you're ashamed of resenting her." A pause and another of those strange smiles: "Don't you?"

Again I felt the sweat start and I said: "I've done all I could, all I could and I'm exhausted." Then I whispered: "Yes, it's true what you said. What do you mean—a shell?"

He looked at me and suddenly his face became absolutely clear, his eyes all-seeing like Rembrandt's, and he said with an absolute simplicity.

"Death. The shell is death. You must crawl inside of death and die yourself. You must lose your life. You must lose it to yourself."

"What are you talking about?"

"When things become intolerable—and for you they've become intolerable now—you must die within yourself. Your soul is making your body revolt against what you think you have to bear. You can only live again by facing death. Then you outface it. You must say to yourself, and mean it when you say it: 'What difference does it make if she dies? What difference does it make if I die? What difference does it make if I am disgraced? What difference does it make if everything we've done means nothing?' You must say those things and believe them. Then you will live."

I lay still, but my sweat had ceased to run; I lay still, but my nerves had ceased to scream; I lay still, but the room and Jerome remained in focus; I lay still, but I was no longer in a blackness shot through with fiery lights.

"You see, George, I've been through all this. Not once but many times. So have millions of people. Each one of us is everybody, really. What scares us is just that. We want so much to be ourselves, but the time comes when we find we're everybody, and everybody is afraid. That's when you must die within yourself. *Think* of your life as lived. Think of yourself as annihilated. Then death won't matter. Then fear will go away because there will be nothing left to fear. I learned that in Auschwitz from a Jewish rabbi who also knew some medicine. I learned how to do it, too. A few gifted Jews seem to be the only people these days who know how to be Christians."

Again I lay in stillness and for a long time nothing was said. He did not touch me, he was just there. And now I felt he had ceased being me. I felt as though in a few minutes I would be myself again.

"Then what I'm afraid of is death?" I paused and forced the words out: "Not *her* death, but *mine?*"

He smiled at me: "No, I don't think so. I think what you're afraid of isn't death at all. I think it's life."

When he said this I was astonished: not so much by the words but because of a mysterious force which made the words seem the most important I had ever heard. I had said to myself before that perhaps I was afraid of life. It was an old cliché—to be afraid of life. Now I looked at him and I knew it was more than a cliché.

"Not of life *with* her, George. Of life *without* her."

I looked away: "Yes," I whispered.

"You married her for safety against life. So did I. So do most people when they marry—they marry for safety against life. Now Kate is dying. Yes, I don't deny that. Most of us die slowly for the last twenty-five years of our lives, but she's dying rapidly.

Let her live her death without being afraid for you, for how you'll fare afterwards. You've been wonderful for her so far. I helped her when she was younger, and you've looked after her since. And she's looked after us both. That's all marriage is, I suppose. I went away. I ran away from myself. I destroyed what I used to be. I almost destroyed her. But you don't have to do that. I'm too late, but you aren't."

He seemed to go away from me, to go out of me and away from me, and I was stronger and rose and with my back to him I stared at the city. That enormous panorama—she would live to see it and she would love it again.

Then I thought of so many things we had seen and done and loved together: our garden in the country, the first green shoots in the spring, the autumn stillness over the lake. I thought of the unborn pictures in her mind. I remembered her long, her almost endless struggle, and I remembered how thankful she had been, after every assault on her life, to be able to go on living. I thought of Sally and longed for her to be here. Sally must see Jerome again and he must see her. It would be all right, Sally and this new Jerome; it was necessary and absolutely right that she should meet him, and when she did meet him, she would know again that she was his daughter. I thought of Jerome as a boy, not even knowing his own name, coming down that river to the sea in the canoe at night. Who was he? I remembered how this thought had haunted him. I remembered that amazing afternoon in November when he had paddled me on the lake in the Laurentians and told me his story. 'I don't know who I am,' he had said. Now I was none too sure who I was. What is a name after all? What is it to be the son of known parents? They seldom know you, or you them. All of us is Everyman and this is intolerable unless each of us can also be I. What is the struggle worth? How measure a thing like that in terms of ordinary value? Van Gogh painted alone and in despair and in madness and sold one picture in his entire life. Millions struggled alone, unrecognized, and struggled as heroically as any famous hero. Was it worthless? I knew it wasn't.

Behind me I heard Jerome say: "Jesus said, 'I am the resurrection and the life.' He died in order to prove it and He rose in order to prove it. His spirit rose. He died in order to live. If He had not died, He would not have lived." Silence for a long time. "Kate will live, and so will you."

Another long silence and after a while I left him and went into Catherine's room. The nurse met me with a smile.

"She's sleeping peacefully," she said.

"Has Dr. Christopher seen her?"

"He'll be up any time now, but it's all right. There's nothing to worry about now, Mr. Stewart. Absolutely nothing. She's going to get better. I promise you."

I returned to the sunroom and found Jerome as I had left him. But almost immediately I knew he was not as I had left him. He had gone away from me, completely out of me, and the feeling I had was very mysterious. He had been me a moment before, but now he was himself, and I was myself, and we were like strangers. In response to this change we both became formal.

"Will you be staying in town for long?" I asked him.

He shook his head: "No, I'm leaving inside a few days. Do you remember Arthur Lazenby? Somehow he tracked me down and phoned me from Ottawa this morning. He's finding me a job out west—or maybe it's up north. There seems to be some new town they're building out there and they want a doctor. My hands"—he held them out and for the first time I noticed those splayed fingers—"aren't much good for difficult operations. But they can do routine ones, and I'm still able to work. No, I won't come back here again, George."

I felt alone when he said this, but not afraid of being alone.

I said to him: "You must meet Sally before you go. She's a lovely girl. I think she's going to get married this year."

He smiled: "Yes, I'll meet her if she wants to meet me. Kate told me I should."

"You're still her father, Jerome."

"Yes, I'm still her father." A smile and his hand went out: "Good-bye, George."

"Good-bye, Jerome."

I left him and went down in the elevator. When I stepped out on the ground floor I met Jack Christopher, who had been talking on the house phone to the chief nurse on the floor where Catherine lay. The tight parentheses around his straight mouth yielded to a sheepish smile, and for the first time since I had known Jack, I thought of him as younger than myself.

"You've met him?" he asked me, and there was anxiety in his voice.

"Yes, I've met him. He's still up there."

Jack continued to look sheepish: "Listen, George, you don't mind this, do you?"

"Not at all."

"He's still a wonderful doctor. He got in touch with me and—well, we consulted. There are dozens with more science than he has, and he's out of touch with a lot—but he still has that mysterious thing, George. He has it more than he ever had it. Don't ask me to explain."

"I don't ask you to explain. He's got it. I know. He told me he didn't do anything, though."

"Of course he didn't." Jack became professional again. "There was nothing medical he could have done. But I'm glad he was with her this afternoon, just the same."

"So am I."

"It's wonderful she's going to recover. I didn't—" Jack, embarrassed by such a show of feeling, half-guilty because this whole situation outraged his professional sense, turned and went into the elevator. I was glad to be quit of him.

For something new and strange had begun to happen to me. Light seemed to be shining inside of me when I stepped outside and walked down the driveway toward the city. The weather had turned still warmer, and on the precipices of the mountain tiny rivulets of icy water were making musical sounds. Romeo Pronovost had been right: winter was ending and this night was lovely with the first sounds of spring, and where is spring more gaily virginal, colder or more fresh than in this northern land where it comes when there still is snow? The soft air was as sweet as a healthy childhood, and the sky was not merely a night sky but a radiance illuminating my fatigue. Such a sky I had not recognized since I was ten years old, and I remembered its wonder and how I had almost wept on account of it. The chaos which had been dark within me for days had disappeared and my soul was like a landscape with water when the fog goes and the moon comes out and all the promontories are clear and still. The whole city shone and seemed to have a voice and I heard it, the voice of them all, the lights shaking and standing up, the sky opening to receive that volume of sound and color from underneath, all of it glad and good. As I walked along the familiar street chipped out of the rock of Mount Royal, with the city luminous below and the sky luminous above, there was music within me, so much that I myself was music and light, and I knew then that what she had upheld from childhood was not worthless, that she was more than a rat in a trap, that the loves she had known and inspired had not cancelled one another out, were not perishable absolutely, would not entirely end with her but would be translated into the mysterious directions of the spirit which breathed upon the void. I reached home, found Sally there, kissed her forehead and told her that all was well. Then with that music in my mind, Bach's music, I fell asleep and lay motionless until eight in the morning when I woke to see Catherine's painting on the wall, its colors singing, and the joy she had when she painted it was mine again.

Epilogue

I COULD end here because my story is told. But if this has been a story into which the reader was led gently, I think it may also be one out of which he should be led factually.

As Jerome predicted, Catherine underwent a second operation. It was performed in mid-March and again she rose to it like a champion. Dr. Andrewes did a perfect job in record time, and when it was over her convalescence was so rapid it amazed us all. Once again Jerome had been right: she was bound to live because her life was not completed.

On the long afternoons when the last snows melted on the slopes of the mountain and the squirrels foraged over dry, brown grass, the sunlight striking against the white birches, mazes of shadows on the blue rocks, the occasional pheasant absurdly flamboyant in that setting of tree and rock above the city—in the midst of all this, the color returned to Catherine's wasted face, a little strength to her damaged body, and a flood of joy to her mind. Even while lying in bed she made sketches for pictures she intended to paint the moment she was strong enough to stand. Seed catalogues arrived and she made out lists of vegetables and annuals she wanted to plant as soon as we got down to the country. Shortly after Easter she came home, and we were down in our country place in time to see the irises.

Now began our last phase together. Catherine would never again have the appearance or the life of a well woman. The full curves of her body had faded away, and she looked tiny, frail and so light she seemed like a gossamer. Her heart was much weaker and was beginning to fail in its duty to the other vital organs. That strange sentence of Jerome's: "She _must_ be allowed to _live her own death._" She was doing it now. The tranquillity I used to observe in her face in rare moments now became constant. Her features were, if you looked at them individually, wasted; yet her face had never seemed to me so beautiful as it was then. Like Jerome's, only much more so, it had become so transparent one almost felt one looked at a spirit. Light was in it. Light came out of it. Light came from her constantly into me.

The beloved movements of everyday living returned, the familiar sharing of sights and sounds and of smells as ordinary as coffee on a summer morning while a kitten played in the sun. Our garden shone in June: poppies, peonies and roses, and then all around us in the country a welter of wildflowers in July. The sword was still over her as the bomb was over the world, but she lived, and that summer was the richest we ever had together. I would watch her sitting at her easel—she sat at it now—and her face was happy and serene, the eyes younger than when she had been a girl, and she moved at last into her own style. Sometimes when I looked at her painting I would feel a pang of agony at the knowledge that she would not have time to leave enough work behind for the world to remember her, but by the summer's end I did not mind that thought any more. She was beyond ambition. She was painting because she loved it. There was joy in her face, she saw friends, she even gave a few parties for them. Her sense of humor became quietly delicious, there was gratitude in it, as though being able to make a joke was something for which to be grateful. Gratitude—it was the thing she felt most of all that summer.

Omnia exeunt in mysteria.

What we saw in Catherine's face now that she was visibly dying is something I would not venture to describe. Everyone who knew her then will always remember it. She was so transparent. She seemed to be closer to us than she had ever been, yet to be somewhere else most of the time, somewhere beyond from which she came back to visit. She was alive and yet she was not; she was half-translated and yet she was still here.

The clouds crossed the sky, country rains washed the gardens, moons shone on the lake and the hillsides, cicadas sang in the August grass, boys and girls fell in love. In the early October of that year, in the cathedral hush of a Quebec Indian summer with the lake drawing into its mirror the fire of the maples, it came to me that to be able to love the mystery surrounding us is the final and only sanction of human existence. What else is left but that, in the end? All our lives we had wanted to belong to something larger than ourselves. We belonged consciously to nothing now except to the pattern of our lives and fates. To God, possibly. I am chary of using that much-misused word, but I say honestly that at least I was conscious of His power. Whatever the spirit might be I did not know, but I knew it was there. Life was a gift; I knew that now. And so, much more consciously, did she.

One evening of a towering sunset after rain, Catherine looked at me across the porch and said: "You know, I've been so incredibly lucky all my life. I can't get over it, how lucky I've been. And I've never felt luckier than I feel now."

We became quiet with each other. When Sally went away it was as though all the words had been spoken and no more were needed. So much life we had seen and felt. Its purpose? It did not seem to matter that one could not answer that question. Our past was not dead but now the present had flowed over it, as the future would flow over the present until the time came, and we both knew it would come soon—when she would be gone and I would be left.

Nobody—this I knew—can ever know in advance how he will feel when he encounters the finality. Often I dreaded it; often I rebelled against this fate of ours. But toward that summer's end I had almost ceased to think about the future, and she never thought of it at all. Remembering the years when she had wrung life and joy out of pain and perpetual exhaustion, I knew, deep inside, that this struggle was not valueless. Sometimes I tried to imagine what it would be like when she went, and to prepare myself for the shock of solitude. It was impossible to do so. Jerome in his obscure wisdom, Jerome with his obscure power, had made it possible for me to live her death with her, and for that I was tranquilly grateful to him. What if only a handful of people enjoyed her pictures? What if the ocean of time overwhelmed her? It overwhelms us all. The kingdom of heaven is as a man travelling into a far country, who called his own servants and delivered unto them his goods. And unto the one he gave five talents, and to another two, and to another one; to every man according to his abilities, and straightway he took his journey. . . . And the Lord said, Well done, thou good and faithful servant; thou hast been faithful over a few things, I will make thee ruler over many. Enter thou into the joy of the Lord.

So, in the end, did Catherine, and her face showed what I can only describe as the joy of the Lord. I knew its light would remain with me. I believed, though I would not know until the time came, that I would be able to say with a whole heart *nunc requiescas in perpetuum*. Already the world surrounding me was becoming a shadow. I loved it more than I had ever loved it and so did she, but it was a shadow in which politics, the echoes of which passed into the work which still earned my living, seemed the most unreal of all.

Enough for now. Later, when the time came when I would have to continue alone, later would be the time for the prayer I knew she hoped would be answered: *nunc requiesce in me.*